Naples Sorrento & the Amalfi Coast

Marina Carter

HUNTER

HUNTER PUBLISHING, INC,
130 Campus Drive, Edison, NJ 08818
☎ 732-225-1900; 800-255-0343; fax 732-417-1744
www.hunterpublishing.com

Ulysses Travel Publications
4176 Saint-Denis, Montréal, Québec
Canada H2W 2M5
☎ 514-843-9882, ext. 2232; fax 514-843-9448

Windsor Books
The Boundary, Wheatley Road, Garsington
Oxford, OX44 9EJ England
☎ 01865-361122; fax 01865-361133

ISBN 1-58843-578-4

Manufactured in the United States of America

This and other Hunter travel guides are also available as e-books through Amazon.com, NetLibrary.com and other digital partners. For more information, e-mail us at comments@hunterpublishing.com.

This guide focuses on recreational activities. As all such activities contain elements of risk, the publisher, author, affiliated individuals and companies disclaim responsibility for any injury, harm, or illness that may occur to anyone through, or by use of, the information in this book. Every effort was made to insure the accuracy of information in this book, but the publisher and author do not assume, and hereby disclaim, liability for any loss or damage caused by errors, omissions, misleading information or potential travel problems caused by this guide, even if such errors or omissions result from negligence, accident or any other cause.

Cover photo: Villa Rufolo, Ravello, © Art Kowalsky/Alamy
Interior color photographs © Marina Carter

Maps by Toni Carbone, © 2006 Hunter Publishing, Inc.
Index by Nancy Wolff
1 2 3 4

Contents

Maps

Going Metric

To make your travels in this region easier, we have provided the following chart that shows metric equivalents for the measurements you are familiar with.

GENERAL MEASUREMENTS

1 kilometer = .6124 miles

1 mile = 1.6093 kilometers

1 foot = .304 meters

1 inch = 2.54 centimeters

1 square mile = 2.59 square kilometers

1 pound = .4536 kilograms

1 ounce = 28.35 grams

1 imperial gallon = 4.5459 liters

1 US gallon = 3.7854 liters

1 quart = .94635 liters

TEMPERATURES

For Fahrenheit: Multiply Centigrade figure by 1.8 and add 32.

For Centigrade: Subtract 32 from Fahrenheit figure and divide by 1.8.

Centigrade	Fahrenheit
40°	104°
35°	95°
30°	86°
25°	77°
20°	64°
15°	59°
10°	50°

Introduction

Known to the Romans as *Campania Felix*, the "fruitful country," and popularized by artists and intellectuals as "the land lapped by the sea, the land where every word, bitter or sweet, speaks of love," the Bay of Naples is also characterized by chaos and complexity. The quintessential Italy of *O' Sole Mio* is at the same time the inheritor of a bewildering array of colonizers and cultures: Greeks, Saracens, Normans and Spaniards among them.

In this Chapter

Despite being one of Europe's largest cities for 300 years, by the end of the 18th century, Naples was an anachronism, with a large non-productive population of clerics and aristocrats and too few entrepreneurs. While other parts of the world were rapidly industrializing, southern Italy remained largely feudal. It is significant that, in the early 19th century, the region's only railway was built to link the three royal palaces of Naples, Caserta and Portici. After the unification of the country, the problem of the Mezzogiorno became increasingly apparent, and the southern question eventually led to injections of capital, producing the infamous "cathedrals in the desert" – unfinished industrial installations amid massive financial scandal. In the face of large-scale corruption Neapolitans remain stoically self-reliant, and optimistic, a state of mind summed up in local playwright Eduardo De Filippo's phrase "Ha da passa a nuttata," or "the night will soon be over." In recent times, Naples and the towns around its bay have experienced a cultural regeneration, albeit with continuing problems generated by uncontrolled urban sprawl and organized crime.

For visitors, Naples and its environs present a world of surprising and mainly pleasurable contrasts. Hedonistic resorts on the coast and islands are counterpoised by Greek and Roman excavations, and the drama of volcanic fumaroles. A beach getaway amid dramatic scenery can be enjoyed on the Sorrento and Amalfi coasts and the islands, while quieter resorts can be found in Cilento and Campi Flegrei. Classical sites include not only the well known excavated Roman towns of Pompeii and Herculaneum, but also villas at Stabia and

Oplontis, ruins on Capri, superlative Greek temples at Paestum and, in the Campi Flegrei region, a host of dramatic structures, including a Roman amphitheater and a submerged city. Medieval Arab-Norman architecture abounds in Naples and on the Amalfi Coast, while the superb Bourbon palaces are a match for any of the Parisian royal residences. Most dramatic of all are the myriad examples of the region's violent geology: hissing beaches and bubbling spas on Ischia, sulphur-laden fumaroles at Pozzuoli, and the sublime Vesuvius, with its verdant slopes, craggy craters and majestic tides of lava. And, of course, wherever you go the superb gastronomic specialties of Campania: mouth-watering pizza, handmade pasta, sophisticated seafood and tangy lemon flavors served up with the infectious smiles and guttural tones of the irrepressible Neapolitans and their near neighbors.

Vesuvius

■ The People & their Culture

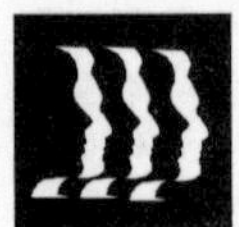

Writer and humorist Luciano De Crescenzo sums up the ethic of Neapolitans with two phrases – "penzamm' a salute" (one must consider one's health) and "e patr e figlie" (one has a family to provide for), claiming that the one is justification for the relaxed outlook on life, while the other provides a useful explanation for the frequent infringement of laws. This and the numerous other amusing depictions of southerners provided by themselves and by generations of visitors are usually exaggerations but often reflect sombre realities. Years of unremitting poverty spent in overcrowded urban slums, in situations of precarious employment, ruled over by distant authority figures, have nurtured strong support networks within families and close communities, but correspondingly weaker links to state organisations. And with the family rather than government taking on the role of provider, the position of women is particularly important. Thus the mother figure has a primary symbolic role within a sometimes shockingly macho culture. As the Neapolitans say: "Amore e mamma nun te nganna" (The love of a mother is true).

An offshoot of the deep-rooted suspicion of government has been to perpetuate politics for private gain and prolong the survival of the Camorra, a mafia-like organization. At the same time, this has created within Neapolitan society a strong sense of protectiveness, both for themselves and for their visitors. Tourists will find this expressed through constant reminders to watch one's bag, and to conceal jewelry and valuables. They may also be surprised, initially, by the willingness of people to engage with strangers, offering advice and information freely and often unsolicited. The exuberance and tenacity of the southerners finds its greatest expression in their artistic creations, whether it be a heartfelt rendition of a Neapolitan song by a restaurant singer, in the Baroque architecture of their magnificent churches, or indeed the grave pleasure they take in the celebration of traditional festivals.

Modern Customs & Ancient Practices

Traditional customs and crafts, which have died out in many Western societies, not only flourish in southern Italy, but continue to provide a living for a surprising number of people. Age-old festivals once celebrated in every village have mostly died out elsewhere, along with their small, settled communities, in this age of globalization; whereas, in hamlets and towns around the Bay of Naples, such traditions have not only managed to survive but continue to be celebrated with great panache. A visit to any one of the seasonal festivities that punctuate the calendar of the south provides a journey to a forgotten heritage for jaded urbanite tourists. Even food has a long tradition here. At Easter, Neapolitans still prepare the *pastiera*, which Lewis described in 1944 as a "springtime cake made with soft grain of all kinds, removed from their husks months before ripe, and cooked with orange blossom," remarking that the tradition was so old that mention was made of it by one of the Latin authors. The original pagan rite has now been subsumed within a Catholic festival, and certainly the celebration of one's saint's day is almost as important to Neapolitans as a birthday.

The Presepe

The makers of nativity figures, centered around the Via San Gregorio Armeno in the *Centro Storico* of Naples, are the example par excellence of a group of local craftsmen keeping alive a centuries-old tradition, and continuing to derive a living from a skill handed down from generation to generation. Known to have existed since at least the 13th century, the craft has now become a Neapolitan institution. The makers of nativity cribs and figures are most in demand in the winter months leading up to Christmas, but they are open all year round and do a healthy trade with the summer tourists. The figures are still produced using materials and methods little changed since the 17th century: modelled by hand from terracotta and baked in brick ovens. Nowadays, some of the figures are recognizably modern, demonstrating how this traditional craft is able to keep pace with new trends.

The Street Performer

Naples street performer1860

Naples has a great tradition of street theater, and countless descriptions of the inventive and dramatic performers survive in the memoirs of Grand Tour visitors. As late as 1944, Norman Lewis remarked upon the storytellers or *Cantastorie* who stood in front of canvas backgrounds depicting wars and chanting recitations of the deeds of Charlemagne and the Paladins. On Via San Pasquale he saw a *Pazzariello* whose function was to drive away evil spirits and who wore a costume dating from the Napoleonic period, including a cocked hat. The sellers of water and lemonade, or *Acquaiolo* beloved of 18th- and 19th-century travelers were also still in evidence. Lewis remarked that their equipment seemed scarcely to have changed over centuries, since they still carried round earthenware vessels exactly like those shown with watersellers on Pompeian frescoes. Sadly, these picturesque figures have now vanished from the Neapolitan scene, but itinerant minstrels continue a centuries-old tradition of street entertainment and are one of the joys of eating out in Naples. A man with a mandolin does the rounds most evenings on the *Lungomare*, and is happy to demonstrate his usually excellent singing skills at close range by serenading diners in return for a small financial reward.

The Sport of Gambling

Travelers have always associated Neapolitans with a love for gambling. Interest in the lottery is described as reaching almost mythical proportions. During World War II, Allied visitors remarked that "luck" played such a large part in the lives of local people, that every jeweller's shop sold good luck charms, or amulets to ward off evil spirits, such as a small horn, worn on a necklace. These small amulets, called "corni" are still worn or carried by many Neapolitans. Today, one of the most obvious manifestations of belief in luck and love of gambling is the continuing popularity of the lottery. And in true Neapolitan style, a hefty dose of the supernatural is involved. Numbers are given individual meanings, and events prior to the lottery can help players decide on propitious choices. For the confused, a book exists – the *Smorfia* – which explains the meanings of numbers, while helpful "interpreters" can translate dreams or events into likely numbers for a fee. Numbers in the *tombolella* game have many meanings. Some represent body parts.

The Seasonal Calendar of Festivals

Popular local traditions can be witnessed at almost any time of year and often involve processions of the Madonna. Many of those associated with seasonal events such as harvest and springtime or the production of local foods and beverages, also offer the opportunity to sample regional specialities. A summary of the principal events in the region is given below. Further information can be obtained from tourist offices.

❖ February-March

Carnival time is 40 days before Easter, so usually in February or early March, when street festivities and masked balls are held in Naples and all over the region. Sorrento hosts a lively festival to celebrate its Patron Saint, with concerts and other special events, on **Valentine's Day**. The coming of **Easter** sees church processions across the region: in Piano and Meta di Sorrento, Massa and Torca, the "arciconfraternite" or local brotherhoods (charitable organizations), wearing traditional hoods, lead processions through the town. On the island of Procida a colorful procession of the statue of Christ is held, with the festival lasting from 7 am until evening. On **Palm Sunday** the people of Sorrento carry olive palm or sugar almond branches to church. The Easter processions on Maundy Thursday and Good Friday should not be missed. The Easter cake – *la Pastiera* – is delicious.

❖ May-June

On the first Saturday in May, the city of Naples celebrates the ***Festa di San Gennaro***. The miracle of the liquefaction of his blood is attempted (this also takes place on September 19th each year). On May 14th, Capri celebrates its **Patron Saint Costanzo** with a procession in Marina Grande. The Saint's day is also celebrated in Termini, with a procession to the top of Mount St Costanzo. During this month ***Sagre del Pane*** and ***delle Alici*** (bread and sardine feasts) are held in Procida. At the beginning of June the Marine Republics (Pisa, Genoa, Venice and Amalfi) stage a **boat race**, preceded by a procession with participants dressed in period costume. The event, called a ***palio***, is hosted by each of the former republics in turn. A traditional festival celebrating nature and known as ***Festabiente***, with local products on sale, is held in Sorrento. On June 13, a procession of boats at Marina del Cantone celebrates **St Antonio's feast day**. The same event is marked by a procession through the streets of Anacapri with a statue of the Saint. At Monticchio in Massa Lubrense, on June 29th, at the **Patron Feast of Saint Peter and Paul**, special meals of spicy snails are served. Saint Peter is also celebrated at Crapolla with a procession of boats.

❖ July

With the arrival of summer, numerous open-air concerts are held. Sorrento's **Summer International Music Festival** begins, and the Piazza San Domenico Maggiore in Naples is the scene for free concerts in July. Top artists perform free at Palinuro on the Cilento coast, and the **Ravello Music Festival**, one of the most famous in Italy, takes place, chiefly at Villa Rufolo, in commemoration of Wagner's visit there. Details are on www.ravellofestival.com. Also in July, a **zucchini fair** is held in Massa Lubrense, and at the **Sea Festival** in Sant Agnello model boats and other associated crafts are on display. A procession in honor of **Sant'Anna** is held in Marina Grande, Sorrento with fireworks and dancing in the evening. In the village of Montepertuso, fireworks commemorate a local legend about the Madonna, every July 2nd. On the first Sunday of the month, the **Procession of S Maria delle**

Grazie leaves from Marina di Cassano on the beach of Piano di Sorrento, continuing by boat for a traditional Blessing at sea. The **Festival of the Madonna del Carmine** on July 16th culminates in a spectacular fireworks show in Naples, and at Piazza Tasso in Sorrento. Further information is at www.sorrentotourism.com. On July 26th, the **Festa Sant'Anna** is held in Ischia, when the folk dance known as the *Ndrezzata*, which simulates fighting with sticks and wooden swords, can be seen. This dance can also be seen on the ***Lunedi dell'Angelo*** and on the **Festival Day of St John the Baptist**. **St Anne's Day** is also celebrated at the church of the same name in Marina Grande, Sorrento. The bay is filled with boats that launch a firework display, and dancing continues on the beach until late in the night.

❖ August

In August, the **Feast of St Salvatore** is held in Schiazzano, Massa Lubrense, with displays of locally made fresh mozzarella and other agricultural products. The **Melon Festival** in Piano di Sorrento, and a **Cheese Fair** in Meta offer a chance to sample local products. A **regatta** is held off the beach of Marina della Lobra and seafood specialties are served on the pier. Visit the little mountain village of Casarlano to see the **celebrations in honour of Mary**, where a tasty sausage dish with eggplant and zucchini is served. The village of Maiano hosts the **St Rocco Meatball Fair** and Massa Lubrenze holds a **Lemon Fair**. The music festival continues and many sports competitions are held. On August 10th and 15th **beach parties** are held to celebrate St Lorenzo and Ferragosto. On the first Sunday of the month, a **boat procession** leaves Marina Piccola in Sorrento in honor of Santa Maria della Grazie.

At the Feast of the Assumption in Positano, the recreation of the landing and **defeat of Saracen pirates** takes place each year on August 15th. As part of the commemoration, a statue of the Madonna is carried from the Church of Santa Maria Assunta. Farther up the hillside, at Montepertuos, a ***Sagra del Fagiolo*** **(bean feast)** is held on the last Saturday of the month. In the Cilento Park, organic products are celebrated from August 9th to 11th, and a ***Sagra del Salame*** **(salami fair)** is one of many feasts celebrating local produce.

❖ September

During September the ***Colli di Fontanella* festival** is held in Sant'Agnello to celebrate the start of autumn, and the **Alimuri Fair** at Meta di Sorrento re-enacts an invasion of the town by Saracens. Models of the ancient boats and of the town's old tower are made for the occasion. Seamen celebrate the **Feast of the Madonna del Lauro**. On the second Sunday of the month, a mass is celebrated on the Vervece rock to honor the **underwater statue of Mary** – divers take flowers 40 ft down to her. A **pizza fest** is held in Naples during this month, around the same time as the miracle of San Gennaro's blood. See www.verapizzanapoletana.org for details. On September 29th the patron saint of Piano, **St Michele Arcangelo**, is commemorated. Procida holds a **Culture Week**.

❖ October

The **Grape Festival** in Priora during the first week of October is a chance to taste local wines and watch the traditional wine-making process. A **Chestnut Festival** is held in Faito. The Meta Open Door organization offers a **historical tour** through the *Centro Storico*.

❖ November

During November Procida holds a ***Sagra del Vino* (wine fair)**. And preparations for the **nativity scene** are made in churches throughout the region – San Liborio, a suburb of Piano, is famous for its *presepe* (nativity scenes) with many visitors taking a stroll along the narrow town streets to see them. In Naples, Via San Gregorio Armeno is abuzz with craftsmen preparing and arranging beautiful nativity scenes.

❖ December

Held in the second week of December, the week-long **Sorrento Cinema Festival** offers several screenings a day, concentrating on low-budget European films and American independents. At the ***Terra delle Sirene*** in Sant'Agata local products are on display. Christmas and New Year is a great time to be in southern Italy; parties and lively celebrations begin in mid-December with the **Festival of Santa Lucia** on December 13th, when log fires are lit and sausage dishes prepared. **Christmas** is seen in with elaborate restaurant meals, midnight masses and a procession of Baby Jesus through the streets. The streets are illuminated with food stands and *tombola* (lottery) stalls. At Meta di Sorrento, a dramatic, **living nativity** is staged in Via Casa Piccio. Living *presepe* can also be seen in Procida, and the villages of Torca and San Francesco in Massa organize a **Nativity Pageant**. ***Capodanno*** or **New Year's Eve** is celebrated in Naples with the *zampognari* (bagpipe players) and *capitone* (eel) dishes. A traditional New Year's Eve meal is served, and people play *tombola*, the lottery. At midnight, the residents flock to their balconies to light fireworks, or congregate on the Piazza del Plebsicito in Naples, the Piazzetta in Capri, and the Piazza Tasso in Sorrento.

Art & Architecture

Doric temple, Paestum

The 2,000-year history of the Bay of Naples, stamping ground of Greek seafarers, Roman Emperors, Norman barons, Aragonese nobles, and French kings, has left its mark in the diverse architecture and multi-layered character of the region's cities. Underfloor excavations in the cellars of Naples and in foundations of buildings around the bay regularly reveal buried layers of Greek and Roman settlements. Medieval structures have been built around fragments of pre-existing classical walls, and centuries of damage from earthquakes and other phenomena have resulted in a complex mixture of styles as edifices have been successively restored.

Greek & Roman Structures

The Doric temple at Paestum (shown above) and the Sybil's sanctuary at Cumae are superb relics of the Greek communities of Campania. Their original settlement at Naples – Palaeopolis – has disappeared, but the grid layout of their second settlement, Neapolis, founded in the seventh century BC, can still be seen, particularly when looking down on the city from a panoramic viewpoint like Vomero. A section of the original Greek wall can be seen in the Piazza Bellini, and beneath the present Cathedral of Naples, along with columns and sections of pavement dating from both the Greek and Roman periods. Sections of the defensive Greek wall around Sorrento can also be seen there at Porta Parsano Nuova and Marina Grande.

The Roman street plan of Naples followed that laid down by the Greeks, its main arteries corresponding with Via Anticaglia, Via dei Tribunali and Via San Biagio dei Librai. One of the monuments that best reveals the historic layers of construction is San Lorenzo Maggiore. Beneath the Gothic church, itself reconstructed on several occasions, the ground level in Roman times is revealed, with its *macellum* (market) and other structures, while lower still the ground level from Greek times is visible.

Around the Bay of Naples, the excavations at Pompeii and Herculaneum are the best-known of several Roman sites, but magnificent Roman villas can also be seen at Stabia and Oplontis. In the Campi Flegrei, marvels of Roman engineering include immense water reservoirs (the Piscina Mirabilis and Cento Camerelle among them), an impressive amphitheater and the road tunnel of Fuorigrotta. On the Sorrento Peninsula, sunbathers lie among the ruins of the Villa Pollio Felice and swimmers enjoy the baths of Queen Joanna. Capri's Roman villas date from the last decade of Emperor Tiberius' life, when he settled on the island, building Villa Jovis near the Punta del Capo, Villa Damecuta above the Blue Grotto, and the Villa of Augustus in the environs of Marina Grande.

Byzantine & Medieval Architecture

The early Middle Ages are perhaps most famously represented in the religious architecture of the Amalfi Coast. The 11th-century bronze doors of the Amalfi and Ravello cathedrals, interlaced arches, colored stone and glass chip décor, and other features of the Arab-Norman style are replicated in numerous churches of the region. The Villa Rufolo in Ravello was also built in this period. The Byzantine and Norman periods are well reflected in and around Caserta, particularly the village of Caserta Vecchia. The Veniero Palace on Via Pietà in Sorrento, while much altered, remains a rare example of late Byzantine and Arab architecture. Byzantine influence on Capri is reflected in the names of the churches: Santa Maria di Costantinopoli, Santa Sofia, and San Cataldo, for example. The Certosa of San Giacomo is the best-preserved of the medieval structures.

With the arrival of Charles of Anjou came the French Gothic style, represented in several of Naples' churches, such as Sant'Eligio and San Domenico Maggiore. The Duomo, San Lorenzo, Santa Chiara, San Pietro a Maiella and Donnaregina all date from this period. Castel Sant'Elmo was also part of the Angevin flurry of building.

Renaissance & Baroque Buildings

The triumphal arch of the Castel Nuovo is perhaps the most significant Renaissance work in Naples – a mythological rendering of Alfonso I's achievements. The Sala dei Baroni in the castle was designed by the Majorcan Guillermo Sagrera in this period. The Renaissance style with a Tuscan flavor found its way into the architecture of noble residences: Palazzo Maddaloni, Palazzo Gravina, and the façade of Gesu Nuovo (originally also a palace) are good examples. Much of the new tendency to create pretentious aristocratic urban residences may be laid at the feet of viceroy Pedro da Toledo, in the mid-16th century, who encouraged the nobles to move closer to the court, thereby removing them from their feudal fiefdoms and effectively emasculating them. At the same time, his energetic building plans razed slums, paving the way for the creation of the Via Toledo and the network of streets still known today as the *Quartieri Spagnoli*.

Castel Nuovo

By the 17th century the rich Baroque decorative style, which so gratified the Neapolitan desire for flamboyance, was transforming the squares of the city, as shown by the extraordinary *guglie* or spires in the *Centro Storico*, which date from this period, and the sometimes extravagant, sometimes ghoulish drapery of churches. Examples of Baroque churches in Sorrento include the Church of the Pietà on Corso Italia and the façade of the Church of our Lady of Sorrows, in Via Tasso.

The 18th century was the era of grandiose projects under the Bourbon rulers, who arrived in 1734. The royal palaces of Capodimonte, Caserta and Portici and their poor cousin, the Albergo dei Poveri, were all monumental architectural designs. The Theater of San Carlo and the Vesuvian villas also date from this period. The architects employed are in themselves a roll call of great names – Fuga, Sanfelice, Luigi and Carlo Vanvitelli among them. The magnificent palaces, with grandiose staircases, courtyards and colonnades remain a testimony to the genius of their creators. Noble residences in Naples built around this time include the Palazzo Serra di Cassano and Palazzo Casacalenda.

Destruction & Regeneration

The 19th century witnessed both a continuation of the masterly construction of the Bourbon period, with the work of architects like Antonio Nicolini, and the destruction of historic areas of the city center, in a bid to rid Naples of its dilapidated housing stock. While clearance of city slums left the way clear for the construction of glorious seafront palaces on Riviera di Chiaia, of which Villa Floridiana is a crowning example, the redevelopment work led to the loss of some medieval and Renaissance buildings, and historic *fondaci* (commercial shops and dwellings). The Second World War brought further destruction to the *Centro Storico*, but enabled postwar restoration projects to recover hidden gems like the church of Santa Chiara, shorn of its added Baroque décor.

Twentieth-century building has provided the region with some striking Fascist architecture, of which the Palazzo delle Poste in Naples and Casa Malaparte on Capri are well-known examples, along with elegant new residential districts in Vomero and Posillipo. At the same time, poor planning produced a concrete sprawl, disfiguring the coastal towns along the Bay of Naples. More recent urban development bodes well for the future: the Centro Direzionale has reclaimed a derelict industrial site and marshland to provide smart, new office blocks and apartment buildings, while the current extension of the urban transport system has produced impressive showpieces of modern art and architecture in the form of new metro stations.

Artists & Artistic Treasures

An extraordinary collection of precious ancient paintings and sculptures, largely recovered from the excavations of Roman sites, remains in Naples, despite the best efforts of souvenir hunters from the 18th century onwards. The artistic treasures of the classical period include some very rare examples of Greek funerary painting recovered from tombs around Paestum. Most of the ancient treasures are housed at the Archeological Museum in Naples, but many Roman frescoes can still be found *in situ*. Early Christian art can be seen in the catacombs.

Guido Mazzoni sculpture

While the authorship of priceless works of classical art remains largely speculative, in later periods, the foreign rulers of Naples brought in artists of international repute whose names and creations have by and large been preserved for posterity in the numerous churches and palaces of the region, despite the many adversities that the region has encountered. Angevin rule in the 13th century brought Pietro Cavallini from Rome to decorate the church of Donnaregina Vecchia, among other tasks. Giotto worked in Naples from 1328-1334, but the frescoes he painted have been lost and only traces of his art survive. During the rule of Ferrante, sculptor Guido Mazzoni produced his life-size terracotta figures for the church of Monteoliveto, while the triumphal arch of Castel Nuovo was the work of several artists.

The art of numerous early Renaissance painters can be seen in the Museo Capodimonte, while tombs by Donatello and Michelozzo and by Antonio Rossellino are found in the Sant'Angelo a Nilo and Monteoliveto churches. Sculptures by Giovanni da Nola, and work by Romolo Balsimelli decorate several religious edifices in Naples.

The late 16th and 17th centuries saw the arrival of artists from Northern Italy like Cosimo Fanzago, Domenico Fontana, and Francesco Picchiatti, who labored on the Royal Palace, the Certosa of San Martino, and the Monte di Pietà. Fanzago also designed the spire in Piazza San Domenico, and

Santa Maria Egiziaca at Pizzofalcone – he is perhaps the greatest exponent of Neapolitan Baroque. Caravaggio, in Naples to escape a murder enquiry, produced his *Flagellation* and *The Seven Acts of Mercy* here. The contribution of his followers – artists like Jose Ribera and Mattia Preti – and Luca Giordano, helped to make Naples an important center of Italian artwork in the 17th century. The chapel at the Certosa di San Martino is a showcase of Neapolitan painting from this period The female artist Artemisia Gentileschi lived in Naples from 1630 until her death. Her *Judith and Holofernes* can be seen in Capodimonte. Native Neapolitan artist Salvator Rosa was also painting at this time. In Capri, remarkable examples of Baroque art can be seen at San Michele and Santa Sofia.

The 18th century belongs to artists like Francesco Solimena, Ferdinando Sanfelice, Giuseppe Sammartino, and above all to the Vanvitellis. Sanfelice's monumental staircases are among his greatest claims to fame, while the sculptures by Sammartino in the Sansevero chapel are extraordinary pieces by any measure. Examples of Solimena's work can be seen at the churches of San Paolo Maggiore and Gesù Nuovo.

Pierre Jacques Volaire, Eruption of Vesuvius

Landscape painting became popular in the 18th century, helped by the increase of tourism in the region. Gaspar Van Wittel, and Pierre Jacques Volaire, who drew dramatic scenes of an erupting Vesuvius, are among the better known names. The works of another Dutch painter, Anton Pitloo, inspired the Posillipo school of painters, of whom Giacinto Gigante was the undoubted star. His works can be seen in Capodimonte.

Among more recent and innovative showcases for modern art in Naples are the recently opened metro stations at Dante, Cilea, Salvator Rosa and Materdei. They are worth a visit both for their modern design and the numerous art works on show. Dante station – designed by Gae Aulenti – hosts works by contemporary artists such as Joseph Kosuth, Jannis Kounellis and Nicola De Maria. Materdei station – designed by the Atelier Mendini – features a glass spire, mosaics by Sandro Chia and colored panels by Lucio Del Pezzo. Salvator Rosa station, also designed by the Atelier Mendini, has mosaics, a playground and a number of sculptures by Barisani and Longobardi among others. In the park, the remains of an ancient Roman bridge, and a small 19th-century chapel can be seen. Quattro Giornate station, designed by Domenico Orlacchio, recalls Neapolitan war combatants with female figures by Marisa Albanese, and other art works by Sergio Fermariello and Betty Bee among others. The Museo station will house a gallery for four Neapolitan photographers when it is opened.

Music & Musicians

Enrico Caruso

Think of Naples, and music will not be far from your mind. The region will surely be forever identified with its melodramatic love songs from the 19th and early 20th centuries, but musical traditions have a long pedigree here. In the 15th century, Ferrante enticed some of the best musicians in Europe to his court with the offer of high salaries, and the resulting compositions of the courtly retinue produced important innovations. Later, Naples would become a renowned center for Baroque musicians. The conservatories were particularly famous for producing exceptional violinists, like Francesco Durante. Grand Tour visitors provide some interesting accounts of musical traditions and operatic performances at Naples in the 18th century, and in the early 19th century San Carlo hosted world premieres of the Rossini operas *Mose in Egitto* (1818) and *La Donna del Lago* (1819). Donizetti's *Lucia di Lammermoor* was also performed for the first time at San Carlo. However, it was through the large-scale migration of southern Italians from the late 19th century that the world was introduced to the popular musical culture of the Neapolitans.

Traditionally Neapolitan songs had been anonymously written, but in 1880 *Funiculi-funicula*, composed by Peppino Turco and Luigi Danza to a Russian folk tune, propelled its authors to a brief stardom, helped by the Tsar's enthusiastic support. The song was written to commemorate the funicular railway that once took visitors up the slopes of Vesuvius. It was based on Russian folk music, and the Tsar had it performed for him by the Italian tenor Marconi, then on tour in St. Petersburg. Soon afterwards, *O' Sole Mio* was written by another duo of impoverished Neapolitans. Its success has proved enduring. *Torna a Surriento*, originally composed for a politician, is also popular for its romantic lyrics.

The great Naples-born tenor Enrico Caruso used his operatic training to sing his home town songs to great effect, launching a tradition that many have since followed, and contributing greatly to their longevity and popularity. Caruso, born in Naples in 1873, grew up on the Via San Giovanni e Paolo and was baptized at the nearby church. His family was poor, and as a young man Caruso earned extra money by singing Neapolitan songs in cafés and by performing at church festivals. It was at Caserta Cathedral one day in 1895 that he was recommended for a role in an opera, making his debut two months later at the local Teatro Nuovo. His first overseas engagement was in Egypt, followed by successful performances in Sicily and then at La Scala, Milan in December 1900. Caruso debuted at the Metropolitan Opera, New York in 1903, singing the part of the Duke in *Rigoletto*, and went on to have worldwide success. In 1921 the ailing Caruso returned to Italy and went by boat across the bay to Sorrento to stay at the Hotel Vittoria. A few days later he returned to Naples, dying there in a room at the Hotel Vesuvio. Popular musicians in Naples today include Eduardo de Crescenzo, Pino Daniele and Enzo Avitabile, a folk singer.

Literary Figures

Petrarch

Almost as long as the Bay of Naples has been inhabited, writers have extolled its beauty. The antics of the Roman Emperors who enjoyed themselves here filled many pages by Latin authors – Cicero wrote disapprovingly of the ostentatious displays of wealth but kept three villas on the bay himself – and almost as many wrote about its curative waters, delightful wines, pleasant landscapes and tranquil countryside.

Virgil loved Naples so much that he asked to be buried here. Pliny the Elder famously died during the eruption of AD 79, and his nephew Pliny the Younger left a unique account of events.

The Angevin and Aragonese courts later attracted new generations of writers: Petrarch and Boccaccio were two of many authors who spent time in Naples. Ferrante surrounded himself with men of letters and poets like Giovanni Pontano, Jacopo Sannazaro and Giovanni Brancati. Under his patronage, Naples became a major printing center. Home-grown literary figures included Torquato Tasso, who wrote an epic poem, famous for centuries, but little known now, and two 18th-century philosophers: Gaetano Filangieri and Giovanbattista Vico.

By now, Naples was well established on the Grand Tour and a host of major literary figures left accounts of visits to the classical sites and to the city. The enthusiasm of men like Stendhal, who called Naples the most beautiful city in the world, and Goethe, who wrote "Naples is a paradise: everyone lives in a state of intoxicated self-forgetfulness, myself included," no doubt contributed to the reputation which the region was acquiring. However, American author Henry James was less than overwhelmed while Shelley reported that his first experience in the city was witnessing the murder of a thief, and Charles Dickens followed him in drawing attention to the "depravity, degradation and wretchedness" of many inhabitants. By the time Ruskin arrived, in 1874, Naples had been metamorphosed into "the most disgusting place in Europe." Fortunately, the resorts along the Bay of Naples continued to enthral visitors. Robert Browning's poem *An Englishman in Italy* was written during a stay in the hills above Piano di Sorrento, while John Steinbeck did much to popularize the Amalfi Coast and generations of writers on the islands have added to the mystique of Capri and Ischia.

Language & Gesture

The unusual dialect of Naples, an amalgam of foreign influences grafted onto the melodious Italian language, and the vociferous gesturing that accompanies or sometimes supplants conversation entirely, was much discussed by Grand Tour visitors, and continues to characterize and distinguish the Neapolitans.

Recent studies have underscored the longevity of the local gestural traditions. Andrea de Jorio, an expert on Greek antiquities, has authored a book on the subject that describes the similarities between gestures depicted on ancient Greek vases and contemporary sign language in Naples. The crowded and outdoor lifestyle of generations of Neapolitans is believed to have helped perpetuate these traditions.

As with gesture, the popular sayings of Naples and its environs document centuries-old customs and rivalries. The folk saying "Meta p'astipa, Caruotto pe pensa, e Surriento p'agghinda" (Meta retains, Piano sells, Sorrento boasts) reveals perceived local characteristics and the desire of villagers to differentiate themselves. Post-unification, the Neapolitans mourned the passing of their status as an independent kingdom and their perceived subordination to the north, with sayings such as: "Tutt'e solde d'o Tesoro d'o Stato d'e Doje Sicilie fujeno arrobbate e carriate o nord" (All the wealth of the state of the Two Sicilies has been stolen and taken to the north). For poor southerners emigration became a way of life, as thousands left for America, Australia and the wealthy industrial sectors of northern Europe. This is expressed in the phrase "E meridiunale pe ffaticà, hann'a stà appriparate a jí luntano d'e case loro" (Southerners who want to work have to be prepared to do so far from their homes). At the same time, local pride in their beautiful homeland has remained a characteristic. Hence phrases like: "Chi Capri non vede, Paradiso non crede" (He who has not seen Capri does not believe in Paradise). This is also reflected in many of the songs. One famous line runs "Napule bella mia, terra d'ammore, lacreme e canzone" (My beautiful Naples, land of love, tears and song). A selection of Neapolitan phrases and proverbs is given below:

Common Neapolitan Phrases

- *Statte buono!* (Keep well, or keep calm)
- *E quanne buono buona?* (What can happen?)
- *C'avimma fa?* (What can we do?)
- *Tien a capa fraceta!* (You are not right in the head!)
- *Nun torna cchiu!* (Go away!)

Neapolitan Proverbs

- *Vatte o fierro quann'e cavero.* (Strike while the iron is hot.)
- *Mannaggia a pressa, dicette a maruzza.* (Don't rush, says the snail.)

- *L'auciello s'apparano ncielo, e chiavecche nterra.* (Birds mate in the sky, and rascals mate on the earth.)
- *Fa chello ca dici, e nu chiello ca facci.* (Do what I say, and not what I do.)
- *Chi che pecura sa fa, s'o manga o lupo.* (If you act like a sheep, the wolf will eat you)
- *Fa l'arte ca saje, ca si nun t'arrechisce, camparaje.* (Find a job that you know how to do. If you don't get rich, at least you'll make a living.)
- *E denare fanno veni a vist e cecate.* (Money makes sight return to the blind person.)
- *Mazza e panella fanno e figlie belle; panella senza mazza fanne 'e figlie pazze.* (Punishment and reward makes children good; reward without punishment makes them mad.)
- *Chisto e o munno: chi naviga e chi va nfunno.* (The world is like this: some sail and some sink.)
- *L'ammore nun s'accate e nun se venne.* (You can't buy or sell love.)
- *Doppo e quarant'anne nun s'adimanda chiu "Cumme staje?" ma "Cumme te sienti?"* (After the age of 40, one doesn't ask "How are you?" but rather "How do you feel?")

A Southern Subculture: the Camorra

The Camorra is a secretive criminal organization which is Naples' version of the Mafia. Its roots have been fed by the "southern question" – the economic dualism of Italy that has perpetuated the neglect of Neapolitans by the state and encouraged unhealthy forms of patronage, while at the same time enabling racketeers to benefit from development funds channelled to the region by the "Cassa per il Mezzogiorno."

The origins of the Camorra are shrouded in mystery. Some contend that it dates from a 15th-century Spanish secret society, the *Garduna*, others that it was spawned at the end of the 18th century. The name may derive from a combination of the words "capo," boss, and "morra," a street game. In 1735 one gaming house in Naples was "Camorra avanti palazzo" (Camorra in front of the Royal Palace) in the Piazza del Plebiscito. After Nelson's suppression of the 1799 Neapolitan revolution, it is believed that the resulting power vacuum helped the growth of the Camorra. In 1820 the existence of the organization was official – a police report described its initiation rites and fund collections for imprisoned members –

rather like the pirate articles of the 17th century. Fatally, in the early 19th century the Naples police chief called on the Camorra to help restore order. As he later wrote in his memoirs, "I thought of making use of the evil skills of camorristi, offering the most influential leaders a means to rehabilitate themselves." Recruiting men who had been convicted of numerous offences into the police force unfortunately served chiefly to make smuggling and extortion easier, and state revenues plummeted.

Over the 19th century, the Camorra made money from brothels and gambling; merchants moved into politics and forced other merchants to pay for their "supervisory" services. In the late 19th century a backlash occurred with the arrest of some high-profile camorristi and a clean-up campaign of local politicians. In response, the Camorra went underground, but succeeded in maintaining a popular base even as Socialism eroded their support networks by fostering working-class over regional loyalties. A mass trial in 1911-12, which led to long prison sentences for 35 leaders of the Camorra, was followed by further repression of the society during the Fascist period. Perversely, however, the victorious arrival of the allies after World War II prompted a resurgence of criminality as the Americans and British forged an unholy alliance with Mafiosi, who in turn brought in the Camorra.

By 1960, sources again claimed the Camorra was moribund, and yet, in the 1970s, the contraband industry was being run by the organization, with one camorrista boasting that he shifted $100 million worth of cigarettes a year. This renewed period of activity was again interrupted by police crackdowns and infighting but ironically received a boost after the 1980 earthquake when relief funds were channelled into Camorra-controlled construction businesses. In response, students organized protests and demonstrations teaming up with shopkeepers to challenge the organization, emphasizing that both the Mafia and Camorra were "inside the state." One Camorra boss who was arrested in 1992 had personal assets believed to be more than a billion dollars. His headquarters were in the town of Nola, 15 miles northeast of Naples.

The Camorra differs from the Mafia in being an urban as opposed to a rural phenomenon and, while the Mafia is better known, some analysts claim that the Camorra is "an even more efficient killing machine." Its top hit man in the late '80s and early '90s claimed to have committed 90 murders himself, while his group was estimated by police to be responsible for 500 killings in a two-year bloodbath. The modern Camorra has distinct wings – a mass movement, a business wing and a political wing. It differs from the Mafia in other ways – more vendettas, and more groups operating semi-independently. This makes it harder to stamp out than the Mafia – as one group is destroyed others quickly grow up.

The Camorra survives because it can apportion scarce jobs in an area with high unemployment, usually topping 25%, thereby winning popular support. That in turn helps influence voters' choices and cements alliances with local politicians. To understand the pervasive influence of the Camorra, one point will suffice – if a Neapolitan's car is stolen he would usually find it more useful to contact the local Camorra chief, rather than report the matter to the police. If he does the former, he has some chance of getting it back, even if he has to pay for it. The system of paying the thief to return your item even has a name – "cavallo di ritorno." As long as unemployment is high, theft and the appeal of organizations like the Camorra will be hard to defeat. Individual attempts to fight the Camorra carry a high personal risk. A priest, Don Peppino Diana, who took a stand against the organization, was murdered in 1994. Specific Camorra outrages caused mass indignation. When innocent bystanders are killed in shooting incidents, for example, as occurs all too often, it is front page news.

Tourists are unlikely to see much evidence of the Camorra, although car owners may wonder about the ubiquitous bystanders who demand cash for "keeping an eye" on your vehicle. The travel writer, Eric Newby, claimed in 1984 that he saw a young Camorra recruit, known as "a Picciotto d'Onore," an unpaid apprentice to the Camorra, evidently anxious to prove his worth and loyalty to the cause, ride up on a scooter to the Trattoria Agostino in Mergellina. He took several potshots at Mario dello Russo, a fellow Camorrista, who was taken away in an ambulance.

Recent arrests demonstrate that the Camorra maintains a hold on traditional businesses while also moving into new areas. Maria Licciardi, arrested in 2001 having taken over her brothers' role in the organization, was dealing simultaneously with businesses involving drug trafficking, contraband cigarettes, extortion and procurement. Today the organization is believed to have 7,000 members and to be actively engaged in money laundering in Holland, Britain and Germany. Recently it has also moved into the lucrative business of waste disposal (*ecomafia*). This involves the use of illegal landfill sites in Italy or offloading dangerous waste in Africa. In 2004 the Camorra was implicated in a match-rigging scandal involving several Serie A Italian football clubs. Even more disconcerting was the revelation of links between the organization and Islamic terrorist groups. Pierluigi Vigna, formerly Italy's national anti-Mafia prosecutor, reported evidence that "groups of the Camorra are implicated in an exchange of weapons for drugs with terrorist groups."

■ History

The archeological richness of the Bay of Naples owes as much to its long history of foreign domination as to the awesome powers of Vesuvius. Romans built on and expanded the original Greek settlements, and after the fall of their Empire, Byzantines, Normans and Spaniards followed. It was under Bourbon rule that the great 18th-century palaces were built and the systematic excavation of Roman towns began. Foreign rule was ended by Garibaldi's triumphal march from the south in 1860. However unification brought its own problems, and the economic stalemate was highlighted by waves of out-migration. Development remains patchy, and youth unemployment high, but the local inhabitants are at last harvesting a good vintage from their cultural pride and legendary hospitality as ever-increasing numbers of vacationers arrive to enjoy the stunning views and architectural wealth of the region.

The Greeks

Eight centuries before Christ, Greeks colonized Campania, making it the northernmost province of Magna Graecia. They founded a city which they called Parthenope – after the sirens who were said to lure sailors onto dangerous rocks – on the promontory of present-day Pizzofalcone in Naples. Greek seafarers and traders also settled on the island of Ischia, at Cuma in the Campi Flegrei, and Elea, in the Cilento Valley. The magnificent Greek temple dedicated to Hera, at Paestum, dates from the sixth century BC.

Tribes already inhabited the region – Samnites, Oscans and Opics – who soon became Hellenized, adopting Greek customs and art forms. Greek influence in Campania was challenged by Etruscans and Carthaginians, but the Greeks defeated them in a series of battles, holding onto power until the fifth century BC, when they lost an important naval confrontation at Cuma and were driven out of Ischia by volcanic eruptions. Infighting had already prompted the decline of Parthenope, and the Greeks who fled Cuma now established a new settlement called Neapolis. It is this Greek city, laid out on a rectangular grid plan, which has survived in the layout of the Decumani of the present-day *centro storico*.

Roman Campania

By the fourth century BC, Roman expansion threatened both the Greek settlements in Campania and the Samnites. Taking Neapolis, around 330 BC, they expanded the city, turning it into a byword for beauty and civilization, and by 27 BC, the Bay of Naples had become a magnet for intellectuals and vacationers.

Puteoli (Pozzuoli) became an important trading and naval port under the Romans, thriving until the construction of a rival port at Ostia. St Paul famously came here in 61 AD, en route from Egypt, founding an early Christian community in the town. Nearby Baia was more devoted to pleasure, as a popular seaside resort and spa town, and Seneca summed it up as a "resort of vice." By the first century BC wealthy villa owners in and around Baia included Julius Caesar (Cleopatra was staying here, when he was murdered), Marcus Antonius, and Lucullus. Caligula reportedly rode a horse over a bridge of boats that he had constructed across the bay of Puteoli, and it was at nearby Bauli (Bacoli) that Nero famously took forcible possession of villas belonging to his mother Agrippina, and his aunt Domitia, assassinating both.

Misenum, which played an important part in the battle of 474 BC, and was later attacked by Hannibal, had, by the first century BC, become a pleasure resort as well as a working naval port – the official base of the Roman fleet in the Tyrrhenian Sea. On the other side of the Bay of Naples, Surrentum was also a favorite haunt of Roman nobles, who built a number of villas at panoramic locations along the coast. The residence of Pollius is still visible at Capo di Sorrento, and the Emperor Augustus had a villa on the promontory between the Marina Grande and Marina Piccola. Ischia was having a much tougher time: a series of volcanic eruptions, landslides, mudflows and earthquakes help to explain why Augustus was keen to hand the island over to the authorities on Naples, in return for Capri, despite its smaller size and lack of hot springs.

It is known that Augustus visited Capri in 29 BC, but it was under his successor, Tiberius, who went to live there around 26 BC, that it became an island of palaces. Tiberius would rule his empire from several fortified hill-top residences on Capri for the next 10 years. Among family members invited to Capri by Tiberius was Caligula, who spent some of his formative years there. After his death in 97 BC, Capri continued to be a holiday resort for Roman aristocrats but, without the large retinue that accompanied Tiberius, the island inevitably was heard of less and less.

AD 79 & its Aftermath

Alongside the written stories of aristocrats and emperors we also know a great deal about everyday life in Roman Campania, and this is due to two of its less glamorous towns. Pompeii and Herculaneum, originally settled by Italic peoples, Greeks and Samnites, came under Roman rule in the first century BC, and were thriving commercial centers. Pompeii in particular was known for its wine, fruit and oil exports, while Herculaneum was a more elegant town of some 5,000

Herculaneum fresco

inhabitants. During the first century AD, towns around Vesuvius, like Pompeii and Herculaneum suffered a series of repeated earthquakes that damaged many structures. The local residents, however, did not connect the earth tremors with Vesuvius, which had not erupted for nearly 2,000 years.

On August 24th, AD 79, Vesuvius gave them a sign that could no longer be ignored. Like an exploding pressure cooker, ash and pumice spewed out of the mountain at a rate of 100,000 tons a second, forming a column that stretched several miles upwards. Watching across the bay at Misenum, Pliny the Elder's nephew described what he saw: "a cloud of very unusual size and appearance. It resembled a pine tree, for it shot up a great height in the form of a trunk, which extended itself at the top into several branches." Within about 45 minutes, cooling ash and pumice began to fall onto Pompeii, filling the streets to a height of three metres (nine feet) or more. Early in the morning hours of August 25th, a second, deadlier phase of the eruption began. As the volcano began to collapse, a pyroclastic wave rushed down the slopes of Vesuvius at 70 mph. A mixture of rock, ash and toxic gases, many times hotter than boiling water, annihilated all living creatures in its path. Herculaneum was the first to disappear as the upper floors of houses were compressed downwards and covered by a thick volcanic blanket. Successive pyroclastic waves reached Pompeii with the same devastating effect.

Initially declared off-limits, to protect property, the depth of rubble that remained proved impenetrable even to the hordes of clandestine treasure-seekers, and the towns beneath were gradually forgotten. It was not until 120 AD that the roads around the area were reopened to traffic. As time went on the bodies buried beneath ash and pumice decayed, leaving voids

in the solidified rock-like material that encased them. Centuries later, an excavator would have the brilliant idea to pour plaster into these holes. The casts that emerged have brought many of these ancient dead back to view. Their twisted limbs and contorted facial expressions recall forever the moment of terrible drama in AD 79.

Even Sorrento, farther away from the volcano, sustained damage from the earthquake that accompanied the fearful eruption. Roman Campania had suffered a blow, but the halcyon days of the bay as a destination for classical vacationers were not quite over. Baia, across the bay in the Campi Flegrei, continued to be a fashionable resort for at least another 300 years. By the fourth century, however, bradyseism (ground movements cause by volcanic activity) was already having its effect – and the shoreline began to sink, although the resort probably continued to thrive for at least another hundred years, as decorations from local Roman villas testify. Puteoli was already in decline, from the second century, when the port of Ostia was developed – conveniently closer to Rome. But the death knell to Roman Campania would be given in the fifth century AD, after the transfer of the imperial capital and division of the empire left the region exposed to attacks from Goths and Vandals. The last Western Roman Emperor died in Naples in AD 476, signaling the final end of the empire.

Byzantines & Normans

Over the next few hundred years, following the fall of the Roman Empire, a succession of challengers presented themselves, but Naples, nominally now part of the Byzantine empire, managed to retain a degree of independence, and economic success. During the sixth century Lombards captured much of Campania, but Naples survived their sieges, while

Baia continued to be admired for its oysters, and its baths, now by the Ostrogoths, who transferred Misenum's fleet to their own capital. Saracens next began to raid towns all along the coast, necessitating the intervention of a fleet from Sorrento on at least one occasion to relieve Ischia. Capri, too, fared badly, attacked by barbarians and pirates, and repeatedly struck by earthquakes.

In the seventh century, Naples and Sorrento both asserted their independent status as duchies, and continued to trade, surviving by playing off one challenger against another. Amalfi took the hint, and in the 800s rebelled against the domination of Naples to declare its own independent status, forming strategic alliances with the Saracens in order to combat the Byzantine threat. In 958 Amalfi elected its first doge, in imitation of the Maritime Republic of Venice. Thus began that town's golden age, when its mercantile links stretched to Constantinople and other Muslim territories, and the Tavola Amalfitana system of maritime law was adopted across the Mediterranean.

At the turn of the 11th century, the reigning Duke of Naples teamed up with Norman forces to oust the Lombards. In so doing, he opened the door to a long period of Norman rule. The Normans took Amalfi in 1073 and then besieged Naples – its Duke changed sides more than once and died, still fighting, in 1137, while his erstwhile Duchy was incorporated into Roger de Hauteville's Kingdom of Sicily. Roger made a triumphal entrance to the city through Porta Capuana. Under Roger's rule Naples thrived, and the city showed its loyalty by supporting his grandson Tancred against a rival, Henry of Hohenstaufen. The victorious Henry demonstrated his displeasure by destroying much of the city's defensive wall. His death, soon after, did not bode well for his infant son Frederick but, despite their initial support for his rival Otto IV of Brunswick, Frederick II would later appease his Neapolitan subjects by restoring the fortifications and walls, completing the Castel Capuano and the Castel dell'Ovo and, most importantly, founding the University that still bears his name.

Sorrento too became part of the Norman kingdom, but remained largely self-governing through its resident aristocratic families. Capri also fell under Norman domination for a time, but Ischia, ravaged by another damaging earthquake in 1228 and by a volcanic eruption in 1300, which killed at least 700 islanders, was little enough of a prize for anyone. The Amalfitans struggled against Norman rule, but also had to defend themselves against Pisan attackers and began a long slide into decline.

Frederick II's death in 1250 prompted another battle for succession, as his legitimate son Conrad, and illegitimate offspring Manfred, both attempted to reassert Hohenstaufen rule, abetted by the Saracens. But Naples preferred to side with Pope Innocent IV against the anti-clerical family, offering their kingdom to the Angevins at the first opportunity. In 1266 Manfred was defeated at the Battle of Benevento and Conrad's public execution in Naples on October 26, 1268 by Charles of Anjou ushered in a new period of rule.

The Houses of Anjou & Aragon

Robert the Wise

As capital of the Angevin kingdom, Naples witnessed a flurry of building projects designed to show off the new dynasty to his peers, headed by a brother of the King of France. The Castel Nuovo, San Martino, the Duomo, and the church of Santa Chiara – some of Naples' best-loved monuments – date from Charles' rule. During this time, trade and commerce flourished, encouraged by the arrival of Florentine and Catalan craftsmen and merchants.

Robert the Wise took over as Angevin ruler of Naples in 1309, ushering in another period of cultural creativity – he was a patron of Giotto, Petrarch and Boccaccio, who wrote enthusiastically of the jousting tournaments then hosted in the city – and building the Castel Sant'Elmo. Robert's son had died young and, after his death in 1343, he was succeeded by his grand-daughter Queen Joanna I. Her long reign was marked by a destructive seaquake in 1343, by the Black Death (1347-48) and by the outbreak of civil war among the Angevins, which was to fatally weaken the dynasty. Joanna was eventually overthrown by Charles III, who ruled Naples between 1381 and 1386. His son Ladislas succeeded to the throne until his death in 1414, when the equally controversial Joanna II, his sister, took over the reins. Her designated successor, René of Anjou, was driven from Naples after her death, by Alfonso, King of Aragon who took power in 1442.

Joanna's dithering about her choice of heir ensured the continuance of bitter fighting in southern Italy as René's armies continued to battle those of Alfonso. Until his death in 1480, René stubbornly used the traditional title of Naples' rulers, "King of Jerusalem and Sicily."

Ferrante

In Ischia Alfonso sent away followers of René and installed a colony of Spanish and Catalans, set up game reserves, and built the bridge connecting the castle to the harbor. Unfortunately, Alfonso, like Joanna, died without a secure heir, but having promised his illegitimate son Ferrante (probably by a Catalan woman) the position. Ferrante ruled from 1458 to 1494, gaining a reputation for cruelty, largely based on his cunning murders, notably of one-time chief conspirator the Count di Sarno and other baronial guests, whom he put to death after inviting them to a banquet at the Castel Nuovo. It was said that he kept the dressed corpses of his victims at the castle in a "museum of mummies." On the plus side, Ferrante introduced a number of important economic reforms. Under his rule, outlying strongholds of the Angevin kings, like Massa Lubrense, were also brought into the Aragonese fold, and Naples was again united with Sicily.

Disputes over Ferrante's entitlement to the throne, nevertheless, continued to plague his successor Alfonso II, who reigned for less than a year before Naples fell to Charles VIII of France, and he was obliged to flee – first to Ischia castle and then to Sicily. Alfonso's son, Ferrante II, regained control after a brief period of French rule, during which wild talk of Naples as the starting point for a crusade to recover Constantinople and Jerusalem was circulated. Ferrante, however, died prematurely in 1496, and his successor was soon driven out by an alliance of French and Spanish forces.

The Spanish Viceroyalty

Spain, under Ferdinand and Isabella, was a dominant power in Europe when Naples was subordinated to its rule in 1502 as a viceroyalty. The century that followed saw Naples continue to grow and develop, becoming Europe's second-largest city. But this expansion was not without cost: overcrowding and poverty brought disease and disaffection in its wake. Mid-century was punctuated by rebellions, but it was ultimately not the power of the people, but international intrigue that led to the secession of Naples to Austria in 1707, bringing an end to Spanish rule.

Spain's commanding role in Europe was not easily held on to, however, and the military might needed to keep control of far-flung territorial possessions required vast resources. The grand martial strategies of the Spanish king had to be paid for, and to secure the enormous subsidies it was necessary to bring Naples' barons to heel. Strong viceroys like Pedro Alvárez de Toledo proved adept at playing factions one against the other, and using harsh methods when necessary. Toledo is credited with a successful urban renewal program in the city – the famous Quartieri Spagnoli date from this period – and with improving the coastal towns in the Campi Flegrei after the eruption of Monte Nuovo in 1538. The eruption also disrupted the thermal spas of Baia, and necessitated the rebuilding of the castle there, begun by Alfonso II.

Meanwhile the towns of the Sorrento Peninsula, from Massa to Vico, were sacked by Turkish pirates, who carried off numbers of the inhabitants into slavery. The Spanish even imposed taxes on the ransoms paid to the Turks to free their Neapolitan prisoners! Scores of watchtowers were constructed along the coast and on the islands to provide a warning system against the raiders, as Barbarossa and then Dragut continued their incursions – attacking Ischia and Procida on several occasions.

The increasingly heavy taxation imposed on Naples by the Spanish viceroys prompted a famous revolt in July 1646 when Tommaso Aniello (Masaniello) – a fisherman's son from

Amalfi – led a vast mob on the rampage in Naples, breaking open the prisons and grabbing arms from the stores. Outnumbered, the Viceroy was temporarily forced to proclaim support for Masaniello by abolishing taxes, and naming him Captain General. Very quickly afterwards, however, Masaniello was outsmarted, and beheaded.

Masaniello

The disorders in Naples did not pass unnoticed elsewhere. Villagers in Sorrento seized the opportunity to launch their own rebellion, besieging the town with the assistance of Genoan troops. Inhabitants of Ischia and Capri also took sides in the dispute between ruled and rulers. Worse, however, was to come as a plague epidemic swept through the region in the 1650s. Even the islands were affected – Capri was temporarily abandoned, and the population of Ischia decimated.

In 1688 an earthquake struck Naples, damaging many buildings. Outstanding memorials of this epoch – which ended in 1707 after the War of the Spanish Succession placed Naples under the control of the Habsburgs – include the Palazzo Reale, the lavish Baroque decoration of many monuments, and the Neapolitan paintings of Caravaggio and his followers.

The Bourbons

The Austrian Habsburgs ruled over the Kingdom of the Two Sicilies only until 1734 as a result of the outbreak of hostilities between them and their French counterparts, the Bourbons. The 18-year-old Charles, son of Philip V and Elisabetta Farnese, entered the city with his army in May 1734, crowning himself Charles III in 1735, a move confirmed by the Peace of Vienna four years later. During the quarter-century of his reign, Charles ordered the construction of a number of prestigious buildings and made some attempt to deal with the city's problems through channelling funds from churches to public works and industry, and commissioning an immense "Hotel for the Poor." The San Carlo opera house – Europe's finest – and the grandiose palaces at Portici, Capodimonte and Caserta, all date from his reign. He also oversaw excavation work at Pompeii and Herculaneum and ordered the building of the Archeological Museum to house the treasures found at those sites. The exciting finds brought visitors from all over Europe. This, together with the new monuments built by Charles, who had restored the city to the status of a great capital, meant that Naples' place on the Grand Tour was henceforth assured.

Charles III by Goya

In 1759 Charles abdicated and left for Spain to succeed his father as king there. His appointed heir and third son was only eight years old and, left to the care of advisers in Naples, grew up wild and untutored. A true Neapolitan, whose preferred language was the local dialect, Ferdinand became known as the Lazzarone King, for his familiarity with the young layabouts so often remarked upon by visitors to the city. His wife, Maria Carolina, daughter of the Austrian Empress, quickly saw the opportunity to take charge, dismissing her husband's advisers and installing as her prime minister John Acton, a French-born navy man of British origin.

Over the 18th century, Naples had become a center of Enlightenment thinking, second only to France in the quality of its jurists and philosophers. Among them, Giambattista Vico, Antonio Genovesi and Gaetano Filangieri were luminaries. In many respects they were the precursors of the Neapolitan Jacobins who would come to an unfortunate end in 1799. The events of the short-lived Parthenopean Republic had their origin in the outbreak of the French Revolution. The queen of Naples, Maria Carolina, was the sister of Marie Antoinette, and understandably shocked and dismayed at the rapidly moving popular uprising that saw first the arrest, and then execution of the French Queen in 1793. Naples joined the anti-French alliance, but fled before the advance of General

Above: Beverello Harbor in Naples

Below: Café Gambrinus, in Piazza Trieste e Trento near the Teatro San Carlo and the Palazzo Reale in Naples

Above: View across the Bay of Naples to Vesuvius
Below: Marina di Corricella, on the island of Procida

Santa Maria della Pietà on Procida

Above: View from the Greek ruins at Cumae in the Campi Flegrei region.

Below: Sacellum or sunken chapel of the Augustales, Miseno

Championnet, who led French forces into Rome at the end of 1798, and arrived in Naples itself in early 1799.

Admiral Nelson

Events were now complicated by the unfortunate circumstance of the British Admiral Nelson's infatuation with the notorious Emma Hamilton, ex-prostitute and now wife of the British envoy to Naples, William Hamilton. Emma had become close friends with the Queen and identified vehemently with the royalists. She convinced Nelson to take the royal couple, with the Prime Minister Acton and the Hamiltons, away from danger, to Sicily. In Naples itself, the Republicans failed to win over the mainly monarchist masses, who rounded on the Neapolitan liberals as soon as French troops left the city, supported by a Christian army from the south. In June of 1799 the liberals capitulated and were then rounded up and executed. Nelson, goaded by Emma's fanatical royalism, played a singularly ill-judged and inappropriate part in this bloodbath, even staging the "trial" and murder of the much-respected Admiral Francesco Caracciolo – who had defected to the rebels – aboard his ship. More executions were carried out on Nelson's orders at Ischia where inhabitants had decorated a "tree of freedom" with the revolutionary cockade.

Emma Hamilton

The King himself did not return to the city until 1802, only a minor player in the war that now engulfed Europe. He could do little more than barter his kingdom's independence for some minor possessions in Tuscany. On January 14, 1806, French forces under Napoleon's brother, Joseph Bonaparte, again took Naples, and the King and Queen once more escaped into exile on Sicily. Joseph was declared King but, on becoming ruler of Spain, was replaced by his brother-in-law Joachim Murat in 1808. Despite a series of reforms including land redistribution, and the weakening of aristocratic power, the people of southern Italy were unenthusiastic about their new rulers, staging a number of popular protests around the region. Among positive measures taken by the Bonapartists, was a renewed interest in Pompeii.

The French erected new fortifications on Ischia and at Massa, as a defence against the English, who, under Hudson Lowe, occupied Capri. Despite fortifying the island, the French regained it in 1808 – an event described by writer and long-term Capri resident Norman Douglas, as "a discreditable Lowe business." In June 1809 the British retalitated, taking Procida and Ischia. In 1815, Murat was forced to abdicate and, later that year, attempting to retake his kingdom, was shot and killed by Bourbon troops.

After the final victory over Napoleon, Ferdinand was reinstated as ruler. But, despite paying lip service to constitutional reforms, he remained unable to adjust to the changing status of the monarchy. He died in 1825. Ferdinand II, who became king in 1830, presided over a number of important public works. The first railway line in Italy, between Naples and Portici, opened in 1839, and was soon extended to Pompeii, bringing streams of visitors to the Sorrento Peninsula. Byron, Keats, Dickens and Goethe, were succeeded by many other figures of note. A road was also constructed, linking Sorrento to Massa Lubrense. Ischia had a less happy time: In 1825 an earthquake reduced Casamicciola to a pile of rubble.

Piecemeal reforms, however, could do little for a suffering city, overpopulated and prey to disease. Cholera killed thousands in 1836-37, and in 1848, the year of popular insurrections across Europe, Ferdinand granted a liberal constitution to Naples, while simultaneously supporting conservatives within and outside the city. He would be nicknamed King Bomba, after his troops shelled Messina during the revolutionary ferment of that year. The Bourbons were by now seriously out of step with Neapolitans who increasingly supported the ideals of the Risorgimento. When Garibaldi's expeditionary force began its march from the south in 1860, riots erupted in Naples to support it. In a desperate attempt to restore order, the Camorra was called in, and the King made yet another half-hearted attempt to introduce constitutional reform. To no avail.

Unification & After

Garibaldi

Garibaldi entered Naples on September 7, 1860 to popular acclaim. Neapolitans had bought into the promise of Italian unification, and displayed banners of the northern Italian Savoy royal family. Disillusion would come later. They voted enthusiastically in favor of joining an Italy ruled by Victor Emmanuel II of Savoy on October 21st, and on February 13, 1861, the last of the Bourbon rulers capitulated to Piedmontese troops led by Garibaldi. The Bourbon entourage with a number of its defeated troops moved to Ischia where many of them died soon afterwards in a typhus epidemic.

Ferdinand was an anachronism, but his regime had also laid the foundations of modern industry and built that great engineering feat – the Amalfi coastal road. Capri – a favored hunting and tourist destination of the Bourbons – also flourished, as many visitors followed in their wake. Procida had been another royal domain, while its fortress was turned into a prison. The renewed interest in antiquity also prompted the rediscovery of the Phlegrean Fields. Many sketches were made of Baia's ruins, which became a mandatory part of the Grand Tour for European visitors.

The late 19th century would see further industrial development in the region with the growth of the shipbuilding industry in the bay of Naples. However, with the focus of the new Italy firmly centered on Rome after 1870, Naples declined in importance, and was economically disadvantaged by new tariff policies that favored northern interests. The problem of the Mezzogoiorno was thus, in many respects, as much created by the new Italy, as it was entrenched in the long, dolorous history of foreign rule in the South.

By the 1880s, decades of neglect of a city beset by problems of overcrowding and poor sanitation, aggravated by the unfair trade policies adopted after unification, came home to roost in a devastating cholera epidemic. By 1911, when a second outbreak killed more than 2,000 inhabitants, Naples' port was crowded with emigrants fleeing to America and a better life. This, on the 50th birthday of a united Italy, was an ironic comment on the failures of national politicians to deal effectively with the southern question.

Elsewhere, tourism flourished. The islands in the bay were annexed to Naples in 1862, and Ischia was graced with the presence of artists like Henrik Ibsen, who spent the summer of 1867 in Casamicciola, hard at work on his play, *Peer Gynt*. At Pompeii, excavations continued, new roads opened up the hills of San Pietro, beloved of Robert Browning, to the carriages of more and more visitors, and Capri was deluged with tourists, drawn to the Blue Grotto, among other attractions.

World War II & Postwar "Reconstruction"

The people of Naples suffered immensely and showed great courage during the course of World War II. One of the best English-language accounts of the region in wartime is that of Norman Lewis, who served in the Field Security Service during the war and sailed with US troops to Salerno in early September 1943. Lewis recounts "ineptitude and cowardice spreading down from the command, (which) resulted in chaos." During the war, the city of Naples suffered more than 100 Allied bombing raids, which rendered 200,000 homeless. Toward the end of September, when the Germans tried to round up the young men to press them into further service, a revolt flared up. Known as the Four Days of Naples, this remarkable feat of resistance forced the Germans to leave the city. As they went, they left a trail of destruction around the waterfront. Many damaged buildings had to be blown up by the Allies after they took over the city in late October. They found a population desperate to survive. Prostitution was rampant, and the black market increasingly siphoned off Allied supplies. The Camorra resurfaced amidst bungling Allied attempts to make use of Mafia connections, and in the general release of prisoners.

Postwar reconstruction was no less lawless. The still-monarchical Neapolitans (80% in 1946) found little solace in the Republic's attempts to ease their lot. Major projects like the Bagnoli steelworks had ended up scarring the landscape while producing little benefit. Now more money from the Cassa del Mezzogiorno, allocated to development projects, lined the pockets of unscrupulous men, and buildings were left unfinished, or erected indiscriminately and unsafely. As Achille Lauro's populist but rightwing Uomo Qualunque movement gave way to an even more unholy alliance of Christian Democrats and Camorristas, things seemed set to go from bad to worse. The islands of Capri and Ischia, meanwhile, continued to bewitch the world's exiles, even as the glorious hillside of Posillipo, overlooking them, succumbed to concrete eyesores.

Modern Times

In 1973 the unthinkable happened when cholera broke out yet again. It is not so shocking when one considers that at this time Naples was suffering Third World levels of infant mortality and high rates of infectious disease, but the renewed presence of epidemic disease again drew attention to inadequate sewer systems and appalling slums. Hard on its heels came the 1980 earthquake, which wrecked the homes of 100,000 city dwellers. Once again, a generous reconstruction budget served chiefly to line the pockets of unscrupulous contractors and engineers, and boosted Camorra activities. Fortunately, and despite continuing problems with dishonest politicians and organized crime, Naples was able to begin a process of regeneration in the 1990s, which is still ongoing. The city hosted the G7 summit in 1994, and a meeting of the G8 in 2001 when US President Clinton came to town. The futuristic modern office development known as the Centro Direzionale is about to be linked to the city via extensions to the metro network, and the shipbuilding, aerospace, automobile, telecommunications, food and fashion industries of Naples are growing. In typical Neapolitan fashion, the performance of big state companies is still outstripped by the massive underground economy, which keeps many of the officially unemployed in work.

■ The Land

Naples lies between two active volcanoes – Vesuvius and the Campi Flegrei, both of which have had an important influence on the life and history of the city and the surrounding region. Campania is also close to a fault line that runs along the Appennine mountains, and is the cause of the tectonic earthquakes which have struck the area many times in the past. The volcanic nature of the region is responsible both for many of its dramatic landscapes and its renowned fertility. Procida, like Ischia, is of volcanic origin, made up of four extinct craters, as both belong to the Flegrean zone. Capri, however, is an island of limestone rock, which represents the tip of the Monti Lattari mountain chain of the Sorrento Peninsula.

A Violent Geology

The geological feature that best defines Naples and the bay area is Vesuvius. The most densely populated (with almost half a million residents in the 20 towns around its flanks), Vesuvius is also the best-known volcano in the world, and a complex one. Its oldest dated rock has been around some 300,000 years. The cone of Vesuvius itself formed 17,000 years ago, after the ancient volcano Somma was partially destroyed by eruptions. Two of the largest known eruptions in Europe occurred here in 5960 BC and 3580 BC; earth tremors were frequent.

Greek and Roman scholars were well aware of the volcanic nature of Vesuvius. Vitruvius, writing between 46 and 30 BC, reported that it "sometimes spouted flames on the surrounding fields" and commented that the rock known as Pompeian pumice "seems to have been formed from some other sort of rock by the heat." Strabo has left us the best description of the region prior to AD 79: "Mt Vesuvius, save for its summit, has dwellings all round, on farm-lands that are absolutely beautiful." He paid close attention to the rocks on the ash-colored summit and inferred that "in earlier times this district was on fire and had craters of fire, and then, because the fuel gave out, was quenched."

Vitruvius also remarked upon the unusual properties of local volcanic material. He noted "there is a naturally-occuring powder that produces remarkable results. It is found near Baia.... When mixed with lime and gravel it produces a strong building material, especially useful for piers built out into the sea, as the mixture hardens even under water." Modern scientists identify the local volcanic rock as tephrite – basaltic, but containing a number of minerals including augite and leucite.

In fact Naples is surrounded by four quaternary caldera: Campi Flegrei, Procida and Ischia, as well as Vesuvius. The earliest eruption history of the region is disputed by scholars, but from Roman times onwards, many eyewitness accounts of successive eruptive events have been recorded. Mount Epomeo on Ischia was created by volcanic uplift some 30,000 years ago, and the thermal springs and fumaroles occur at fractures along its flanks. Fumaroles with temperatures near 100°C/212°F are found on the flank of Monte Nuovo and Monte Cito and along the Maronti coast. In other areas (San Michele, Monte Rotaro, Fundera and Scarrupo di Panza), the temperature of the fumaroles does not exceed 46°C/115°F. The hot springs at Forio and Casamicciola have temperatures between 20° and 80°C/68-176°F. Scientists consider them possible sites for future eruptions, noting that a fumarolic field called Solonaria, used for the extraction of sulphur, was close to the site of the last eruption of 1302. Fumaroles and hot springs are also found in the Campi Flegrei region, but their location and use as thermal spas has been affected by bradyseism (volcanic ground movement), and many are now underwater.

Volcanic activity on Ischia is among the first recorded eruptive events in Campania. It is known, for example, that Greek colonists on the island were compelled to abandon their settlement after successive eruptions, culminating in that of Monte Rotaro around 600 BC. Syracusan settlers, who then arrived, were also driven off the island by another eruption, possibly around the present location of Ischia port between 474 and 470 BC. During Roman times, an eruption took place in 91 BC, and another in the Augustan period, which led to the Emperor's exchange of the island for Capri, in a deal with the settlers on Naples. Around Vesuvius, the first sign of a resumption of activity for the local population was the earthquake of AD 62. Seneca wrote: "Statues were thrown from their pedestals amd smashed, people wandered about completely out of their senses."

In AD 79, when Vesuvius erupted, it had been silent for more than 800 years. However, as recent scientific research has demonstrated, the people of Pompeii had plenty of time to escape, if only they could have interpreted events. A time line of the stages of eruption indicates an 18-hour window between the first Plinian event and the pyroclastic flow which would engulf the Vesuvian towns and kill all in its path.

EVENTS OF AUGUST 24, 79

- 10 am: Earth tremors begin, and continue for several hours.
- 1 pm: Vesuvius explodes, creating ash and rock column many miles high.
- 1:45 pm: Pumice begins to fall on Pompeii.
- Midnight: The first of several pyroclastic flows occurs.
- 7 am: Pyroclastic flow reaches Pompeii.

Scientific analysis of the volcanic deposits found in the excavations of Pompeii, Herculaneum, Oplontis and Stabiae indicate their different types, which in turn reflect the method of transportation from Vesuvius, and help to facilitate a more accurate reconstruction of the event. The pyroclastic rocks (consisting predominantly of pumice and volcanic ash) found at the sites have been distinguished variously as air fall pumice, material from pyroclastic flows, and ground surge deposit. They serve to indicate the phases of volcanic activity. The initial explosion, which sent a cloud of ash and rock several miles into the air, created the first type of material – pumice fall. This is now known as a plinian phase. Flat roofs of some houses collapsed during this phase – as are in evidence at Oplontis, where columns, which supported the portico roof, lie horizontally. Wind direction meant that Herculaneum was less affected by the plinian phase. However, when the pyroclastic surges began, several hours later, in the middle of the night, Herculaneum was in the path of the initial flow. Vesuvius now unleashed waves of burning ash, rock, and dust particles, which rolled down the mountainside instead of rising into the sky.

Pyroclastic flows can move at high speeds but their path is determined by the local topography, i.e., they usually flow along valleys and come to a stop in depressions or on lowlands, where deposits of several yards thickness form. This first Vesuvian avalanche tore tiles off roofs, heated wood to at least 400°C/750°F and killed any living creatures in its path. The discovery of 80 skeletons buried in caves used as boathouses along the beach initially confused scientists by their natural, relaxed posture – unlike the contorted figures in the Pompeii casts. This anomaly has now been explained by a team of scientists working with Naples University. They have concluded that the bodies were caught in a pyroclastic flow of intense heat – around 500°C. Indeed, so fierce was the heat that the victims died in a fraction of a second, not long enough for any reactions of self-protection (such as would produce contortions); the insides of their skulls blackened, the enamel on their teeth cracked; skulls fractured due to the violent vaporization of their brains. In under a second, only bones remained. Twisted feet and hands indicate post-mortem heat-induced muscle contraction.

Volcanic rocks covered the dead of Herculaneum. Mudflows also occurred, created by the renewed movement of other deposits. Meanwhile, several more pyroclastic flows surged from Vesuvius. One moved southwards toward Pompeii. Scientists believe that several pyroclastic waves were generated, of which at least one was of the kind known as a ground surge deposit. This usually precedes pyroclastic flows, in many cases by only a few seconds, and was observed when Mt Pelée erupted on Martinique in 1902. Traveling at speeds of more than 60 mph, it killed all but two of the 28,000 inhabitants of a nearby city. The deposit left behind was only eight to 12 inches thick, yet it had been spectacularly destructive, flattening stone buildings. This most violent form of volcanic activity is now known as Pelean. Deposits of this type have been found in the excavations around Vesuvius.

After the eruption of AD 79, Emperor Titus set up a rescue effort and put measures in place to control looting, but initial attempts to rebuild were affected by further eruptions. Galenus reported around 172 AD that Vesuvius was still burning, and in 202-3 AD so violent an eruption occurred that it was heard in Capua, 56 km/34 miles away. A further event occurred on November 6, 472, when an eyewitness testified that "Vesuvius... erupted the burning interiors, caused night during the day and covered all Europe with fine ash." A more detailed description was made of another eruption in 512. Cassiodorus wrote "a burnt ash flies in the sky, and, forming ashy clouds, it rains with ash droplets also in the provinces beyond the sea.... It is possible to see ash rivers flowing like liquid, bringing hot sands and... the fields grow suddenly up to the top of the trees... and are ravished by the sudden heat." Vesuvius continued to be active, with reports of further lava flows in 685, 787 and 968. There then followed a quiescent period until June 1st, 1139, when a strong explosive eruption occurred, lasting eight days, ashes from which reached Salerno, Benevento, Capua and Naples. No further reliable evidence of volcanic activity is available until a less severe incident around 1500. For the next 131 years, Vesuvius remained quiet.

Instead it was at Ischia that the next volcanic eruption in the region occurred. In 1301-2, lava flowed from Mt Epomeo to Ischia Ponte, destroying all in its path, and prompting residents to evacuate the island. Next it was the turn of the Campi Flegrei: in 1538 a new volcano named Monte Nuovo formed in a matter of days. The 17th century was then marked by a series of geological catastrophes. In 1627 a violent earthquake shook southern Italy and destroyed the city of San Severo, causing an estimated 5,000 deaths. Four years later, Vesuvius again erupted with an extraordinary violence that left thousands dead. Once again the inhabitants had forgotten the volcano in their midst. Large trees covered the Great Cone; thus its reawakening during the night of December 16th, 1631 took everyone by surprise. An eyewitness ruefully reported on the extent of the damage: "Densely inhabited lands, wonderful villas, with rich and sumptuous gardens, and many large palaces with lovely orchards and gardens" were razed to the ground while the large tracts of cultivated land had been ruined "part from the fire, part from the ash, some from the fallen stones and much more from the water." It seems likely that more pyroclastic flows had occurred because it was noted that at San Giorgio a Cremano, San Sebastiano, Massa, Pollena and Trocchia all was destroyed. Only a few houses were left standing at Torre Annunziata while "ash rose several feet high at Herculaneum." Yet more was to come. In 1638 one of the biggest known earthquakes of southern Italy destroyed a large swathe of Calabria. And Vesuvius kept blowing its top, with further eruptions in 1694, 1767, 1794 (which again devastated Torre del Greco) 1822, 1834, 1850 and 1872, followed by a series of slow lava effusions.

Then came a great blow to the long-suffering inhabitants of Ischia. Two earthquakes, in 1881 and 1883, occurred at the town of Casamicciola. The first killed 129 people and wrecked or damaged hundreds of buildings there and in Lacco Ameno and Forio. Then, on July 28, 1883, another earthquake, lasting 16 seconds, proved even more deadly. Nearly 2,000 died on Casamicciola, many of them tourists; numerous houses and some churches collapsed. The casualties extended to Forio, Serrara Fontana and Barano.

In the early 20th century, Vesuvius erupted yet again – beginning with slow lava flows in May 1905, exhibiting strombolian (explosive) activity in January 1906, and culminating with lava fountains and earthquakes in 1906, during which an eruptive column of gas and ash rose over 30,000 feet into the sky. The shape of the mountain altered, with the formation of a new crater. Further lava flows filled the crater and then beyond the Somma caldera rim in 1929 down to the village of Terzigno on the eastern slope. By 1944, the original crater had been almost entirely effaced by the new lava field. In that year a final eruption occurred at Vesuvius, following the now familiar pattern of lava flow, succeeded by lava fountains and terminating in an explosive phase characterized by an eruption column. Once again Terzigno was affected, and allied planes stationed nearby were destroyed, as were the villages of San Sebastiano and Massa. Since then, the volcano has been quiescent, without even the plume of smoke that was once a familiar landmark.

The evidence of past and present volcanic activity can be seen all around the region. The deposits from AD 79 can be seen both on the slopes of the volcano and as far away as Castellammare. The tuff cliffs of Sorrento are themselves a volcanic covering. In Herculaneum the events of that year created a subsidence along the coast as the volcano deflated, while subsequent volcanic deposits have caused the coast to retreat by 750 feet. Thus in one place two contrasting effects of volcanic action can be seen: land subsidence and land formation.

Even more striking are the effects of bradyseism in the Campi Flegrei area and on Ischia. Bradyseism is the name given to slow ground movements caused by volcanic activity. The land alternatively rises or sinks. The instability of the region has been highlighted by travel writer Bill Bryson, who wrote, "the citizens of Pozzuoli enjoy the dubious distinction of living on the most geologically unstable piece of land on the planet.... They experience up to 4,000 earth tremors a year, sometimes as many as a hundred in a day." The effects of bradyseism are localized so that, while today sections of the ancient Roman road at Baia are 18 feet underground, at Lake Avernus, by contrast, the land is at much the same level as in the days of the Emperor Augustus. In ancient times, bradyseism was attributed to divine punishment. Thus in the sixth century St Paul was said to have caused the city to sink into the sea as a punishment for the inhabitants of Puteoli who had sentenced him to death.

Vesuvius' Last Eruption

Norman Lewis, *Naples '44*

March 19th, 1944: Today Vesuvius erupted. It was the most majestic and terrible sight I have ever seen or ever expect to see. The smoke from the crater slowly built up into a great bulging shape having all the appearance of solidity. It swelled and expanded so slowly that there was no sign of movement in the cloud which, by evening, must have risen 30 or 40,000 feet into the sky, and measured many miles across.

At night the lava streams began to trickle down the mountain's slopes. By day the spectacle was calm but now the eruption showed a terrible vivacity. Fiery symbols were scrawled across the water of the bay, and periodically the crater discharged mines of serpents into a sky which was the deepest of blood reds and pulsating everywhere with lightning reflections.

March 20th 1944: Today the sky was fogged over and ash was falling, and everything – the buildings, streets and fields – was covered to a depth of a half-inch in a smooth grey pall. At Sorrento, and on Capri and Ischia the ash lay already in places several inches deep.

At San Sebastiano: The lava was pushing its way very quietly down the main street, and about 50 yards from the edge of this great, slowly-shifting slagheap, a crowd of several hundred people, mostly in black, knelt in prayer. Holy banners and church images were held aloft, and acolytes swung censers and sprinkled holy water in the direction of the cinders.... I had been prepared for rivers of fire, but there was no fire and no burning anywhere – only the slow, deliberate suffocation of the town under millions of tons of clinkers. The lava was moving at a rate of only a few yards an hour, and it had covered half the town to a depth of perhaps 30 feet. A complete, undamaged cupola of a church, severed from the submerged building, jogged slowly toward us on its bed of cinders. The whole process was strangely quiet.... A house, cautiously encircled and then overwhelmed, disappeared from sight intact, and a faint, distant grinding sound followed as the lava began its digestion."

Flora & Fauna

Naples and its bay area is a densely populated region not immediately associated with nature reserves and abundant fauna. In fact there are a number of protected areas where indigenous plant and animal species can be enjoyed, and lots of pleasant clifftop walks. The Vesuvian and Cilento national parks publish information booklets about local flora and fauna and suitable itineraries. The Sorrento Peninsula and the islands are criss-crossed by ancient paths, which offer visitors an opportunity to escape from the bustle of resort towns and commune with nature.

The Mediterranean-type vegetation that grows on **Vesuvius** owes its existence to a silver lichen, *Stereocaulon vesuvianum*, which grows first, preparing the way for other species. Of the hundreds of plants that have colonized the volcano, there are 20 species of orchids, and several endemic plants. Foxes, rabbits and hares are also found on Vesuvius, together with more than a hundred types of birds, and several reptiles, including the rat snake. Some 44 different butterflies have been seen in the region. In the summer months the area is strongly perfumed by the yellow-flowered broom that grows here in profusion.

Primula palinuri

There are around 1,800 different plant species in the **Cilento National Park**, 10% of which are endemic or rare, of which the best known is the park's symbol, the primula of Palinuro (*Primula palinuri*). The primula, carnations, centaurea, iberis, and the Neapolitan campanula are coastal cliff dwellers that give the landscape a rare beauty. On the beaches, the increasingly rare sea lily (*Pancratium maritimum*) can be found. In the interior, watch for Cilento brooms, carob trees, red junipers, and groves of Aleppo pines. At higher altitudes, oaks, maples, lime-trees, elms, ash and chestnut trees cover and protect the slopes. On the mountains are the stately beech trees and a variety of maple (*Acer lobelii*). Even higher up amid the peaks of the Alburni Mountains, lives the very rare *Berberis aetnensis* bush. Among more common plants in the park are groves of birch trees, white firs, boxwood and eastern plane trees.

The animals of the Cilento National Park are very diversified due to the range of different natural environments within the reserve. On the peaks, at high altitude grasslands and on the cliffs, the bald eagle and its favorite prey, the coturnix quail and the Appennine hare can be found. The latter is now extinct elsewhere. Other predatory birds that can be seen include species of hawk and the imperial crow. On the plains, a species of field mouse (*Microtus savii*), foxes, and wolves are in evidence. Numerous types of butterflies, wall lizards and chalcides, which resemble small snakes, also reside in the park. Among the rich birdlife of the beech forests, typical species include black woodpeckers, the related sitta europaea and the bullfinch.

Coturnix

Various species of small mice are preyed upon by the wild cats, and in the rivers the population of otters is among the most important in Italy. In colder waters, in thick woods, resides a rare salamander (*Salamandrina terdigitata*). Trout, the water blackbird and numerous frogs and toads also inhabit the park. Vipers, several species of lizard and the rare harrier eagle (*Circaetus gallicus*) also grace the Cilento valley.

There are fewer rare species, but superb walks can be taken in the **Monti Lattari** along the **Sorrento Peninsula**, particularly around the 3,000-foot **Monte Faito**, with its alpine-style villages. Beech and cedar woods give way to myrtle, prickly pear, juniper and rosemary. Between March and May a small orchid (*Serapias lingua*) may be seen. Fauna that can be glimpsed while walking includes the rat snake (*Coluber viridiflavus*), hares, foxes, weasels, lizards, the Sardinian warbler (*Sylvia melanocephala*), wrens, ravens, robins, and kestrels. The **Le Tore Wood**, under the protection of the World Wildlife Fund, is particularly rich in this characteristic Mediterranean flora and fauna. In general, white heather, cyclamen, croci, poppies, thyme, mint, geraniums, lilies and honeysuckle are abundant. Lemons are everywhere in the spring, as are olive groves and vineyards. Note the characteristic *pagliarelle* coverings made of straw and chestnut wood, which protect the citrus fruit.

Capri, which broke away from the Sorrentine peninsula in the quaternary period, took with it elephants and tigers, as fossil discoveries have revealed. The island's name itself is believed to derive from the Greek word "Kapros" or wild boar, of which many fossils have also been found. Nowadays, you are more likely to see seagulls, although Capri is also home to a rare blue lizard and the endangered monk seal. With more than 800 plant species, the island is in effect a large garden perched on limestone. Pines, laurels, wild orange trees, and myrtle are common, but look out for rarities like the dwarf palm. Larger **Ischia** has pine, chestnut and oak woods.

Travel Information

Traveling to and around Naples is liable to give rise to a variety of emotions: "shock and awe" might well be appropriate reactions to the breathtaking drive along the Amalfi Coast; while negotiating traffic jams and kamikaze drivers in the towns of the region are more likely to produce irritation and expletives. Luciano de Crescenzo, the great purveyor of Neapolitan folklore, has provided a superb caricature of the local taxi driver, who goes through a red light, then, when stopped by a policeman, demands that his customer pay the fine, and finally, after passersby intervene and persuade the lawman to let him go, asks his hapless passenger at the end of the journey to decide himself what the fare should be. There are certainly more than a few dodgy characters in Naples, but the alert traveler who avoids taking risks can concentrate instead on all that the region has to offer: exceptional restaurants, panoramic hotels, haute couture, dazzling walks on volcanic cliffs and boat trips to submerged cities among them.

In this Chapter

■ Transport

Getting to Naples

Scheduled flights to Naples operate from major European cities. **British Airways** flights leave from Gatwick airport (☎ 0870 850 9850, www.ba.com), and **BMI** flies direct from Heathrow (☎ 0870 607 0555, www.flybmi.com), as does **Alitalia**, but via Milan and Rome, which adds considerably to the time and inconvenience of the journey. In addition, the budget airline **EasyJet** runs daily flights from Stansted (UK) and a seasonal service from Gatwick, Berlin and Paris (☎ 0870 600 0000, www.easyjet.com). If you plan your trip well in advance this is the cheapest option, but is a no-frills, no-refreshment journey. Flights from Nice and Athens to Naples (www.alpieagles.com) from Berlin (www.hix.com) and Brussels (www.flysn.com) are also available in summer. Visitors from North America can alternatively fly directly to

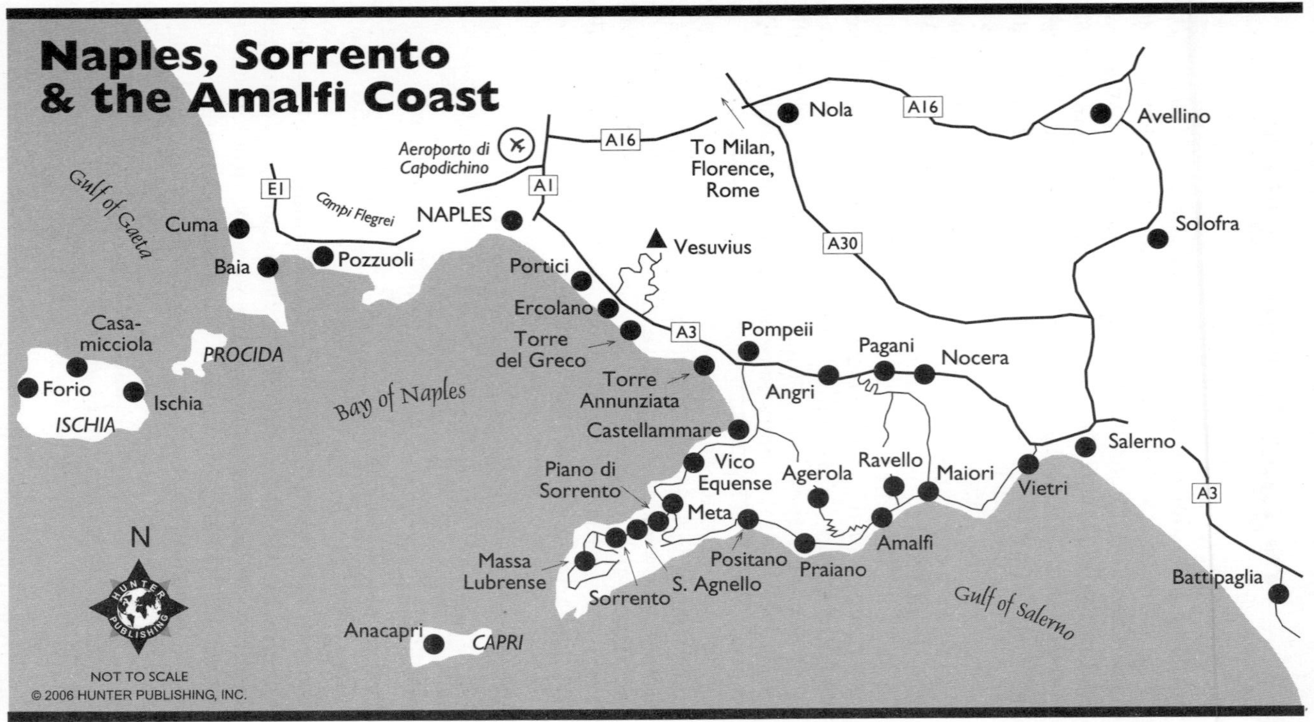
Naples, Sorrento
& the Amalfi Coast
Nola
A16
Avellino
A16
Aeroporto di Capodichino
To Milan, Florence, Rome
E1
A1
Gulf of Gaeta
Campi Flegrei
NAPLES
Cuma
Solofra
Vesuvius
A30
Baia
Pozzuoli
Portici
Ercolano
Casa-micciola
A3
Pompeii
Torre del Greco
PROCIDA
Pagani
Nocera
Forio
Ischia
Bay of Naples
Torre Annunziata
Angri
ISCHIA
Castellammare
Salerno
Vico Equense
Piano di Sorrento
Agerola
Ravello
Maiori
Vietri
A3
Meta
Amalfi
N
Massa Lubrense
Positano
Praiano
S. Agnello
Sorrento
Battipaglia
Gulf of Salerno
HUNTER PUBLISHING
Anacapri
CAPRI
NOT TO SCALE
© 2006 HUNTER PUBLISHING, INC.

Rome for onward transfer to Naples and the coastal resorts. **American Airlines** (www.aa.com) and **Delta** (www.delta.com) operate direct flights from the US to Rome.

Naples Capodichino International Airport (☎ 081 789 6259, www.gesac.it) is located seven km/4.8 miles northwest from the city center, on Viale Umberto Maddalena. An airport bus (☎ 800 639 525) goes to the main railway station on Piazza Garibaldi and to the Molo Beverello where hydrofoils arrive and depart for the islands in the Bay of Naples and Sorrento, and car ferries go farther afield – to Sicily and Sardinia. The journey from Naples airport to the town center takes around 30 minutes, depending on traffic. A taxi service is also available from the airport, and a free shuttle service goes to the nearby car rental bays. A bus service also goes directly to Sorrento from the airport but is not very frequent. A direct bus service, run by the Curreri company (☎ 081 801 5420), operates from the airport to Sorrento, but services are not very frequent.

Journey time between Naples airport and the Sorrento Peninsula varies between one and two hours, depending on traffic, and costs around €5. The same trip by taxi would cost between €70 and €100. Alternatively, a bus, taxi or shuttle can be taken from the airport to the Circumvesuviana rail station in Naples. The airport ANM bus goes from outside the arrivals terminal to the station, stopping at the side entrance on Via G. Ferraris. When making the return journey from the Naples railway station to the airport, the Alibus leaves at 55 and 25 minutes past the hour. The bus stop is outside the post office on the Corso Novara which is to the right of Piazza Garibaldi as you exit the railway station.

The train service from Rome is frequent; and takes two hours on average. The travel time depends on the type of the train; Eurostar trains are the fastest but also the most expensive. Alternatively, you may travel by Intercity or regional rail services (the slowest) the latter are, however, more frequent. Most trains arrive at the Stazione Centrale (www.trenitalia.com) on Piazza Garibaldi. A left luggage office is open 24 hours, and tourist information is available. Underneath the station is the Metropolitana service to Campi Flegrei. There are two further train services to the Campi

Flegrei from Naples Montesanto: the Circumflegrea train goes to Cuma and the Ferrovia Cumana to Pozzuoli, Baia and Bagnoli (☎ 089 551 3328). A bus service also operates from Rome to Sorrento twice daily departing from Tiburtina station and arriving at Tasso Square. Journey time is between 2½ to four hours depending on traffic.

Moving Around Naples

American travel writer Bill Bryson's account of arriving in Naples is a classic: "I emerged from the train and was greeted by 27 taxi drivers, all wanting to take me someplace nice and probably distant, but I waved them away and transferred myself by foot from the squalor of the central station to the squalor of the nearby Circumvesuviana station, passing through an uninterrupted stretch of squalor en route. All along the sidewalks people sat at wobbly tables selling packets of cigarettes and cheap novelties.... The city had a strange, knocked-about appeal to it – a tantalizing surfeit of grubbiness and commotion, quite unlike any city I had seen before." You have been warned!

Within the center of Naples, the simplest way to see the sites is to walk. There have been a number of initiatives in recent years to make visiting the *Centro Storico* easier. Free maps at the tourist office list important monuments, with short texts about them. While at the tourist office, make sure to pick up a copy of the monthly free ***Qui Napoli*** magazine, which also lists up-to-date prices for museums and other paying sites.

Significant historic buildings and churches have small plaques, and a recent tourist innovation – Museo Aperto Napoli – has provided useful signage on important monuments. The **Main Center of the Museo Aperto of Naples** is in the Via P Colletta. For €6 you can obtain the audio guide for one day along with a map and a guide book to the sites. The latter are to keep; the audio guide must be returned at the end of the day. The price also includes a pizza and soft drink at the center. In the same building is a museum which costs €5 to visit (or €10 as an all-in-one price with the audio guide). The map costs €1 and the booklet €2 if you do not take the guided tour. The exhibits change and recently included "la magia del sesto senso" and "arte preseppiale" – "the magic of the sixth sense" and "Nativity art." There is also a good book and souvenir shop open every day except Wed from 10 am to 6 pm at the center. (☎ 081 563 6062). The Museo Aperto audio tours are a good do-it-yourself alternative to a guided tour through the historic center.

Travelers who have the time and intention to visit numerous sites of interest should pick up a **Campania Arte Card**. There are three options. 1) A three-day card is valid for all sites in **Naples and the Campi Flegrei**, which offers two free visits and half-price entry to all other sites, together with free use of public transport in Naples and the Campi Flegrei. The card costs €13, or €8 for those aged 18-25. 2) The second option is the three-day card, valid for all sites in **Campania** (thus including Caserta, Paestum, Pompei and Herculaneum). The cost is €25, or €18 for 18-25 year olds. 3) Finally, dedicated tourists can purchase the **seven-day Campania Arte Card**, which offers free admittance to all sites for €28 or €21 for 18-25 year olds, but does not include transport. The cards can be purchased at Naples airport, the main railway stations and the port of Naples, and also in hotels, travel agencies, newstands, and at the museums and archeological sites. Internet users can also buy online (☎ 800 600 601, www.campaniartecard.it).

Visitors wanting to join organized tours can call **Itinera**, a private company which operates guided excursions to museums, theaters, churches, palaces, castles, handicraft shops and the archeological sites (☎ 081 664 545).

Driving is almost impossible in the *Centro Storico*, where most of the historic churches are located. Visitors arriving in Naples by car should expect heavy traffic jams, particularly in the morning, at lunchtime and in the early evening. On weekends late evening jams also build up as everyone goes out to their favorite restaurants at around the same time. Aggressive car towing is in operation, and even in designated parking spaces, touts are likely to demand money in return for "keeping an eye" on your vehicle. Thus, while they are relatively expensive, the supervised parking lots are definitely the best option. Major car rental companies have desks at the main railway station in Naples and at the airport.

The city is actually quite spread out and for some sightseeing it is necessary to take the bus, a funicular train, or the *Metropolitana* (more like an infrequent train service than a city metro at present, although new stations are being built). Line 6 of the metro is currently under construction and connects the western part of the city with the port of Naples and to Metro Line 1 via an interchange junction in Piazza Municipio. Plans are being made for a new 2.4-mile/four-km, five-station track to run from the Centro Direzionale to Capodichino Airport. Work is also underway for a line from Dante to Centro Direzionale which will lead to the creation of new Toledo, Municipio, University, Duomo and Garibaldi stations. The historical importance of the area has required a close working relationship with the authorities in charge of Archeological and Architectural Conservation and consequently further delays may occur if sites of archeological interest are discovered. When the new lines are open, Naples should be a much easier city to travel around; at present going from one end to the other is time-consuming.

For the present, the *Metropolitana* is really only useful for trips between the central station, Vomero and Mergellina and the Campi Flegrei. While planning journeys, it is wise to remember that the area around Piazza Garibaldi (currently undergoing restoration work, as a new metro is being built) and the central station is notorious for its underworld, seedy air. The Chinese and Arab quarters between the *Centro Storico* and the Piazza Garibaldi are colorful by day, but can be less welcoming, and possibly dangerous, at night.

The **Unico Napoli Card** allows travel by bus as well as by metro and train within the city and its outskirts. The **ANM bus** services are numerous but if your destination is at a terminus be prepared to sit on the bus for 50 minutes as the routes are often circuitous and the slow progress is further impeded by heavy traffic. While some routes are served by buses that run every 10 minutes, others may operate only at half-hourly or hourly intervals. It is usually quicker to walk short distances, or to check the whereabouts of the place you want to visit, and take the first bus that will head you in the right direction. There is a limited bus service in the late evening, operating until around 1 am from Piazza Garibaldi.

Vomero and Posillipo are among the intra-city routes, while outside Naples night buses serve Pozzuoli, Torre del Greco, and Herculaneum.

The brightly colored open-topped **Citysightseeing Napoli bus** (☎ 081 551 7279) is an alternative way to visit the city, although it is much more expensive than the one-day travelcard, at €18 for adults, €9 for children and €54 for a family ticket. It is unlikely that you will have the time or energy to do all the major sites in one day, but if your time is limited, and you want to see a lot quickly, the three routes run by this bus take in most of the difficult-to-access tourist attractions. Route A, the Art Tour, covers the Archeological Museum and Capodimonte, as well as the Castel Nuovo and the *Centro Storico*. Route B follows the Lungomare and the scenic Posillipo road, and Route C goes up to Vomero, for a visit to Villa Floridiana. A commentary in eight languages is provided.

The **Funicolare di Chiaia** and the **Funicolare Centrale** – both near Piazza Vanvitelli in Vomero – are a quick way of going up and down the city slopes. The first goes to Piazza Amedeo and the second to Augusteo near Piazza Municipio. The Montesanto funicular was closed for lengthy repairs in 2004 but has now reopened.

Taxis are expensive, and it is important to make sure that the meter is working correctly. Taxi ranks can be found at the train stations, and on the main piazzas. They are not, however, as ubiquitous as London and New York taxis, so call from your hotel first if you are making an important journey (☎ 081 556 4444 or 081 556 0202).

Farther Afield

Towns along the Bay of Naples are well served by public transport, with both rail and bus services; the **Circumvesuviana** rail service, which threads through the Vesuvian region from Naples to Sorrento, is the most convenient way to visit Pompeii, Herculaneum and the towns of the Sorrento Peninsula (www.vesuviana.it). The Amalfi Coast – on the other side of the peninsula – can only be reached by road or boat, while trips to the islands can be made from Naples and the larger

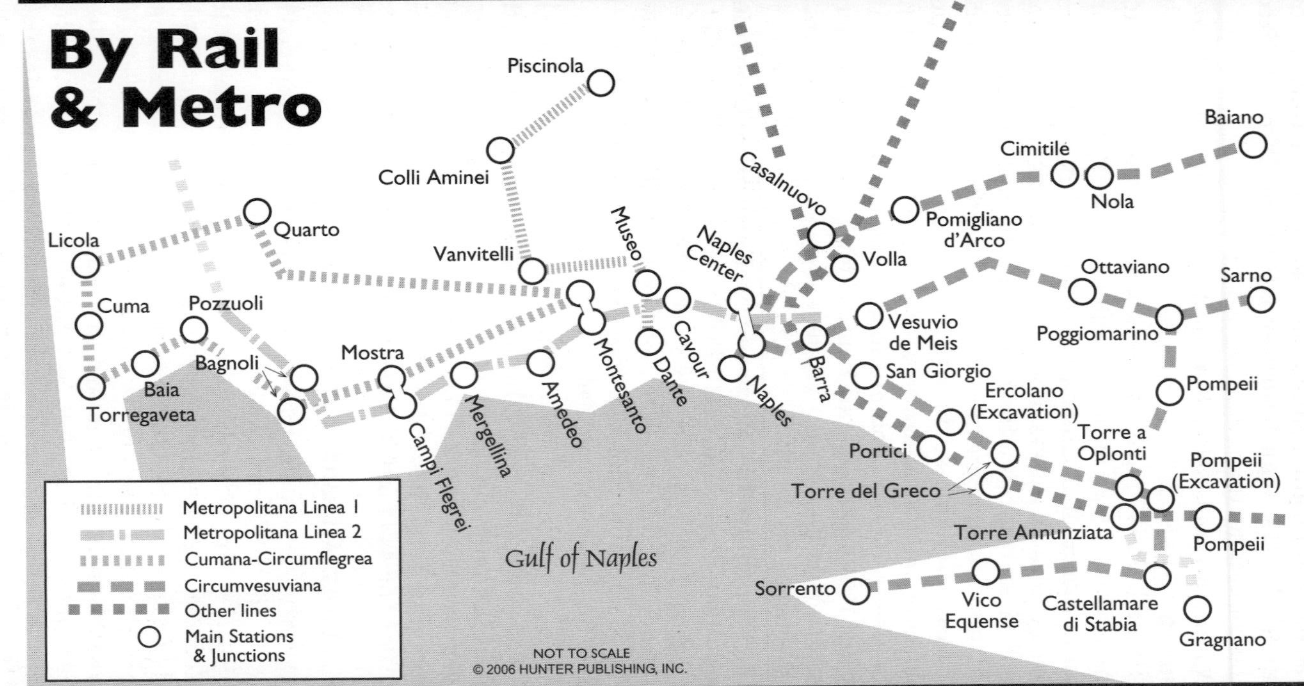
By Rail & Metro
Piscinola
Colli Aminei
Vanvitelli
Museo
Licola
Quarto
Cuma
Pozzuoli
Baia
Torregaveta
Bagnoli
Mostra
Campi Flegrei
Mergellina
Amedeo
Montesanto
Dante
Cavour
Naples Center
Naples
Casalnuovo
Volla
Pomigliano d'Arco
Cimitile
Nola
Baiano
Ottaviano
Sarno
Poggiomarino
Vesuvio de Meis
Barra
San Giorgio
Pompeii
Ercolano (Excavation)
Portici
Torre del Greco
Torre a Oplonti
Pompeii (Excavation)
Torre Annunziata
Pompeii
Sorrento
Vico Equense
Castellamare di Stabia
Gragnano
Gulf of Naples
Metropolitana Linea 1
Metropolitana Linea 2
Cumana-Circumflegrea
Circumvesuviana
Other lines
Main Stations & Junctions
NOT TO SCALE
© 2006 HUNTER PUBLISHING, INC.

coastal resorts. Caserta and Cilento can be reached by bus (☎ 081 700 1111) and rail, but the train service can be infrequent and slow. The Campi Flegrei are accessible from Naples by rail, but onward travel by bus is required to reach outlying sites of interest.

Trains leave from the Naples terminus of the Circumvesuviana rail network every 30 to 45 minutes. The journey to Sorrento takes 1½ hours and costs around €3; trains are often crowded. The towns of Pompeii and Herculaneum (Ercolano in modern Italian) are also located along this line, between Naples and Sorrento. Bill Bryson's account of a journey to Sorrento on the Circumvesuviana railway is both amusing and instructive: "We traveled out of the slums of Naples and through the slums of the suburbs and onward into a slummy strip of countryside between Vesuvius and the sea, stopping every few hundred feet at some suburban station, where 100 people would get off and 120 would get on. Even Pompeii and Ercolano looked shabby, all washing lines and piles of crumbled concrete, and I could see no sign of the ruins from the train. But a few miles farther on... the villages were stunningly pretty with long views down to the blue sea." This is a fairly accurate portrayal of the route, and it should be added that in summer the Circumvesuviana becomes very crowded, as Neapolitan day-trippers, heading for the beach, join the throngs of tourists going to Sorrento or the excavations.

Visitors wanting a more stylish train journey to Sorrento can travel in a 1940s carriage, refurbished in period style, with air conditioning and music, by booking a ticket on the privately run **Sorrento Express**, which offers Saturday and Sunday excursions, including lunch in a restaurant and a guided tour of Sorrento for an inclusive price of €52 per person, or €57 including a visit to Pompeii.

Boat travel is, of course, part of the joy of tourism in the Bay of Naples, and a choice of ferry or hydrofoil is available to most destinations. Tickets are best purchased locally. Hydrofoils are called *aliscafi* and run to Sorrento, the islands and the Amalfi Coast from Beverello Harbor in Naples every half-hour. Tickets for these and for the slower ferries (*traghetti*) can be purchased at the quayside kiosks. **AliLauro** (☎ 081 551 3352) and **SNAV** (☎ 081 761 2348) are the two major companies operating on these routes. Boat services also run from Mergellina at the other end of the Lungomare. From the harbour – Marina Piccola – in Sorrento, take a yellow bus to Piazza Tasso in Sorrento town center; it's a 10-minute walk for those unencumbered with luggage.

From Sorrento, boats also go to **Capri** (half an hour), to **Ischia** (one hour) and other venues along the coast. The **Metro del Mare** (MM) runs services along the coast from Monte di Procida to Sapri on the Cilento Coast, with an additional route to Capri (☎ 199 446 644). A *Unico Terra & Mare* transport ticket valid for both land and sea travel can be purchased at the MM ticket counters and a link with the private Archeobus service which goes to the Roman excavation sites is also provided at Torre Annunziata port.

The **Archeobus** service offers an opportunity for tourists to visit those archeological sites of the **Vesuvian region** and the **Campi Flegrei**, which are not easily accessible by rail. There are two routes. The first serves the Vesuvian region, with stops at Pompei, Boscoreale, Torre Annunziata, Pompeii and Stabia. The second route serves 16 archeological sites in the Campi Flegrei, with stops at Pozzuoli, Cuma, Bacoli and Baia. Purchase of the three-day **Campania Arte Card** (which offers free entry to museums) also entitles tourists to use the Archeobus free of charge.

For those traveling by **car**, **Sorrento** can be reached from the A2 Rome-Naples motorway, or the A16 Bari-Naples road. Take the A3 Naples-Salerno motorway and exit at Castellammare di Stabia to join the coastal road – SS 145 – which offers lovely views, but is often clogged with traffic in summer.

For **Positano** take the same route, and at Meta, take the SS 145 Nastro Azzurro route towards Salerno. If traveling from Salerno, take the Amalfi Coast road SS163. For **Ravello** and **Amalfi**, continue on the A3 until the Angri exit, and follow signs to the Valico di Chiunzi pass and Ravello. A longer but

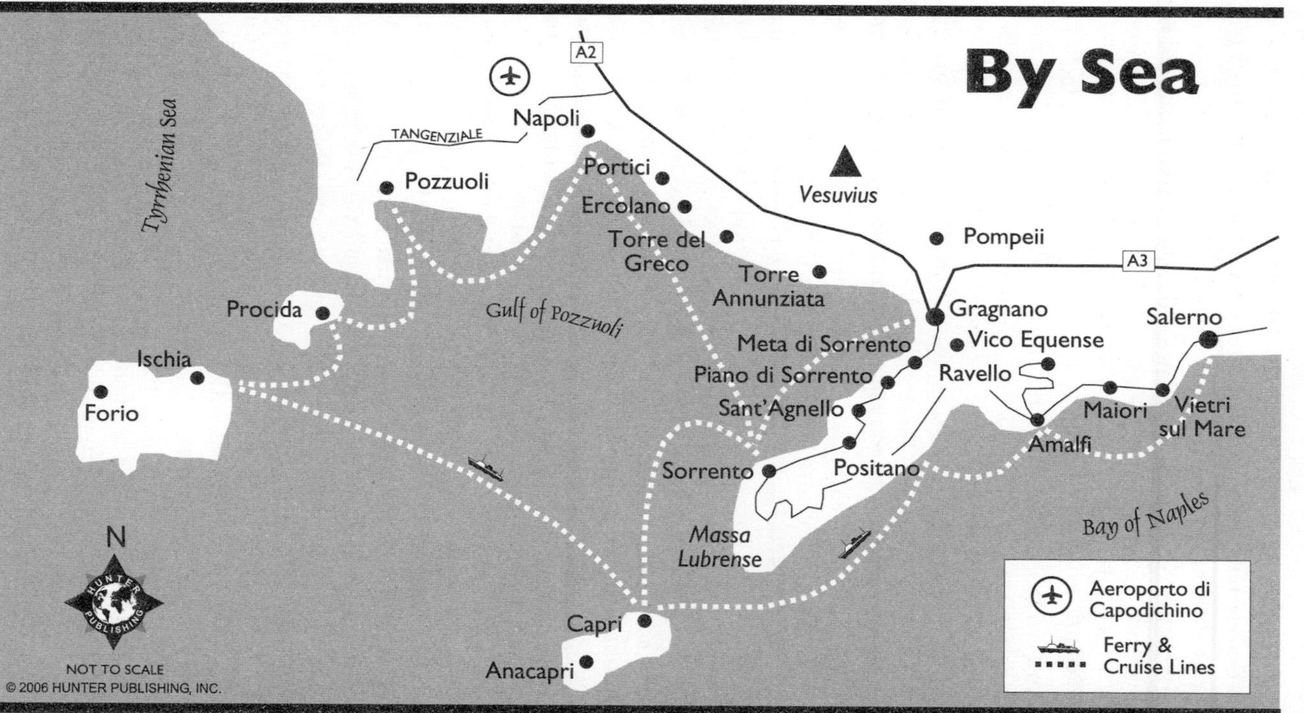
By Sea
A2
Napoli
TANGENZIALE
Pozzuoli
Tyrrhenian Sea
Portici
Ercolano
Torre del Greco
Vesuvius
Pompeii
A3
Torre Annunziata
Gragnano
Procida
Gulf of Pozzuoli
Meta di Sorrento
Vico Equense
Salerno
Ischia
Forio
Piano di Sorrento
Ravello
Sant'Agnello
Maiori
Vietri sul Mare
Amalfi
Sorrento
Positano
Bay of Naples
Massa Lubrense
N
Capri
Anacapri
Aeroporto di Capodichino
Ferry & Cruise Lines
NOT TO SCALE
© 2006 HUNTER PUBLISHING, INC.

more scenic route is on the SS 366 from Castellammare di Stabia via Gragnano which connects with the coast road two km west of Amalfi.

Around the Sorrento Peninsula itself, the **SITA buses** are an inexpensive, relatively efficient and, above all, stress-free way to travel along the often narrow coastal roads. Look for the *Fermata SITA* signs, which indicate the bus stops. Tickets should be purchased in advance in a bar, or tobacconist, and are validated by machine on the bus.

Current timetables are usually available in local tourist offices. On the timetables, *giornaliero* means daily, *feriale* means workdays (i.e., Monday to Saturday) and, conversely, *festivo* indicates Sundays and holidays. The Amalfi Coast towns are a 30-minute to one-hour bus ride from Sorrento and the SITA bus service is as reliable as the sometimes busy roads allow; it is impressive to see how skilled the drivers are at negotiating the hairpin turns. Prices are very reasonable, and for around €2 you can travel from Sorrento to Amalfi. The day tickets, where available, enable you to hop on and off the bus – but be aware that you will have around 45 minutes to wait for the next bus, and up to one hour at certain times of the day. Check the timetable for your return journey – in the summer season some buses take an alternative route to Sant'Agata sui due Golfi before continuing on to Sorrento.

At the Circumvesuviana station of Stabia, there is a funicular railway which takes travelers up the Monte Faito. Called the Funivia del Faito, the eight-minute ride leaves every half-hour or so, from 7:25 am to 7:15 pm in summer and from 9:35 am to 4:25 pm in winter.

If you are driving – and there are a number of car and scooter rental companies in Sorrento and other resorts – the winding roads on the **Amalfi Coast drive** require concentration, good driving skills, and a calm disposition. Nicknamed the "road of a thousand bends," carved out of the cliff in the mid-19th century, the views are superlative, but parking is difficult along the way, and nerves of steel are needed to deal with oncoming buses. John Steinbeck remarked ironically that the road was "carefully designed to be a little narrower than two cars side

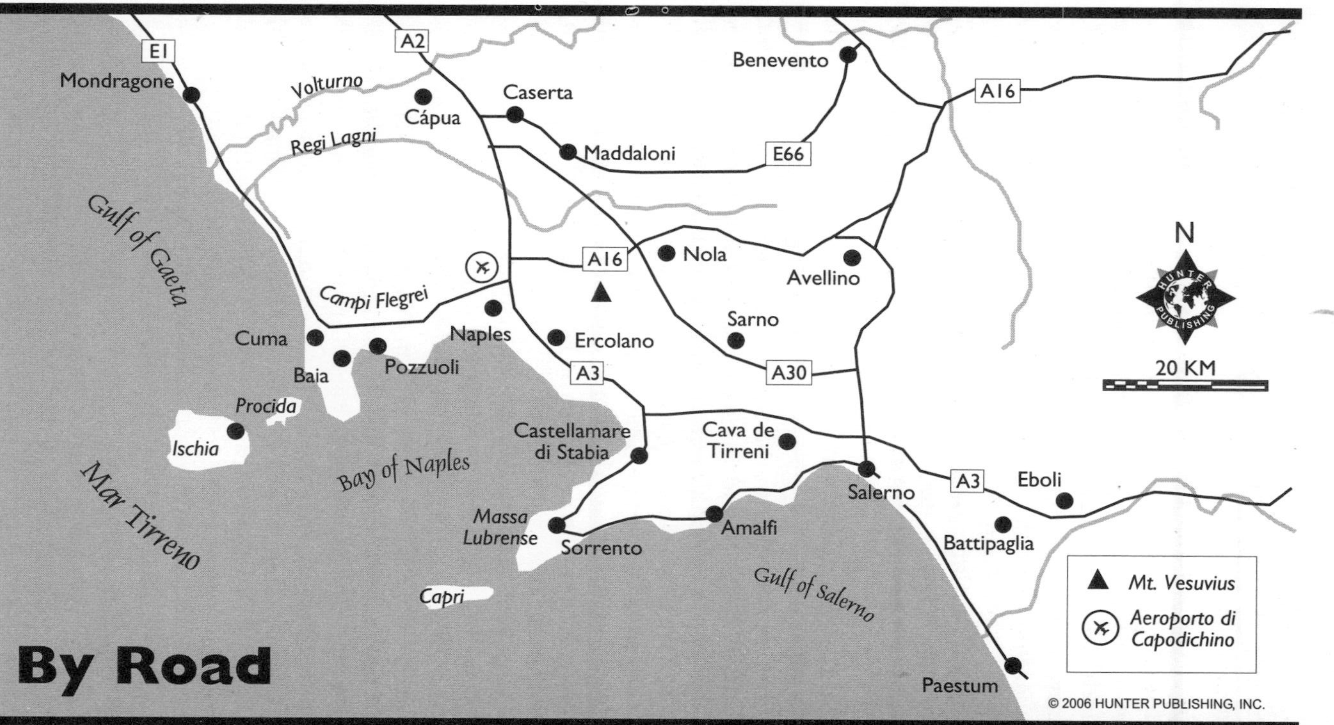
By Road
E1
A2
Mondragone
Volturno
Cápua
Caserta
Benevento
A16
Regi Lagni
Maddaloni
E66
Gulf of Gaeta
A16
Nola
Avellino
Campi Flegrei
Naples
Sarno
Cuma
Ercolano
Baia
Pozzuoli
A3
A30
N
20 KM
HUNTER PUBLISHING
Procida
Ischia
Castellamare di Stabia
Cava de Tirreni
Bay of Naples
Mar Tirreno
Salerno
A3
Eboli
Massa Lubrense
Sorrento
Amalfi
Battipaglia
Gulf of Salerno
Capri
Paestum
Mt. Vesuvius
Aeroporto di Capodichino

by side." The Amalfi resorts are 160 miles from Rome and 34 miles from Naples. The journey takes 3½ hours and 1½ hours respectively.

For luxurious travel to **Capri**, **motorboats** can be hired with steward service from **Taxi del Mare** (☎ 081 877 3600, www.taxidelmare.it) or an exclusive **helicopter** service can take travelers (☎ 081 738 7257 and 800 915 012, www.capri-helicopters.com) from the airport to their accommodation – or the nearest heliport. Excursions along the Amalfi Coast and the islands of the Bay of Naples are also offered. On Capri itself, the **Staiano brothers** run a fleet of vehicles to take guests around the island. Their clients include royals and celebrities (☎ 081 837 1544, www.staianogroup.it). Most tourists, however, take the funicular to go up to Capri and then walk or use buses to visit the island.

On **Ischia** the **SEPSA** bus service travels around the island in clockwise and anticlockwise directions at 30-minute intervals. Daytrippers are best advised to purchase a one-day ***Ischia Unico*** card and stop off at various locations. The card also enables visitors to use the smaller bus networks, for example the Inteforio transport between the Forio resort and La Mortella, two miles north of the town.

Paestum's Greek ruins can be visited on a day trip from Naples, or the coastal resorts. Located 25 miles south of Salerno, and just over 60 miles southeast of Naples, the site is accessible by bus or train from Naples and Salerno. The Salerno bus leaves half-hourly from Piazza Concordia (☎ 089 255 899) and the journey takes around one hour. To reach Paestum by car, take the A3 motorway, and exit at Battipaglia if arriving from the North, or at Eboli if arriving from the South, then follow Strada Statale (SS) 18 southbound and exit at Paestum.

Travel Contacts

Airlines

Alitalia, ☎ 081 7511494 (Naples office)

Air Canada, ☎ 800 919 091 (throughout Italy)

Air France, ☎ 081 7896259 (Naples airport)

American Airlines, ☎ 02 679141 (Milan office)

British Airways, ☎ 081 7803087/7517354 (Naples office)

British Midland, ☎ 028 0663025

Continental, ☎ 800 296 230 (throughout Italy)

Delta, ☎ 06 42010340 (Rome office); 800 864 114 (elsewhere in Italy)

Easy Jet, ☎ 848 887766

Lufthansa, ☎ 081 7804797 (Naples office)

Meridiana, ☎ 081 7517614/7801424 (Naples office)

Thomsonfly, ☎ 023 600 3582

Car & Scooter Rental

Avis, 44 Via Piedigrotta, Naples, ☎ 081 761 1365

Europcar, 10 Via Scarfoglio, Naples, ☎ 081 570 8426

Hertz, 21 Via N. Sauro Naples, ☎ 081 764 5323

Autoservizi De Martino, 253 Corso Italia, Sorrento, ☎ 081 878 2801

Jolly Scooters & Car Rental, 29 Via Fuorimura, Sorrento, ☎ 081 877 3450

Persico Autonoleggio, 33 Viale Filangieri, Massa, ☎ 081 878 9144

Rent A Scooter Milano, Fontanella SS 163, Praiano, ☎ 089 813 071

Sprint, 28 Via Roma, Procida, ☎ 081 896 9435

Taxi Services

Naples, ☎ 081 556 4444 or 081 556 0202

Sorrento, ☎ 081 878 2204

Sant'Agnello, ☎ 081 878 1428

Castellamare di Stabia, ☎ 081 870 6251

Capri, ☎ 081 837 0543

Anacapri, ☎ 081 837 1175

Rail Services

Ferrovia dello Stato, ☎ 081 567 2991

Metropolitana FS, ☎ 081 554 3188

Metropolitana Napoli, ☎ 081 748 4111

Circumvesuviana, ☎ 081 772 2444

Sepsa-Cumana, ☎ 081 551 3328

Funicolare di Capri, ☎ 081 837 0420

Ferry & Hydrofoil Services

Caremar, ☎ 081 551 3882

Alilauro, ☎ 081 761 1004

SNAV, ☎ 081 761 2348

Lauro, ☎ 081 552 2838

Car Parking Services

Parcheggio Brin, ☎ 081 763 2855

Parcheggio Colli Aminei, ☎ 081 763 2252

Parcheggio Chiaiano, ☎ 081 763 2252

Parcheggio Frullone, ☎ 081 763 2767

Parcheggio Scampia, ☎ 081 763 2769

Tour Guide Services

Itinera, 74 Corso Vittorio Emanuele, Naples, ☎ 081 664 545

Museo Aperto Napoli, 89/95 Via Pietro Colletta, Naples, ☎ 081 563 6062, www.museoapertonapoli.com

City Sightseeing Napoli, Piazza Municipio, Naples, ☎ 081 551 729

ACLI Campi Flegrei, 135 Via G De Rosa, ☎ 081 804 0620

Associazione Aliseo, 49 Via Lucullo, Baia, ☎ 081 854 5784, www.associazionealiseo.it. Tours of undersea archeological sites.

Transport Websites

www.gesac.it – Naples International Airport; arrival and departure information.

www.fs-on-line.com – Buy Italian rail tickets online and check timetables.

www.trenitalia.it – A similar service.

www.vesuviana.it – Information and timetables for the Circumvesuviana line.

www.ctpn.it – Information on bus services around Naples.

www.snavali.it – Ferry and hydrofoil services from and to Naples and the bay.

www.campaniatrasporti.it – General transport services in Campania.

www.ctpn.it – Regional bus services in Campania.

www.radiotaxinapoli.it – Taxi services in Naples.

www.metrodelmare.com – Boat taxi information on the Bay of Naples.

www.museoapertonapoli.com – Information about audio tours of Naples.

www.campaniartecard.it – Information about discount entry prices to sites.

Tourist Information Websites

www.comune.napoli.it – Official website of the comune di Napoli.

www.provincia.napoli.it – Official website of the Provincia di Napoli.

www.regione.campania.it – Official website of the Campania region.

www.touringclubcampania.it – General information about travel in the region.

caprionline.com – General information for travelers to Capri.

www.procida.net – Useful site for visitors to Procida.

www.pompeiisites.org – Official portal on cultural heritage of the Vesuvian area.

www.arethusa.net – Information about guided visits to Pompeii.

www.ravello.it/aziendaturismo – Tourist information for Ravello.

www.sorrentoinfo.com – Information about Sorrento.

www.comune.sorrento.na.it – Official site of Sorrento.

www.sorrentotours.com – Excursions in the Bay of Naples.

■ Finding a Place to Stay

In the days of the Grand Tour, visitors opted for the luxury hotels on the Lungomare and Via Posillipo or – like Shelley and his wife – rented apartments in Chiaia. Victorian poet Robert Browning stayed in a house in the Campania countryside, lent to him by the Prince of Colonna. Today visitors to Naples and the bay area have many of the same choices, indeed even a few of the very same hotels – thankfully renovated. The biggest difference between our 18th-century tourist forebears and ourselves is surely on the islands. Only the adventurous went out to Capri and Ischia then, peopled as they were mostly by donkeys and peasants. Society was shocked when the occasional aristocrat eloped with a glamorous but illiterate village girl. Nowadays, Capri and Ischia are full to bursting with hotels and holiday homes, and even little Procida has opened up to tourism. The range of accommodation available, from campsites to five-star luxury hotels, has been broadened in recent years by the proliferation of ***agriturismo*** farms and homes – countryside properties offering bed and breakfast, and more than a little exposure to the Campanian way of life.

Options, Rates & Bookings

Italian hotels are graded according to a star system, which will also reflect the cost of rooms at the establishment. There are often substantial differences in pricing according to the season. July and August are the most expensive months at coastal resorts, while the heat of Naples at this time may make a visit here uncomfortable. May, June and September offer great weather, and reasonable prices, with the added bonus of fewer crowds at the main sites. Nowadays a range of price options is available in most locations, although Capri, Sorrento, Positano, Amalfi and Ravello are generally more expensive across the board.

Visitors on a budget can opt for camping sites close to the resort towns, or for reasonably-priced family holidays you can try the less well known resorts like Piano di Sorrento, Atrani, Vietro and the Cilento coast.

Agriturismo prices vary greatly. Some have very basic accommodation and are reasonably priced. Others are in renovated palaces and offer a much better quality of accommodation at an understandably higher cost. Bookings can be made by telephone, although smaller, independent venues might require a knowledge of Italian, or through travel agents. More and more properties offer online bookings. A list of relevant websites is given at the end of this section.

Hotels & Pensioni

Top-of-the-range hotels in Naples are grouped around the Via Partenope and in locations with panoramic views such as Posillipo and Corso Emanuele II. A few of the more reasonably priced *pensioni* are also located in smart districts such as Chiaia, so check the addresses and go for the option that best suits your sightseeing itinerary. If you are keen on visiting the historic churches and monuments of Naples, you may well prefer to stay in one of the smaller *pensioni* around the *Centro Storico*. If, however, you plan to make several visits to the coast and to the islands, the Lungomare or Piazza Garibaldi areas will be preferable. The latter, however, has yet to shake off its downbeat reputation, and it is wise to visit a room in this area before you pay.

When booking hotels on Capri, the Sorrento Peninsula or the Amalfi Coast check their location carefully if you are not fully fit and mobile, or if you have small children in tow. They may not be easily accessible by car or public transport. For travelers who cannot afford to stay in the revamped Grand Tour hotels of Sorrento, there are a number of well-located *pensioni* or bed and breakfasts in or near the center. Be prepared, however, to share with the owners in some cases.

Houses, Apartments & Campsites

Private houses and **apartments** can be booked at weekly rates, ranging from €500 to €1,250. This type of accommodation has the advantage of kitchens so you can cook for yourself and they can often also be booked on Internet websites.

Youth hostels are located at the Via degli Aranci in Sorrento and at Mergellina in Naples. The Youth Hostel organization – Associazione Italiana Alberghi per la Gioventu (AIG) – offers shared sleeping quarters from €16 a night, but also has private rooms with washing facilities and breakfast at a higher cost.

Campsites at Solfatara, Meta, Piano and Capo di Sorrento, Paestum, and Nerano generally offer spaces for pitching tents and parking motorhomes together with accommodations that have kitchens in rustic bungalows. They frequently also have a swimming pool on site and offer reasonably priced accommodation in relatively good locations. The bungalows are often cheaply built, however, and light sleepers are likely to be disturbed by their neighbors when the campsites are full in summer.

Agriturismo: Rural Retreats

For those who want to escape the bustle of the town, there are a number of countryside villas and tourist villages. Some of these are adjacent to campsites, others are in lovely private properties with stunning views. The *agriturismo* properties offer visitors an exceptional opportunity to sample life away from the tourist crowds, with local hosts who generally offer not just home cooking but also guided tours of their localities and an insight into their lifestyles. Visitors without cars can usually arrange to be picked up from the nearest railway station. Hikers can take advantage of the increasingly numerous *agriturismo* facilities to explore the hills of Campania, spending each night at a different address. Visitors with cars can also take the opportunity to visit a range of sites during their holiday.

Useful Websites

www.napolihotel.it – More than a hunded hotels bookable online.

www.agriclub.it – Has links to *agriturismo* sites in Campania.

www.hotelclub.net – Hotel website with online specials.

www.venere.net – Hotel reviews by clients.

www.hotel.portanapoli.com – Links to a good selection of rental apartments.

www.sorrentotourism.com – Sorrento guide including accommodation details.

www.vacanzeprocida.it – Holiday homes to rent on the island of Procida.

■ What & Where to Eat

"Food, for the Neapolitans, comes even before love, and its pursuit is equally insatiable and ingenious," wrote Norman Lewis. Granted, his account refers to 1944 when postwar scarcity left even the city's aristocrats grateful for a can of Allied corned beef, but even in today's relatively prosperous times, it is evident that eating and drinking rank high in the scale of local pleasures. Fortunately for visitors, the *cucina povera* traditions of Southern Italy mean that delicious food and drink are not necessarily expensive. At the same time, Naples and its bay resorts boast some of the best restaurants in Italy and gourmets will not be disappointed.

Regional Specialties

Naples calls to mind mouthwatering pizza served in unpretentious establishments down narrow cobbled streets where wood-fired ovens turn out this simple but delicious dish with remarkable speed. Men with mandolins weave through al-fresco diners on the Lungomare, while playing haunting melodies. Sorrento, Amalfi, Capri and Ischia – the names conjure up memorable meals on flower-filled terraces, the offering of toasts to the panoramic vista below, the natural light sparkle of a white wine at lunchtime, and forkfuls of incomparable seafood pasta and risotto.

The key to Campanian cuisine is simplicity. The classic Neapolitan pizza and pasta dish is made with tomato, garlic, basil and little else. Mozzarella is added to make "gnocchi alla sorrentina." These potato dumplings are filling but, prepared correctly, are light and fluffy. Try also the richer oven-baked dish with lashings of cheese, or a creamy version served with shellfish or broccoli. The food works because the ingredients are all full of flavor and very fresh.

The artisanal, homemade pasta served in many restaurants is an interesting variant on the usual spaghetti but very filling. Other local specialties include a bean dish, *pasta e fagioli*, sometimes served with mussels or pork (*cotica*), spaghetti with clams, *vongole*, and *sartu di riso*, an elaborate rice dish.

If you are lucky enough to be invited for Sunday lunch with a Neapolitan family you might be served *carne al ragu* (also called *braciola*) – meat rolls served in a tomato sauce. Lovers of the nutty *rucola* (rocket salad) will be in heaven in Naples where it is served also in pasta dishes and on pizza. Try it!

Seafood is excellent. Mussel soup, spaghetti with clams, octopus, squid, swordfish – there is an endless choice. The superb linguine or *risotto alla marinara* (seafood pasta and rice) are best when tasted al fresco, by the sea. What better way to combine the tastes and sights that you have come for! It's a moment to savor, after you have selected your sea view, settled yourself comfortably, and sipped your first glass of lightly bubbling mineral water, Greco di Tufo or Falanghina wine, to dip your fork into a plate piled high with fresh linguine or creamy rice on which are perched mounds of mussels, clams and prawns. So choose the time and place carefully for your seafood feast – a late afternoon lunch in Sorrento, is especially recommended.

A specialty of the Vesuvian region is the cherry tomato that grows on its slopes, known as the *pomodorini da serbo*. Local orchards also produce apricots and cherries. At Stabia, a local snack, called *caponato* – a biscuit garnished with pickles – is served from stalls along the waterfront. An unusual specialty on the Amalfi Coast is the ancient dessert of *melanzana alla cioccolata* (fried eggplant served with chocolate and ground almonds). Another Roman delicacy that is still served up in Vietri is *colatura*, or essence of anchovies, used as an accompaniment to savory dishes.

Cilento is home to buffalos and their produce is world-famous: not just the melt-in-the-mouth *mozzarella di bufala* but also delicious yoghurt and ice cream. Finally, the lemon desserts and liqueurs are a great way to round off a meal in traditional style.

A Day in the Life of Food

As befits a nation for whom food is important, there are rituals to be observed. This section provides information about the typical composition of meals and a glossary of the dishes which you are likely to find on the menu. While breakfast is usually a rapid, stand-up affair, lunch and dinner can be lingering and gargantuan, involving several courses. A typical meal begins with starters or antipasti, and is followed by two savory courses – the *primo* and *secondo piatto*. This may be too much unless you have the heartiest of appetites, so feel free to skip one of these courses. Pasta is a usual component of the primo piatto and meat or fish is commonly chosen for the second course, with a side dish (*contorno*). The main meal of the day is often preceded by a drink (*aperitivo*) and a snack, and will end with a liqueur (*digestivo*).

Early Morning Treats

You have a 6 am start and a long day of traveling ahead. You only have a few minutes to grab a much-needed bite to eat. No problem! Head for one of the region's many cafés where you will be served a steaming café latte by a bright-as-a-button *cameriere* and grab a crunchy *sfogliatella* (pastry with ricotta filling) or a *cornetto* – Naples' equivalent to the croissant. If you prefer to start the day with the tiny, strong black coffee that kick-starts most Neapolitans in the early hours, and if you want to impress the packed bar, ask for *na tazzulella e caffè* – that's local lingo for an espresso. With a drop of milk, it becomes a *macchiato*. With added liqueur – for the particularly adventurous, or strong of constitution – it's a *corretto*. Locals prefer to drink *cappuccino* in the morning, but are used to serving it at any time of day to tourists. Coffee is so important to the locals that plays, and a song by Pino Daniele, have been written about it.

Aperitifs & Starters

Street food in Naples is mainly fried snacks or pizza slices. Bars will also serve the traditional starters with a drink. A selection is described below.

Crocché – Fried potato ball with mozzarella and ham

Arancini – Savory rice balls with melted cheese and green beans

Fiorilli – Zucchini flowers in batter

Alici or zucchini a scapece – Fresh anchovies or zucchini, dipped in flour, and fried

Alici marinate – Fresh anchovies, filleted and marinated

Caprese – Mozzarella and sliced tomato salad, with basil and olive oil

Freselle – Bread with tomato, herb and olive oil topping

Panzarotti – Dough-balls filled with meat, fish, cheese, or tomatoes

Polipi sott'aceto – Octopus in vinegar

Bresaola con rucola e parmigiano – Smoked beef served with rocket salad and parmesan cheese

The Primo Piatto

After sampling one or two of the local starters, it is time to get serious with a pasta dish. Be warned, that you may not have room for a second meat or fish course, especially if you try *paccheri*, *scialatelli*, and other types of the homemade, thick pasta. Neapolitan pasta dishes are generally simple, and made with fresh ingredients. Some of the favorite options are listed below:

Gnocchi alla sorrentina – Potato dumplings served with tomato, mozzarella and parsley

Linguine ai frutti di mare – Linguine with cherry tomatoes, seafood and parsley

Manicaretti with ricotta – Homemade pasta filled with ricotta and ham

Ravioli alla caprese – Ravioli served with cheese, tomato and herbs

Risotto alla pescatora – Rice with seafood, fresh tomatoes and parsley

Spaghetti alle vongole – Spaghetti with clams fried in olive oil and garlic

The Secondo Piatto

Following the pasta, many Neapolitans have a relatively light course of grilled fish and salad. A number of alternatives with explanations are listed below:

Grigliata mista – Grilled calamari, prawns and other small fishes

Parmigiana di melanzane – Oven-baked layers of eggplant, cheese, and tomato

Pesce spada alla griglia – Grilled swordfish seasoned with olive oil and garlic

Pollo / coniglio alla cacciatore – Chicken or rabbit stew

Cheeses

Neapolitans generally eat cheese after the main course (*secondo piatto*). Various names are given not only to the different cheeses but in some cases to the method of serving them. The important varieties are described below:

Bocconcini – Small balls or "mouthfuls" of mozzarella

Provolone – Southern cheese, which can come in a variety of shapes, and smoked

Ricotta – Soft cheese used like yoghurt and often in cooking

Ricotta salata – Aged, hard and salted variety of Ricotta; used to grate over pasta

Scamorza – Local cheese, fermented, cooked and sometimes smoked

Treccia – Braided string of mozzarella or scamorza cheese

Delightful Desserts

If you have not been completely overwhelmed by the antipasti, pizza and seafood, and still have room for something more, be sure to try a *delizia al limone* – a lemon-filled sponge cake, which is Naples' worthy version of the profiterole. Last, but definitely not least, a tiny glass of the delightful local liqueur, *limoncello*, will add the finishing touch to your *menu alla meridionale.* An alternative dessert – the *baba* (rum baba) is a throwback to Naples' Arab-influenced past.

Baba – Sponge cake soaked in rum often served with cream and a cherry

Delizia al limone – Lemon profiteroles with a lemon cream sauce

Torta di mele – Apple cake baked in the oven

Torta caprese – Chocolate cake, a specialty of Capri but served all over the Bay of Naples.

Seasonal Specialties

The Neapolitans are lovers of tradition and have maintained customs for centuries. This is also reflected in their food and, depending on when you visit the region, you can enjoy sampling some of the seasonal dishes outlined below:

Carnival & Shrove Tuesday

Lasagne with ricotta, ragu and small meatballs is traditionally served, followed up with pastries such as *chiacchiere* (a wheat and egg cake) and *migliaccio* (made with eggs, sugar and ricotta).

San Giuseppe

To celebrate the feast day of San Giuseppe, which falls on March 19th, fried or baked *zeppole* (doughnuts) are eaten. The doughnuts are usually decorated with cream and cherries.

Easter

In Naples each day of Easter is characterized by a different culinary specialty. On Maundy Thursday *zuppa di cozze* or *maruzze* (soup with mussels or sea snails) is traditionally eaten. Tourists can fortunately try this dish all year-round. Fish is served on Good Friday, simply cooked with lemon and olive oil in most cases. *Casatiello* – a round pie stuffed with salami, eggs, cheese and pepper – is prepared on Easter Saturday. On Sunday, Neapolitans might tuck into a salami known as *fellata*, *minestra maritata* (vegetable soup), and oven-cooked pasta, and will usually finish up with the celebrated *pastiera* dessert, a flan made with ricotta, cinnamon, eggs and wheat. On Easter Monday, families organize a picnic at which a macaroni dish is served.

All Saints' Day

On this day of commemoration for Catholics, which falls on November 1st, *torrone dei morti* (nougat with chocolate and/or almonds) is a favorite.

Christmas

On Christmas and New Year's Eve a fish dish is traditionally served. *Capitone* (eel) and *fritelle di baçala* (cod fritters) are favorites. An *insalata di rinforzo* (salad) made with cauliflower, broccoli, olives and peppers accompanies the meal. Christmas time pastries include *struffoli* (fried pastry balls with honey and candied fruit), *roccoco* (almond cake), and *mustaccioli* (a filled chocolate pastry).

Capodanno

On New Year's Eve, from 11 pm to 1 am, meals of seafood, especially *capitone* (eel) and *cotechino* (pigs' trotters) with lentils and mashed potatoes, are served.

Wines of Campania

Ancient Roman authors praised the wines of Campania, and while the sulphurous reds served here may not be to everyone's taste, there are also light whites and fragrant *fragolino* dessert wines. A selection of the best is given below:

Lacryma Christi – This is the one tourists like to take back, because of the evocative name (Christ's Tears). Made from Falanghina, Piedirosso and Coda di Volpe grapes grown on the slopes of Mount Vesuvius; red and white varieties available.

Aglianico del Taburno – A great, robust Southern red wine, from the grape which is believed to be Greek in origin.

Taurasi – Another good red, derived from the *aglianico* grape.

Greco di Tufo – A famed Campanian white wine.

Fiano di Avellino – Another good local white.

Biancolella – A white wine from Ischia.

Bianco / Rosso Campi Flegri – Declared DOC wines since 1993 and among a number of wines from the Campi Flegrei, e.g. *falanghina*, which have been given this appellation.

Where To Eat

Few places in Italy can beat the restaurants of Naples in terms of ambiance and value for money. Their greatest claim to fame is of course the pizza – the *margherita*, *marinara* and *capricciosa* varieties in particular, are Naples' gift to the culinary world. Whether you want inexpensive fast food or a sumptuous feast, the city seems to have an endless supply of eateries to suit every budget. From Thurs to Sun, locals crowd the restaurants on the Lungomare (seafront) — and you could find yourself standing for half an hour on the street. But it's generally worth the wait if you want superb pizzas at rock-bottom prices and don't mind the hubbub of a packed restaurant dominated by exuberant groups of Neapolitans. Alternatively, you can go for a more genteel dining experience at one of the many seafood restaurants that line the coastal road between Castel dell'Ovo and Posillipo hill. The Amalfi Coast towns and the islets also have a range of good restaurants serving seafood and local specialties, often with the added bonus of great views.

The itinerant minstrels are one of the joys of eating out in Naples. Some of Italy's most famous songs – like *O' Sole Mio* – originated in Naples and, unless you've chosen a really isolated spot, you are bound to be approached by a man with a mandolin doing the rounds. Show the slightest enthusiasm for his usually excellent singing skills and you can expect to be serenaded at your table, and invited to make a request. Be warned, however, that the restaurants do not pay these wandering singers and he will expect you to show your appreciation by offering a bank note. Before the switch to the unified European currency, a 1,000 lire note would have sufficed. Now €5 – the lowest denomination banknote today – is a bit more expensive, but if you're a music lover, keep a few of these in your pocket and allow yourself to succumb to the virtuoso performances of the Neapolitan minstrels. The restaurant **A' Canzuncella** (Neapolitan for a little song) is dedicated to music, for those who want an accompaniment of traditional local songs with their meal.

Restaurants & Trattorie

❖ Naples

The more famous and plush restaurants are located on the Posillipo road. They include **Don Salvatore, Il Delicato, Lo Scoglio** and **Ciro A Mare**, which all serve superb fish dishes. **La Sacrestia** in Via Orazio is considered one of the best restaurants in Naples and has a great view over the bay. The Michelin guide rates **Caruso** in the Grand Hotel Vesuvio, the **Megaris** in the Grand Hotel Santa Lucia and **La Cantinella** highest. **Fenestella**, **Transatlantico**, **Le Due Palme** and **Giuseppone a Mare** all rate a mention for great traditional Neapolitan food. The smaller family-run trattorias are often closed during the annual August holiday. **Vini e Cucina** is a good place to sample the simple, trattoria-style cuisine.

On trips outside Naples to the Campi Flegrei, Pompeii and Herculaneum, there are fewer choices.

❖ Bacoli

Bacoli has two good restaurants – **La Misenetta** and **Fefe**. The cafés at Pompeii and Herculaneum are acceptable. Pompeii now has a McDonalds! Some restaurants in the smaller coastal towns and on the islands are closed during the winter, reopening around Easter time. The Amalfi Coast towns each have a number of good restaurants.

❖ Ravello

In Ravello city center, the family-run **Cumpa Cosima**, once a wine shop, now famous for its pasta with pesto sauce, is a safe bet.

❖ Amalfi

Da Gemma, in Amalfi, has a lovely terrace, and superlative seafood – the place to have *fritto misto* or scorpion fish soup. The interior dining area remains open in winter.

❖ Positano

The beach restaurant of **La Buca di Bacco**, at Positano, is a celebrity haunt, but also worth visiting for the *arancini* – fried rice balls with mozzarella. **La Cambusa**, on the beach, is overcrowded in summer, but a good venue for the local favorite – linguine alla marinara.

❖ Sorrento

In Sorrento, combine a swim with dinner at one of the restaurants at the Marina, or sample one of the scores of ice creams available at the **Gelateria Bougainvillea**. Admirers of La Loren will enjoy dining at the small harborside **Di Leva** restaurant and snack bar, where her pictures line the walls. In 1955 Sofia made a film in Sorrento and one of her scenes took place here. In 2004 she returned for another film project, and made a nostalgic visit to Marina Grande, insisting on dining at her old haunt – the Di Leva. She tucked in to *farfalle al sugo*, and fried calamari, rounding off her meal with the house specialty rose petal ice cream, and *torta caprese*. Why not sample the Loren menu yourself and enjoy a chat with the friendly Di Leva sisters who still run the place. **O Parrucchiano** is a well-established restaurant in the town. For the greatest gastronomic adventure of the region, go to **Don Alfonso** at Sant'Agata sui due Golfi. Liva and Alfonso Iaccarino have acquired a fabulous reputation with this restaurant, using ingredients from their own farm. A member of the Relais & Chateaux, their specialties include *paccheri al ragu di scorfano e peperoni* (homemade pasta with fish sauce and pepper). Expect to pay at least €100 per person plus wine.

❖ Capri

People-watching is a well-known pastime in Capri, and the cafés around the Piazzetta are the best venue for this, but prices reflect the trendiness and popularity of this tiny square. The **Grotelle** restaurant on the island offers al fresco dining with a superb sea view and is an ideal place to sample *spaghetti e vongole*. A popular pizza restaurant is **Anem e Core** near Quisisana Hotel. And, of course, there is no more appropriate place to sample the local *limoncello* than in the lemon groves of the **Da Paolina** restaurant, overlooking the Marina.

❖ Ischia

Ischia offers a number of seasonal specialties for the adventurous of palate. In summer, risotto is de rigueur; in autumn, polenta with capers and snails, or one of the local rabbit dishes is popular. **Il Focolare** also offers unusual combinations such as gnocchi with broccoli.

Pizzerie

The justly beloved pizzas of the Neapolitans are given pride of place in many of the city's restaurants, and are on the menu almost everywhere – from the swankiest restaurant to the cheap and cheerful eateries. In 1883, when English traveler Augustus Hare was offered a pizza to try, he called it "a horrible condiment made of dough baked with garlic, rancid bacon and strong cheese." Fortunately, today's visitors are more familiar with the delights of the pizza, and a stop at Naples' **Brandi** restaurant is popular with tourists. The pizza margherita is said to have been first created here in 1889 for the Queen of Savoy. The **Da Michele** pizzeria serves only the margherita and is always busy during office hours. Remember, when it comes to pizza, the best is not necessarily the most expensive. Try pizza with rucola (rocket salad), if it's offered. Naples city center is the best place to find an unpretentious and inexpensive meal at one of the many pizzerie, but they are everywhere across the region. Lovers of the innovative and eccentric should go to **Ristorante Miracapri** at Termini on the tip of the Sorrento Peninsula to order pizza cooked in a portable oven brought to your table! A tasty and abundant repast washed down with a palatable house wine can cost as little as €6.

Cafés & Bars

Many bars have only stand-up counters, and there may be an additional charge for seating where available. They often serve pastries and ice creams, as well as snacks. Bars and cafés are the ideal stop for breakfast, or for afternoon coffee and pre-dinner drinks. The region is dotted with bars and, as a general rule of thumb, those located on a town's main piazza are likely to be the most expensive. Of these, the bars on the Piazzetta in Capri are surely the costliest. Avoid them unless you are determined to celebrity-watch. One of the most elegant in Naples, and a former haunt of intellectuals, is **Café Gambrinus**, in Piazza Trieste e Trento near the Teatro San Carlo and the Palazzo Reale. The **Bar dell'Ovo** on the seafront is also a good place to stop for an aperitif, while a coffee at the **Gran Bar Riviera** or in **Caffetteria Bernini** is recommended. The **Scaturchio** in Piazza San Domenico Maggiore is well-known for delicious *sfogliatelle* (crispy, cream-filled pastry). **La Caffettiera** in Piazza dei Martiri is one of the best places to enjoy that quintessential Italian experience: the pre-dinner aperitif. Try the house cocktail (alcoholic or non-alcoholic) and drink it at the bar, where you will be served an array of snacks ranging from large green olives to tiny hot pizzas. To do it justice, go there when you are dressed in your best, prior to the opera, for example. Young and old alike enjoy an ice cream; and the best shops here offer great choice and quality. Look out for signs that read *produzione propria* or *artigianale*, meaning made on the premises, or home-made. In summer a *granita* (a fruit drink with crushed ice) is a refreshing alternative.

Tips & Charges

Arrive early to avoid the crowds on weekends – locals tend to eat late, and most restaurants serve until 2 am. If you want to dine well on a budget, check out the number of people waiting for a table. In places like the Lungomare of Naples, a crowd bustling outside an unpretentious-looking eatery is a sure sign that it will be serving simple but good pasta and pizza at unbelievable value prices. They will be noisy, however. House wine served in carafes or *vino sfuso* is inexpensive and generally good. Some restaurants serve a small antipasto such as *bruschette* with fresh cherry tomatoes free of charge. Service charges are usually included; a 10% tip would be appreciated by your waiter. The larger restaurants accept credit cards.

■ Shops & Markets

From handmade haute couture to bric-a-brac stalls, creative Naples is a joy for shoppers. Souvenir hunters will find endless ceramics, products made from or featuring lemons and oranges both

Above: The Roman Arco Felice in Pozzuoli
Below: Solfatara volcano, Pozzuoli

Above: Temple of Jupiter at Cuma in the Campi Flegrei

Below: The Gardens of Augustus, on the island of Capri

Above: Castello Giusso in the town of Vico Equense
Below: Villa Campolieto,
one of the Vesuvian Villas near Ercolano

Above: The port and resort of Bacoli, in the Campi Flegrei
Below: View from Capri over the Marina Grande to the tip of the Sorrento Peninsula

Above: Looking down fromCapri's cliffs

Below: I Faraglioni on Capri

Above: Riding Capri's cable car

Below: Certosa di San Giacomo cloister on Capri

Mosaic from the House of Neptune & Amphitrite, Herculaneum

here and in the coastal and island resorts. Choice and price is much better in Naples than in the more popular seaside resorts of Sorrento and Amalfi or on the island of Capri. Shops are generally open in the mornings from 9 or 10 to 1 pm, close for the siesta time until 4 pm and then open until 8. Most shops are shut on Sundays, and often also have a closing day during the week, together with a holiday closure, generally August in Naples. Annual sales are held in the summer and from January to March.

Food Shops

In Naples, as elsewhere in Italy, small shops selling specialty goods still prevail over the supermarket culture of the UK and USA. This is part of the charm of shopping in Naples, but it means trawling the streets if you have a number of items to buy. In case you need to ask where a particular item can be found, here are the main types of food shop:

A ***salumeria*** is equivalent to a delicatessen.

An ***enoteca*** sells wine.

Bread is bought from a ***panetteria***.

Cakes and sweets are obtained from a ***pasticceria.***

Buy fruit and vegetables from a ***fruttivendolo***.

A ***pescheria*** sells fish.

Red meat is sold in a ***macelleria***.

White meats like chicken and rabbit can be bought in a ***polleria***.

Fashion & Accessories

In **Naples**, the elegant designer shops are mostly located around the Piazza dei Martiri in Chiaia, and in Scarlatti and Luca Giordano streets of Vomero. The handmade clothes of Naples have been prized for literally hundreds of years and a tailoring industry – making suits for Blasi, Isaia, Kiton, Marino, Monetti and Luigi Borrelli among others – continues to flourish here. **Mario Valentino**, **Ferragamo** and **Tods** are world-renowned as shoemakers and have showrooms in the Calabritto area near Piazza dei Martiri. Grand tour visitors raved over the silk hats and buckskin gloves; modern tourists can still buy bespoke suits, shirts, ties, gloves, hats and shoes. **Tramontano** on Via Chiaia is reputed to be the best leather store in town, with gorgeous handmade bags and shoes (☎ 081 668 572). On the same street is **Canestrelli**, where handmade children's clothes are cute enough to empty a fond parent's wallet all too quickly (☎ 081 401 954).

Designer stores, like **Ferragamo**, **Versace**, **Valentino** and **Armani** line the streets around the pedestrian zone of Piazza dei Martiri. Along Via Roma and Via Toledo are more everyday shops and department stores, selling a wide range of goods. Vomero is also a great shopping area. Jewelry shops abound in Spaccanapoli but the most famous modern jewelry designer is **Ventrella**, whose store is in Via Carlo Poerio, Chiaia (☎ 081 764 3173). The shop also contains prêt à porter designs.

Bargains can be bought in the stores of Via Roma and around Piazza Garibaldi. Via Forcella has cut-price clothing and general stores. Beware of pickpockets in these areas. Fakes are everywhere outside the designer stores, and the Galleria is usually full of Senegalese street entrepreneurs flogging handbags.

Even unwilling shoppers will enjoy traversing the narrow streets of **Capri**, the **Sorrento Peninsula and the Amalfi Coast** in search of designer wear or knick-knacks, or just as window-gazers. Modern boutiques in Sorrento are concentrated around Corso Italia. Popular buys include leather gloves. Capri is crammed with designer shops around the Piazzetta and even on calmer Ischia, great jewelry (at **Maia** in Ischia Ponte) and footwear (at **Corsi**, on the port) can be purchased. Positano is the clothes-shoppers' mecca on the Amalfi Coast, while lovely handcrafted leather sandals can seemingly be found in all of the bay and island resorts.

Crafts, Antiques & Souvenirs

Visitors hunting for quirky gifts and souvenirs should start at the **Via San Biagio dei Librai** in the *Centro Storico* of Naples, where an amazing collection of stores sell all kinds of ornaments, bric-a-brac and antiques. Off this street, the **Via**

San Gregorio Armeno is a treasure-trove of the traditional Neapolitan *presepe* figures which decorate nativity cribs. **Via Domenico Morelli** is the place for antiques, with dealers specializing in 18th-century paintings and furniture, lithographs, engravings and other objets d'art. Another set of antique stores can be found on **Via Santa Maria di Costantinopoli**. Many artists' studios and workshops will gladly open their doors to potential buyers: wander around the Pizzofalcone and Toledo backstreets to find them. Jewelry craftsmen still work in the area traditionally allocated to their profession, around the **Borgo degli Orefici**.

Cheap and cheerful souvenirs include the artisanal food products and liqueurs which are found everywhere, but will indubitably be cheaper in Naples. **Mandara** on Via Santa Caterina a Chiaia (☎ 081 417 348) sells mozzarella and ricotta cheeses and smoked meats. Quality chocolate and sweet stores are also ubiquitous in this region. **Gay Odin**, a traditional chocolate manufacturer on Via Colonna is one of the best of a great bunch of shops for the sweet-toothed. The most famous chocolate shop is probably **Dolce Idea** on Via Solitaria at Pizzofalcone (☎ 081 764 2832). Appointments can be made to watch the chocolate-making process.

Gaily decorated ceramics are on sale everywhere, but it is **Vietri**, on the Amalfi Coast, that is the recognized center for this craft. Amalfi itself is home to the traditional papermaking industry. Examples of the "carta amalfitana" can also be bought at **Ettore Smith** in Naples (☎ 081 551 6989). Coral, another local craft, is centered in **Torre del Greco**, a Vesuvian town, which can be reached by rail. Perfume shops can be found in the coastal resorts and on the islands, usually claiming to produce scents based on centuries-old techniques perfected by religious orders. The **Officina Profumo** at Via Santa Caterina a Chiaia in Naples offers similar products (☎ 081 407 176) and hand-wrapped soaps and scented candles.

In **Sorrento**, the craft par excellence is *intarsia*, or inlaid woodwork. Visitors can buy modern examples of this 19th-century tradition and see craftsmen at work in their ateliers, as well as great historic examples in the Museo Correale and the Cathedral. Cabinet makers Antonino Damora and

Luigi Gargiulo introduced the art of inlaying or marquetry to Sorrento around 1830. In 1844, King Ferdinand II himself visited Gargiulo's workshop. Today visitors can see a recreated intarsia workshop at the Sorrento Intarsia Museum and Craftshop. Local produce and crafts can be purchased on Via S. Cesareo in Sorrento. Tarsia work is on sale at **Attardi** on Via P.R. Giuliani. Musical boxes and Capodimonte figurines are also popular souvenirs.

Wine and gourmet cheeses are on sale at **Bollicines** in Via Accademia and lemon liqueur, at **Limonoro** on Via San Cesareo. The Bay of Naples resorts are all well known for their citrus groves, as well as liqueurs, soaps, chocolates and ceramics with lemon motifs are all popular souvenirs.

Markets

Visitors to Naples have always been fascinated by the open-air markets, and fortunately these are as lively and flourishing today as ever, although some of the beloved peculiarities recorded by past travelers, like the odd-sized shoe market, have now vanished. Such events produce good pickings for street thieves, so hide valuables and stay alert while you are browsing. The markets start early and traders are usually packing up by 2 pm.

Food and flowers are sold at the **Borgo di Sant'Antonio Abate market**, behind Via Foria, and the **Porta Nolana fish market**, near the central railway station, and on Via Forcella. A **morning flower market** is held daily near the Castel Nuovo. Fruit, vegetables and seafood are sold daily on **Via Pignasecca**. General **daily markets** selling clothing and accessories as well as food are held at **Antignano in Vomero**, **Fuorigrotta**, **Via Ponte di Casanova** and **Ercolano**. There is a Sunday market on **Corso Malta**.

Clothes markets are at **Via Casanova** (daily), near the main Naples railway station, and at **Via Virgilio**, in **Posillipo** (Thurs only) and **Via delle Rose in Piano di Sorrento** (Mon). There is a Tuesday morning market in Sorrento itself. Antiques are sold every other weekend at markets on the **Lungomare** and in **Spaccanapoli**. A Sunday market is also held at **Casoria** on the outskirts of Naples.

LEMONS & LIMONCELLO

The citrus fruits of Naples and the bay resorts have inspired a range of products and souvenirs. From ceramics, to sweets, and liqueurs, lemons are displayed everywhere in the shops and markets. The fruit trees with their characteristic pagliarelle – protective coverings for the citrus groves – are one of the characteristic features of the region, much loved by tourists. And the lemon features in almost every meal – from the refreshing granita drinks, to salads and grilled fish flavored with fresh lemon juice, the delicious lemon dessert "delizia," and the tiny glass of limoncello to round off your evening.

One of the secrets of a good lemon liqueur is to peel the fruit so that only the yellow skin is kept and the bitter white interior is removed. Many Neapolitan families still make the lemon liqueur at home.

■ Sporting Activities

Watersports and walking are the most popular sporting activities for visitors to Naples and its bay resorts. In addition, the city and the larger coastal towns offer facilities for tennis, gym and cycling. The luxury hotels have fitness and spa centers. Football (soccer) is a passion in Naples, as across Italy, and lovers of the sport will enjoy the match-day ambiance. Home games of the Napoli Serie A side are played in the Stadio di San Paolo at Fuorigrotta, which can be reached by train on the Ferrovia Cumana from Montesanto to Mostra. There is a **fitness club** at Via Nuova San Rocco, a **female-only gym** in Via Luca Giordano and **saunas** at Via delle Murate.

Beaches & Bathing

Access to beaches in the popular coastal resorts is generally via beach concessions, while the beaches themselves are often pebbles or grey, volcanic sand. Some of the smaller coastal resorts, like

Piano have a mixture of free and paying beach areas. The free beaches get dirty very quickly (local day-trippers do not seem disposed to clean up after themselves). In Naples, locals sun themselves on the rocks at the Lungomare, but visitors will probably prefer the beach concessions on Via Posillipo and at Marechiaro. Baia and Bacoli in the Campi Flegrei also have pleasant beaches, some with naturally warm thermal waters and sauna-type facilities. Ischia is the best of the islands for long, relatively uncrowded beaches, while in the Gulf of Salerno the Cilento coast beaches are probably the best in the region.

Diving, Fishing & Boat Excursions

The clear waters, caves, and underwater classical ruins along the coastline of the Bay of Naples and around the islands make this a great location for enthusiastic divers and snorkelers. The best diving is certainly along the 12-mile/20-km **Massa Lubrense coast**, and particularly the marine reserve of **Punta Campanella**, but the submerged Roman city of **Baia** is unbeatable. The **Bay of Puolo** just outside Sorrento is good for night dives. Cave-dwelling rare fish can be seen in the **Grotto of Mitigliano** – a 30-foot dive at **Punta Bacoli**. Beneath **Fossa Tower** on Punta Campanella a 120-foot dive provides an opportunity to see a variety of marine fauna. The **Sapphire Grotto** opposite the rocky outcrop island of Isca at nine feet depth has stalactites and an ethereal blue illumination. Dives in the **Marine Park of Punta Campanella** can be arranged through the **Sorrento Diving Centre** (☎ 081 877 4812), which will also organize your accommodation.

Every weekend in summer the Bay of Naples is filled with fluttering white sails and the foam trail of speeding motorboats as every boat owner heads to the islands. The less well-heeled head for the ferry and hydrofoil services, but for visitors who would like to enjoy the privilege of diving into the super-clear waters around the islands, boats can be rented from a number of companies. Alternatively, day-trippers in Capri can take boat trips around the island or excursions to specific marine sites like the **Grotta Azzurra**. The round-Capri boat tour takes around 2½ hours.

Walking & Hiking

Numerous walking itineraries have been devised for the national parks of Campania. The Vesuvius and **Cilento parks** are easily reached on day-trips from the coast. The **Sorrento Peninsula** is famous for its network of old footpaths, and walks along the coastline and through the citrus groves have been popular since Roman times. The **Lattari mountains** in the spine of the peninsula rise to nearly 5,000 feet and are well worth exploring. Guided walks can be arranged through the tourist offices in the Sorrento and Amalfi Coast resorts. Maps are provided by the **Club Alpino Italiano** (CAI), which has also waymarked some routes. Walking tours of Capri and Ischia are also popular. Dress for rain from October to May, and wear a sunhat and long-sleeved shirt in the summer months as sun protection. Drinking water and comfortable walking shoes are a must.

Walks in the Campi Flegrei

In addition to the urban parks and gardens of Naples, a number of interesting nature reserves and countryside walks can be seen on day-trips out of the city. At **Agnano** an ancient volcanic crater can be explored – at the bottom of which are the ruins of an old thermal bath. The surrounding park has a rich variety of flowers, bushes and trees. The nature reserve of **Astroni** can be visited only by prior appointment. At **Monte Nuovo** in the Campi Flegrei, guided excursions can be taken to visit this recent example of a mountain created by local volcanic activity. **Monte Nuovo** is the youngest volcano in Europe, formed in the 16th century, when the village of Tripergole was destroyed. A nature park was set up here in 1990 and walks are organized by the **Ali di Dedalo** organization (☎ 349 547 1559) around the crater, taking in the panoramic views of the **Campi Flegrei** and pointing out sites of interest relating to the history of volcanoes in the region, and on the eruptive effects of the Monte Nuovo. Two-hour walks are also organized by the same group around the **Lake of Avernus**, and on **Cape Misenum**. The sand dunes of **Licola** and the lakes of **Lucrinus** and **Fusaro** can also be visited.

Walking Tours of Vesuvius

The 23,600-acre National Park of Vesuvius extends across 13 municipalities and includes a Special Protection Zone, a Wilderness Area and a National Forest Reserve. The nine nature trails enable visitors to discover the unusual beauty of the Somma-Vesuvius volcanic complex. Each trail has been carefully signposted and made safe for walkers, who are advised to bring a wind-proof jacket, gloves and a hat, as well as plimsolls or hiking shoes, binoculars and drinking water.

To reach the park, drivers should take the A3 Napoli-Salerno motorway and exit at Torre del Greco or Ercolano. From here, turn left under the motorway bridge and continue along Via Boscocatene onto Via B. Cozzolino, following directions for Vesuvius. Park at the terrace, which marks an altitude of 2,800 feet, for the walk to the crater. Visitors traveling by public transport should take the Circumvesuviana train to Ercolano Scavi, from where bus or taxi services continue to the terrace.

Trail no 1, the **Valle dell'Inferno**, follows a circular route, which takes four hours to complete. The Valle dell'Inferno exhibits lava from the last eruption of the volcano in 1944, and separates Mt Somma from the newer Mt Vesuvius. A **second trail** takes in the ridges of the **Cognoli of Ottaviano** and **Levante**, where rope-like lava formations can be seen, and numerous fern species. **Trail 3** follows the ridge of **Mt Somma**, while **Trail 4** goes through pine forests to the 1944 lava flow where there is a great view of the Gulf of Naples. **Trail 5** is along the **Great Cone**, and walkers make a series of hairpin turns to take in panoramic views. Tickets costing €4.50 per person must be purchased to take the trail leading to the crater, and admission is from 9 am to 6 pm in summer and to 3 pm in winter. A guide takes visitors on the two-hour round-trip.

Coast & Hill Walks on the Sorrento Peninsula

The "passeggiate" or historic footpaths that were once the only routes for villagers down to the coast and from town to town are still preserved and, while little used nowadays, offer tourists a wonderful means of exploring the peninsula, provided suitable walking gear is worn.

From **Castellammare di Stabia** the 3,700-foot summit of **Monte Faito** is the starting point for some of the most exciting walks in the Monti Lattari down to the Amalfi Coast. Hikers can either walk up to Monte Faito from the town of Stabia or take the cable car, which operates from a platform of the Circumvesuviana train station. From Stabia the walk to Faito takes in the royal palace of Quisisana, and the Bourbon aqueduct, on a panoramic route. The trail continues along **Via Tuoro** to **Pizzo delle Monache**, and **Acqua dei Porci** before passing the cable car station en route to the Belvedere which offers superb views.

A four-hour walk from **Meta di Sorrento** can be taken to the mountain of **Sant'Angelo**, also known as Casini, from where views over Vico Equense can be seen. **Alberi**, and the **monastery of Camaldoli** are also on this trail.

Camaldoli

Tourists looking for little-known, deserted beaches can take a walk from **Piano di Sorrento**, a short distance along the SS 163, which leads to the Amalfi Coast, taking a right-hand turn at the 8,500 km marker down to the small pebble beach. From here boats can be hired to visit coves farther along the coast.

Alternatively, follow the sign from the SS 163 to **Scaricatoio**, which winds through conifers and old olive trees, for a half-hour walk to the sea. A lovely panoramic view of the gulfs of Naples and Salerno leads from the Corso Italia, along **Via Cavone** to **Trinità**, and farther up to the village of **Arola**.

Tourists already at the coast can take a walk inland from **Sant'Agnello** to **Malacoccola**. This five-km/three-mile trail takes two-three hours and ends at **Sant'Agata**. En route, there are citrus and olive groves, chestnut and oak woods and dwarf palm trees. The 1,500-foot-high **Malacoccola ridge** offers wonderful views of the two gulfs: Vesuvius can be seen on one side, and the Li Galli islands on the other.

Vacationers in Sorrento have a number of options for interesting walks. Take the bus or go on foot to **Capo di Sorrento**, for a walk down to the Roman villa and baths of **Pollio Felice** by the sea. To go by foot from Sorrento, follow the Corso Italia out of town in the direction of Massa Lubrense, and onto the Via Pantano to the Cape of Sorrento. Turn left down a track, signposted for the Roman ruins, where sunbathers lie among the ancient stones.

A further walk to the west of Sorrento, past the Cape, leads to the delightful fishing village of **Marina di Puolo**. Turn right off the main road onto the track that passes the Hotel Dania, and follow signs for Marina di Puolo.

Punta Campanella

In spring or autumn the uphill climbs around **Massa Lubrense** and **Punta Campanella** are spectacular. Massa is only four km/2.4 miles from Sorrento but the climb can be tiring and summer hikers will need plenty of water. The main road up to Massa curves to give good views of the coast. After the Francischiello restaurant, continue on the main road to the small step road of Via San Montano, which leads to Massa and Termini. At a fork in the road, take a right to go to Massa, which is a pleasant town with a belvedere, cathedral and a number of welcome bars and restaurants. From here buses return to Sorrento, or walkers can return by Via Rachione, Bagnulo and Monte Corbo along paths to Via Capodimonte, and a series of hairpin bends with lovely views over Sorrento and the Bay of Naples. A longer walk along footpaths goes from Sorrento to Massa, Sant'Agata and up to Termini.

The walk from **Termini** to **Nerano** and down to the beach at **Marina del Cantone** is a lovely excursion. Alternatively, from Nerano take the two-km/1.2-mile panoramic mule trail to the small white stone beach at **Jeranto** where the bay is a protected site, with transparent seas and an abundance of marine life. **Capitello Cave** here has a submerged entrance through which shafts of light filter and reflect on the rocks. The **Fontanelle to Sant-Agata walk** is also above a delightful stretch of the coast, with views towards Positano and over to Capri.

For stunning views of Capri and a delightful walk through Mediterranean flora, wild olive trees and plums, rosemary and juniper, take the **Termini to Punta della Campanella walk**. The final stretch of the walk, to the promontory, is part of the nature reserve – no cars are allowed. At the point, the ruins of a Saracen tower can be seen, and an ancient Roman path. A Roman villa and temple once occupied this spot. This excursion covers seven km/4.2 miles and takes around five hours to complete.

Amalfi Coast Walks

The fabulous cliffside paths that date from Roman times take in views of what is considered by many the most beautiful coastline in the entire Mediterranean. No wonder that the most famous of these routes is called the **Sentiero degli Dei** or Path of the Gods. The 15-mile/25-km route links **Amalfi** and **Positano**, 2,000 feet above sea level, with incredible panoramas. A variety of different half-day walks can be taken along this route, which is well signposted, as well as more extensive hikes with overnight stops en route.

Around **Ravello**, the footpaths, which at one time were the only links of the hillside towns with the sea, offer a number of scenic walks, through terraced lemon groves to small hamlets seemingly untouched by time, and where unexpectedly grandiose churches testify to a more glorious past. The **Via Santa Barbara stairway** from Ravello leads to **Atrani**, with lovely views from **Valle del Dragone** en route. The walk takes in the **Torre dello Ziro**, a watchtower at Pontone, and continues along Via Santa Barbara, following first signs to Amalfi and then signs to Atrani. This is the second-smallest munici-

Torre dello Ziro

pality in Italy, and the birthplace of famous fisherman and revolutionary, Masaniello. Buses stop at Atrani for the return journey.

The area covered by the **Cilento National Park** is daunting, and tourists wishing to visit the region as a whole will prefer to rent a car. The itineraries provided at local tourist offices within the park area have been designed for drivers, but the detailed park map available from regional tourist offices will be helpful for walkers. In addition, specialist companies offer guided walks in Cilento.

Walking on the Islands: Capri & Ischia

The panoramic paths of Capri and the volcanic slopes of Ischia provide yet more opportunities for hikers to enjoy the natural splendors of the Bay of Naples. One of the most beautiful walks on **Capri** is the Roman path from **Anacapri** to the **Migliera Belvedere**. Taking **Via Caposcuro** and then **Via Migliera**, from the **Piazza Vittoria**, the path winds past orchards and vineyards on the slopes of Monte Solaro to the Belvedere with a lovely view of Punta Carena. A path on the left leads to another belvedere with a view of the southern coast and the Faraglioni, huge rocks that stick up out of the sea. Return to Anacapri via the Torre della Guardia and Torre di Materità.

Along the western coast of the island another itinerary leads between the **Blue Grotto** and the **Punta Carena Lighthouse** past 19th-century defensive structures and medieval fortifications. From the piazza, **Via Pagliaro** leads through vineyards and olive trees to the Roman **Villa Damecuta** and the **Grotta Azzura** – a one-hour walk.

Day-trippers can also take one or more of the shorter walks from the Piazzetta of Capri town. The **Gardens of Augustus** are a short walk along **Via F Serena**. From here the Faraglioni and Marina Piccola can be seen, with a good view from above of the incredible, winding Via Krupp. Taking Via Krupp, it is a 20-minute walk down to the charming beaches of **Marina Piccola**.

Alternatively, a 45-minute walk from Capri town leads to the summit of **Monte Tiberio**, where the remains of the Roman Villa Jovis are located. **Via Matermania** leads to the **Arco Naturale**, and on to the **Grotta**, transformed into a Ninfeo by the Romans. Follow the path farther down to the terrace of **Tragara**, to take in the panoramic view of the Faraglioni.

The volcanic island of **Ischia** offers a number of geologically interesting walks. The path to the **Grand Crater** leads through chestnut woods and offers great views of the Aragonese castle and the Gulf of Naples.

From **Vatoliere** a two-hour walk through vineyards and woods leads to the **Sanctuary of the Madonna of Montevergine** at **Schiappone**, where a lovely view of Barano can be seen.

Useful Addresses & Websites

Fitness Centers & Spas

Sinergy Club, 72 Via Nuova S. Rocco, Naples, ☎ 081 744 4777. Fitness and health center.

Imma Gym, 77 Via Luca Giordano, 77, Naples, ☎ 081 556 0022. Female-only gym.

Greenblu Sauna, 4 Via delle Murate, Naples, ☎ 081 570 7002.

Terme Puteolane, 1 Via Gerolomini, Pozzuoli, ☎ 081 526 1303.

Scrajo Terme, 10, Strada Statale 145, Vico, ☎ 081 801 5734. Open April to October for thermal therapies.

Nuove Terme Stabiane, 3 Viale delle Terme, Stabia, ☎ 081 871 4422. Thermal treatments.

Terme Vesuviane Nunziante, 36 Via Marconi Sorrento, ☎ 081 861 1285.

Parco Termale Giardini Eden, Via Nuova Cartaromana, Ischia, ☎ 081 993 909.

Parco Termale Castiglione, 36 Via Castiglione, Casamicciola, Ischia, ☎ 081 982 551.

Parco Termale Giardini Poseidon, Spiaggia Citara, Ischia, ☎ 081 907 122.

Negombo, Baia di San Montano, Lacco Ameno, Ischia, ☎ 081 986 152.

Giardini Tropical, Sant'Angelo, Ischia, ☎ 081 999 215.

Nautical Sports

Motonave Falerno, 179 Corso Garibaldi, Portici, ☎ 335 719 6187. Day cruises to Capri and Amalfi.

Sea Point Diving Center, 14 Molo di Baia, Baia, ☎ 081 868 8868. Dives to the underwater Roman city.

Associazione Aliseo, 49 Via Lucullo, Baia, ☎ 081 854 5784. Glass-bottom boat excursions to the sunken Roman city.

Sorrento Diving Center, 32 Vico III Rota, Sorrento, ☎ 081 877 4812.

Corsi di Vela, Canoa, Sci Nautico, Citara-Forio, Ischia, ☎ 081 981 943. Sailing, canoe and waterski lessons at the beaches of Citara and Forio in Ischia.

Scuola di Windsurf, Forio, Ischia, ☎ 081 997 286. Lessons in windsurfing.

Giro dell'Isola, Capri, ☎ 081 837 0973. Boat tours around Capri.

Sercomar, 64 Via Colombo, Marina Grande, Capri, ☎ 081 837 8781. This company offers diving trips in and around the island of Capri

Noleggio Barche, Spiaggie Corricella e Chiaiolella, Procida, ☎ 081 992 383. Boat rental information on the island of Procida.

Capitaneria di Porto, Via del Brigantino, Positano, ☎ 089 875 486. Information about boat rental on the Amalfi coast.

Teresa Lucibello, Via Marina Grande, Positano, ☎ 089 875 032. Rents boats, pedalos, canoes and offers waterskiing.

Delegazione di Spiaggia, Municipio, Maiori, ☎ 089 814 211. Information on beach activities and water sports at Maiori on the Amalfi coast.

Posidonia, 11 Lungomare Trieste, Marina di Camerota, ☎ 0974 939 127. Boat excursions in the Cilento National Park.

Cooperative Porto, Via Santa Maria, Palinuro, ☎ 0974 938 294. Information about boat excursions.

General Sporting Clubs

Tennis Club Napoli, Viale Dohrn, Naples, ☎ 081 761 4656.

Complesso Turistico Averno, Via Licola Patria, Pozzuoli, ☎ 081 804 2666. Tennis, pool and go-karting.

Ippodromo di Villa Glori-Agnano, Via R Ruggero, Agnano, ☎ 081 570 4222.

Circolo Sportive Caprese, Via Roma, Capri, ☎ 081 837 7147.

Circolo Tennis Yacht Club Capri, 41 Via Camerelle, Capri, ☎ 081 837 0261.

Sport ClubCapri, 10 Via G Orlandi, Anacapri, ☎ 081 837 7980.

Maneggio, 17 Via Cretaio, Fiaiano - Barano, Ischia, ☎ 081 982 069.

Tennis Club Punto, 50 Via Montagna, Fiaiano – Barano, Ischia, ☎ 081 901 881.

Tennis Comunale, Via Piano, 2 - Testaccio - Barano, Ischia, ☎ 081 99 09 09.

Tennis Club Forio, Via Matteo Verde, 41 - Forio, Ischia, ☎ 081 99 81 98.

De Sanctis, 22 Via Giovanni da Procida, ☎ 081 896 7571.

Walking Tours, Guides & Parks

Le Ali di Dedalo, 12 Via Compagnone, Pozzuoli, ☎ 349 547 1559, www.lealididedalo.it. Cultural association that organizes guided walks around the Campi Flegrei.

Servizio Guide del Comune, Baia, ☎ 081 868 7541. Guides to the area.

Oasi Naturalistica di Monte Nuovo, Via Virgilio, Pozzuoli, ☎ 081 804 1462. Guided visits through the nature park of Monte Nuovo by appointment.

Solfatara, 161 Via Solfatara, Pozzuoli, ☎ 081 526 2341. Visits to this privately owned area where volcanic activity can be witnessed are at 8:30 am to 7 pm in summer and 8:30 to 4 in winter.

Riserva Naturale degli Astroni, 24 Via Agnano Astroni, ☎ 081 588 3720. Morning visits to the crater and ancient baths at the Astroni Nature Reserve.

Bosco di S. Silvestro, Caserta, ☎ 082 3361 300. Visits by appointment to these woods near Caserta.

Collegio Regionale Guide Alpine Campania, 302 Via Panoramica, Sorrento, ☎ 081 777 5720. Information about mountain walks in the region.

Posidonia, 11 Lungomare Trieste, Marina di Camerota, ☎ 0974 939 127. Walks and horseback riding in the Cilento National Park.

Capri Trekking, Anacapri, ☎ 081 837 3407. Guided walks around the island.

Specialist Sports

Federazione Speleologica Campana, Castel dell'Ovo, Naples, ☎ 082 3868 798, www.campania.speleo.it. Information about cave exploring.

Useful Websites

www.faito.it – Excursions on and around Monte Faito.

www.vesuviana.it – The National Park and other Vesuvian sites.

www.associazionealiseo.it – Excursions to Campi Flegrei sites.

www.capitanmorgan.it – Boat tours around Capri and Ischia.

www.protours.it – Boat taxis in Procida.

www.progettoceano.com – Boat rentals on Procida.

■ Entertainment

Like all big cities, Naples has much to offer visitors, whether seeking high culture or family entertainment. The long, good summers also provide opportunities for outdoor entertainment, and there are numerous open-air concerts held in the region. Anglophone visitors, however, will find that most theaters and cinemas only show dubbed films, and Italian-language performances. An exception is the **Theater Tasso** in Sorrento, which caters specifically for tourists. An additional source of irritation is the fact that many of the historic churches, not a few ancient sites and even museums are closed indefinitely or require that "custodians" be called to open them, with the usual demands for money. Finally, visitors with families should note that many of the large sports and entertainment complexes are outside the city, and a car or taxi is needed to visit them. The same is true of many nightclubs, particularly in summer, when the beach, rather than the town, becomes the focus of entertainment.

Summer Concerts

A number of summer musical events are organized in and around Naples. In July **Festival Napoli** holds comedy and musical events at the **Castel Sant'Elmo**. The **Neapolis Festival**, also in July, sees top artists coming to Naples to perform. Peter Gabriel and David Byrne were among recent international invitees who held concerts at the **Arena Flegrea**. A **Napoli Blues Festival** is held every summer, and lovers of world and folk music will enjoy the **Musiche Migranti Festival**. South African group, Ladysmith Black Mambazo, and Cesaria Evora have been among recent artists. The **International Festival of Ethnic Music** is also held each year, with a mixture of free and paying events at a number of venues in and around Naples. Entry price to summer concerts is generally around €10.

Outside Naples, the **Napoli Jazz Festival** is an annual event, and features top performers each July, with performances at the Arenile di Bagnoli. **Pomigliano** also hosts a jazz event on four evenings in mid-July at the Public Park of Pomigliano d'Arco. The performances are free. An annual music festival is held at **Palinuro** on the Gulf of Salerno each summer. Performances are free and the beachside location is idyllic. Restaurants are booked well in advance for the occasion.

Theater

The opera season of the world-famous **San Carlo Theater** in Naples runs from December to May. At other times, classical concerts and ballets are held. Tickets cost from €35 for the opera and from €20 for ballet. Last-minute tickets can be obtained one hour before the show at €15. The box office is open from 10 to 1 pm and 4:30-6:30 Tue-Sun (☎ 081 797 2111).

The **Teatro Mercadante** on Piazza Municipio has a long avant garde tradition and is located in a charming 18th-century building. Performances are in Italian, as they are at the **Teatro Bellini**, the **Teatro Diana** and the **Teatro Augusteo**, also in the City. The **Teatro Toto** is an homage to the great Neapolitan comic actor and puts on performances based on his legendary film achievements. The **Galleria Toledo** and the **Teatro Tintadirosso** host more serious dramas.

Outside Naples, the **Teatro Le Nuvole** in **Fuorigrotta** near Edenlandia, reenacts fairytales on alternate Sunday evenings. In **Sorrento**, a **Musical Show** is held each evening with a 1½-hour performance that includes traditional dances in costume and local songs. **La Mela**, also in Sorrento, hosts a **Tarantella Show**.

Nightclubs & Winebars

Nightlife in Naples revolves around the elegant residential districts of Chiaia, Vomero and Posillipo. Trendy cafés and wine bars for the bourgeois youth of Naples proliferate here. Bars on the Via Partenope are popular and generally less expensive than those in Posillipo. Neapolitans eat late so the move from restaurant to dance club is not made until the early hours. In summer many out-of-town venues come into their own, offering seaside open-air dance venues. Famous nightclubs are in Positano, Capri and Sorrento, and there are late night traffic jams on the coastal roads during weekends as the gilded youth make their way to the places that are in vogue.

Family Entertainment

Aside from the coastal resorts and ice cream shops that make the Bay of Naples as attractive to children as to their parents, a number of theme parks are located on the outskirts of the city, perfect distractions for the occasional rainy days. In addition, the cultural sites offer great educational opportunities for children.

In Naples itself, adults and children will both enjoy a visit to the **Dolce Idea chocolate factory** in Pizzofalcone, which can be visited on Sunday mornings by appointment. The **Aquarium** on the Lungomare, in the middle of the public gardens, is the oldest in Europe, and will keep children amused for an hour or two. It's open Tues-Sat 9 am to 6 pm in summer and to 5 pm in winter; Sunday 9 am-2 pm.

A short drive or taxi ride from Naples, **Edenlandia** will fascinate children occupied for a whole afternoon with its ghost train, boating rink and Disney sets. Open from 3-10 pm in summer, and from noon to 8 pm in winter. **Magic World** and **Aqua Flash** in Via Nullo offer further amusements and a water park for children. Visitors of all ages will enjoy the **Città della Scienza**, a huge site in an old factory with a science gym, planetarium, and children's workshop, among many other interactive exhibits. Open 9 am to 6 pm Tues-Sat and 10 am-8 pm on Sun. Closed August and Mon.

In **Portici**, on the Circumvesuviana railway line between Sorrento and Naples, the **Museo Nazionale Ferroviano** will be enjoyed by adult train spotters and children with an eye for old steam engines. There is also a pleasant garden. Open 8:30 am to 2 pm Mon-Sat; closed Sun. Free admission. Educational tours are offered to the **Solfatara Volcano**, see page 96, where the hissing fumaroles are sure to provide dramatic entertainment for all the family. The plaster casts of ancient Pompeians will help to make the Roman site an interesting visit for children.

Useful Addresses & Websites

Teatro Tasso, Piazza San Antonino, Sorrento, ☎ 081 807 5525, www. teatrotasso.com.

Teatro Bellini, 14 Via Conte di Ruvo, Naples, ☎ 081 549 9688, www.teatrobellini.it.

Travel Information

Teatro Diana, 64 Via Luca Giordano, Naples, ☎ 081 556 7527, www.teatrodiana.it.

Teatro Augusteo, 263 Piazzetta Duca d'Aosta, Naples, ☎ 081 414 243, www.teatroaugusteo.com.

Teatro Toto, 12 Via Frediano Cavara, Naples, ☎ 081 296 051, www.teatro-toto.com.

La Mela, 263 Corso Italia, Sorrento, ☎ 081 878 1917.

Teatro Le Nuvole, 26 Viale Kennedy, Fuorigrotta, ☎ 081 239 5653. Open Oct-May, 11:30 am every second Sunday. No credit cards.

Bowling Oltremare, 12 Viale Kennedy, Naples, ☎ 081 624 444. Largest bowling alley in Naples.

Dolce Idea di Bottone Genaro, 718 Via Solitaria, Pizzofalcone, ☎ 081 764 2832. A chocolate factory.

Museo Nazionale Ferroviano, Via Pietrarsa, Portici, ☎ 081 472 003.

Aquarium, Stazione Zoologica, Villa Comunale, Viale A Dohrn, Naples, ☎ 081 593 3111.

Acquaflash, Via S. Nullo, Naples, ☎ 081 804 7122. Waterpark.

Bolle di Sapone, Via Colli Aminei, Naples, ☎ 081 744 4848. Childrens' party organizer.

Edenlandia, Viale Kennedy, Naples, ☎ 081 239 9693. A children's amusement park.

Il Grottino, 34 Via Morghen, Naples, ☎ 081 558 1197. Children's party organizers.

Magic World, Via S. Nullo, Licola, ☎ 081 804 7122. Aquatic park, open only in summer.

Complesso Turistico Averno, Via Licola Patria, Pozzuoli, ☎ 081 804 2666. Go-karting track.

Città della Scienza, 104 Via Coroglio, Posillipo, ☎ 081 735 2260, www.cittadellascienza.it.

Vulcano Solfatara, 161 Via Solfatara, 161, Pozzuoli, ☎ 081 526 2341, www.solfatara.it.

www.napolicabaret.it – Information about the July comedy and music festival.

www.neapolis.it – Information about the annual music festival held in Naples.

www.napolijazzfestival.it – Held every July.

www.pomiglianojazz.com – Details on the upcoming four-day annual event.

www.labazzarra.com – Information site for Ethnos, the ethnic music concert organizers.

NEAPOLITAN GESTURES

In addition to their unique verbal language, Neapolitans can call upon a range of hand signals to convey their emotions. The following are a few of the most common gestures, which authorities now say continue a tradition dating back to antiquity.

Ma che vuò? Literally what do you want? Can convey a rebuke, or a threat.

E corna. Literally means you are a cuckold but, with the fingers pointing to the ground, is a way to ward off the evil eye, *malocchio*.

Ma chi t'ha fatt fa? Why did you do that? An expression of disapprobation when hands are shaken toward an interlocutor.

■ Special Interest Trips

For visitors who wish to combine a vacation in Italy with the acquisition of a skill, or the indulgence of a favorite hobby, a number of organizations offer special interest tours. Couples wishing to get married in the Bay of Naples have an impressive range of options to choose from.

Language & Culture Classes

The Centro Italiano, 17 Vico S. Maria dell'Aiuto, ☎ 081 552 4331. A selection of Italian language and culture courses are offered, including an intensive two-week course. Specialist courses on Neapolitan nativity scenes and archeology are also offered.

Centro Linguistico Internazionale, 9 Via S. Francesco, Sorrento, ☎ 081 807 5599. Located in a 16th-century palazzo, the school offers courses in Italian language for foreigners, voice training by a tenor from San Carlo, and lessons in local culinary and ceramic-making skills.

Capritime Tours, 9 II Traversa La Guardia, Anacapri, ☎ 081 838 2188, www.capritime.com. 11-day/10-night Art & Archeology in Capri tour, with visits to important sites on Capri, the Amalfi Coast and Pompeii.

Cooking Courses

Sorrento Cooking School, Giardino delle Esperidi, Sant'Agnello, ☎ 081 878 3255. Offers individual and group lessons over four-eight days for up to 15 participants. Includes cookery courses, tastings, and gastronomic tours. Lessons last for up to four hours and include the preparation of a complete menu.

Mami Camilla Cooking School, 4 Via Cocumella, Sant'Agnello, ☎ 081 878 2067. Located in a large garden, with an emphasis on organic ingredients. Lessons in vegetable growing also offered. A one-week course, including bed and breakfast accommodation and excursions, costs from €1,350. Alternatives are a one-week language and cookery course, from €1,150, and a four-day course at €576.

Capri Dolce Vita, 9 Via Tito Minniti, Anacapri, ☎ 337 367 2794, www.capridolcevita.com. Culinary vacation, offering personal interaction with local food producers and chefs, and hands-on cooking experience at an *agriturismo* farm. The owners are Massimo, from Capri, and Elizabeth, an American.

Italian Travel, www.italiantravel.it. Seven-day food, wine and culture in Campania. Includes an excursion to Paestum to visit a water buffalo farm where mozzarella di bufala is made.

The Food Maven, www.thefoodmaven.com. Culinary vacation at Tenuta Seliano, the *agriturismo* farm of Baronessa Bellelli. Olive trees, vegetables, fruits and, over the road, a water buffalo herd. Four trips annually with three half-day cooking classes and two full days of touring.

Sports Activities

Up Level Travel, 67 Via degli Aranci, Sorrento, ☎ 081 877 4742, www.upleveltravel.com. Walking and fishing holidays on the Amalfi Coast, Sorrento Peninsula and Capri. Guided walks along the *Sentiero degli Dei*, in Massa Lubrense, Capri and Vesuvius, and boat tours with fishing off the Sorrento coast and in the Jeranto Bay.

Exodus, www.exodus.co.uk. Cilento Park specialty walking excursion, 11 days walking (and sightseeing), two free days on the tour, staying in *agriturismo* farms and small local hotels.

Ciclismo Classico (Classic Cycling), www.ciclismo-classico.com. Amalfi Stroll & Roll multi-activity hiking and biking tour, taking in Capri, the Amalfi Coast and Cilento.

Vacanze a Procida (Holidays in Procida), www.vacanzeaprocida.it. Diving holidays on the island of Procida, in the Bay of Naples.

Weddings in the Bay of Naples

More and more couples are choosing to combine the ceremony and the honeymoon by getting married in the Bay of Naples. The civil wedding can be held in a number of romantic settings, including the cloisters of St Francis, and the Basilica di Sant'Antonino in Sorrento, the medieval castle in Castellammare di Stabia, and the Cathedrals of Amalfi and Ravello. The Hotel Cocumella in Sant'Agnello has a special chapel in its grounds that is used for weddings. The bride and groom need to be in Sorrento four days prior to the wedding. A number of specialist companies and some hotels – such as Corallo and La Tonnarella – can do all the organizing for you.

Wedding receptions can be hosted at some of the most popular restaurants in Sorrento, including O'Parrucchiano, Zi'Ntonio Mare and Antico Francischiello in Massa Lubrense. Hotels in Positano, Amalfi and Ravello are also available for wedding receptions. On Ischia and Capri similar arrangements are in place.

■ Practicalities

Immigration Formalities

For short visits (up to three months) no visas are required for citizens of the European Union, the United States, Canada and New Zealand. A valid passport (or an ID card for EU citizens) must be carried at all times. Addresses of foreign consulates in Naples are given below.

Canada . . . . 29 Via Carducci, ☎ 081 401 338
UK . . . . 122 Via Francesco Crispi, ☎ 081 663 511
USA . . . . Piazza della Repubblica, ☎ 081 583 8111

Property

Since petty crime is a problem in Naples, it is wise to take out travel insurance for valuables. Do not walk around the city with expensive jewelry or cameras on display. Drivers should leave cars in supervised car parks. There is a lost property office at the Central Railway Station in Naples (☎ 081 567 2927). In case of theft or loss, a report should be made to the local police station (Polizia di Stato or Carabinieri). Call ☎ 112 or 113 to speak to a police officer.

Money Matters

The currency of Italy is the Euro. Bank notes in denominations of €5, €10, €20, €50, €100, €200 and €500 are available. There are also €1 and €2 coins, and smaller denominations in cents.

Banks are open from 8:30-1:20 and from 2:45-3:45 in the afternoons Mon to Fri. Outside banking hours, use the Bureaux de Change at the airport, railway stations and in towns.

Credit cards are accepted in most restaurants and hotels, but carry some cash for bars and cafés.

Post Offices

Main post offices are open from 9 am to 6 pm, Mon to Sat; smaller post offices may be open mornings only. Stamps can be purchased from tobacconist (*tabaccaio*) shops. Post offices around the region are listed below:

Naples – Piazza Matteotti.

Sorrento – 210 Corso Italia.

Positano – Viale Pasitea.

Amalfi – 35 Corso delle Repubbliche Marinare.

Ravello – 3 Piazza Duomo.

Caserta – Viale Ellittico.

Ischia – Via Alfredo de Luca.

Procida – 72 Via della Liberta.

Pompeii – 3 Via Sacra.

Telephones

Prefixes are always used within Italy. The prefix for Naples is 081 (including Sorrento and the islands). Amalfi Coast towns use the prefix of Salerno, 089. Caserta numbers begin with 0823. Free phone numbers begin with 800. The international code for Italy is +39.

Public telephones are located in main streets of towns and in many bars. Telephone cards can be purchased from a tobacconist (*tabaccaio*) or bar. For international directory inquiries, dial 176. International operator assistance is 170. As elsewhere, telephone calls made from hotel rooms will be charged at well above standard local call rates.

Health Issues

International travelers are entitled to free emergency health care, but private treatment for non-urgent medical problems is expensive and it is advisable to take out a travel insurance policy that covers doctors' bills. EU citizens are entitled to the same health care as Italian nationals, provided they have the necessary (E111) forms. In the event of an emergency dial 118. The emergency department of a hospital is called *Pronto Soccorso*.

Pharmacies (*farmacia*) are open during normal shop hours, and late at night by rotation (a list of on-duty pharmacies is usually posted on the door). Advice on minor ailments will be given, but over-the-counter drugs are more expensive than in the UK or USA, so take adequate supplies with you.

Voltage

Electric current in Italy is 220 volts. Two- or three-pin round pronged plugs are used, and Continental adaptors can be purchased that will work with most UK and USA electrical appliances.

Internet Access

There are a number of places to access the Internet in Naples, and new outlets are being opened continually. In Sorrento, there is an Internet café within the Matilda nightclub, and most resort towns now have at least one Internet access point. Prices vary, and are currently slightly more expensive than in UK or USA, but it is worth shopping around. Addresses of some are given below:

Naples – Internet Globe, Via Carrozzieria.

Naples – FNAC, 59 Via Luca Giordano, Vomero.

Naples – Internet Bar, 74 Piazza Bellini.

Naples – Internet Napoli, 146 Piazza Cavour.

Naples – Jericho Internet, 121 Via S Biagio dei Librai.

Capri – Internet Point, 13 Piazza Vittoria, Anacapri.

Capri – Capri On Line, 37 Via Longano, Capri.

Capri – Pomodoro Café, 23 Via Lo Palazzo, Capri.

Sorrento – Blublu.it, 20 Via Fuorimura 2.

Sant'Agata – Internet Point, 67 Corso S. Agata, S.A. sui Due Golfi.

Caserta – Cyberspazio Palazzo ETA, Via Unita Italiana.

Tourist Offices

The official tourist offices are generally very helpful, and have free maps and publications listing useful numbers and ongoing events. There are also some commercial offices that look official, but will steer you toward their own products and services. A list of tourist information offices is given below.

Naples – Capodochino Airport, ☎ 081 780 5761.

Naples – Central Station, ☎ 081 268 779.

Naples – Mergellina Station, ☎ 081 761 2102.

Naples – Piazza Gesù Nuovo, ☎ 081 551 2701.

Naples – 58 Piazza dei Martiri, ☎ 081 405 311.

Sorrento – Piazza del Plebiscito, ☎ 081 418 744.

Sorrento – Piazza del Gesù, ☎ 081 552 3328.

Sorrento – 35 Via De Maio, ☎ 081 804 4033.

Stabia – 34 Piazza Matteotti, ☎ 081 871 1334.
Vico Equense – 15 Via San Ciro, ☎ 081 801 5752.
Pompeii – 1 Via Sacra, ☎ 081 850 7255.
Positano – 2 Vai Saracino, ☎ 089 875 067.
Amalfi – 19 Corso Roma, ☎ 089 871 107.
Ravello – 10 Piazza Duomo, ☎ 089 857 096.
Maiori – Viale Capone, ☎ 089 877 452.
Paestum – 151 Via Magna Grecia, ☎ 0828 811 016.
Capri – 11 Piazzetta Cerio, ☎ 081 837 0424.
Ischia – 116 Corso Colonna, ☎ 081 507 4211.
Procida – Porto, ☎ 081 810 1968.
Pozzuoli – 9 Via Campi Flegrei, ☎ 081 526 5068.
Caserta – Palazzo Reale, ☎ 082 3322 233.

Climate

The Bay of Naples has a warm, pleasant climate from April to October, but can be cold in winter, though snowfall, except on high ground, is comparatively rare. August is the hottest month of the year, and cities like Naples close down as everyone leaves for a beach or mountain holiday. Walkers and hikers will find spring and autumn much more pleasant. Budget travelers should consider visiting the region in May-June and September-October when accommodation is cheaper, the main sites less crowded, and the weather is generally good. A guide to annual temperatures is given below.

Jan-Feb	Temperatures range from 4 to 15°C/39 to 59°F.
March-Apr	Spring-like temperatures from 8 to 20°C/46 to 68°F.
May-June	Very pleasant temperatures; generally 16-28°C/61-82°F.
July-Aug	The main tourist season with great weather for swimming, but difficult for long and dusty days of sightseeing. Temperatures from 18 to 32°C/64 to 90°F.
Sept-Oct	Grape harvesting, with temperatures of 12-26°C/54-79°F. The weather generally stays fine but storms can arrive toward the end of September and onwards.
Nov-Dec	Olive production; snow on Vesuvius, and temperatures between 5 and 17°C/41 and 63°F.

Time Zone

Italy is one hour ahead of Greenwich Mean Time. Thus New York is six hours behind Italian time. Clocks go forward one hour in March and back one hour in September.

Tips for Travelers

- Bring good, comfortable walking shoes. You will need them if you intend to do the rounds of the Naples monuments, the Roman sites, or any walks along the Sorrento Peninsula. Remember that walking is the easiest way to get around central Naples, and is obligatory on Capri, where many paths are small, and cars are discouraged, or in parts of the Amalfi Coast.
- If staying on the Amalfi Coast try to make sure that you have a sea view from your hotel room.
- The beaches are often pebbly and plastic shoes can save tender feet!
- Avoid visiting the region in July and August if you don't like crowds, especially Capri and Sorrento. If you cannot visit at any other time, consider accommodation in one of the smaller resorts like Piano or Meta, Cetara or Vietri.
- If you want hospitality in a rural Italian setting, check out the *agriturismo* websites, or ask your travel agent.
- Bring some extra cash to rent a boat and go out for lunch along the Amalfi Coast or off the islands. It's a great way to join the local jet set.
- If visiting in summer make sure you get to at least one of the wonderful outdoor summer musical concerts.
- There are local festivals or *sagre* throughout the year; try to find out whether there will be one where you are during your stay, as this is a lovely means of experiencing local culture and sampling regional dishes.

To Get You in the Mood

To steep yourself in local color and culture, or simply to fill in those quiet moments during your trip, here are a few ideas for books to read before you travel or to take with you, along with DVDs and music.

Bill Bryson, *Neither Here nor There: Travels in Europe*. The incomparable American travel writer rather glosses over Naples in his book, but does devote one chapter to the delights of the bay resorts, with suitably hair-raising accounts of his passage through the city and some amusing, gossipy accounts of fellow tourists in Sorrento, and the delights of Capri.

Luciano de Crescenzo, *Thus Spake Bellavista: Naples, Love and Liberty*. The superb vignettes, by a Neapolitan, capture with wonderful humor the particularities and peculiarities of his countrymen. If you want an insight into what makes Neapolitans tick, buy this book. It is delightful.

Norman Lewis, *Naples '44*. This classic account of World War II is still a real eye-opener and remains a masterful account of a low point in Neapolitan history told with a curiously detached and ironic air by a participant in the glories and misdeeds of the Allied take-over.

Jay Parini, *The Apprentice Lover*. A novel about a young American who arrives on Capri to work for a Scottish writer and becomes entangled with the novelist's women. Not particularly well-written, but the gossip about the celebrity author residents of the island like Norman Douglas, W H Auden, and Graham Greene – albeit not first-hand – is interesting.

Susan Sontag, *The Volcano Lover*. Well researched though somewhat romanticized account of Sir William Hamilton, erudite British envoy to Naples in the late 18th century, with an interest in geology and ancient vases, whose ex-prostitute mistress persuaded the besotted ageing diplomat to marry her and then cuckolded him with Admiral Nelson, prompting one of the greatest scandals of the age, and reducing that great British naval hero to his most appalling act – executing the Neapolitan revolutionaries of 1799.

Harold Acton, *The Bourbons of Naples*. Serious lovers of history will enjoy this account of Bourbon rule – when the great palaces of Naples were built – by a descendant of the famous Anglo-French Prime Minister of the King. Outdated but still very readable.

Pavarotti, Andrea Bocelli and Caruso. Most of the great tenors have recorded CDs of the many haunting Neapolitan melodies that are one of this region's claims to world fame. Hear *O Sole Mio* and other great songs sung by the masters, or look out for a recording by the greatest Neapolitan tenor of all time – Enrico Caruso.

The Postman, *The Gold of Naples*, and *Marriage Italian Style*. Look for a showing or a video of *The Postman,* a sensitive Italian film set in 1950s Capri where writer Pablo Neruda – exiled from Chile for political reasons – spent some time. *The Gold of Naples*, also a 1950s film by Vittorio De Sica and starring Sofia Loren, is available on DVD. In the 1960s Sofia Loren again starred in a film directed by De Sica, and based on Neapolitan playwright Eduardo De Filippo's comedy, *Marriage Italian Style*. Other screen depictions of Naples include Rossellini's *Viaggio in Italia* (1953) and the more recent *L'Amore Molesto* by Martone.

EDWARD LEAR'S NONSENSE POETRY

Artist, and author of amusing poetry, Edward Lear spent the summer of 1838 in southern Italy. Children will enjoy reading his innocent and fun limericks, of which the following is from his *Book of Nonsense Poetry*, first published in 1846.

There was an Old Person of Ischia
Whose conduct grew friskier and friskier;
He danced hornpipes and jigs, and ate thousands of figs,
That lively Old Person of Ischia.

Exploring Naples

Neapolitans are proud of their city's unique character and eccentricities. They will be the first to exaggerate its problems and difficulties, even as they speak with enthusiasm of its unmatched beauty, awesome history and ever-vibrant cultural heritage. In order to enjoy your stay in Naples, it is wise to take note when you are advised – in what sometimes seems to be every other shop or café you visit – to watch your purse, and keep valuable jewelry out of sight, and not to take unnecessary risks like wandering at night in out-of-the-way backstreets. But you should not miss the pleasure of making day-time forays into the winding alleys of the *Centro Storico*. Here you can still see the archetypal Naples – families living almost on the street in the one-room dwellings known as *bassi*, laundry flapping on lines above your head, makeshift shrines to local heroes, whether it be Maradona or Padre Pio, with elaborate churches and magnificent, crumbling palazzi every few steps.

The royal palaces and Angevin castles of central Naples, the breathtaking waterfront views on the Lungomare, the ever-splendid seaside dwellings of Posillipo, the elegant shops of Chiaia, and that unique Italian treasure – the National Archeological Museum – undoubtedly remain the chief attractions of Naples, and secure its place in the top three Italian cities. Add to this the fact that Naples continues to be many cities in one. This is both a physical fact, with its layered architecture, and a cultural one through the centuries of foreign rule. Within a few days, you too are likely to succumb to the infectious charm of this extraordinarily vibrant and rich heritage.

The obsessions of the Neapolitans sometimes seem difficult to comprehend. Religious fervor has helped to perpetuate a degree of superstition and mythology which is almost medieval, and yet which goes hand-in-hand with a modern tolerance for sexual diversity. Note the well-integrated transvestite population and, more disquietingly, the lawlessness in its manifold manifestations (from jumping red lights as a matter of course, to the petty and grandiose extortion rackets of the Camorra).

One of the more charming aspects of Neapolitan life for the tourist is the long association of its people with some of the finest musical traditions and compositions in Italy. Visitors on the Grand Tour made sure that an evening at the San Carlo opera house was part of their itinerary, and even if opera is not your style, you can still take a guided tour of this venerable building. Whatever your musical tastes, you are unlikely to be disappointed by the itinerant minstrels who, mandolin in hand, will give you a stirring rendition of *O Sole Mio*, or another of the great Neapolitan tunes that strive to encapsulate the bubbling vitality of this great city.

■ Royal Naples & Via Toledo

Naples is full of great cultural adventures, and the striking Angevin castles and impressive Bourbon edifices of central Royal Naples are top of the list with most visitors to this wonderful city.

Piazza del Plebiscito

The Piazza del Plebiscito is a good place to start your tour, for around this spacious square are some of the city's most famous landmarks. Furthermore, a Tourist Office is located on the Piazza itself. Get here in the morning for free maps and very useful advice from the friendly staff.

With the Palazzo Reale on one side of the square, the church of San Francesco di Paolo on the other, and the elegant Café Gambrinus and San Carlo opera house a few feet away, this is the stately heart of Naples. The original name of the square – Largo di Palazzo – was changed to Foro Ferdinandeo in the early 19th century, to herald the completion of a Neo-Classical transformation of the area. Initiated by Joachim Murat in 1809, succeeding decades saw the demolition of the 15th-century San Luigi church, and that of Santo Spirito, then the building of San Francesco di Paolo in 1815. This period also saw the construction of guest quarters for the Royal Palace, now the Prefettura, and the renovation of Palazzo Salerno, to accommodate the Bourbon State Ministers (Palazzo dei Ministri).

In past centuries, the Largo di Palazzo was the scene of celebratory appearances by Neapolitan monarchs and visiting dignitaries. Now closed to traffic, and recently renovated, the square is becoming a popular venue in the evenings, with works of art sometimes displayed here. The two grandiose statues in the center of the square represent the Bourbon Kings Charles III and his son Ferdinand IV (on horseback), by Cali and Canova respectively.

San Francesco di Paola

This church was built to fulfil a promise made by Ferdinand IV, following his restoration to power. Modelled on Rome's Pantheon, and designed by architect Pietro Bianchi, the impressive exterior looks most dramatic when lit up at night. The dome is 150 feet high, and the statues on its façade represent St. Ferdinand of Castiglia and, of course, St. Francis of Paola. The bare interior is disappointing, but it contains a fine high altar, designed by Ferdinando Fuga in 1751 for the Church of the Holy Apostles.

Palazzo Reale

The statues on the palace façade are a roll-call of local monarchs – Roger the Norman, Frederick II, Charles of Anjou, Alfonso of Aragon, Charles V, Charles III of Bourbon, Joachim Murat, Vittorio Emanuele II – and are amusingly over-dignified. These giant statues were added by Umberto I. The Royal Palace dates from the 17th century, designed and partly built by Domenico Fontana, but was renovated in the mid-18th century, under the Bourbon King Charles with the help of Luigi Vanvitelli. Today the historic

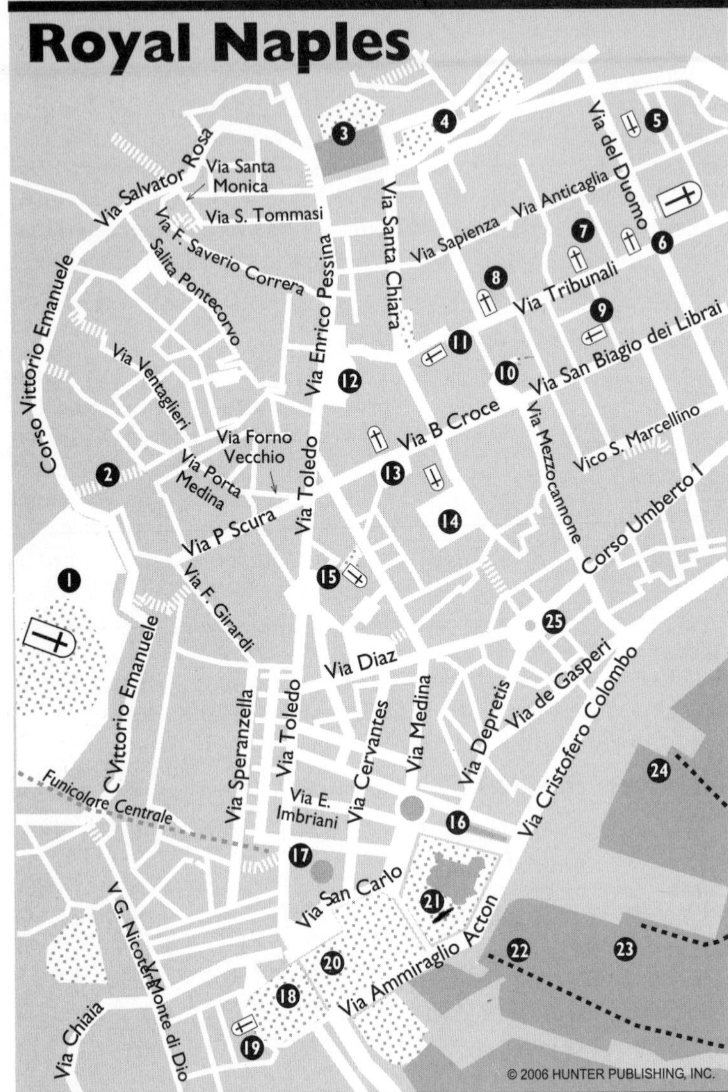

1. Certosa di San Martino
2. Scala Montesanto
3. Museo Archeologico Nazionale
4. Piazza Cavour
5. Santa Maria Donnaregina
6. Duomo; Girolamini
7. San Paolo Maggiore
8. Santa Maria Maggiore
9. San Gregorio Armenio
10. Piazetta del Nilo
11. San Domenico Maggiore
12. Piazza Dante
13. Piazetta del Gesù Nuovo
14. Santa Chiara
15. Piazza di Carita; Santa Anna di Lombardi
16. Piazza Municipio
17. Galleria Umberto
18. Piazza del Plebiscito
19. San Francesco di Paola
20. Palazzo Reale
21. Castel Nuovo
22. Ferry to Ischia, Procida & Capri
23. Ferry to Sardinia, Sicily
24. Ferry to Sardinia

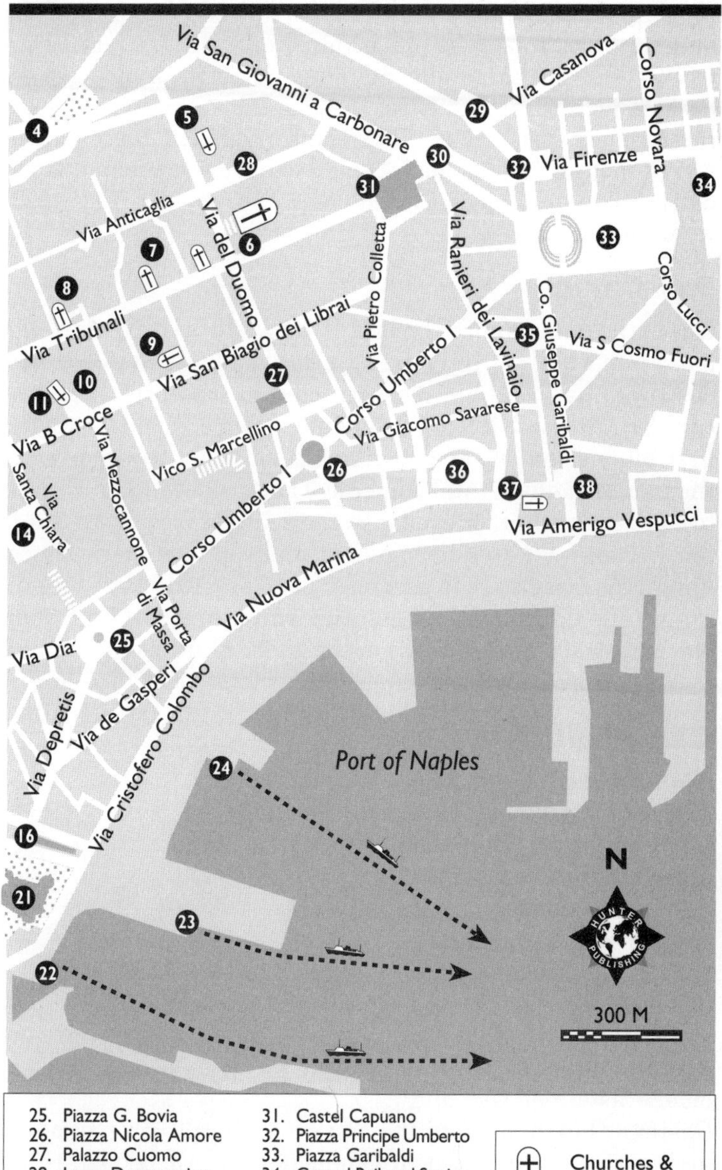

25. Piazza G. Bovia
26. Piazza Nicola Amore
27. Palazzo Cuomo
28. Largo Donnaregina; Via Santi Apostoli
29. Piazza San Francesco di Paola
30. Porta Capuana
31. Castel Capuano
32. Piazza Principe Umberto
33. Piazza Garibaldi
34. Central Railroad Station
35. Piazza Nolana
36. Piazza del Mercato
37. Santa Maria del Carmine
38. Piazza G. Pepe

Churches & Cathedrals

Ferries

royal apartments are a museum, open to the public, and the building also houses an important library. More recently, a facelift was given to the building in 1994, when the G7 nations held a summit here. Besides the sumptuously decorated rooms with original Bourbon furnishings, highlights of a visit include the delightful small chapel and theater. Open daily 9 am to 8 pm. Closed Wed. €4. ☎ 081 794 4021, www.museionline.it.

San Carlo

One of the famous opera houses of the world, and arguably the most important in Italy, San Carlo was built in 1737, was destroyed by fire, then reconstructed in the early 19th century by Antonio Niccolini. Stendhal wrote of San Carlo, "the first impression one gets is of being suddenly transported to the palace of an oriental emperor. There is nothing in Europe to compare with it, or even give the faintest idea of what it is like." There are frequent guided tours of the opera house, unless rehearsals are in progress. The San Carlo summer program runs until mid-July and the winter program begins on November 30. Guided tours every 15-20 minutes Mon-Sun 9 to 6:30 pm. €5. Call ☎ 081 664 545, www.teatrosancarlo.it.

Castel Nuovo

Also known as the *Maschio Angioino*, this 13th-century Angevin castle was later converted into the residence of the Aragon kings, and today houses the Museo Civico (Civic Museum). It was known as the New Castle to distinguish it from the older Castel dell'Ovo and

Castello Capuano. Note the superb 15th-century triumphal arch at the entrance, which commemorates Alfonso I's arrival in Naples. As a former royal residence, the castle has a great deal of history. Petrarch and Boccaccio were among the visitors here. The most memorable of its rooms are the Cappella

Palatina (Palatine Chapel), and the Sala dei Baroni (Hall of the Barons), with its lovely vaulted ceiling by Spanish architect Guillermo Sagrera. Below the Palatine Chapel, the dungeons can also be visited. Legend has it that prisoners held here were fed to an enormous crocodile. The museum itinerary begins in the 14th-century Palatine Chapel, where a few fragments of Giotto's original frescoes can still be seen, along with some Neapolitan Renaissance sculptures. On the first floor of the museum are paintings, sculptures and silver crucifixes commissioned by the Church between the 15th and 17th centuries. The 15th-century bronze doors – complete with a cannonball wedged in the lower panel – are an interesting reminder of past skirmishes with the Genoese. More modern (18th- to 20th-century) paintings are displayed on the second floor. Of particular interest are those depicting historical events of Naples' past such as the massacre of Altamura, and views of Old Naples. Mon-Sat 9 am-7 pm. €5. ☎ 081 795 5877.

San Giacomo degli Spagnoli

Opposite the Castel Nuovo, on the Piazza Municipio, is the imposing Church of San Giacomo. Built in the 16th century together with its adjoining hospital, for the Spanish nobles of the city, and renovated in the 18th century, between 1819 and 1825 the church was incorporated into the Palazzo San Giacomo.

Via Medina

Leading off Piazza Municipio toward the *Centro Storico*, Via Medina is rich in historical buildings. The 14th-century church of **Santa Maria dell'Incoronata** was built to celebrate the coronation of Joan I of Anjou. When excavations began for a second moat around Castel Nuovo in the 16th century, the church ended up below street level, and was not reopened until the 18th century, after Baroque renovation. Frescoes by Roberto d'Oderisio were restored more recently. Opposite the Incoronata is the church of **Pietà dei Turchini**. Originally built in the late 16th century for deprived children, the church houses works by famous artists such as Battistello Caracciolo and Luca Giordano. Look out for a number of historical palazzi on this street. **Palazzo Caracciolo di Forino** is attributed to Ferdinando Fuga, while **Palazzo Fondi** was rebuilt according to a design by Vanvitelli. **Palazzo Carafa di Nocera** has an interesting 19th-century façade. At the end of this street, Via G Sanfelice leads to the Piazza Giovanni Bovio with its glorious 17th-century **Fountain of Neptune** (the square is now undergoing renovation as the new underground line is built) and on to the Corso Umberto I, a busy street which leads to the central railway station on Piazza Garibaldi.

Piazza Trieste e Trento

Returning to the Piazza Trieste e Trento by the Palazzo Reale, a day exploring Royal Naples would not be complete without a stopover to observe life in the heart of the city from the terrace of the historic **Caffè Gambrinus**, once the haunt of Guy de Maupassant, Oscar Wilde and numerous other luminaries. From here, the favored place of worship of local writers, the 17th-century church of **San Ferdinando**, can be seen across the square. Marble statues by Domenico Antonio Vaccaro are housed in the church, together with frescoes by Paolo de Matteis, and the tomb of Lucia Migliaccio, Duchess of Floridia and the morganatic wife of Ferdinand I.

Galleria Umberto I

This late 19th-century gallery, with its elegant glass roof and marble floor, was once a favored haunt of local musicians. Despite the glamorous stores within its interior, it's nowadays oddly empty of life, apart from the ubiquitous Senegalese handbag salesmen. Note the central floor decoration featuring the signs of the zodiac.

Via Toledo

One of the principal shopping streets of Naples, and described by a celebrated visitor on the Grand Tour as "the most populous and gayest street in the world," Via Toledo stretches across Naples up to the National Archeological Museum.

Along its route are a series of fascinating buildings, demonstrating a range of architectural styles – from the Baroque **Palazzo Carafa di Maddaloni** to the Fascist-era Post Office. To its left the sprawling, notorious streets of the **Quartieri Spagnoli** can be glimpsed. On the right, the elegant **Piazza Dante** and the second-hand bookstalls of Port'Alba offer a more cultured perspective on this diverse city.

Santa Brigida

Notable for its cupola with fresco by Luca Giordano, this 17th-century church was named for Saint Brigid of Sweden. Santa Brigida was restored during the reign of King Ferdinand II in the mid-19th century.

Quartieri Spagnoli

The Spanish Quarter, so-called because it was part of an extension to the city ordered by Viceroy Don Pedro de Toledo, notably for quartering troops, is well known to tourists for its characteristic narrow streets, festooned with washing lines, so beloved of photographers. Despite its Baroque churches and historic links – the poet Leopardi once lived here – tourists should venture into this area with caution.

Piazza Carità

On this recently renovated square, the 17th-century church of **San Nicola alla Carità**, restored in subsequent centuries, houses works by Francesco Solimena and Paolo di Matteis. The **Palazzo Cavalcanti**, on the square, is the work of Mario Gioffredo (1762). Note also the fine 18th-century gate of the **Palazzo Mastelloni**. A short detour along the Via C. Battisti leads to the Piazza G Matteotti, with its bombastic **Palazzo delle Poste e Telegrafi** – a typical Fascist-era building.

Carafa di Maddaloni & Doria d'Angri Palazzi

Returning to the Via Toledo, and continuing northwards, on the left note the Palazzo Maddaloni, enlarged by Cosimo Fanzago, and next to it the Palazzo Doria D'Angri – a fine example of the work of Carlo Vanvitelli, who completed a project entrusted to his father, Luigi Vanvitelli, by Marcantonio Doria, Prince of Angri. If you are allowed inside, visit the Rococo-style conference hall with its 18th-century frescoes by Fidele Fischetti.

Palazzo Doria D'Angri

Piazza Dante

Long known as the Largo del Mercatello or Little Market Square, the transformation into Piazza Dante was the work of Luigi Vanvitelli. San Michele Arcangelo, the church on the edge of the square, dates from the 17th century. Via Porta Alba, at the back of the Piazza, is well known for its second-hand book stalls and is an entry point into the *Centro Storico*.

Via Chiaia

Like Via Toledo, this is another major shopping artery for the well-heeled of Naples which leads off Piazza Trieste e Trento. Landmarks to look out for are the **Ponte di Chiaia**, a restored 17th-century gate, and the 16th-century **Palazzo Cellamare**, rebuilt in the 18th century by Antonio Giudice, prince of Cellamare. The portal is by Ferdinando Fuga.

Pizzofalcone

A lift on Via Chiaia takes visitors up to the **Piazza Santa Maria degli Angeli** and the hill of Pizzofalcone. This is the historic site of the original Greek settlement of Parthenope founded in the seventh century BC, and later named Palaepolis. The fortified Roman Villa Lucullus is believed to have been nearby. In the medieval period, a number of monasteries were sited here, but in the 15th and 16th centuries the area was reclaimed and many aristocratic residences were built on Pizzofalcone. The **Via Monte di Dio**, then one of the smartest streets of the city, still bears some traces of its noble past.

Santa Maria degli Angeli

The church dates from the 17th century and is notable for its impressive façade, the dome of which is a landmark of Naples, and its beautifully designed three-nave interior. A cycle of frescoes by Giovan Battista Beinaschi can be seen in the cupola and vaults, as well as a painting by Luca Giordano in the choir.

Palazzo Serra Di Cassano

Constructed in the early 18th century by Ferdinando Sanfelice, the original entrance on Via Egiziaca was closed after the death of Gennaro, son of its owner, who was executed for his part in the Neapolitan Revolution of 1799. Notable for its monumental double staircase, the palace today houses the Italian Institute for Philosophical Studies.

Nunziatella

Constructed on the orders of a noblewoman in the 16th century, and subsequently gifted to the Jesuits, the church and convent were rebuilt in the early 18th century by Ferdinando Sanfelice, and the Royal Military College was installed here. It still houses the military college, and special permission must be obtained to visit. However, it is worth making the effort, because the decoration is spectacular. The frescoes of the *Adoration of the Magi*, the *Assumption of the Virgin* and of *The Virtues* are by Francesco De Mura. The high altar, constructed in 1756-57 by Giuseppe Sanmartino, possibly after a design by Sanfelice, is a superb example of Neapolitan Baroque.

Santa Maria Egiziaca

Originally conceived by architect Cosimo Fanzago for the nuns of Sant-Agostino, the church was completed by Picchiatti, Galluccio, and Guglielmelli, who altered parts of Fanzago's design. The altars of the side chapels feature paintings by Paolo De Matteis. The church also has an early 18th-century majolica floor, and wooden statues by Nicola Fumo.

Museo Artistico Industriale

Situated to the rear of the Piazza Plebiscito, this building has a lovely façade of majolica tiles. Founded in 1878 by Prince Gaetano Filangieri as an art institute to teach young men trades such as metalwork, the institute was given a number of art objects designed to serve as models. Enlarged over time, the collection includes fifth-century Coptic fabrics, work in ebony and jewelry. Run by the Scuola Palizzi, visits are by appointment, except during May when there is free entry on Saturday and Sunday. ☎ 081 764 7471.

GIAMBATTISTA VICO

Born and spending most of his life on the Via San Biagio dei Librai, Vico has been called the "first political scientist" for his great work, *La Nuova Scienza*, and is much respected by modern philosophers. Like so many great historical figures, he received scant recognition in his lifetime, and spent much of it dreaming up ways to escape poverty. He was thwarted at every turn – less deserving colleagues won promotion, while he was overlooked. Even his funeral was farcical. A street disturbance led to the abandonment of his coffin in the Via dei Tribunali. He is buried in the Girolamini church.

■ The Centro Storico

The historic center of Naples is a crowded mass of cultural heritage on a web of streets intersected by three parallel Roman roads, and corresponds to the original city – Neapolis. They are today's Via dell'Anticaglia (*Decumanus Superior*), Via dei Tribunali (*Decumanus Major*) and the road which starts as Via Benedetto Croce and becomes Via San Biagio dei Librai (*Decumanus Inferior*) – also called Spaccanapoli, because it literally cuts through the center of town. The only sensible way to visit the *Centro Storico* is on foot, as the streets are very narrow. This part of Naples is densely packed with cultural monuments and to see all of them would require a great deal of stamina. Fortunately the area is also one of the best in Naples to sample the traditional pizza, and there are numerous cafés for a quick pick-me-up.

Spaccanapoli

Piazza del Gesù Nuovo

A good starting point for the Spaccanapoli cultural route is at the Piazza del Gesù Nuovo – where a tourist office is open in the mornings. In the middle of the square is the distinctive 17th-century spire known as **Guglia dell Immacolata**, and around it are some important monuments. The church of **Gesù Nuovo** on the square was constructed from the 15th-century **Palazzo Sansevero**, which accounts for its unusual diamond piperno (volcanic stone) façade. The interior is triumphal Neapolitan Baroque, with walls and floors of colored marble, and important frescoes by Solimena, as well as works by Giordano, Fanzago and Ribera.

Santa Chiara

An important Angevin monument, the majolica-tiled cloister here is one of the top 10 sights of Naples. Dating from the 14th century, the church and adjoining convent were built for the wife of Robert of Anjou. It was restored in the 18th century in Baroque style, but bomb damage after World War II necessitated extensive repair work, when the original Gothic style was reinstated. Funerary monuments of several Bourbon sovereigns, as well as of Robert of Anjou, can be seen here. There

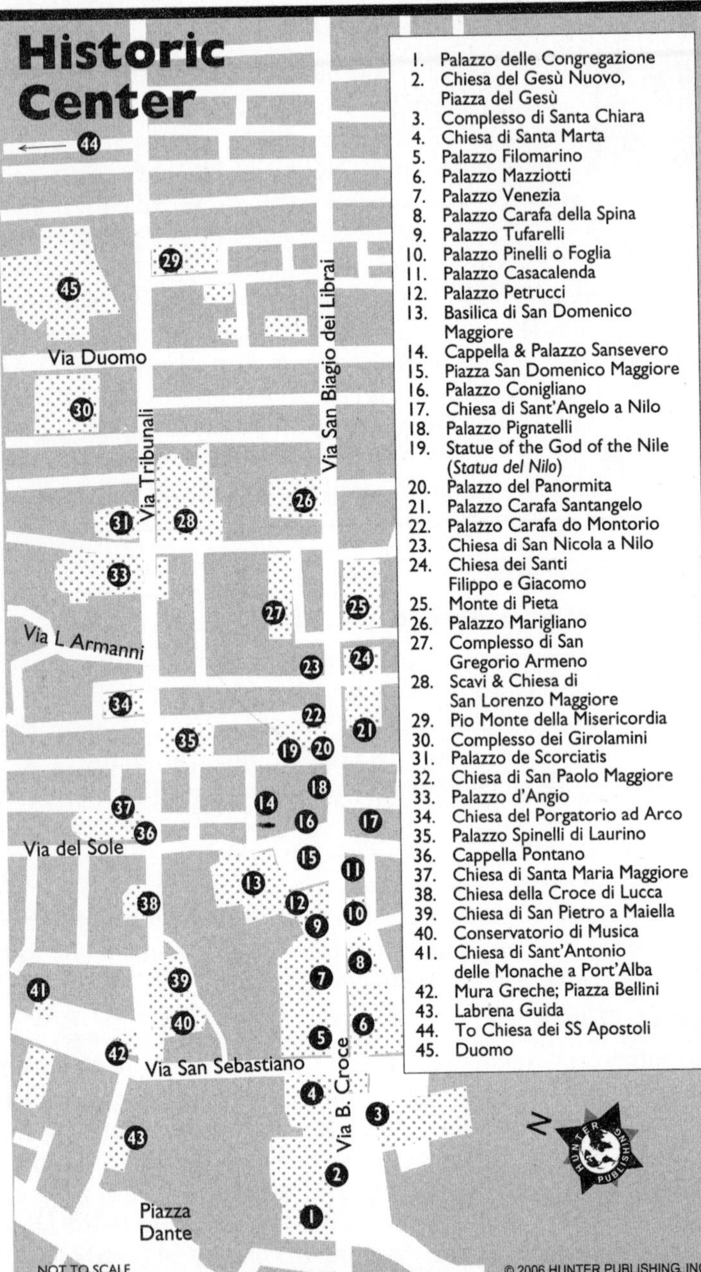
Historic Center
1. Palazzo delle Congregazione
2. Chiesa del Gesù Nuovo, Piazza del Gesù
3. Complesso di Santa Chiara
4. Chiesa di Santa Marta
5. Palazzo Filomarino
6. Palazzo Mazziotti
7. Palazzo Venezia
8. Palazzo Carafa della Spina
9. Palazzo Tufarelli
10. Palazzo Pinelli o Foglia
11. Palazzo Casacalenda
12. Palazzo Petrucci
13. Basilica di San Domenico Maggiore
14. Cappella & Palazzo Sansevero
15. Piazza San Domenico Maggiore
16. Palazzo Conigliano
17. Chiesa di Sant'Angelo a Nilo
18. Palazzo Pignatelli
19. Statue of the God of the Nile (Statua del Nilo)
20. Palazzo del Panormita
21. Palazzo Carafa Santangelo
22. Palazzo Carafa do Montorio
23. Chiesa di San Nicola a Nilo
24. Chiesa dei Santi Filippo e Giacomo
25. Monte di Pieta
26. Palazzo Marigliano
27. Complesso di San Gregorio Armeno
28. Scavi & Chiesa di San Lorenzo Maggiore
29. Pio Monte della Misericordia
30. Complesso dei Girolamini
31. Palazzo de Scorciatis
32. Chiesa di San Paolo Maggiore
33. Palazzo d'Angio
34. Chiesa del Porgatorio ad Arco
35. Palazzo Spinelli di Laurino
36. Cappella Pontano
37. Chiesa di Santa Maria Maggiore
38. Chiesa della Croce di Lucca
39. Chiesa di San Pietro a Maiella
40. Conservatorio di Musica
41. Chiesa di Sant'Antonio delle Monache a Port'Alba
42. Mura Greche; Piazza Bellini
43. Labrena Guida
44. To Chiesa dei SS Apostoli
45. Duomo
Via Duomo
Via Tribunali
Via San Biagio dei Librai
Via L Armanni
Via del Sole
Via San Sebastiano
Via B. Croce
Piazza Dante
N
HUNTER PUBLISHING
NOT TO SCALE
© 2006 HUNTER PUBLISHING, INC.

Santa Chiara

is a separate large campanile (bell tower) but the highlight of the visit is the brightly-decorated majolica columns and seats in the garden cloister, the work of Domenico Vaccaro and the father-and-son team of Giuseppe and Donato Massa who depicted lively 18th-century town and country scenes. The entrance fee covers the cloister, a museum and an archeological area. Open 9:30-1 pm and 2:30-5:30 weekdays; 9:30-1 pm weekends and holidays. €4. ☎ 081 797 1256.

Via Monteoliveto

A short detour takes in the fine Renaissance **Palazzo Gravina**, where busts of the original owners – the Orsini family – can be seen, and the **Church of Sant'Anna dei Lombardi**, a veritable museum of Renaissance sculpture, including a superb group of eight life-size terracotta figures by Guido Mazzoni. The nearby **Palazzo Penna** is a rare example of 15th-century secular architecture.

The Palaces of Via Benedetto Croce

Continuing along Spaccanapoli, a number of historic noble residences can be admired. The **Palazzo Filomarino**, which dates from the 14th century, has an 18th-century doorway by Sanfelice, but is best known for the famous philosophers associated with it. Giambattista Vico was a frequent visitor, and Benedetto Croce lived here. The adjacent **Palazzo Venezia** has a courtyard with open three-arch staircase and 18th-century balconies. The 17th-century **Palazzo Mazziotti**, has a staircase with Neo-Classical columns, while the Baroque **Palazzo Carafa della Spina**, has a magnificent portal decorated with open-jawed lions.

Piazza San Domenico

The Baroque spire in the square was built as a votive offering after the plague of 1656. The Gothic-style church of **San Domenico Maggiore**, constructed in the late 13th century, houses a number of important works of art and is linked to St Thomas Aquinas, who lived in the monastery next door. More imposing palatial buildings line this piazza. **Palazzo Petrucci**, on the corner of Via B. Croce and Piazza San Domenico, has a 15th-century gateway and an 18th-century façade. **Palazzo Corigliano** dates from the 16th century, but was restored in the 18th century, as was the **Palazzo Cascalenda**, rebuilt by Gioffredo and Vanvitelli. Finally, the **Palazzo Sansevero**, designed by Giovanni da Nola, was renovated by Prince Raimondo, an important figure of his day, whose family chapel, on a nearby side-street, is a popular tourist attraction.

The Capella Sansevero

Veiled Christ by Sammartino

From the Piazza San Domenico turn into the Via Francesco de Sanctis toward this extraordinary chapel, decorated by 18th-century sculptor Sammartino. His pièce de résistance is the veiled Christ, a wonderful carving in marble of a reclining figure covered by a delicate shroud. Other sculptures of veiled figures are equally impressive. The masonic iconography in the chapel provides a clue as to why Prince Raimondo was excommunicated. Another reason for the popularity of the chapel – and for the entry price – are the skeletons in the crypt, relics of the Prince's anatomical experiments. Open 10-2:40 daily and 10-1:10 on Sun. Closed Tues. €5. Guidebooks in English cost €8.

Statue of the Nile God

At the beginning of Via San Biagio dei Librai, an interesting sculpture dominates the street. The reclining, bearded figure is believed to have been erected by Alexandrian merchants, who occupied this quarter of Neapolis, around the second century AD. Lost for many centuries, it was placed in its present location around 1667. The nearby church, **Sant'Angelo a Nilo**, originally the family chapel of the Cardinal Brancaccio, houses a sculpture by Donatello and Michelozzo, made in Pisa in 1427, and considered to be the earliest Renaissance work in Naples.

Via Paladino

A detour along the Via Paladino leads to the church of **Santa Maria Donnaromita**. Founded by a group of Romanian nuns in the 14th century, and rebuilt 200 years later, the carved and painted wooden ceiling and the dome, decorated with frescoes by Luca Giordano, are notable features. Across the road, the **Monteverginella** has been restored to a Neo-Classical design.

University Museums

Taking the vico S Marcellino, one reaches the entrance of the former church and monastery of **Saints Marcellino and Festo**. The monastery entrance leads to a wide cloister, similar to that of St Gregorio Armeno, for it was designed by the same architect, Giovan Vincenzo della Monica. Now part of the University of Naples, the cluster of buildings houses a library and several museums (with a main entrance on Via Mezzocannne). The **Palaeontology Museum** was once the west wing of the monastery, and has a precious majolica-tiled floor. The beautiful church dome, tiled with majolica, was restored in 1762. Luigi Vanvitelli was commissioned to undertake further work. He designed the wooden choirs and his floral work can also be seen on the Scala Santa. Of particular interest in the anthropological museum are the collections documenting the palaeobiology and prehistory of southern

Italian peoples, the fossilized remains from Vesuvian eruptions and skeletons from Pompeii. The museum of mineralogy houses interesting items from the Vesuvian and Phlegrean regions, and several extinct species are on display in the zoological museum. The entry fee is €1.50 per museum, or €3.50 to visit them all. Guided visits, €1.50. In the nearby church and monastery of **Santi Severino and Sossio**, frescoes by Francesco de Mura and valuable 16th-century paintings can be seen.

Palaces of Via S. Biagio

Returning to and following the Via S. Biagio dei Librai, another series of palaces can be seen. The **Palazzo Carafa Santangelo** is an interesting example of Neapolitan Renaissance architecture, built in the mid-15th century. The original carved wooden door is still in situ. The **Palazzo del Panormita** also dates from this period. The **Palazzo Marigliano**, its front gate shown at right, is typical of the style of building in the 16th century, when airy gardens and courtyards, offset from the road, were built to compensate for the lack of light on the narrow streets.

Santi Filippo e Giacomo

In the late 16th century, this church was being used as a school for the daughters of the city's silk workers. The current rich décor dates from 18th-century restoration work. The emblem of the Silk Guild is worked into the elaborate design of the tiled floor.

Monte di Pietà

This 16th-century charitable institution houses some interesting paintings and frescoes, and an unusual 18th-century marble and tile floor. Currently owned by the Bank of Naples, the chapel and the art collection of Monte di Pietà can be visited on Saturdays, and on Sunday mornings, free of charge.

Above: View of the ruins, Herculaneum

Below: House of Aristide, Herculaneum

Above: The ruins at Pompeii

Below: Painting of Venus, House of Venus, Pompeii

Above: Mosaic from the Villa di Cicerone, Pompeii, now in the National Archeological Museum

Below: Thermopolium, a small food shop, at Herculanium

Above: Villa Campolieto fresco

Below: The seaside Roman villa of Oplontis, near Pompeii

San Gregorio Armeno

San Gregorio Armeno belfry

Across the street from the Monte di Pietà, turn into the Via San Gregorio Armeno, a famous street where craftsmen still make and sell traditional items such as figures for the traditional nativity or *presepe* scenes – a Neapolitan symbol as powerful as pizza and sfogliatella. This centuries-old craft incorporates contemporary elements in some of the figures portrayed. There are numerous souvenir and knick-knack shops here. A little farther along the street is an important religious edifice of Naples – the church and cloister of San Gregorio Armeno, founded in the eighth century, but subsequently rebuilt. The Baroque interior is magnificent. Look for frescoes by Luca Giordano, the two gilded organs, and the ornate wooden ceiling. In the cloister is a delightful 18th-century fountain and sculptures. The Chapel of the Madonna dell'Idria was decorated by De Matteis. Open mornings only.

Palazzo Marigliano

Returning to Via S. Biagio dei Librai, immediately on the left is the church of **San Gennaro all'Olmo** and next to it the 16th-century Palazzo Marigliano, left, a wonderful example of Neapolitan Renaissance architecture, with its white marble and grey piperno/volcanic stone façade. In the 18th century, the portal was replaced, and openings were cut for ground-floor shops. The interior has a double staircase, and once boasted hanging gardens. The De Mura fresco inside was badly damaged during World War II.

San Giorgio Maggiore

At the junction of Via S. Biagio dei Librai and Via Duomo stands one of the most ancient churches of Naples. The imposing edifice of San Giorgio Maggiore, today, however, is the result of 17th-century rebuilding work by Cosimo Fanzago, after the original structure was destroyed by fire. Although its classic symmetry was ruined when 19th-century work on the Via Duomo led to the demolition of one wing of the church, there are some fine paintings and frescoes in the interior. On this street are also **Roman excavations**, and the **Filangieri Museum**, housed in a 15th-century Palazzo, but both were closed at the time of writing, with no date set for reopening.

Forcella & the Annunziata

If you feel adventurous, you may wish to continue your tour into the Vicaria Vecchia, passing the Gothic church of **Sant'Agrippino** with its 15th-century portal, and through the notorious Forcella district to reach the Annunziata. A former stronghold of the Camorra, Via Forcella is still a place to keep a firm grip on your handbag, but it is also fun to visit, with its proliferation of market stalls, and cut-price Asian clothing stores. At the end of the street, on the Piazza V. Calénda, are the remains of the ancient Greek walls, and the famed **Trianon Theater**, founded in 1911, where Neapolitans indulge their love of song, and which currently houses the Enrico Caruso multimedia library. The **Santissima Annunziata**, on the road of the same name, was a charitable institution for orphans, in operation from the early 14th century, until recently. Restored by the father and son Vanvitelli team, and again after World War II, 16th- and 17th-century statues and frescoes can still be seen in the chapel and sacristy.

Santa Maria del Carmine

Heading along Via Garibaldi toward the seafront, the **Porta Nolana** is a 15th-century city gateway, which is today located near the main fish market. Taking a left turn on the Piazza G. Pepe into the Via del Carmine, the Santa Maria del Carmine church on the Piazza of the same name is a famous Naples landmark. Its 225-foot campanile is the tallest in Naples, while a popular celebration – the feast of the Madonna del

Carmine – is celebrated here annually in mid-July, when a fireworks display is organized. A 14th-century painting of the *Madonna Bruna* in the church is especially venerated. The spot is also associated with the Neapolitan revolution, led by the fisherman Masaniello.

Via dei Tribunali (Decumanus Major)

Corresponding to the Decumanus Major – the central of the three main arteries of the Greco-Roman city – the Via dei Tribunali offers another exhaustive tour of historical monuments.

Piazza Bellini

The delightful Piazza Bellini, with its outdoor cafés, is a good place to start a tour of this section of the *Centro Storico*. Part of the ancient Greek city walls, brought to light by 20th-century excavations, can be seen here. Some venerable palazzi dominate the square. The **Palazzo Conca** is an important example of 15th-century architecture, with its arched doorway and wall décor. Incorporated into the monastery of Sant'Antonio in the 17th century, it underwent considerable structural transformation when the monumental double staircase and stucco work was added. The Baroque 17th-century **Palazzo Firrao**, on the other side of the square, is believed to have been designed by Cosimo Fanzago.

San Pietro a Maiella & the Conservatory

Named for a hermit who became Pope Celestine V, and the founder of the order of that name, the church is one of the most important Gothic structures in Naples. Among notable works of art in the Baroque interior of San Pietro are a series of 17th-century paintings by Mattia Preti and sculptures by

Fanzago, da Nola and Lorenzo Vaccaro. A respected music academy, with a fine collection of antique musical instruments, is located in the complex.

Santa Croce di Lucca

This 16th-century church, built by the Carmelite order, was given a Baroque facelift in the mid-1600s, designed by the architect Francesco Antonio Picchiatti and carried out by Pietro Barberiis.

Cappella Pontano

This grey piperno chapel is considered to be one of the best Renaissance buildings of Naples, and was commissioned by Giovanni Pontano, who wrote many of the Latin epigraphs that adorn the walls. Francesco di Giorgio Martini is believed to be the principal architect. The decorative majolica-tiled floor is especially noteworthy.

Santa Maria Maggiore

Built onto Roman and early Christian structures, this church has an interesting campanile, which is a rare example of medieval Neapolitan architecture. Also known as Pietrasanta, "holy stone" after a popular relic once located here, today's Baroque structure with its distinctive dome, is the work of Cosimo Fanzago. A superb tiled floor was added later and is believed to be by Giuseppe Massa. Indeed, so much history is crowded onto this tiny square, that you may well want to stop for lunch at the well-located Locanda del Grifo, in order to gaze on the lovely bell tower, chapel and church. Afterwards, a short walk up the Via Atri – where Goethe and Torquato Tasso once stayed – will enable you to catch a glimpse of the wonderful ceiling at the entrance of the Palazzo Acquaviva.

Palazzo Spinelli di Laurino

Back on the Via dei Tribunali, this 16th-century palace is another of Naples' historic noble residences that benefited from refurbishment by the talented Ferdinando Sanfelice, who constructed one of his trademark double stairways here. Palazzo Spinelli boasts a unique elliptical courtyard. Bas reliefs by Nicola Massari and a majolica clock are among the interior features.

Purgatorio ad Arco

The name derives from the decision made by a group of Neapolitan aristocrats at the turn of the 17th century to collect funds for the celebration of mass on behalf of the many souls in purgatory. The skull-and-bone motif of the façade and interior testify to this concern for the dead, and add greatly to the macabre theatricality of this little Baroque church. Highlights are the winged skull by Cosimo Fanzago, above, and the underground cemetery.

Palazzo Valois

This is a rare – if not the sole – example of a secular building from the Angevin period which has survived in Naples. It was constructed for Philip of Anjou, Prince of Taranto, in the early 14th century. The nearby church of **Sant'Angelo a Segno** was built to commemorate a sixth-century military victory over the Lombards.

Napoli Sotterranea

A group of enterprising young geologists, speleologists and engineers from the University of Naples are currently organizing tours of a part of the "underground city" – the labyrinth of subterranean passages criss-crossed with ancient structures, which was last in service during World War II, when many Neapolitans sheltered from air raids here. Among sites to see is a small section of the Augustan aqueduct. The tour, currently being run from the Napoli Sotterranea office on Piazza San Gaetano, is short on thrilling archeological finds and long on humorous, unhistorical anecdotes, but children will surely enjoy the candlelit walk. Wear proper shoes, as you will have to walk through watery caverns. The best part of the tour is when you enter a typical "basso," a traditional Neapolitan home, a one- or two-room dwelling with no windows. Inside this basso, steps lead down to a Greco-Roman theater underfoot. The external arches of the theater can still be seen overground on the Via Anticaglia. It is said that Emperor Nero performed one of his own operas here.

San Paolo Maggiore

Also on the Piazza San Gaetano, this church, built on the site of a Roman temple, has an imposing double staircase, by Francesco Grimaldi. Highlights are the Baroque chapel, the paintings by Solimena, and the interesting crypt.

San Lorenzo Maggiore

Another chance to visit the Greek and Roman excavations of underground Naples is provided at this Gothic basilica. Indeed, visiting the premises is a journey back through Neapolitan history, for alongside the Baroque and Gothic features of the church itself, there is a charming 18th-century cloister, with a well by Fanzago, the ruins of a medieval Neapolitan courthouse, and the remains of an ancient Roman market, treasury and shops. San Lorenzo Maggiore is also notable as the place where Boccaccio – author of the *Decameron* – met and fell in love with the girl who would become his model for the beautiful Fiammetta of his writings. Among notable monuments are a 14th-century wooden crucifix, and the tomb of Catherine of Austria. Open 9 am-5 pm daily and 9:30-1:30 on Sun. €4. A small guide is available to the site for €1.50.

Girolamini

A turn left into the Via Duomo leads to the Girolamini church and art gallery, and to the Cathedral across the road. The Neapolitan philosopher Giambattista Vico lived nearby and was buried in this attractive Baroque church. Dating from the late 16th century, the façade was remodelled by Ferdinando

Fuga around 1780. There is an attractive, recently restored cloister and a picture gallery that displays paintings by Solimena, Ribera, Vaccaro and Durer, among others – one of the most important art collections in Naples.

The Duomo

Naples' Gothic Cathedral, which dates from the 13th century, is characterized by its overlapping styles, as centuries of alterations have transformed its structure. There are for example, Greco-Roman foundations, early Christian mosaics, and a Baroque chapel. Dedicated to San Gennaro, patron saint of the city, martyred at Pozzuoli, around 305 AD, and whose tomb is in the superb Renaissance crypt, one of the most famous processions of Naples starts from here. The "miracle" of the liquefaction of San Gennaro's blood was for generations a crucial event. Today it is notable chiefly for the large procession that winds from the Duomo to Santa Chiara. For modern-day tourists, a visit to the on-site museum that houses the "Treasures of San Gennaro" is a must. With an impressive collection of silver objects such as candelabra and crucifixes, it is a showpiece of Neapolitan craftsmanship from the 15th to the 18th centuries. There are also stuccoes and paintings, as well as the 14th-century blood reliquary – a container for the ampoule of San Gennaro's blood. Allow 30-40 minutes for the visit – there are five rooms and sacristies to see. €5.50, including an audio guide. Open Tue-Sat 9 am-6:30 pm. Holidays 9:30-7. ☎ 081 421 609, www.museotesorsangennaro.com.

Guglia di San Gennaro

On the Piazza Riario Sforza, at the side of the Cathedral, the 70-foot spire, designed by Cosimo Fanzago, dates from the 17th century, and was constructed in gratitude for protection from the eruption of Vesuvius a few years earlier. The bronze statue of San Gennaro is by Tommaso Montani.

Pio Monte della Misericordia

Back on the Via dei Tribunali, this is another of the characteristic 17th-century buildings created in Naples to fulfil a charitable role, in this case for the benefit of the Christians enslaved by Barbary pirates. The two-storey structure was built with five arches. The pièce de résistance of the octagonal chapel is Le Sette Opere di Misericordia, a magnificent painting by Caravaggio, shown at right. An art gallery on the first floor houses an interesting collection, including 41 paintings by Francesco de Mura. Visits by appointment only.

Santa Maria della Pace

Built between 1629 and 1659, the church commemorates the peace treaty signed between Philip IV of Spain and Louis XIV. Restored in the 18th century, the interior floor tiles are the work of Donato Massa. The attached hospital was founded to care for plague victims and lepers; it has a marble altar and lovely frescoes.

Santa Maria del Rifugio

Designed as a refuge for girls in danger of being ensnared into prostitution, the church has ceiling paintings from the 17th century, and marble décor by Pietro Ghetti.

Castel Capuano

At the end of the Via dei Tribunali, this castle dates from the 12th century, and was built for the Norman king William the Wicked. The Angevin and Aragonese kings later enlarged it, and it served for a while as a private noble residence. The Viceroy Don Pedro of Toledo made it a courthouse in the 16th century, which function it has preserved to this day, after substantial renovation in the mid-19th century. The Cappella della Sommaria, with its lovely 16th-century frescoes, is of particular interest. On the other side of the Piazza de Nicola, is the **Porta Capuana**, an ancient city gate rebuilt in the 15th century. Its towers are important 15th-century monuments to the Neapolitan Renaissance.

Santa Caterina a Formiello

Also on the piazza is this beautiful 16th-century church with its imposing dome. Notable features inside are the ceiling frescoes by Luigi Garzi, and the Spinelli family tombs. The floor dates from the late 18th century, and incorporates 16th-century tombstones.

Decumanus Superior

The upper parallel road of the *Centro Storico*, the ancient Roman Decumanus Superior, changes its name several times – from Via della Sapienza to Via Pisanelli, and then Via Anticaglia. This route takes in a number of important churches.

Santa Maria della Sapienza

Situated at the start of the Via della Sapienza, this Baroque church has a majestic marble altar. Across the Via S. Maria di Costantinopoli, San Giovanni has a splendid 18th-century façade by Giovan Battista Nauclerio.

Santa Maria Regina Coeli

At the other end of the Via della Sapienza, this 16th-century church has a Baroque interior. The wood ceiling with its gilt décor is by Piero de Martino. Paintings on the walls and ceiling are by Domenico Gargiulo, young Luca Giordano and Massimo Stanzione.

Santa Maria di Gerusalemme

On the Via Pisanelli, the church of Santa Maria dates from the late 16th century, and has stucco decoration and an 18th-century majolica floor.

Palazzo Caracciolo di Avellino

The façade is early 16th century, but the palace was enlarged a century later by Prince Caracciolo, incorporating a lake connected by two arcades.

San Giuseppe dei Ruffi

The church was founded in the 17th century, but was demolished and rebuilding work not completed until the early 18th century. The present façade and the marble and piperno (volcanic stone) portico are by Arcangelo Guglielmelli. The rich Baroque interior was designed by Lazzari, and features frescoes by Francesco de Mura. The chapel of Saint Augustine houses a painting of the *Trinity* by Luca Giordano and statues of Saint Peter and Paul by Giuseppe Sanmartino.

The Archbishop's Palace

Dating from the 14th century, the remains of a much earlier pre-Christian structure were found during renovation work. The present building owes more to 17th-century restoration and enlargement, probably by Bonaventura Presti. The interior houses frescoes by Giovanni Lanfranco and an art collection. Note the beautiful old carriage in the courtyard.

Santa Maria Donna Regina Nuova

Opposite the archbishop's palace, on the Vico Donnaregina, this 17th-century church has a monumental stairway, and a richly decorated marble interior. Especially notable are the wall frescoes by Francesco Solimena featuring the life of Saint Francis.

Santa Maria Donnaregina Vecchia

The older church of the Donnaregina complex houses the marble tomb – by Tino di Camaino – of Queen Mary of Hungary, wife of Charles II of Anjou. The church also contains a famous cycle of early 14th-century frescoes, exceptionally important for students of Neapolitan painting.

Santi Apostoli

At the end of the Decumanus Superior, set back from the Via Santi Apostoli, this ostentatiously decorated church is considered to be one of Naples' most magnificent Baroque monuments. The chapel altars are by Francesco Borromini – his only work in Naples – and Ferdinando Sanfelice. There are also several paintings by Luca Giordano, and superb frescoes by Giovani Lanfranco.

San Giovanni a Carbonara

Taking the Via S. Sofia past the church of the same name and turning left on Via Carbonara, it is a long walk up to San Giovanni, but the trek is worth it, as this is considered among the most beautiful churches of Naples. Dating to the 14th century, this monumental complex has exceptional sculpture and artwork, particularly in the chapels of Caracciolo del Sole and Caracciolo di Vico. The lovely double staircase, right, is by Sanfelice, and also noteworthy are the funerary monuments of King Ladislao and Ser Gianni Caracciolo, lover of Queen Giovanna.

Via Foria & Capodimonte

Naples boasts two world-class museums: the Museo Nazionale Archeologico houses the precious antiquities rescued from Pompeii and Herculaneum, while Capodimonte has a superb collection of Old Master paintings and porcelain. The Via Foria, and the Sanità district, around these museums, contain a number of other interesting sites which are discussed in this section.

National Archeological Museum

The world-famous Roman sites around Naples are essentially empty houses and villas, with only a few floor and wall decorations. Instead, the most valuable treasures of antiquity from these important excavations are found in the National Archeological Museum in Naples, including the erotica kept in the so-called Secret Room. The museum's Roman collection has also been boosted by the Farnese family who purchased

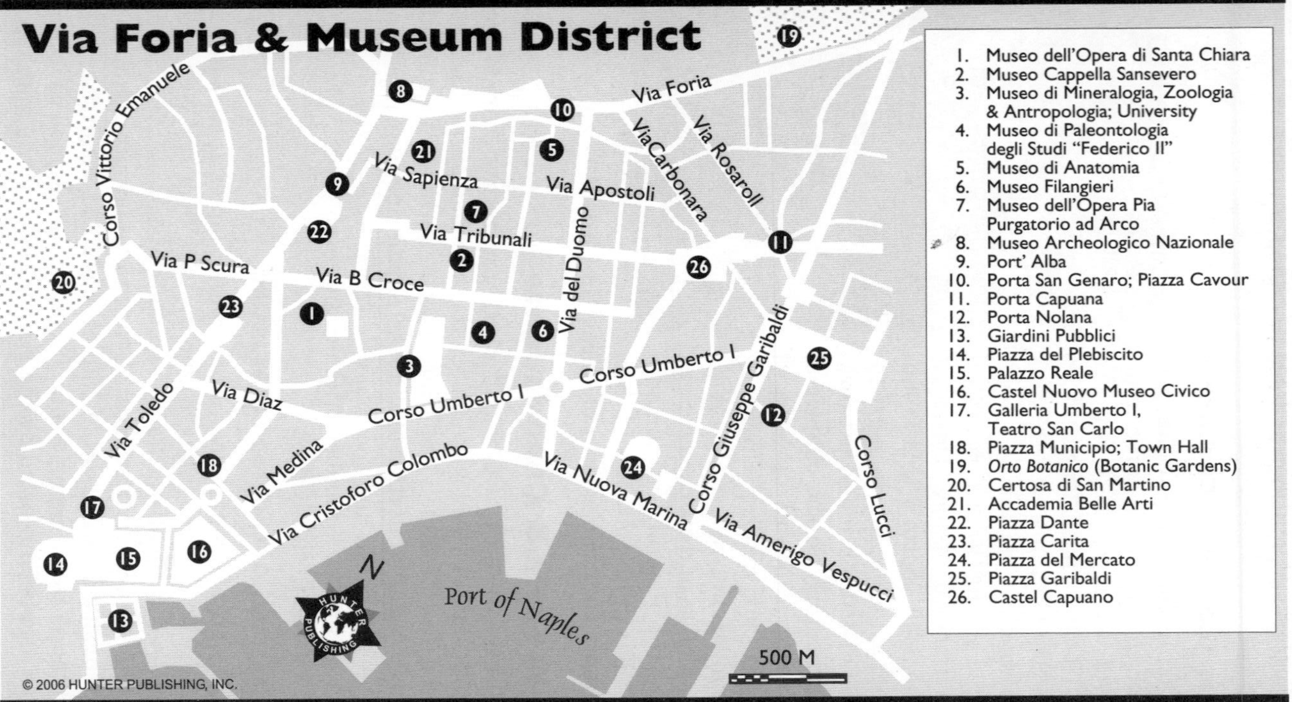
Via Foria & Museum District
1. Museo dell'Opera di Santa Chiara
2. Museo Cappella Sansevero
3. Museo di Mineralogia, Zoologia & Antropologia; University
4. Museo di Paleontologia degli Studi "Federico II"
5. Museo di Anatomia
6. Museo Filangieri
7. Museo dell'Opera Pia Purgatorio ad Arco
8. Museo Archeologico Nazionale
9. Port' Alba
10. Porta San Genaro; Piazza Cavour
11. Porta Capuana
12. Porta Nolana
13. Giardini Pubblici
14. Piazza del Plebiscito
15. Palazzo Reale
16. Castel Nuovo Museo Civico
17. Galleria Umberto I, Teatro San Carlo
18. Piazza Municipio; Town Hall
19. *Orto Botanico* (Botanic Gardens)
20. Certosa di San Martino
21. Accademia Belle Arti
22. Piazza Dante
23. Piazza Carita
24. Piazza del Mercato
25. Piazza Garibaldi
26. Castel Capuano
Corso Vittorio Emanuele
Via Foria
ViaCarbonara
Via Rosaroll
Via Sapienza
Via Apostoli
Via Tribunali
Via del Duomo
Via P Scura
Via B Croce
Corso Umberto I
Corso Giuseppe Garibaldi
Via Diaz
Via Toledo
Via Medina
Via Cristoforo Colombo
Via Nuova Marina
Via Amerigo Vespucci
Corso Lucci
N
HUNTER PUBLISHING
Port of Naples
500 M
© 2006 HUNTER PUBLISHING, INC.

The Farnese Bull

numerous important artifacts over a 300-year period. There is so much to see here that you need to keep a whole day free. Visitors on the Grand Tour used to spend a week or more here!

Highlight of the Farnese collection is the magnificent Farnese Bull, the largest sculpture from antiquity in the world. In addition to statues, paintings and mosaics, the everyday objects from the Roman cities of Campania are what many visitors remember best: petrified foods, crockery and toilet articles rescued from the homes of ordinary people. The museum also houses a collection of Etruscan and Egyptian art and ancient coins. Open 9 am to 7:30 pm every day except Tues. €6.50 (€3.25 reductions). Free entry for those under 18 and over 65. A place on the twice-daily guided tour (at 10:30 am and noon) costs €3.50 and an audio guide costs €4. Classical concerts are held here on Saturday evenings in the summer. ☎ 081 440 166.

Galleria Principe di Napoli

Opposite the museum is the entrance to this ornate 19th-century shopping gallery. Designed by architects Nicola Breglia and Giovanni De Novellis, the Galleria has a cast-iron and glass roof and stucco wall decorations.

Santa Maria di Costantinopoli

This church celebrates the Madonna of Constantinople, protector against epidemics, on behalf of grateful survivors of plague in 16th-century Naples, and was designed by Fra Nuvolo in the early 17th century. Cosimo Fanzago is responsible for the Baroque interior and imposing high altar. Paintings from the ateliers of Giordano and Solimena can be seen here.

Ospedale degli Incurabili

To the left of the Archeological Museum is Piazza Cavour, where the nearest subway station is located. Opposite the square, take Rampa M Longo to the historic Hospital and Pharmacy of the Incurables. The hospital dates from the 16th century, and was built for the benefit of the poor. Also on the site, the 18th-century **Pharmacy**, at the end of Via Armanni, houses an important collection of majolica vases.

San Carlo all'Arena

On the other side of the Via Foria, this church was partially built by Fra Nuvolo, but not completed until the late 18th century. Used as a barracks by the French, the façade and dome were restored by Francesco De Cesare. The life of San Carlo is depicted in bas-reliefs on the front of the building.

The Botanical Gardens

Farther along the Via Foria, for those who want to escape the rush of Naples traffic, the Botanical Gardens are worth the long walk up. Founded in 1807, the gardens are today part of the University of Naples and can be visited by appointment only. Once you are inside, however, they are lovely, recreating diverse plant habitats, in greenhouses or in the open air. The aquatic plants, palms, and cacti are especially splendid. ☎ 081 449 759.

Albergo dei Poveri

Next to the gardens is a monumental structure. Designed in the 18th century by Ferdinando Fuga, around the same time as the Palaces of Capodimonte and Portici, this Hotel for the Poor is similarly gigantic in scale and conception. Originally intended to provide housing for all the poor who needed it, this was to be a city within a building, with five piazzas and a church. Left unfinished in a city where accommodation for the poor was to remain an unresolved problem, the Albergo is nonetheless a testament to the paternalism of the Bourbons, and the most grandiose of the many historic buildings that express the charitable – if somewhat unpragmatic – visions of past Neapolitan rulers. It is currently being restored to function as a cultural center.

Porta San Gennaro

This historic city gate, on the Via Foria dates from the mid-15th century – and is the only one bearing a fragment of the 17th-century fresco decoration by Mattia Preti that once also graced the other old gateways into Naples.

From here a walk through the Sanità district leads up to the palace museum and park of Capodimonte. The Sanità is a poor part of Naples, however, and visitors should proceed with caution. The less adventurous may prefer to take a bus or taxi directly up to Capodimonte and the catacombs.

Palazzo dello Spagnolo

From the Via Foria, take Via Crocelle, which leads on to Via Vergini. Look out for this striking 18th-century palace, which has a superb external double staircase, the work of Ferdinando Sanfelice. The palace is named after Tommaso Atienza, a Spanish aristocrat, who lived here in the 19th century.

Palazzo Sanfelice

On Via Sanità itself, Sanfelice built his own family home in 1728. Here can be found the prototype external staircase which would become associated with his name.

Santa Maria della Sanità

Farther along this winding road, on the Piazza Sanità, this basilica is considered to be one of the most important of the surviving early 17th-century monuments of Naples. There is a superb double semicircular stair leading to an elevated presbytery, and a number of important works of art by Luca Giordano among others. Beneath the presbytery, a paleochristian basilica can be visited, which has a ninth-century fresco and various tombstones that date from the fifth century. Entry to the Catacombs of San Gaudioso is via a 15th-century crypt. Ancient fragments of frescoes and mosaics can be seen alongside the rather gruesome tombs. Open 8:30 am to 12:30 pm and from 5-8 pm weekdays; 8 am to 1:30 pm Sun. ☎ 081 544 1305, www.santamariadellasanita.it. There are guided tours of the catacombs in the mornings. Evening tours with guides in historical costume can also be arranged.

Catacombs of San Gennaro

Lifts link the Sanità district with Corso Amedeo, the main road leading to Capodimonte. En route to the museum, you can visit the vast catacombs, where the mortal remains of the city's bishops were kept. Here you can find the first known portrayal of San Gennaro, from the fifth century, and see the important collection of early Christian wall paintings. Guided tours are offered in the mornings.

Cimitero della Fontanelle

Alternatively you can continue along the Via della Sanità and into Via Fontanelle to the cemetery where caverns containing bones and skulls frightened Ingrid Bergman in Rossellini's *Viaggio in Italy*; since then tourists have made determined efforts to put it on their itinerary.

Capodimonte Palace Museum & Garden

Built on top of a hill, with lovely views of the city, the royal residence of Bourbon King Charles III can also be reached by buses from Piazza Garibaldi or Piazza Dante. Begun in 1738, but completed much later, there are three areas to visit: the royal apartments, the collections of paintings, china and majolica, and the surrounding park. The Sala di Porcellana – a room covered in Capodimonte porcelain – is a great feature. Highlights of the art collection

Antea by Parmigianino, Capodimonte Museum

include two works by Brueghel, a Botticelli *Madonna*, Caravaggio's *Crucifixion*, and paintings by Titian and Raphael. One hall has a superb series of 19th-century watercolors of Naples and the surrounding countryside. The park is open from 8 am until one hour before sunset every day and can be visited free of charge. ☎ 081 749 9111. Museum open Tue to Sun 8:30 am to 7:30 pm. Closed Mon. €7.50.

Astronomical Observatory of Capodimonte

Built in 1819, during the reign of Bourbon King Ferdinand I, the first observatory in Italy, and with an excellent view over the Bay of Naples, it is currently open to the public by appointment only. ☎ 081 557 5111, www.na.astro.it.

CAPODIMONTE PORCELAIN

The famous porcelain owes its origins to Charles of Bourbon, who brought craftsmen to Naples and set up a royal porcelain factory in the mid-18th century. The complex production process, requiring several firings for the varnishing and decorating phases, produced the delicate coloring which can be seen on examples from the period in the city's museums.

The Lungomare & Chiaia

The Lungomare is the coastal road of the city which stretches from Santa Lucia to Mergellina. This delightful, picturesque area of Naples includes an ancient castle as well as the glamorous residential and shopping area of Chiaia.

Santa Lucia

South of Piazza del Plebiscito, the Via Santa Lucia runs through an area close to the sea front, which is immortalized in the famous song, *Santa Lucia*. With its lively markets, it is a typical Neapolitan neighborhood. Some of the streets around it are rather run-down, and it would not be advisable to linger too long, before heading to the Via Partenope.

Lungomare di Napoli
Via Tasso
STAZIONE CUMANA
Corso Vitorio Emanuele
Via Tasso
Piazza Amedeo
S. Teresa a Chiaia
Palazzo Cellamare
S. Maria dei Angeli a Pizzofalcone
Via Francesco Crispi
Via G Martucci
Chiesa d'Ascensione a Chiaia
S. Caterina a Chiaia
S. Francesco di Cassano
Via Michelangelo Schipa
Via Chiaia
Via Monte di Dio
S. Maria in Portico
Villa Pignatelli (Museum)
Via Andrea d'Isernia
CHIAIA
Nunzia- tella
Palazzo Serra di Cassano
Via Principessa Pignatelli
S. Maria di Vittoria
PIEDIGROTTA
STAZIONE MERGELLINA
Piazza della Repubblica
Riviera di Chiaia
Villa Comunale
Piazza Vittoria
Gran Quartiere di Pizzofalcone
Via D. Morelli
SANTA LUCIA
Via Francesco Caracciolo
Via Piedigrotta
Rotonda A. Diaz
Colonna ai Caduti del Mare
Via Chiatamone
Via Mergellina
Viale Antonio Gramsci
Via Partenope
S. Maria di Piedigrotta
Via Francesco Caracciolo
Castel dell'Ovo
Tunnel
Ferries to Ischia, Procida, Sorrento & Capri
Bay of Naples
Via Orazio
Via Sannazzaro
MERGELLINA
Funicolare di Mergellina
S. Maria di Parto

Via Partenope

One of the favored places for young locals and tourists to gather in the evenings, with its lively bars and discotheques. Some of the city's classier hotels and restaurants are here, but this is also the place where you can enjoy a good and inexpensive meal in great surroundings at an establishment like Antonio & Antonio. The **Immacolatella fountain**, which marks the beginning of the Lungomare promenade here, was built in 1601.

Castel dell'Ovo

The old fishing district of Santa Lucia – known as the Borgo Marinaro – is today a cluster of picturesque seafood restaurants, which are crowded with tourists for lunch and dinner. By its side is the oldest castle of Naples – the **Castel dell'Ovo**, built on the ruins of a Roman villa and extended by Norman, Angevin and Aragonese rulers. There is free entry to the castle, but not much to see within the building itself. However, Roman columns are still visible in the dungeons and good views of the Lungomare, Vesuvius and the Bay of Naples can be had for those who take the elevator or walk up to the top floor. There is a bar up here, but it is not always open. Cultural events, such as art exhibitions, are often held in the Castel dell'Ovo. An ethno-prehistoric museum is also in the castle, with documentation, implements, and other aspects of early human settlement, especially in southern Italy. The museum, principally designed for educational visits, can be seen by appointment. ☎ 081 764 5343.

Le Crocelle

The early 17th-century church of Le Crocelle is on Via Chiatamone, which runs parallel to Via Partenope. This is the tomb of the artist Paolo de Matteis, and many of his works are found here, including the painting of the *Immaculate Conception* on the high altar. The **Villa Ebe**, on this street, with its distinctive square tower, was built by the Anglo-Indian designer Lamont Young, in the early 20th century.

Via Francesco Carraciolo

Named after the Neapolitan admiral Francesco Caracciolo, who was hanged as a result of his participation in the Neapolitan Revolution of 1799, this waterfront promenade is a lovely place for a stroll in the early evening.

Villa Communale

Though it sounds like a residence, this is in fact the name of the park that runs between Via Carraciolo and the Riviera di Chiaia. Commissioned in the 18th century, and later enlarged, today the park is an enchanting blend of pine, palm and eucalyptus trees with 19th- and 20th-century statues and fountains. The famous Farnese Bull once stood here, but was replaced by a basin from Paestum, now incorporated into the Fontana delle Paparelle. The bandstand dates from 1887. An antiques and bric-a-brac market is held here on Sunday mornings.

The Aquarium

Located inside the park and set up in 1873 by German naturalist Dr Anton Dohrn, a friend of Darwin, the Stazione Zoologica or Aquarium is one of the oldest continually functioning research stations in Europe. English engineer Alfred Lloyd designed the system brought into operation here for recycling water, which enabled specimens to be kept for longer periods in the display tanks, and the aquarium still uses this "semi-closed" system of water filtration and circulation. The Aquarium's 23 display tanks house a superb collection of marine life from the Bay of Naples, where moray eels and crabs hide inside Roman amphorae and Neapolitan water jars. Visits take around 30 minutes, and the Aquarium is open year-round. €1.50 (€1 reductions). Open weekdays 9 am to 6 pm in summer, and 9 am to 5 pm in winter. Closed Mon. Shorter hours on Sun and holidays.

Villa Pignatelli

This delightful villa, on the Riviera di Chiaia, was designed in 1826 for Ferdinand Acton, son of the Prime Minister of Naples, Sir John Acton. It was purchased in 1841 by the Rothschild family, who enlarged and refurbished the villa. In 1867, Diego Pignatelli, Duke of Monteleone, acquired the residence. Today, the ground floor of this important example of

Neo-Classical architecture retains many reminders of its illustrious inhabitants: the library is the former smoking room of Acton's original house, while the ballroom and the Red Salon also retain many original features. The first floor houses part of the art collection of the Bank of Naples. The gardens, which preserve many features of the original English design, with winding avenues, can be visited, and a carriage museum is also here. Open Tue-Sun 9 am to 2 pm. €2. (€1 for minors and the elderly). ☎ 081 669 675.

San Giuseppe a Chiaia

Farther along the Riviera, this 17th-century church functioned as a military academy and a hospice before its restoration in the mid-19th century. It was here that Percy Shelley reputedly took his love child – born during his stay with wife Mary in Naples – to be baptized.

Santa Maria in Portico

Turning inland from the Riviera, into the street, also named Santa Maria in Portico, the 17th-century piperno façade of the Santa Maria church looms into view. The interior houses works by Paolo de Matteis and Domenico Vaccaro.

Ascensione a Chiaia

Continuing along Via G. Piscicelli, on the left-hand side, this 14th-century church, restored by Cosimo Fanzago some three centuries later, houses two paintings by Luca Giordano, among other artworks.

Piazza Amedeo

Superb palaces surround this 19th-century square, where a subway station is located. They include the Art Deco **Palazzo Regina Margherita**, and, to the rear, Lamont Young's Neo-Gothic **Aselmeyer Castle**, now divided into separate residences.

Santa Teresa a Chiaia

From the Piazza, Via Vittoria Colonna leads to a three-storey church, originally called St Theresa by the Beach, an indication of the closer proximity of the sea in previous times. Restored by Cosimo Fanzago in the 17th century, and given its double staircase at this time, more works by Luca Giordano are preserved here.

Christ Church

To the left of Via San Pasquale, steps lead to the funicular railway of Chiaia, which takes travelers up to Vomero. To the right, is the Anglican church, built on land donated by Giuseppe Garibaldi in gratitude for the English community's support of his unification struggle. In use since 1865, among interesting plaques in and around the church is that commemorating the men who fought at Salerno during World War II, and another remembering a particularly unfortunate assassination of tourists at Paestum in 1824 – Thomas Welch Hunt of Wadenhoe Northamptonshire and his wife Caroline. The inscription reads: "The end of this youthful and amiable pair furnishes an impressive instance of the instability of human happiness. A bullet fired by an assassin, on the 3rd of December pierced at the same time the husband and the wife and consigned them both to the same grave."

EMMA HAMILTON

Born Emily Lyon in 1765, the daughter of a blacksmith, she was the mistress of several men, including Charles Greville, the nephew of Sir William Hamilton. He determined to rid himself of her, by passing her on to his newly-bereaved uncle, the British envoy to Naples. Emma, however, used her considerable charms to bewitch the elderly diplomat to marry her in 1791. She was 26 and he aged 60. Later she would make him the most famous cuckold in England, and their household the scene of a scandalous ménage-à-trois when she took up with Britain's naval hero, Lord Nelson, with whom she had a child. She died a lonely alcoholic at Calais in 1815.

Piazza dei Martiri

More elegant palazzi and exclusive shops line the Via dei Mille and Via Filangieri, leading to the Piazza dei Martiri at the heart of fashionable Chiaia. On the square itself the splendid **Palazzo Calabritto** was built by Luigi and Carlo Vanvitelli. **Palazzo Portanna**, rebuilt for Lucia Migliaccio, is Neo-Classical in style. The square itself is dominated by a monument to the martyrs of the 1799 revolution – four stone lions guarding an obelisk. Sir William Hamilton once lived on the nearby vico (the Neapolitan word for a small street or alley), Santa Maria a Cappella Vecchia, and it was here that the fateful introduction of Admiral Nelson to his wife, Emma, was made in 1793. An archway dated 1506 leads into the courtyard of what was a Benedictine abbey until 1788 when it was rented to a string of notables, including Hamilton and Emma.

Mergellina, Posillipo & Vomero

Pausilypon, as Posillipo was known to the ancients, means freedom from pain, a name suggestive of the pleasure resort which this peninsula has been for millennia. Vomero, by its side, has also been developed, albeit more recently, as a popular residential and shopping district. Mergellina, at the foot of Posillipo hill, has a busy port that connects Naples by sea to the islands, and numerous bars and restaurants along the seawalk, and around its piazzas.

Mergellina

Mergellina can be reached by foot from Chiaia – this is the scenic route along the Lungomare. Or you can get there by railway.

❖ Santa Maria di Piedigrotta

From the train station to the Piazza Piedigrotta is a short walk. The piazza is dominated by the popular church of Santa Maria di Piedigrotta, one of the most popular churches in Naples, and the site of an annual festival. Built in the 14th century, the church was reconstructed in 1560 and renovated in the mid-19th century, from when the present façade by Enrico Alvino dates. The interior houses an important wooden statue

of the *Madonna*, long venerated by Neapolitans, and a painting of the *Tabernacle* by Pier Paolo Farinelli.

❖ Parco Virgiliano

The fame of this park is founded upon a myth – that the Roman poet Virgil is buried here. In fact, the ancient funerary monument in the garden has not been identified. It is known that Virgil expressed a wish to be buried in Naples, and even composed his own epitaph: "Mantua gave me life; Brindisi death; Naples a grave."

He was buried on the Via Puteolana, on land that was later acquired by Silius Italicus, who commemorated the Ides of October, Virgil's birthday, at that site. Pliny mentions this fact, but did not give a specific location for the tomb. This has not stopped generations of classically minded tourists from paying their respects, and the park is still an attractive place to visit. In any event, the tomb of another great literary figure, Giacomo Leopardi, is in the park – placed here in the 1930s. Open to visitors in the mornings only, Tue-Sun.

❖ Santa Maria del Parto

The tomb of Neapolitan poet Jacopo Sannazaro (1458-1530) is found here, behind the high altar. Perhaps designed by Sannazaro himself, the church motifs are all pagan. A wooden *presepe* or nativity inside was certainly commissioned by the poet. Also worth a second look is a painting, shown at right, of Saint Michael astride the Devil – who has taken on the form of an attractive woman. It is by Leonardo da Pistoia.

Posillipo

Posillipo has been a residential area for the smart set since Roman times. Around the second century AD, it became fashionable to build glamorous urban residences, and a number of luxurious villas grew up in this spot with its enchanting views. Ever since, the area has attracted the wealthy. Nowadays it is the 19th- and 20th-century villas that capture our gaze. Smart sea-view bars and restaurants complete the picture of jet set living which this area evokes. Those who cannot afford to live here still like to visit – it's a popular place with the hordes of young scooter riders for an al fresco evening ice cream.

❖ Via Posillipo

Taking Via Posillipo from Mergellina, a vista of noble palazzi stretches before the visitor. The splendid **Palazzo Donn'Anna** dates from 1642 and has seen a lot of history: damaged in the Masaniello riots, and again in the 1688 earthquake, it has been reconstructed several times. **Villa Grottamarina** was the 17th-century home of the King of Spain's sister, while **Villa Roccaromana** was the residence of Prince Caracciolo.

❖ Capo Posillipo

Along Via Russo, toward the cape of Posillipo, are more extraordinary residences, among them **Villa Rosebery**, currently owned by the state and reserved for the use of the President of the Italian Republic. These historic palazzi cannot all be seen easily from the road, and one of the best ways to glimpse the elegant seafront homes of the super-rich is by boat. An excursion by sea will also provide an opportunity to see the island of Nisida at close range. It is reportedly on this island that Brutus and Cassius plotted the assassination of Julius Caesar. A Bourbon prison was sited here. Roman ruins, like the so-called Palazzo degli Spiriti, are also visible from the sea.

❖ Marechiaro

A left turn on the Via S Strato or Manzoni leads on to the Via Marechiaro and the fishing village of the same name. Here there are a number of eateries and beach concessions. The small church of **Santa Maria del Faro**, built on the site of an old lighthouse, as the name suggests, is nearby.

❖ Posillipo Park

Also known somewhat confusingly as the Parco Virgiliano (as is the park in Mergellina) and the Parco della Rimembranza, this spot is wonderful for an early evening stroll. Recently upgraded, there are superb views over the Bay of Naples along verdant avenues that criss-cross this promontory. The volcanic islet of **Nisida** and the **Phlegrean Fields** can also be seen from here. From the park, across Via Caro, the fishing village of **Gaiola** can be visited. Important archeological discoveries have been made here recently. Nearby is the original 2,000-foot Roman tunnel built by Seiano, a minister of Tiberius, toward the end of the Republic, through the tuff of Posilippo hill to link the Campi Flegrei with the Vallone della Gaiola. Today, part of the Parco Archeologico del Pausylipon, the **Grotte di Seiano** can be visited by appointment. ☎ 081 230 1030.

Vomero

With its enviable position, high in the hills like Posillipo, it is only from Vomero that a simultaneous view of the western side of the Bay of Naples – Mergellina – and the eastern side, with the port and Vesuvius in the background, can be seen. Now another wealthy residential district of the city, there are scores of smart bars and shops on the Via Scarlatti and surrounding streets. Vomero is served by the subway and by two funicular lines – both near Piazza Vanvitelli. The Funicolare di Chiaia climbs to Vomero from Piazza Amedeo, while the Funicolare Centrale descends to Augusteo near Piazza Municipio. An alternative return route to the city is to take the flights of steps that lead down to Corso Vittorio Emanuele and to the *Centro Storico*. A third funicular line, Montesanto, is currently undergoing repairs.

❖ Villa Floridiana

A walk along the Via Cimarosa from the funicular leads to the entrance gates of the Parco della Floridiana. The English-style garden of this 18th-century villa was laid out in the early 19th century soon after its purchase by Ferdinand I of Bourbon in 1816 for Lucia Migliaccio, the Duchess of Floridia, whom he had married two years earlier following the death of his first wife. It was remodelled by Antonio Niccolini in Neo-Classical style. A British neighbour of the duchess described the ornate and fanciful décor created for the long-time mistress of the King, whose morganatic marriage did not entitle her to reside in the royal palaces: "as if designed for some youthful lover, whose mind was imbued with the luxuriant and poetical fancies of Eastern climes;

instead of the person for whom this fairy palace was created, who is a grandmother, and the lover who formed it, who is an octogenarian." After Migliaccio died in 1826, the property was divided between her children. In 1919 the villa was bought by the state, and became a museum. Today, known as the **Duca di Martina National Museum of Ceramics**, two floors of the villa house ceramics, majolica, glass and enamel ware, some Neapolitan artworks, and Chinese and Japanese porcelain collected principally by members of the Di Sangro family.

The villa has a spectacular location, with glorious views, but only the rear gardens and the Museum are currently open to the public. Renovation work has been ongoing for some time and there is no date set for completion. Open 8:30 am to 2 pm. Closed on Mon. ☎ 081 578 8418. €2.50. The garden is open daily from 9 am to one hour before sunset.

❖ Castel Sant Elmo

This 14th-century castle, built into the tufo rock, occupies the highest point in Naples and has an amazing view over the city. It is also an impressive star-shaped fortification, the present plan of which was designed in the 16th century, with a church and chapel included in the complex. For many years a prison, where revolutionaries and rebels languished, today the Castel Sant Elmo hosts exhibitions and concerts with most visitors coming to enjoy the panorama above all else. ☎ 081 578 3787. Open 8:30-6:30. €2. Closed Mons.

❖ Certosa di San Martino

Close by the castle is this magnificent 14th-century Carthusian monastery, with its superlative collection of Neapolitan painting and sculpture, now a national museum. Cosimo Fanzago's splendid Baroque decoration and sculpture in the church and cloisters are a sight not to be missed. Paintings by

Luca Giordano and Ribera, among others, grace the church. The National Museum of San Martino houses interesting collections of fans and snuff boxes, models of royal ships, and a theater section, but is most notable for its historic nativity scenes or *presepe*, many of which were executed by famous artists, and which represent real-life inhabitants of the area from centuries ago. This is the surely the best collection of this uniquely Neapolitan and delightful artistic genre. Open 8:30-7:30. €6. Closed Mon.

Presepe detail

THE FACE OF NAPLES: SOPHIA LOREN

Born in a Rome hospital, Sofia Scicolone grew up in Pozzuoli, but the attractive girl, discovered in a Naples backstreet, is a true child of the city, coming from a poor background to seduce the world with her bubbly personality and irrepressible wit. She has incarnated the face and character of Naples in several films set in and around the city. Her first big break, appropriately enough, was playing a Neapolitan pizza girl in Vittorio de Sica's production, *The Gold of Naples*. A later film, with a local theme, was *It Started in Naples*, in which she starred alongside Clark Gable. Today, Sophia Loren has over 100 films to her credit and is fêted wherever she goes. Here are a few of her best known quotes:

"The two big advantages I had at birth were to have been born wise and to have been born in poverty."

"Sex appeal is 50% what you've got and 50% what people think you've got."

"Getting ahead in a difficult profession requires avid faith in yourself. That is why some people with mediocre talent, but with great inner drive, go so much further than people with vastly superior talent."

"Mistakes are a part of the dues one pays for a full life."

"There is a fountain of youth: it is your mind, your talents, the creativity you bring to your life and the lives of the people you love. When you learn to tap this source, you will have truly defeated age."

■ Places to Eat

Royal Naples & Via Toledo

Ciro a Santa Brigida, 71 Via S. Brigida, ☎ 081 552 4072. Closed Sunday. €€€. Serving traditional Neapolitan dishes, since the 1930s.

La Bersagliera, Borgo Marinari, Castel dell' Ovo, ☎ 081 764 6016. Closed Tues. €€. One of several restaurants crowded along the waterfront, by the castle, popular with evening diners, particularly tourists, as much for its location and lively ambience as for its fish menu.

Transatlantico, 15 Via Luculliana, ☎ 081 764 9201. Closed Tues. €€. Also in Borgo Marinari; Michelin-starred.

Al 53, 53 Piazza Dante, ☎ 081 549 9372. €€. A brasserie-style restaurant known for its antipasti and soups.

Osteria della Mattonella, 13 Via Nicotera, ☎ 081 416 541. €. A small restaurant which serves typical "cucina povera" – simple Neapolitan food.

Brandi Pasquale, 2 Via Chiaia, angolo S. Anna di Palazzo, ☎ 081 416 928. €. A famous pizzeria reputed to be where the pizza margherita was first served in 1889 in honor of the Queen of the same name.

DINING PRICE CHART	
Price for an entrée	
€	€10-29
€€	€30-49
€€€	€50+

The Centro Storico

La Taverna dell'Arte, 1a Rampe S. Giovanni Maggiore, ☎ 081 552 7558. Closed Sun. €€. Open in the evenings only, and serves typical Neapolitan dishes like *sartu di riso*.

La Locanda del Grifo, 14 Via F Del Giudice, ☎ 081 442 0815. €€. This restaurant has a very reasonable three-course tourist menu and is in an enviable historic location.

Di Matteo, 94 Via Tribunali, ☎ 081 294 203. €. Bill Clinton came here to taste the famous Neapolitan pizza.

Pizzeria del Presidente di Ernesto Cacialli, 120 Via Tribunali, ☎ 081 210 903. €. Popular pizzeria.

Antica Pizzeria da Michele, 1 Via Cesare Sersale, ☎ 081 553 9204. €. Famous for its traditional Neapolitan margherita and marinara pizzas (the latter said to have been invented at this restaurant which has been in operation for more than a century).

Via Foria & Capodimonte

La Corte, 198 Via Foria, ☎ 081 442 1528. Closed Sun. €€

Lombardi, 12 Via Foria, ☎ 081 456 220. €. Wholesome local food at reasonable prices.

Un Sorriso Integrale, 6 Vico San Pietro a Maiella, ☎ 081 455 026. €. One of the few vegetarian restaurants of Naples.

The Lungomare & Chiaia

La Cantinella, 21 Via N. Sauro, ☎ 081 764 8684. Closed Sun. €€€. This classic restaurant, housed in a wine cellar, is considered one of the best in Naples.

Caruso, 45 Via Partenope, ☎ 081 764 0520. Closed Mon. €€€. Michelin-starred restaurant in the Grand Hotel Vesuvio.

La Stanza del Gusto, Vicoletto S. Arpino a Chiaia, ☎ 081 401 578. Closed Mon. €€. Serves gastronomic specialties, and homemade sweets and ice creams.

Antonio & Antonio, 24 Via Partenope, ☎ 081 245 1987. €. Always busy and lively, excellent pizzas and *calzone* (folded pizzas with generous fillings) at great prices.

I Re di Napoli, 29 Via Partenope, ☎ 081 764 7775. €. Open every day for cheerful fare at a very good price.

Marino, 118 Via Santa Lucia, ☎ 081 764 0280. €. The ham, egg, cream and mushroom pizza is recommended.

Mergellina, Posillipo & Vomero

Rosiello, 10 Via Santo Strato, Posillipo. €€€. This restaurant, run by the Concetta family, is renowned for its fabulous views, fresh fish dishes and sorbet desserts.

La Sacrestia, 116 Via Orazio, Posillipo, ☎ 081 761 1051. €€€. Fine cuisine with views of the Bay of Naples from this Posillipo restaurant.

D'Angelo Santa Caterina, 203 Via A Falcone, Vomero, ☎ 081 578 9772. €€€. Sea views from the terrace, interesting antipasti, and good fish dishes.

'A Fenestella, 23 Via Calata del Ponticello, Marechiaro, ☎ 081 769 0020. €€€. Michelin-starred restaurant in Posillipo.

Ciro a Mergellina, 17-21 Via Mergellina, ☎ 081 681780. €€. Serves enormous pizzas, but gets very crowded on weekends.

Don Salvatore, 5 Via Mergellina, ☎ 081 681 817. €€. Very popular restaurant with great pizzas and a Michelin rating.

Dal Delicato, 34 Largo Sermoneta, Mergellina, ☎ 081 667 047. €€. Another very popular pizza restaurant.

Gorizia, 13 Via Bernini, Vomero, ☎ 081 578 2248. Closed Mon. €€. Established by the Grasso family in 1916, the name recollects the Italian troops' arrival at Gorizia at that time. Enjoy a meal in their cool, elegant dining room.

Giuseppone a Mare, 13 Via Ferdinando Russo, Capo Posillipo, ☎ 081 575 6002. €.

Pizzeria Alba, 14 Piazza Immacolata, ☎ 081 578 7800. €. Rustic restaurant, known for the mushroom and ham pizza.

Pizzeria Tonino, 270 Via Cilea, Vomero, ☎ 081 640 901. €. Neapolitan cuisine and pizzas – open for lunch and dinner.

■ Bars & Cafés

Royal Naples & Via Toledo

Gran Caffè Gambrinus, 1-2 Via Chiaia (Piazza Trieste e Trento), ☎ 081 417 582. The glamorous Belle Epoque décor and superlative service reinforce the notion that you are at one of Naples' most historic cafés, once frequented by the likes of Oscar Wilde and Gabriele d'Annunzio. By day you can sample the wonderful coffee and cakes at Gambrinus and, in the evening, try the house aperitif.

Pintauro, 25 Via Toledo, ☎ 081 417 339. Reputedly the inventors of *zeppole* – Naples' version of the doughnut.

Il Caffè Arabo, 64 Piazza Bellini, ☎ 339 882 8120. Enjoy the Arabic ambience of this café within the old Greek walls.

Caffè San Carlo, 4 Via San Carlo, ☎ 081 425 212.

The Centro Storico

Scaturchio, 19 Piazza San Domenico Maggiore, ☎ 081 551 6944. This café is famous for its pastries.

Intra Moenia, 70 Piazza Bellini, ☎ 081 290 720. A well-known "literary" wine bar on the elegant piazza.

Internet Bar, 44 Piazza Bellini, www.internetbarnapoli.it. Late opening hours, and a centrally located bar where you can check your e-mail.

Bar Nilo, 120 Via S Biagio dei Librai, ☎ 081 551 7029. A good place to have a stand-up coffee with the Neapolitans, in the heart of the historic center of Naples.

Via Foria & Capodimonte

Café Letterario, 6 Galleria Principe di Napoli. This café inside the galleria is not far from the Archeological Museum.

Chocolat, 8 Via S. Pietro a Maiella. ☎ 081 299 840. Closed Sun. Hot chocolate and pastries are served in this café on two floors.

The Lungomare & Chiaia

Caffè Amadeus, 5 Piazza Amedeo, ☎ 081 761 3023. Superlative coffee prepared according to a secret blend.

Gran Caffè La Caffetteria, 30 Piazza dei Martiri, ☎ 081 764 4243.

Gran Caffè Cimmino, 12 Via Filangieri, ☎ 081 418 303. The desserts – especially the baba and torta mimosa – are recommended in this long-established but newly renovated establishment.

Le Delizie de Casa Ferrieri, 75 Via Gaetano Filangieri, ☎ 081 405 221.

Grand Bar Riviera, 183 Riviera di Chiaia, ☎ 081 665 026. Good selection of pastries.

Remy il Gelato, 29 Via F Galiani, ☎ 081 667 304. Great choice of ice creams.

La Tana del Pinterre, 12 Via Partenope. ☎ 081 764 9822. Closed Mon. For the price of a beer or a glass of wine (at around €4) you can pile your plate high with the mini-pizzas, ricotta-filled pastries and other Neapolitan snacks. The bar also has a nightclub below ground.

Mergellina, Posillipo & Vomero

Chalet Ciro, Via Caracciolo, Mergellina, ☎ 081 669 928. Closed Wed. A gelateria with a wide choice of flavors.

Gelateria Bilancione, 238 Via Posillipo, ☎ 081 769 1923. Closed Wed. Traditional ice cream shop, popular with the youth of Naples as an evening outing.

Il Faretto, 127 Marechiaro, Posillipo, ☎ 081 575 0407. Closed Mon. This trendy wine bar is frequented by young professionals and also serves excellent antipasti and fish dishes.

MiraNapoli, 62 Via F Petrarca, Posillipo, ☎ 081 769 1482. The bar and gelateria has a long, covered panoramic terrace and is a lovely place to look out over the Bay of Naples while sipping a café frappé or an aperitif.

Daniele, 104 Via Scarlatti, ☎ 081 578 0555. The historic café of Vomero.

Gran Caffè La Caffetteria, Piazza Vanvitelli, Vomero. Another branch of this elegant café for the Vomero clientele.

Fantasia Gelati, Piazza Vanvitelli, ☎ 081 578 8383. Very busy in the evening. You can either have a drink from the extensive and imaginative menu in the elegant veranda on the square or walk into the café any evening – as do hordes of young Neapolitans – to order an ice cream from the counter.

Vintage Wine Bar, 37a Via Bernini, Vomero, ☎ 081 229 5473. Closed Mon. Open all day with a breakfast menu, and cocktails and food for the evening.

Caffeteria Bernini, 9 Piazza Fanzago, Vomero, ☎ 081 556 2890. Serves a range of frappés and yogurt drinks along with the usual Italian bar fare. Smart al fresco covered section.

THE NEAPOLITAN CAFETTIERA

The traditional Neapolitan coffee pot is cunningly designed with a double bottom and handles. Add water in the end without the spout and fill the coffee container. Then screw on the top part. When the water boils, simply turn the cafettiera over to let the water trickle through the coffee grains. Delicious!

■ Places To Stay in Naples

High-profile visitors to Naples are most likely to stay in the magnificent hotels that line Via Partenope on the Lungomare. At the other end of the scale, backpackers tend to gravitate to the colorful but sometimes seedy areas around the railway station on Piazza Garibaldi. Fortunately, there are also plenty of rooms in comfortable hotels and bed & breakfasts that fall between these categories. It is worth browsing the Internet to look for bargain lodgings, especially if your trip is in the off-season.

HOTEL PRICE CHART	
For a double room for two	
€	€50-150
€€	€151-250
€€€	€251+

Royal Naples & Via Toledo

Mercure Angioino, 123 Via A. Depretis, ☎ 081 552 9500, www.accor-hotel.com. €€.

Chiaja, 216 Via Chiaia, ☎ 081 415 555, www.hotelchiaia.it. €€. The former home of a 19th-century nobleman, this hotel is only 200 yards from Piazza Plebiscito.

Toledo, 15 Via Montecalvario, ☎ 081 406 800, www.hoteltoledo.com. €€. Situated in the heart of Naples, with comfortable rooms equipped with bath, shower, hair-drier, phone, satellite TV, safe, central heating, ceiling fan, air conditioning, radio and mini-bar.

Miramare, 24 Via N Sauro, ☎ 081 764 7589. €€. This Art Deco hotel is between the Palazzo Reale and the Castel dell'Ovo. The restaurant has a glorious sea view.

Rex, 12 Via Palepoli, ☎ 081 764 9389. €€. Located in Santa Lucia, opposite the Castel dell'Ovo, this is one of the less expensive options close to the coveted Lungomare.

Il Convento, 137a Via Speranzella, ☎ 081 403 977. €€. Close to the Via Toledo and local transport facilities, in a skilfully restored 17th-century palace.

The Centro Storico

Caravaggio, 157 Piazza Riario Sforza, ☎ 081 211 0066. €€€. In a restored historic palazzo close to the historic center of Naples.

Jolly Ambassador, 70 Via Medina, ☎ 081 410 5111, www.jollyhotels.it. €€€.

Des Artistes, 61 Via Duomo, ☎ 081 446 155. €€. Close to the cathedral, the hotel offers en-suite rooms for one-four with TV, telephone and bar service.

Prati, 4 Via C. Rosaroll, ☎ 081 268 898 www.hotelprati.it. €€. 43-room hotel on Piazza Principe Umberto with restaurant and parking spaces.

Cavour, 32 Piazza Garibaldi, ☎ 081 283 122. €€.

San Giorgio, 9 Via Alessandro Poerio, ☎ 081 281 661 www.albergosangiorgio.com. €. Good value hotel close to the railway station.

Neapolis, 13 Via Francesco del Giudice, ☎ 081 442 0815. €. Popular with younger travelers due to its reasonable prices and the Internet connection, included in the room price.

Nettuno, 9 Via Sedile di Porto, ☎ 081 551 0193. €

Via Foria & Capodimonte

Charming International, 35 Viale U. Maddalena, ☎ 081 231 1004. €€€.

Hotel Villa Capodimonte, 66 Via Moiariello, ☎ 081 459 0000, www.villacapodimonte.it. €€€. Set in a private park with views the Gulf of Naples.

Costantinopoli 104, 104 Via S Maria di Costantinopoli, ☎ 081 557 1035, www.costantinopoli104.it. €€. An Art Deco villa in the courtyard of a 19th-century palazzo with garden and pool.

Real Orto Botanico, 192 Via Foria, ☎ 081 442 1528. €€.

Locanda dell'Arte, 66 Via Pessina. €. Enjoy a family atmosphere at this bed & breakfast at the top end of Via Toledo, 50 yards from the Museo Nazionale. En-suite rooms equipped with telephone and television.

The Lungomare & Chiaia

Vesuvio, 45 Via Partenope, ☎ 081764 0044, www.vesuvio.it. €€€. Oscar Wilde, Clark Gable and scores of other celebrities have stayed here. Superb views from the roof garden restaurant, and celebrated spa facilities.

Santa Lucia, 46 Via Partenope, ☎ 081 764 0666, www.santalucia.it. €€€. Elegant Neo-Classical-style hotel with pool on the roof garden.

Excelsior, 48 Via Partenope, ☎ 081 764 0111, www.excelsior.it. €€€. Historic hotel on the waterfront with an excellent seafood restaurant.

Hotel Pinto Storey, 72 Via G. Martucci, ☎ 081 681 260. €€. Stay in the heart of Chiaia without spending a fortune.

Astoria, 90 Via S. Lucia, ☎ 081 764 9903. €.

Mergellina, Posillipo & Vomero

Grand Hotel Parker's, 135 Corso Vittorio Emanuele, ☎ 081 761 2474, www.grandhotelparkers.com. €€€. Relive the Grand Tour in this vintage 19th-century hotel, refurbished to modern tastes.

Britannique, 133 Corso Vittorio Emanuele. ☎ 081 761 4145. €€€.

San Francesco al Monte, 328 Corso Vittorio Emanuele, ☎ 081 423 9111, www.hotelsanfrancesco.it. €€€. This converted monastery on the slopes of Vomero has been celebrated for its spectacular view for hundreds of years and can now be enjoyed along with its pool by paying guests.

Hotel Paradiso, 11 Via Catullo, ☎ 081 247 5111, www.bestwestern.it. €€€. Set on the Posillipo hillside with the sprawling floors and stupendous views of the ancient palazzi.

Hotel Canada, 43 Via Mergellina, ☎ 081 680 952. €€. Lower down the Posillipo hill, ideally placed for island-hopping from Mergellina.

Casa Carlo, 61 Via Manzoni, ☎ 081 714 1075, www.casacarlo.it. €€. Once a stately home, but now a chic bed and breakfast with three guestrooms.

Splendid, 96 Via Manzoni, ☎ 081 645 462. €€.

Belvedere, 51 Via Tito Angelini, ☎ 081 578 8169. €€.

Margherita, 29 Via Cimarosa, ☎ 081 556 7044. €.

Bonapace, 18 Viale Maria Cristina di Savoia. €. Family-run bed and breakfast in Mergellina.

THE ROMAN VACATION HOME

The Bay of Naples is one of the world's earliest getaway destinations. The first mention of a seaside vacation villa dates from the early second century BC when Scipio Africanus built a palatial residence overlooking the sea. Seneca, left, later described it in a letter to his friend Lucilius: "I write to you from a couch in the villa of none other than Scipio Africanus.... The villa I have seen is built of squared stones. A wall surrounds the woods, with towers to defend the villa rising on both sides. There is a cistern big enough for an army beneath the buildings and greenery, and a pinched little bath-house."

Seneca himself noted how standards of holiday homes had risen even during Roman times: "Who now would put up with a bath like this? A man thinks himself poverty-stricken or cheap if his walls don't gleam with large expensive insets, if his Alexandrian marbles aren't set off by Numidian veneers, if the intricately worked and shaded marbles aren't spread with a protective varnish, if his vaulted ceiling isn't topped with glass. We want the bathing pools into which we lower bodies filthy with sweat to be lined with rock from Thasos, which used to be a wondrous rarity even in a temple, we want our water poured from silver spigots.... We want to get a tan at the same time as a bath, and to be able to see fields and sea from our seat as well."

Seneca's description provides an insight into the luxury accommodation enjoyed by the ancient Romans in Naples and its environs.

■ Shopping

Whether you are shopping for designer clothes, or unusual souvenirs, Naples is unlikely to disappoint. The smartest shops are in Chiaia and Via Toledo, while the quirky souvenir shops are crowded into the narrow streets of the Centro Storico. Vomero (a funicular ride from Chiaia) also has a smart shopping area on Via Scarlatti and surrounding streets. The numerous markets provide an opportunity to see colorful Neapolitan life at first hand, but beware of pickpockets.

Clothes, Leather Goods & Accessories

Designer goods can be found in the elegant stores on Via Calabritto and Via Filangieri in the Chiaia district: Armani, Gucci, Valentino and Prada are all here. More clothing stores are on Via Dei Mille and Via Carducci.

Antonio Panico, 29 Via Carducci, ☎ 081 415 804. Acknowledged as the grand master of Neapolitan sartorial style.

Marinella, 287 Via Riviera di Chiaia, ☎ 081 764 4214. Ties for the famous and discerning, with an international clientele.

Halston di Antonio Rossi, 14 Via Guantai Nuovi, ☎ 081 552 9237. Made-to-measure suits, ready-to-wear fashion and accessories.

Anna Matuozzo, 26 Viale Gramsci, ☎ 081 663 874. High-quality handmade shirts.

Canestrelli, 131 Via Chiaia, ☎ 081 401 954. Handmade children's clothes.

Tramontano, 143 Via Chiaia, ☎ 081 668 572. Handmade luggage, leather shoes and accessories. Bill Clinton shopped here.

Mario Talarico, 4 Vico Due Porte a Toledo, ☎ 081 407 723. Handmade umbrellas.

Martino Cilento, 61 Via Medina, ☎ 081 551 3363. High-quality handmade clothing.

London House di Mariano Rubinacci, 26 Via Filangieri, ☎ 081 415 793. More haut-de-gamme handmade clothing.

La Rinascente, Via Toledo. Six-floor department store with large selection of clothing, perfumes and homewares.

SPI, 22 Via R. de Cesare, Santa Lucia, ☎ 081 764 9191. Casual clothing for men and women.

Pasquale Cané, 97 Via Nardones, ☎ 338 488 6250 www.sandalicapresi.it. Hand-made Capri sandals.

Save, 18 Via Monteoliveto, ☎ 333 664 9064. Cut-price clothing store.

Jewelry

Gallotta, 139 Via Chiaia 139, ☎ 081 421 164. Exclusive designs.

Ventrella, 11 Via Carlo Poerio, ☎ 081 764 3173. Unique and prêt-à-porter designs.

Presta, 2 Via A Scialoia, ☎ 081 554 5282. Established Neapolitan goldsmiths and coral carvers.

Antico Borgo Orefici, Piazzatta Orefici, Corso Umberto I, ☎ 081 554 4030. Long-established Neapolitan goldsmiths.

Craft & Gift Shops

Naples is famous for its *presepe* (nativity scenes) and the best place to buy the cribs and the assorted figures that go with them is along the Via San Gregorio Armeno in the Centro Storico. Passing along the Via San Biagio dei Librai, you will see many, many examples of old bric-a-brac, some of which may strike your fancy.

Bottega d'Arte Presepiale, 87 Via S. Biagio dei Librai, ☎ 081 262 707. Traditional Neapolitan statuettes.

La Scarabattola, 50 Via dei Tribunali, ☎ 081 291 735. Makers of *presepe* or nativity scenes who won a recent commission from the Spanish Royal family.

Pastori, 31 Via S Gregorio Armeno, ☎ 081 552 0883. Cribs and figures.

Ettore Smith, 52 Via Benedetto Croce, ☎ 081 551 6989. Handmade paper goods and stationery.

Officina Profumo-Farmaceutica di Santa Maria Novella, 20 Via Santa Caterina a Chiaia, ☎ 081 407 176. Flower-scented soaps and candles.

Caropreso, 7 Vico Cisterna dell'Olio, ☎ 081 552 2175. Has a good selection of watches.

Neapolitan Ceramics, 2 Vico San Domenico Maggiore, ☎ 81 5517764.

Il Cantuccio della Ceramica, 38 Via Benedetto Croce, ☎ 081 552 5857.

The Doll Hospital (Ospedale delle Bambole), 81 Via S. Biagio dei Librai, ☎ 081 203 067. Quirky, much-photographed shop, ostensibly for the repair of dolls but crammed with all kinds of objects.

Limone, 72 Piazza San Gaetano, ☎ 081 299 429. Homemade local liqueurs.

Spagnuolo, 55 Via Croce, ☎ 081 552 1102. Porcelain.

Raffaele Calace, 9 Vico San Domenico Maggiore, ☎ 081 551 5983. Long-established mandolin makers, who export all over the world.

Books & Music

Many small and secondhand bookstores are located between Port'Alba (behind Piazza Dante) and Via Mezzocannone. The largest bookstoes are Feltrinelli and Fnac.

Feltrinelli, Piazza dei Martiri. Vast bookstore on several floors.

Fnac, 39 Via Luca Giordano, Vomero. Sells books and records, and has an Internet café on-site.

Antiques & Old Prints

The antique shops of Naples are concentrated around the Piazza dei Martiri – particularly in Via Domenico Morelli – and in Via Santo Maria di Costantinopoli (near the Archeological Museum). Numerous shops selling fine old prints are in the backstreets off Via Toledo – around Port Alba and on Spaccanapoli.

Navarra, Piazza dei Martiri, ☎ 081 764 3595.

Fasano, 73 Via Domenico Morelli, ☎ 081 764 3446.

Morelli Antichita, 43 Via Domenico Morelli, ☎ 081 764 4481.

Bowinkel, Piazza dei Martiri and 25 Via Santa Lucia, ☎ 081 764 0739.

Lithographs & Engravings.

Regina, 51 Via Maria Di Costantinopoli, ☎ 081 459 983. Prints and objets d'art.

Luigi XVI, 8 Via Scarlatti, ☎ 081 556 3644.

Food & Confectionery

Mandara, 4 Via Santa Caterina a Chiaia, ☎ 081 417 348. Delicious cheeses and cured meats are among the goodies here.

Dolce Idea, 718 Via Solitaria, Pizzofalcone, ☎ 081 764 2832. Hand-made chocolates, produced here.

Augustus, 47 Via Toledo, ☎ 081 551 3540. Divine Neapolitan pastries and sweets.

Gay-Odin, 427 Via Toledo, ☎ 081 400 063. Long-established chocolate manufacturer.

Outdoor Markets

Borgo di Sant'Antonio Abate – daily: food and flowers.

Porta Nolana – daily: fish.

Castel Nuovo – daily: flowers.

Antignano, Vomero – Monday to Saturday: clothing and food.

Fuorigrotta – Monday to Saturday: general.

Via Ponte di Casanova – Monday to Saturday: new and second-hand clothing.

Corso Malta – Sundays: antiques and general.

Via Virgilio, Posillipo – Thursdays: clothes.

Villa Comunale, Lungomare – occasional weekends and holidays: antiques.

Via Constantinopoli – alternate weekends: antiques.

■ Entertainment

Theater

San Carlo, Via San Carlo, ☎ 081 797 2111. The opera house is open daily for guided tours. The opera season runs from late November to May, with classical concerts and ballet during the summer.

Trianon, 9 Piazza Vincenzo Calenda, ☎ 081 225 8285, www.teatrotrianon.it. Twice-weekly concerts of famous Neapolitan songs, accompanied by the Trianon Orchestra musicians. Call or check online for current schedule of events.

Teatro Mercadante, Piazza Municipio, ☎ 081 551 3396. Avant garde touring theater productions – in Italian only.

Music & Dance

Otto Jazz Club, 23 Salita Cariati, ☎ 081 551 3765. Opens at 9:30 pm; concerts at 10:30 pm.

Malu, 5 Vico San Pietro a Maiella, ☎ 081 295 412, www.maluclub.it. Live bands; jazz, bossanova music.

St James Irish Pub, 73 Piazza Bellini, ☎ 081 442 1538. For those of you who can't do without your Guinness, this is the place. Check out the unusual pub menu – including wild boar, roe deer and Black Forest ham.

Voce e Notte, 55 Via E Pessina, ☎ 081 564 5137, www.voceenotte.it. Food and traditional shows.

Chez Moi, 12-13 Parco Margherita, Piazza Amedeo, ☎ 081 407 526. Elegant club, with a dance floor and lounges with waiter service; Thursday-Sunday 10 pm-4 am.

Dugout, Via Mergellina, ☎ 081 662 183.

Freezer Stereo Bar, Centro Direzionale Isola G6, ☎ 081 750 2437. Music on Fridays; a restaurant the rest of the week.

La Suite Club, 176 Via Manzoni, ☎ 081 769 2523. Lounge music.

Mambo King's, 30b Via Piedigrotta, ☎ 081 761 4812. Latin ambiance.

Verve, 101 Via Petrarca, ☎ 081 5754 882. House music in this venue for the gilded youth.

Virgilio, 6 Via Tito Lucrezio Caro, ☎ 338 3459 007. Long-established night club; popular with the gay scene.

■ Adventures

Sea Sports, Cruises & Beaches

Tortuga, 84 Piazza Municipio, ☎ 081 552 0105, www.pelagus-online.it. Yacht dinner cruises with show.

Vittorino, ☎ 081 790 8201, www.vittorino.it. Dinner cruises and tours in the Bay of Naples, for parties of up to 12 persons in the renovated 1914 tugboat *Vittorino*. Weekend charters also possible.

Bagno Elena, 14 Via Posillipo, ☎ 081 575 5058, www.bagnoelena.it. Beach concession, with loungers, umbrellas and snack bar.

Primavela, ☎ 0340 256 0190, www.primavela.com. Sailing courses.

Around The Bay

The Bay of Naples was a favorite resort of the ancient Romans. They built villas all along the shoreline, from the Campi Flegrei – where they enjoyed the thermal waters – to the Vesuvian region where the towns of Pompeii and Herculaneum boasted some stupendous patrician residences. Much later, it was the discovery and excavation of these Roman ruins in the 18th and 19th centuries that gave a renewed boost to tourism in the region. For many years it was de rigueur for the well heeled on the Grand Tour to visit the Bay of Naples, both to explore Pompeii, and later Herculaneum and Paestum, to climb Vesuvius and to venture into the sulphurous heart of the Phlegrean Fields (*Campi Flegrei*).

In this Chapter

Some of these adventures were exceedingly risky: Vesuvius was active during the late 18th century, and for periods in the 19th century, and more than a few visitors were injured by the volcano's violent ejections. Also, at this time, the health hazards of visiting Italy were great, and few stayed in the summer months – indeed, one reason why the Greek ruins of Paestum have survived relatively intact is that the area was known to be malarious and consequently remained largely undeveloped until recently.

Nowadays, the Vesuvian region and the Campi Flegrei still have their disadvantages, but not usually of the fatal kind. It is the urban sprawl between Naples and the volcano that leads most tourists to visit the area, rather than stay here. Fortunately, good rail and ferry links mean that most travelers can get to Pompeii and the other excavation sites around Vesuvius from their lodgings on the coast or the islands. As for the Campi Flegrei, laudable efforts are being made to rid the region of its tarnished image as an industrial wasteland – for example a new theme park, Edenlandia, and the Science City have been established here, while attractive accommodation can be found in the coastal areas.

The Romans, of course, also took an interest in the islets, especially Capri, where the ruins of Tiberius' villas can still be seen. Nowadays, these offshore destinations are among the most popular tourist spots around Naples, and in the summer Capri, in particular, is massively overcrowded. It is much more pleasant to visit in May or September/October, although, even in these months, you will be among throngs of tourists. The picturesque walkways of Capri will help to compensate for the struggle of riding the ferries and the funicular with hundreds of other visitors, but for longer stays, Ischia, and especially Procida, are more tranquil.

A relatively undiscovered treasure of Campania is the Cilento Valley and Paestum. For nature lovers, the trails of the Cilento National Park will be much enjoyed, and there is still relatively inexpensive accommodation in the beach resorts of this region.

■ The Campi Flegrei

The Campi Flegrei, or "burning fields," so called because of the still-evident volcanic activity in this region, are of great interest to tourists, both because of their unique geological features, hot springs and fumaroles and the extensive Roman remains that can be seen here, particularly around Baia, which was a favored holiday spot for aristocrats and Emperors. As the mythological "underworld" of classical scholars, this area is full of fascinating historical references – and some great beaches, and coastal restaurants.

Pozzuoli

Famous as the ancient port of Puteoli, where St Paul landed on his way to Rome, and more recently as the hometown of Sofia Loren, Pozzuoli has some pleasant waterfront restaurants and impressive Roman ruins. Even more ruins are underwater, thanks to bradyseism – the phenomenon of shifting land levels linked to volcanic activity.

Macellum

A short walk from the railway station is one of the most remarked-upon sites in the region, known as the **Temple of Serapis** to Grand Tour visitors. Scholars have more recently decided that this striking monument was in fact a Macellum,

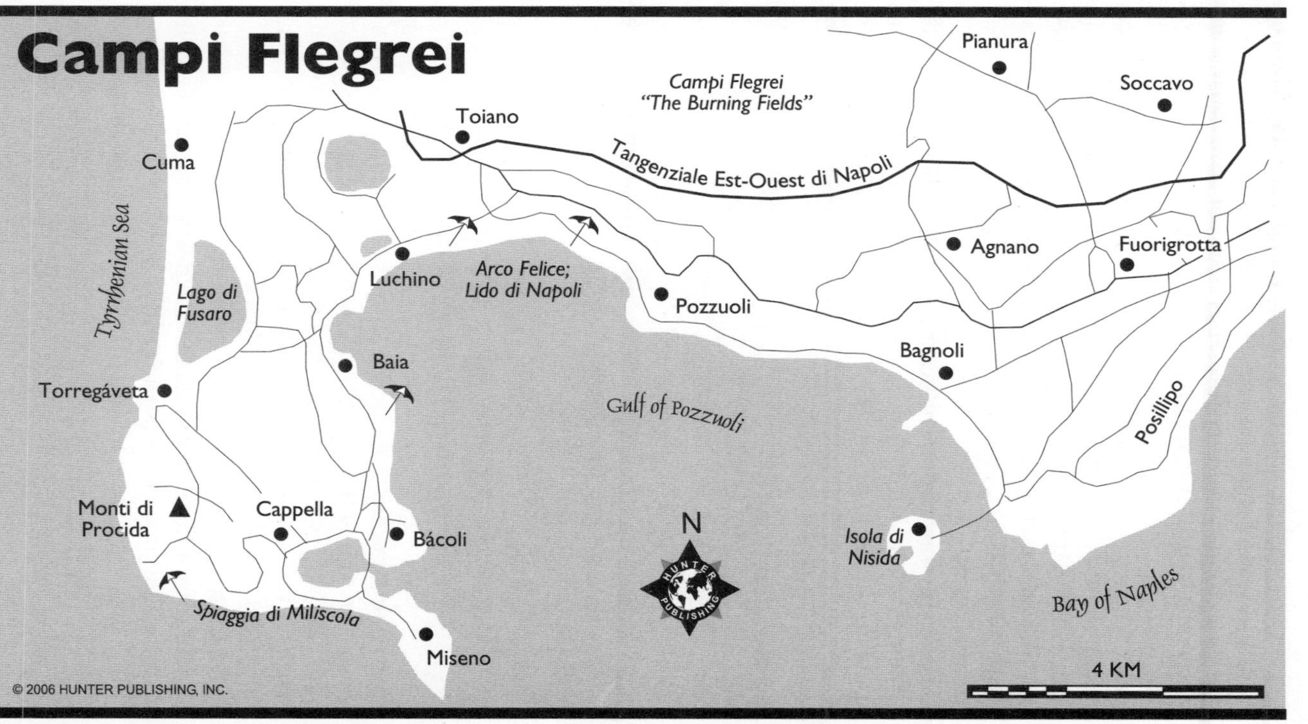

Around the Bay

or Roman market, dating to the second century AD. Originally, the rectangular market would have had a row of *tabernae* (shops) on either side. As a result of bradyseism (volcanic subsidence) it began to submerge not long after its initial building, and a second floor was built. However, by the ninth century it lay some 30 feet below sea level, as marks of marine molluscs on the columns indicate. Shortly before the eruption of Monte Nuovo in 1538, the ground was uplifted, eyewitnesses claim, by about 18 feet. A slow subsidence is currently in effect.

Rione Terra

Close to the waterfront, the acropolis of Puteoli can be visited, although work is still underway on the site. An itinerary led by **Archeobus Flegreo** takes visitors along ancient streets of the Roman colony, past what is believed to have been a bakery and a brothel.

Anfiteatro Flavio

Returning along Via Marconi and Via Rossini, perhaps the most impressive site in Pozzuoli nowadays is this remarkable amphitheater, with its wonderfully preserved underground mechanism for hoisting wild animals from cages up to the arena. It was here, under the rule of Diocletian, that Januarius (San Gennaro), one of seven Christian martyrs, was condemned to die. In fact, it is reported that he was later beheaded near the Solfatara. Open daily from 9 am to one hour before sunset. Closed Sun.

Solfatara

About half a mile from Pozzuoli, this fascinating site is within walking distance of the Metropolitana station; alternatively the P9 bus stops outside the entrance. One of the more recent of the Phlegraean volcanoes, the intense fumarolic and hydrothermal activity has made this a great tourist destination for centuries. It was called the *Forum Vulcani*, or Kingdom of Fire, by Strabo. Later visitors made much of the hot steam,

Above: Maronti Beach, Ischia

Below: Villa Arbusto, Ischia

Above: Marina di Lacco and the Isoletta del Fungo, Ischia
Below: Getting a float ready for the Festa di Mare, Ischia

Above: The Royal Palace of Caserta, northeast of Naples

Below: Villa Cafiero at Colli di San Pietro on the Sorrento Peninsula, an agriturismo or B&B

Cloister in the church of San Francesco, Sorrento

cutting caves into the volcanic rock, where sufferers from skin and respiratory diseases were treated in these natural saunas. There is also a *Fangaia*, a treatment with hot mud, which was considered a remedy for rheumatism. The largest fumarole is known as the *Bocca Grande*. The smell of the sulphurous fumes, the steam spouts, bubbling mud, and hot earth make this a dramatic place to visit, great for children and adults alike. All over the site, the equipment of vulcanologists and apparatus for measuring bradyseism are in evidence. Don't miss the chance for a chat with Gennaro Avalone, whose family have long been selling chunks of the yellow sulphurous rock on site. He calls himself *Caronte*, after the man who guarded the gates of Hell in Dante's *Inferno*. A campsite with restaurant is within this privately owned site. Open 8:30 am-7 pm, www.solfatara.it.

Lake Averno

This is the destination par excellence for classicists. Homer and Virgil evoke Lake Avernus as the entrance to Hades (the Underworld), and it was said that any bird flying over the lake was killed by its noxious fumes. The lake is certainly a volcanic crater in origin, but nowadays the scene is picturesque, rather than hellish. Once the site of a Roman dockyard after Agrippa built a canal linking the lake to the sea, today this is a beautiful, tranquil spot, with lovely views. On the eastern side are baths, known as the Temple of Apollo. To the right of the lake, the cone of Monte Nuovo, created by the 1538 eruption and thus the youngest mountain in Europe, can be seen. If you do not have private transport, it is easiest to visit this and other sites in the Campi Flegrei on the Archeobus.

Arco Felice Vecchio

Taking the road toward Cumae from Lake Averno, the grandiose Arco Felice comes into view. The 60-foot-high and 18-foot-wide structure dates to Roman times, when the Via Domitiana linking Cumae to Pozzuoli was built. Not to be confused with the modern town of Arco Felice near Pozzuoli, this monument is situated closer to Cumae.

Cumae

The first Greek colony of Southern Italy, Cumae was long famous to visitors as the home of the Sibyl and its extensive archeological excavations have the advantage of a panoramic sea view, which makes the hot and dusty climb to the topmost temple even more worthwhile.

The Sibyl's Cave

Close to the main entrance of the excavations, this long corridor, hollowed out of the tufo, with its unusual shape and lighting, is described in Virgil's *Aenead* as the abode of the prophetess, Sibyl. In fact, it is more likely to have had a military function, although some believe it may also be funerary architecture.

Temples of Apollo & Jupiter

Steps lead past the cave onto two terraces. On the first terrace is the Roman foundation of the Temple of Apollo, on which a Christian basilica was built around the fifth century. Farther along the winding Via Sacra is the Temple of Jupiter, above, which was also rebuilt as a Christian church. The remains of the ancient altar and baptismal font can still be seen. The view from here of the curving coastline, Lake Fusaro, and out toward Ischia, is spectacular. Open 9 am to one hour before sunset. ☎ 081 854 3060.

Lake Fusaro

The largest of the Phlegrean Lakes was originally a coastal lagoon. Strabo called it *Palus Acherusia* (literally "wetland of hell") suggesting its marshy origins, while Seneca mentions that oysters could be obtained here. Today, however, the lake is chiefly worth visiting because of its Bourbon prettification in the form of the stunning royal hunting lodge.

Casina Vanvitelliana

One of the loveliest architectural features of the Campi Flegrei, the *Casina*, or hunting lodge, is one of the jewels of Carlo Vanvitelli, who designed it for Ferdinand IV in 1782. The lodge has an octagonal design, and is built on an islet in the middle of the lake. The King and guests had to be rowed out there, but today a small path leads to the lodge. Open only for private functions. The lakeside view is well worth the detour.

Casina Vanvitelliana

Baia

A fashionable seaside resort and spa town in Roman times, most of Baia's Roman ruins are today underwater, as a result of bradyseism, and can only be visited by boat. The Aragonese rulers of Naples built a fortress here in the late 15th century, which was later enlarged by Pedro di Toledo to create the castle, which today houses an important archeological museum.

Stufa di Nerone

Passing by Lake Lucrino, the third of the Phlegraean lakes on the Tritoli hillside at the outskirts of Baia, the entrances of Roman steam rooms can be seen. There were many beach clubs set up by the Romans on the coast to take advantage of thermal springs, but most are now underground. Traces of one are incorporated in the modern "Stufe di Nerone" bathing club. A medieval bath – the Bagno del Figulaio, was also located here.

Parco Archeologico

This monumental complex is set into a terraced hill on several levels and divided into areas that housed baths and so-called temples. Its function is not yet clear, which no doubt accounts for the poor information available at the site. Some believe it may have been an imperial palace. The park is nevertheless worth a visit, not least for its attractive location. Open 9 am to one hour before sunset. The nearby submerged city can be visited using glass-bottom boats. These sites are listed on the Archeobus itinerary, for visitors without private transport. See page 58 for more on the Archeobus tours.

The Castle & Museum

This superb medieval castle, rebuilt in the 17th century, overlooks the gulf of Pozzuoli, and offers lovely views from its ramparts. The Archeological Museum of the Phlegraean Fields, housed in the castle since 1994, is impressive. Finds brought here from the many ancient sites in the region are well-displayed in a series of rooms. Highlights are the reconstructed *Sacellum of the Augustals* from Miseno, and the scene of the *Nymphaeum of Punta Epitaffio*.

Bacoli

Known to the Romans as Bauli, this is today a picturesque seaside resort that stretches as far as Lake Miseno. A number of Roman ruins can be seen, but generally, they are shut up, and a key must be fetched from the local "guardian" of each site, who will expect to be given some money for his or her trouble.

The "Tomb of Agrippina"

The name refers to Nero's infamous act of matricide – when Agrippina was cast into the sea in a staged shipwreck, and killed on reaching the shore. The building is in fact the remains of a small theater, which was once part of a maritime villa complex. The water motifs that can be seen date from its subsequent transformation into a *nymphaeum*, or outdoor Roman bathing area.

The Cento Camerelle

Literally meaning "the hundred little rooms," this interesting structure was in fact a two-tiered series of water tanks, perhaps linked to an adjacent villa, of which no traces now remain.

Piscina Mirabilis

The Piscina Mirabilis

The lovely – but usually inaccurate – names given to the Roman ruins in this region are part of their charm. This is in fact an immense and impressive water reservoir, dating to the Augustan period, and which probably supplied the Roman fleet at Miseno, the town adjoining Bacoli.

Miseno

An important Roman port, attacked by Hanibal during the Second Punic War. Like Bacoli, it had many celebrity residents with sumptuous villas. Most notable was Lucullus. Pliny the Elder was in charge of the port in 79 AD when he set out – with fatal consequences – to assist friends living near Vesuvius. Rampant property development has destroyed much of historic Misenum, but traces of a few Roman buildings remain. They are not yet fully open to the public, but can be visited by appointment. Call the Associazione Misenum at ☎ 081 523 3977. There are a number of commercial resorts on Miliscola Beach.

Naval Reservoirs

Known as the *Piscina Mirabilis* (see above) and the *Grotta della Dragonara*, these Roman remains, despite their romantic 18th-century appellations, were in fact enormous water storage facilities for the fleet. The first is on a hill east of Maremorto; the second is on the shore of Miliscola. The *Grotta* was subsequently connected to the Villa Lucullus.

The Villa of Lucullus

Recent excavations have revealed the remains of this villa on a hillside overlooking the *Grotta*, on Via Dragonara. Scattered buildings – including one in the yard of the local restaurant which has been identified from a 17th-century engraving as a *nymphaeum* (an outdoor bathing area) – point to an extensive seaside villa, possibly that of Caius Marius, later purchased by the phenomenally wealthy Lucius Lucullus, as described by Pliny. If so, this is the spot where Tiberius died in 37 AD.

The Sacellum of the Augustales

Reconstructed in Baia castle, this sunken chapel at the foot of Punta Sarparella was discovered relatively recently. Its inscriptions provided much new information about the *Augustals* – a priestly class. The husband and wife who financed the chapel are shown on a pediment relief. The best of the collection of statues found here – the equestrian figure of Roman Emperor Domitian, reworked after his death to represent his successor, Nerva – can also be seen in the castle. Next to the *Sacellum* is the remains of a Roman theater, which can be visited by appointment only. Numerous Roman necropoli, mostly of members of the former Roman fleet at Miseno, have been enumerated in this region. The main groups of tombs are on the road from Misenum to Cuma at Cappella, and on Via Roma, toward Bacoli.

Domitian / Nerva

Bagnoli

Long blighted by its now-abandoned steelworks, which demonstrates the folly of locating industry in a beautiful natural site with beaches and hot springs, this area west of Naples is now regenerating itself, with newly opened attractions and planned developments.

Città della Scienza

Located in a 19th-century factory, the City of Science occupies a huge site and attracts half a million visitors a year. It is an interactive museum with a "science gym" and a planetarium, featuring a space ship that takes tourists into a giant human intestine. Open 9-5 Tue-Sat and 10-7 on Sun. Closed on Mon. €7. ☎ 081 372 3728, www.cittadellascienza.it.

Museo Didattico del Mare

Housed in the Nautical Institute on the Bagnoli waterfront, the museum has a number of historic nautical instruments on display, together with ship models used by generations of students at the naval school. Open 9-1 and 3-7 pm.

Agnano

A modern conference center, racecourse and theme park are here, along with the ruins of a Roman spa, on the edge of an ancient volcanic crater at Agnano Terme. Nearby is the nature reserve of Astroni.

Edenlandia

This is a great attraction for children. Facilities include a 3D cinema, a mock castle, a Chinese dragon water ride and a number of fairground-style games. ☎ 081 239 4090, www.edenlandia.it.

Riserva Naturale degli Astroni

This former royal hunting ground is now a nature reserve situated in the wooded crater of an extinct volcano, with World Wildlife Fund protected status for its resident and migratory wildlife. In addition to numerous bird species, there are chestnut trees, oaks, elms and poplars. For information on guided tours and opening hours, ☎ 081 588 3720.

■ The Islands

The islands in the Bay of Naples, particularly Capri, receive visitors from all over the world, attracted by their flower-filled walks, superb swimming and spas, and lovely views. The fact that many famous writers, artists and eccentrics lived on these islands from the mid-19th century adds to their charm. Indeed, all have surprisingly long and rich histories of human settlement, along with interesting monuments to visit. Ischia, the largest island, and Procida, the smallest, are both volcanic in origin. They offer more of a getaway from the crush of tourists than Capri in the summer months.

Capri

This 4.3-square-mile island has two towns, and is off the tip of the Sorrento Peninsula. A popular tourist destination since the 19th century, Capri is busy all year round, and terribly so in summer. If possible, avoid making your visit on weekends in the high season when the hordes of foreigners are joined by Neapolitans. But, with its largely car-free roads, it is always a delightful excursion. The limestone island is notable for its stunning residences, gardens and Roman ruins. If you can afford to stay for the sunset, Capri reveals a different ambiance after all the day-trippers depart on the early evening ferries back to Sorrento and Naples.

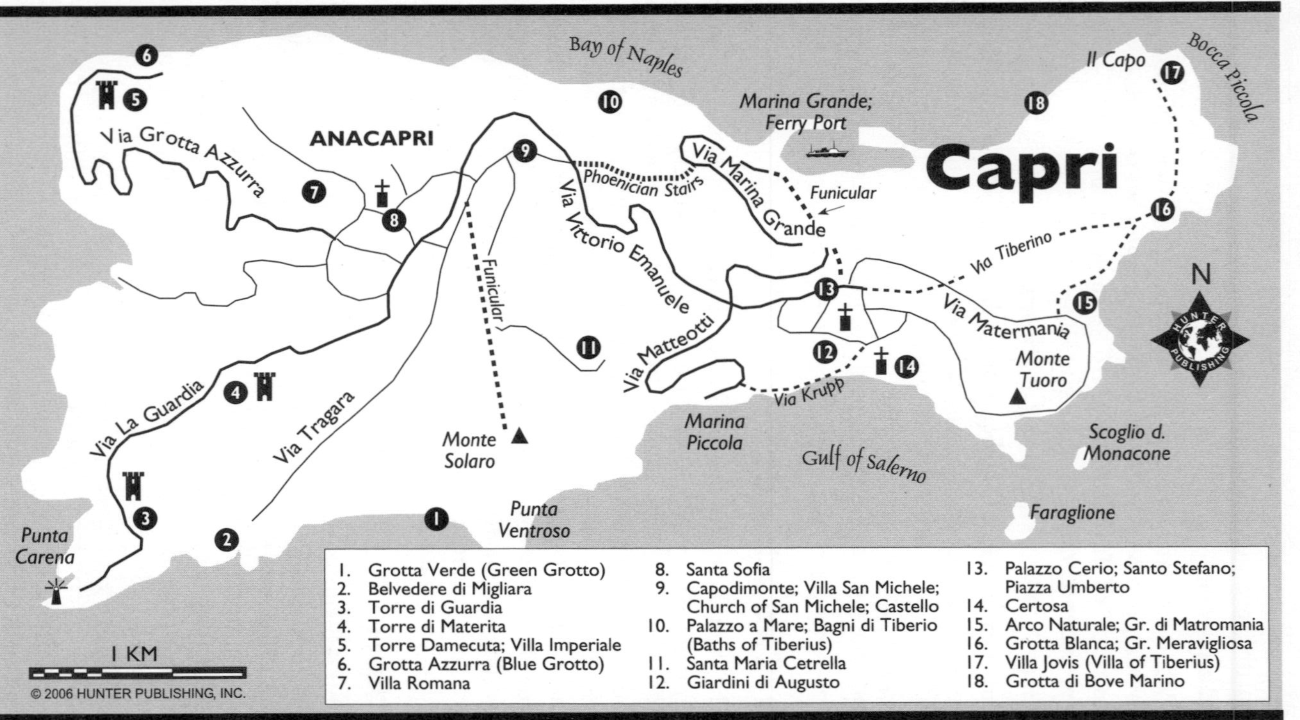
Capri
Bay of Naples
Bocca Piccola
Il Capo
Marina Grande; Ferry Port
Funicular
Via Marina Grande
Phoenician Stairs
ANACAPRI
Via Grotta Azzurra
Via Vittorio Emanuele
Via Tiberino
Via Matermania
Monte Tuoro
N
HUNTER PUBLISHING
Funicular
Via Matteotti
Via Krupp
Via La Guardia
Via Tragara
Monte Solaro
Marina Piccola
Gulf of Salerno
Scoglio d. Monacone
Faraglione
Punta Ventroso
Punta Carena
1 KM
© 2006 HUNTER PUBLISHING, INC.
1. Grotta Verde (Green Grotto)
2. Belvedere di Migliara
3. Torre di Guardia
4. Torre di Materita
5. Torre Damecuta; Villa Imperiale
6. Grotta Azzurra (Blue Grotto)
7. Villa Romana
8. Santa Sofia
9. Capodimonte; Villa San Michele; Church of San Michele; Castello
10. Palazzo a Mare; Bagni di Tiberio (Baths of Tiberius)
11. Santa Maria Cetrella
12. Giardini di Augusto
13. Palazzo Cerio; Santo Stefano; Piazza Umberto
14. Certosa
15. Arco Naturale; Gr. di Matromania
16. Grotta Blanca; Gr. Meravigliosa
17. Villa Jovis (Villa of Tiberius)
18. Grotta di Bove Marino

Marina Grande

Church of San Costanzo, Capri

Arriving at the harbor of Capri by sea from Naples or Sorrento, the entry into the picturesque Marina Grande is a pleasure in itself. The tourist office is here together with numerous bars or restaurants, and some visitors choose to swim and sunbathe around the Marina. Most, however, purchase tickets to take the funicular to Capri town or the bus to other sights on the island. The walk up to the town of Capri can be arduous in summer, and tourists generally prefer to save their energy for the obligatory further walks around Capri. But, should you choose to go by road, you pass the 11th-century **Church of San Costanzo**, and can take the **Scala Fenicia**, steep steps up to the **Castello di Barbarossa**. A separate excursion from Marina Grande takes in the Roman ruins of **Palazzo a Mare** and **Bagni di Tiberio**.

The Blue Grotto

Accessible by boat from Marina Grande, or from Anacapri, the Blue Grotto is perhaps the most famous tourist attraction on Capri, but the crowds may be off-putting. It is certainly enjoyable to take a boat trip around the island, as it provides an opportunity to see the beauty of Capri and its well-known sites from a different vantage point. Known to the Romans, who used it as a *nymphaeum* or outdoor bathing area, the rediscovery of the Blue Grotto in 1826 assured Capri's place on the Grand Tour. The small entrance requires visitors to transfer to a rowing boat and to lie flat in order to go into the grotto. Deflected sunrays produce the transparent, blue effect to the water, which is its claim to fame. The light is said to be at its best in the late afternoon. The acoustics are also impressive, but you cannot swim in the cave. The *Grotta Azzurra* can only be visited if weather conditions are favorable. Immediately above are the remains of the Roman **Villa di Gradola**, which was joined to the grotto by a stairway, now restored.

Capri Town & the Piazzetta

Santo Stefano

A short ride on the funicular leads to the town, from where there are great views of the Sorrento Peninsula and the Gulf of Naples. The **Piazza Umberto**, also called the *Piazzetta*, is the place to spot celebrities, but drinks are very expensive. The sculpted dome of **Santo Stefano** overlooks the square. Built in 1685, the church has Baroque décor and marble flooring from Capri's Roman villas. The streets leading off the square are lined with designer and souvenir shops. Take Via Longano and Via Matermania for the **Arco Naturale**, the **Grotto of Matermania** and the **Tragara terrace**. Alternatively, take Via V Emanuele and Via F Serena for a visit to the **Gardens of Augustus**, the **Certosa**, and **Marina Piccola**. Another walk, by Via Longano or Via Le Botteghe, leads to the church of **S Michele** and the **Villa Jovis** (a steep climb).

The Augustus Gardens & Via Krupp

Formerly part of the villa of the German industrialist, Krupp, who settled here, the gardens were donated to the town by him. They are only a short walk from the Piazzetta and offer lovely views over the sea, and of the magnificent, winding path down to Marina Piccola, called Via Krupp after the German financier who paid for its construction. It takes around 20 minutes on this zig-zag walk – itself considered a work of art – to reach the small but popular beaches of Marina Piccola, from where you can return to the Piazzetta by bus or taxi.

Certosa di San Giacomo

The charterhouse (*Certosa*) is a short distance from the Gardens of Augustus. Founded in the 14th century by Count

Giacomo Arcucci, secretary to Queen Giovanna I of Naples, the *certosa* was attacked during Saracen pirate raids in the 16th century, and fortifications undertaken. There are valuable works of art and two attractive cloisters. Open 9 am-2 pm. Closed Mon. ☎ 081 837 6218. From here, you can take Via I. Cerio, Via Camerelle, and the panoramic Via Tragara to a belvedere offering great views of the Faraglioni rocks.

Villa Jovis

Villa Jovis

One of the more challenging walks from the Piazzetta, the 45-minute trek along Via Botteghe and Via Croce up to the summit of Monte Tiberio, where the Roman villa is located, offers spectacular views. This was the main residence of Emperor Tiberius, built during the first century AD. It was ransacked by the Bourbons, and a more scientific excavation was conducted in the 1930s on the site, which is only part of the enormous villa complex. The multi-layered palace was well provided with water, and the huge tanks can still be seen. Baths, a servants' area, a large kitchen, and the private apartments of the emperor can be visited. A short distance away, are the ruins of the **Torre del Faro**. Originally a Roman construction, probably a lookout post for Tiberius, the 75-foot tower was later used as a lighthouse but has been abandoned since the 17th century. A mosaic in the church of San Stefano in Capri was originally from the Villa Jovis. Open 9 am to one hour before sunset. €2.

Arco Naturale

Returning from Villa Jovis, take a peek at **Villa Lysis**, exquisite former home of the Baron Fersen. At the crossroads of Via Croce, if you have the energy for more walking, follow signs to the Arco Naturale. This curious eroded rock is all that remains of a large grotto.

Grotta Matermania

Returning from the Arco Naturale, retrace your steps to the fork in the road, in order to continue the climb down more steps to the Grotta Matermania. This impressive natural cave was used by the Romans as a *nymphaeum* or bathing area. They built a mosaic wall decorated with shells, a few traces of which can still be seen. A further descent leads to the **Tragara Terrace**, with its views of the Faraglioni and Marina Piccola.

Casa Malaparte

From the Grotta Matermania, a winding cliff path leads to this unusual property on Punta Massullo. Designed by Adalberto Libera, the Malaparte house was built for a controversial member of the Fascist party, who later fell out of favor. Its construction on the cliff-top defied local building restrictions but its strange, low design has created a building that blends surprisingly well with its setting.

Anacapri

The second town of Capri is at the foot of Monte Solaro. There are many interesting sites to see here, but if time is limited, the chairlift to the mountain is not to be missed. It is also possible to reach the Blue Grotto on foot or by bus from here.

Monte Solaro

The chairlift is a fast and thrilling way to reach the top of this 1,800-foot mountain and take in the superb views of Anacapri and the Gulf of Naples. There is an attractive bar with terrace where you can enjoy a drink while you take in the breathtaking panorama. The footpath leading up and down the mountain is considered one of the best walks of the island. It passes **Cetrella** en route, where the small **church of Santa Maria** has a small terrace overlooking the Faraglioni, and if you are lucky enough to be there when it is open, there is a 17th-century sacristy and a balcony with another great view.

Villa San Michele

Axel Munthe (1857-1949) was a Swedish doctor who became well known locally for unstintingly offering his medical skills during epidemics in Naples. His autobiography helped to make his fanciful home – with its Moorish and Norman features, designed by himself – more famous. Built on the ruins of a Roman villa, the house contains ancient artifacts purchased or collected by the owner in and around Capri. There is a lovely garden with a colonnade and terrace with panoramic view. Concerts are held here in summer. During his lifetime Munthe acquired the ruined Castello Barbarossa, established a bird sanctuary and donated the Roman Villa Damecuta to the state. Today, the Munthe Foundation administers the house as a museum, together with the castle. Open 10:3-3:30 in winter and 9-6 pm in summer. €5. ☎ 081 837 1401.

Chiesa di San Michele

The main feature of this church is its superb majolica floor by Leonardo Chiaiese. Depicting Adam and Eve, the work was completed in 1761. A staircase in the church enables paying visitors to view the floor from above. San Michele also has 18th-century altars and paintings by Giacomo Del Po and Paolo de Matteis. Open 9:30-4 pm in winter and 9:30-7 pm in summer. €1. ☎ 081 837 2396.

Casa Rossa

This distinctive red house on the Via G. Orlandi in Anacapri was built by an American colonel, JC MacKowen, in the late 19th century. A historian from Louisiana, MacKowen excavated Roman remains in the Grotta Azzurra. His house, with its Pompeian red walls and tower, is not open to the public.

Capri in Miniature

A lovely installation for children on the main street of Anacapri, and fun for adults too, the pottery and limestone model of Capri on display is a great way to gain an overall view of the island. The sculpture – which takes up a large room – reproduces all the important sites and some of the local festivals and traditions. Scenes, around the room, depict momentous events in Capri's history. Next door, you can see craftsmen and women at work, handpainting ceramics.

Punta Carena

A one-hour walk on foot, or a 15-minute bus ride from Anacapri, leads past the Torre di Materita and the Torre della Guardia, to the seaside resort of Punta Carena, dominated by its lighthouse.

Villa Damecuta

Situated on the cost north of Anacapri, near the Blue Grotto, is the Roman villa of Damecuta. The loggia of the villa is still preserved, but part is obscured by the Torre di Damecuta, a medieval defensive tower, built in the wake of a series of pirate attacks.

Ischia

Volcanic in origin, Ischia is famed, above all, for its thermal waters, but the island has much more to offer than beaches and spas. The **Aragonese castle**, the luxurious gardens of **La Mortella**, the delightful fishing village of **Sant'Angelo** and the museums of **Lacco Ameno**, are among sites to see here. Once inhabited by Greeks and named Pithecusa, today Ischia has a population of 50,000.

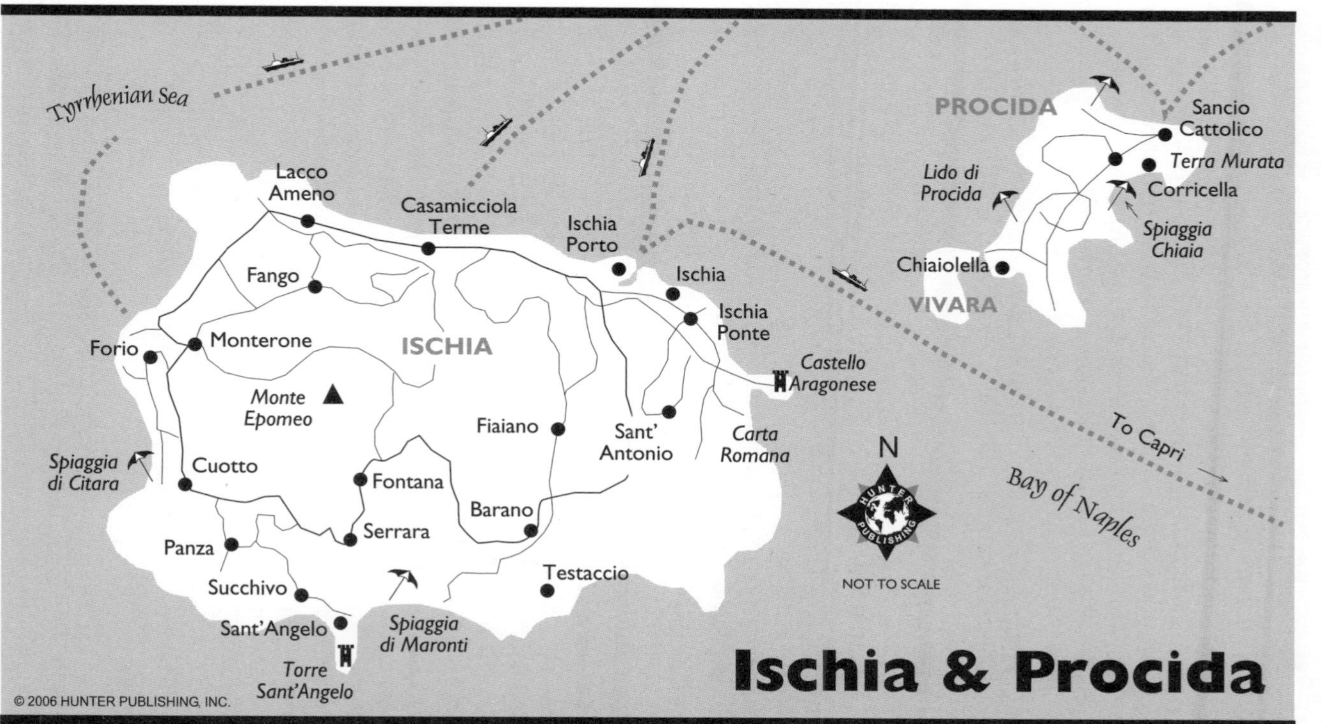

Tyrrhenian Sea
PROCIDA
Sancio Cattolico
Terra Murata
Lido di Procida
Corricella
Spiaggia Chiaia
Chiaiolella
VIVARA
Lacco Ameno
Casamicciola Terme
Ischia Porto
Ischia
Ischia Ponte
Fango
Forio
Monterone
ISCHIA
Castello Aragonese
Monte Epomeo
Fiaiano
Sant' Antonio
Carta Romana
To Capri
N
Spiaggia di Citara
Cuotto
Fontana
Barano
Serrara
Panza
HUNTER PUBLISHING
Bay of Naples
Testaccio
NOT TO SCALE
Succhivo
Sant'Angelo
Spiaggia di Maronti
Torre Sant'Angelo
Ischia & Procida
© 2006 HUNTER PUBLISHING, INC.

THE VITICULTURE OF ISCHIA

Wine has been grown on Ischia since ancient times. On the famous Nestor Cup, found in Lacco Ameno, an inscription praises the local wine, produced by ancient Greek settlers on the island. From the coast to the steep mountain slopes, wine-growing dictated the lives of the islanders for centuries, and has been commercially exported since medieval times.

Among 300-year-old grapes grown on the island are the Biancolella, Forastera, Arilla, and S. Lunardo whites, or Guarnaccia, Pedirosso o Pere e Palummo reds. On Ischia, the vines are pruned from January to March, and the grape harvesting – still done largely by hand – is from August to November.

Ischia Porto

Most visitors to the island arrive by sea at Ischia Porto. This is also the main town, stretching as far as Ischia Ponte – the causeway leading to the Castle. On Via Roma, the main shopping street, is the **Chiesa dell'Assunta**, built in 1300 and since remodeled in Baroque style.

Museo del Mare

Bus no 7 from the port goes to Ischia Ponte, from where there is a short walk to the Castle. Sights not to be missed en route are the magnificent portal of the **Palazzo Corteglia**, and the frieze of the **Church of S Maria di Costantinopoli**. The delightful **Palazzo dell Orologio** houses the Museo del Mare. The museum, on three floors, tells the history of Ischia and particularly of its fishermen, and is run by a voluntary organization. Displays include shells, navigational instruments, photographs and old postcards. €2.50. ☎ 081 902 319. On the side of the Museo del Mare is a memorial to King Vittorio Emmanuele, who visited the afflicted locals, serving as a reminder of the tragic effects of volcanic eruptions that have devastated Ischia in the last century.

Castello Aragonese

The location and imposing character of this fortress make it one of the most impressive sites on the islands. A fort has stood on this site since 474 BC and the present castle is a complex of buildings from different periods, including churches, and a prison. Due to its size, at least 1½ hours should be allowed for a visit. It is probably wise to take the lift up to the castle, and walk back down, enjoying the views. Information booklets are provided at the ticket office.

Castello Aragonese

Sant'Angelo

Ischia has a very good bus service that runs clockwise and anti-clockwise around the island. Buses stop at the top of the hill in Sant'Angelo, giving visitors a chance to take some photographs and take in the views on the walk to the picturesque islet of Punta Sant'Angelo. This is a traffic-free zone and so is reminiscent of Capri – a lovely spot to have a tranquil dinner with a sea view. Climb up the steps to the right of the harbor for a panoramic view of Sant'Angelo and to see the church. The footpath continues on to Cavascura, with its hot springs, used since Roman times, and to Maronti beach – offering lovely views of this part of Iscia's coastline. An excursion can also be made from here to Monte Epomeo.

Maronti Beach

Considered one of the best beaches on Ischia, and definitely its longest, Maronti is famous for its thermal waters, with their steam rising from the hot sand. At the other end of the beach is the town of Barano, where the main Piazza San Rocco boasts two 17th-century churches.

Monte Epomeo

Views over the whole island can be seen from the volcano, which fortunately has not erupted since 1302. It is a tough one-hour climb, or a bumpy mule ride. Some adventurous tourists make the ascent at night, in order to see dawn from the summit.

Forio

Continuing clockwise around the island, the town of Forio has a number of interesting sites. Tennessee Williams and Truman Capote brought some early glamour to Forio by spending time here in the 1950s. Its symbols are its lovely church and tower. Citara beach stretches away to the left of the town. A short bus ride away is the garden of La Mortella.

The Torrione

Built by the Aragonese King Ferrante in 1480 on the site of an even older tower, the aim was to protect the inhabitants from pirate raids. It later served as a prison, and is now an art gallery. Nearby, the Baroque church of **Santa Maria di Loreto** has two majolica-decorated towers and dates from the 14th century.

The Santuario del Soccorso

A pleasant stroll leads to the small white church known as the sanctuary of San Soccorso. Rebuilt over centuries, various architectural styles, especially Moorish, are in evidence. There are lovely majolica tiles on the walls, and numerous wooden offerings, carved – often in the form of ships – by local fishermen.

La Mortella

One of the most famous gardens in Italy, La Mortella is three km/two miles north of Forio – the local bus service is free if you have purchased the daily **Ischia Unico bus card**. It was originally the home of Sir William Walton, the British composer, who died here in 1983. His music is played non-stop in the on-site café, and his life is commemorated in a museum. The property also contains a concert hall. The internationally renowned garden was created by his Argentinian wife, Susana, who came to the island with Walton, 24 years her senior, in 1949. With the help of the great landscape architect, Russell Page, she created this spectacular cliffside house and garden, with its terraces, pools, fountains, palms, and hundreds of species of rare and exotic plants. A highlight of the garden is the huge water lily Victoria Amazonica, with flowers that turn from white to red. For those too enchanted to leave, overnight accommodation can also be arranged. Allow two hours for a visit. Open April to November, Tue, Thur, Sat, Sun 9-7 pm. €10. Guided tours can be arranged. ☎ 081 986 220, www.grandigiardini.it. From La Mortella you can also visit the **Santuario di San Francesco da Paola** or walk back up to the main road to take the bus.

Lacco Ameno

This lovely town, with its elegant bathing concessions and lovely beaches, is Ischia's most popular seaside resort, and is distinguished by the **Isoletta del Fungo**, a 30-foot-high mushroom-shaped rock in the Marina di Lacco. The ancient origins of the town are reflected in the various museums here.

Museo e Scavi Santa Restituta

From the fungo, walk to the left through the town and past the church to reach a charming piazza, to the right of which is the 14th-century **Santa Restituta**, which houses a museum. Santa Restituta is the patron saint of Ischia. The sanctuary, constructed on the site of an early Christian church, dates to the 10th century. The three-room museum displays silver, paintings and Baroque statues. Roman and Greek remains were found underneath the church crypt, and the excavations can also be visited

Villa Arbusto

Built in the 18th century by Carlo d'Acquaviva, the Duke of Atri, in the 1950s the villa was acquired by Angelo Rizzoli, an editor and later a cinematographer. He was a Milanese, born in 1889, who rose from humble origins – he spent part of his childhood in an orphanage – to become a wealthy man, mingling with the stars of the day. He is considered a great patron of Lacco Ameno, having constructed three hotels – the Reginella, Regina Isabella and the Sporting. He also situated a number of his films here in the 1950s and 1960s. After his death the villa was purchased by the local council, and a museum established there to commemorate his life and work. In addition to film posters and other memorabilia of his career, there are numerous pictures of Mr Rizzoli with various celebrities, including Charlie Chaplin. The Museo Archeologico di Pithecusa occupies the main part of the Villa Arbusto, and displays a number of important Greek artifacts, including the famous Nestore Cup described in the Iliad. Open 9:30-1:30 and 3-7 pm in winter; 9:30-1 pm and 4-8 pm in summer. Closed Mon. €5. Students, €1. www.pithecusae.it.

Nestore Cup

Casamicciola

A mile to the east of Lacco Ameno, the spa town of Casamicciola Terme has long been a popular resort; it was here that Ibsen stayed while he was writing *Peer Gynt*. In the late 19th century the town was devastated by earthquakes – that of 1883 killed more than 2,000 people, including hundreds of tourists. The underground fault continues to make this location one of high seismic risk, but Casamicciola has more than recovered its reputation as a spa resort, and offers delightful nature walks through pine and chestnut woods up to the Epomeo mountain. Despite the volcanic activity, a few historical churches have survived.

Procida

The small, 1.8-mile-square Procida has been reluctant to step out from the shadow of its famous sister islands. Now more open to tourism, Procida is nevertheless still relatively underdeveloped. There is a nature reserve on the adjoining islet of Vivara.

Marina di Sancio Cattolico

Immediately on arrival at the port, when the pastel houses and church of **Santa Maria della Pietà** come into view, the charm of Procida is apparent, The church has wide arches and exterior stairs. From here you can walk up to the **Piazza dei Martiri**, where 12 local inhabitants were executed after the revolutionary events of 1799. Nearby, the early 18th-century domed church of **Madonna delle Grazie** houses a popular statue of the Virgin. Continuing on toward the **castle**, which

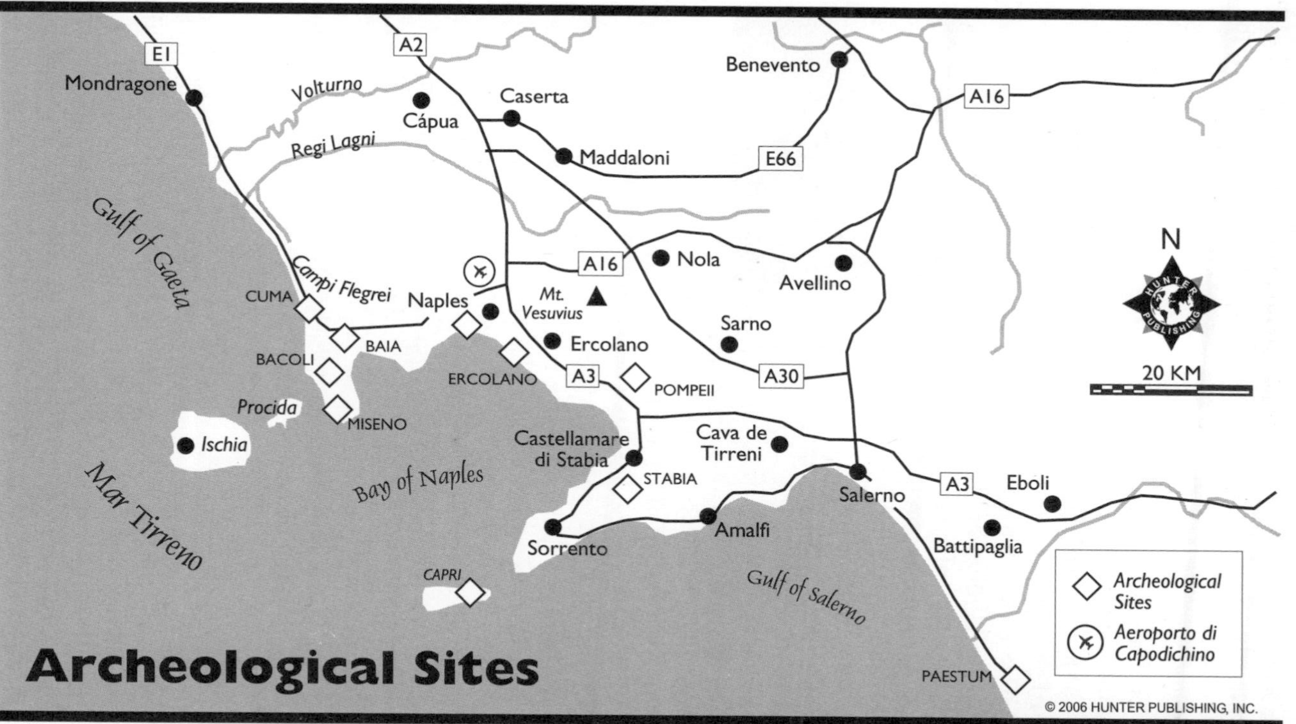
Archeological Sites
N
HUNTER PUBLISHING
20 KM
Archeological Sites
Aeroporto di Capodichino
© 2006 HUNTER PUBLISHING, INC.
E1
A2
A16
E66
A3
A30
Mondragone
Volturno
Cápua
Caserta
Benevento
Maddaloni
Regi Lagni
Gulf of Gaeta
Campi Flegrei
CUMA
Naples
Mt. Vesuvius
Nola
Avellino
Sarno
Ercolano
BAIA
BACOLI
ERCOLANO
POMPEII
Procida
MISENO
Ischia
Castellamare di Stabia
Cava de Tirreni
STABIA
Bay of Naples
Mar Tirreno
Salerno
Eboli
Amalfi
Sorrento
Battipaglia
CAPRI
Gulf of Salerno
PAESTUM

is actually the former Palazzo Reale, used as a prison until recently, the piazza offers lovely views of the village of Marina di Corricella.

Terra Murata

Via San Michele leads to Terra Murata, dominated by the **Abbey of San Michele**. Numerous works of art are housed in the church, including a depiction of San Michele – patron saint of Procida – by Luca Giordano. The painting by Nicola Rooso shows a group of putti (cherubs) saving Procida from Turkish raiders. www.abbaziasanmichele.it.

San Michele, Luca Giordano

Marina di Corricella

This former fishermen's cove is a feast for the eye. Its waterfront was featured in the Oscar-winning Italian film *Il Postino.* The restaurants that line the Marina are very popular with yacht-owning Neapolitans who moor here in summer for a delicious Sunday lunch out. You may not have a yacht, but you can certainly have a great meal with the best of them.

Chiaiolella

On the other side of the island, the small port and beach of Chiaiolella is another popular spot to stop for a drink or a meal while admiring the view of Vivara.

Vivara

This islet is a Nature Reserve, and not generally open to the public, although a bridge links it to the rest of Procida. Vivara is of interest both for its Mediterranean flora, for the diverse bird life it attracts, and also as a site where interesting Bronze Age artifacts have been excavated. Visits can be arranged by appointment. ☎ 081 896 7400.

■ The Vesuvian Region

East of Naples, the familiar outline of Vesuvius soon comes into view. Today it overlooks an urban sprawl interspersed with some of the most famous Roman towns and villas in the world. Visits to Vesuvius generally begin from Ercolano (Herculaneum) or Torre del Greco. The Roman villa of Oplontis is situated in the town of Torre Annunziata, while the more extensive excavations at Ercolano and Pompeii are served by rail stations of the same name further along the Circumvesuviana line. At Portici the Palazzo Reale, and the "golden mile" of Vesuvian villas that surround it, are glorious reminders of Bourbon splendor.

Vesuvius National Park

Vesuvius, one of the best known volcanoes on earth, has killed thousands in a series of deadly eruptions and, with half a million people currently living beneath it, the potential for future devastation is immense. The fertile land around Vesuvius has brought men and women to the region since ancient times. Tourism is a more recent offshoot of the volcano, with the excavation of Pompeii, Herculaneum, and other Roman sites in the 19th century attracting visitors from all around the world. Lately, attention has been paid to the unique flora and fauna of Vesuvius and a number of educational walks around the volcano have been established with the creation of the Vesuvius National Park.

Excursions to the Crater

Today Vesuvius, the only active volcano in continental Europe, is dormant. Reaching a height of 1,281 metres/3,800 feet, the two cones of Somma and Vesuvius are separated by the Valle del Gigante. Somma, the ancient cone, was partially destroyed by eruptions many thousands of years ago. Mt Vesuvius itself was formed later. Vulcanologists have enumerated eight eruptive cycles, each beginning with a "plinian" eruption, characterized by emission of pumice and other pyroclastic products. Visitors wanting to make the ascent can travel by bus from Ercolano, or by car, through vineyards, lava fields and valleys filled with pungent broom to a car park close to the crater, where admission tickets must be purchased. Local guides then accompany tourists on a

Vesuvius National Park

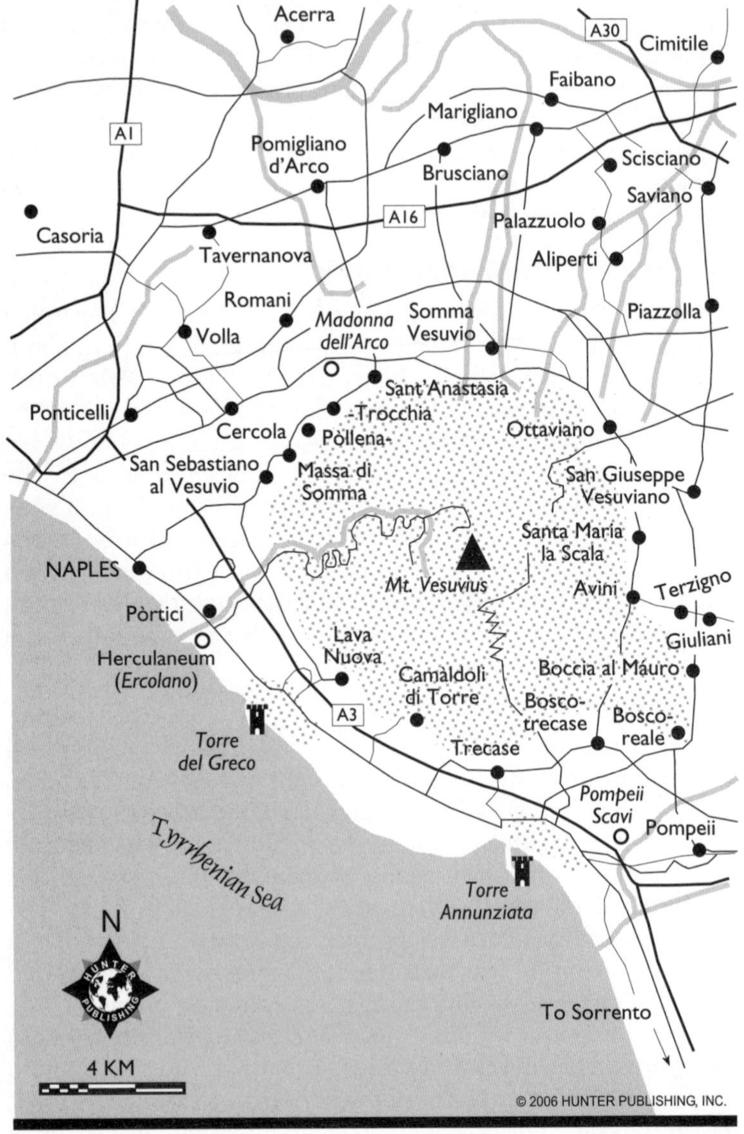

30-minute walk to the crater. The lava flows from the 1944 eruption can be seen, together with a crater caused by that of 1906. At the summit, jagged red rock and occasional plumes of smoke can be seen. Walking along the rim of the crater, fine views can be had of the Gulf of Naples on clear days. €5. Open 9-2 pm. Personal guides are also available, at a price.

Nature Trails

Vesuvius is now a UNESCO World Reserve, and the park authorities have worked very hard over the last few years to create a set of superb nature trails. Using state-of-the-art engineering techniques together with artfully crafted wooden bridges they have succeeded in producing a series of delightful walks that are safe yet exciting. Through information panels, maps and guided tours, visitors can learn to appreciate the unique features of Vesuvian flora and fauna. Currently, some of the trails can only be taken with guides, but the first trail – the **Valle del Inferno** – is open to the public, and 60,000 follow the walk annually. Considering that 10 times this number do the 20-minute crater walk, the nature trails are much less crowded, and are preferable for those with time to spare and who want to explore at their own pace.

An old building on the slopes of Vesuvius – the **Castello Palazzo Mediceo d'Ottaviano** – is being restored and is due to open as a visitor's center. On Saturday evenings in summer a torchlit visit "**Vesuvius by Starlight**" tour is offered. The visit lasts 2½ hours and walking shoes, a pullover, a raincoat, and a bottle of water are recommended. Cost is €10 adults and €7 children. For further information visit www.parconazionaledelvesuvio.it.

The Observatory

Built in the mid-19th century on the site of the historic Hermitage, where Grand Tour travelers used to halt before ascending further, the Vesuvian observatory was the first of its kind in the world and has survived numerous eruptions. It's on the southern side of the Somma caldera, between two deep valleys filled by lava flows. Visits may be arranged by appointment. The observatory also houses a vulcanological museum. ☎ 081 777 7149.

Pompeii

Such is the fame of Pompeii, certainly the most important classical archeological site in Europe, that it scarcely needs an introduction. By the same token, Pompeii is always busy. Fortunately, the area of excavations is large enough to afford plenty of room for the crowds who surge through the barriers every day. Tiring at any time of year, in the summer months, this is a hot, dusty, exhausting excursion. Pompeii covers an area of 123 acres and a whole day or more is needed to visit it properly, so you should prioritize. There is a café within the grounds for lunch, but carry a bottle of water with you. Comfortable walking shoes are essential. If all this sounds too daunting, those who would prefer to visit a smaller area, or a single villa, should go to Herculaneum, Stabiae, or Oplontis. Most of the treasures taken from these Roman sites are at the **Archeological Museum of Naples** or at the **Museum of Boscoreale**.

Another frustration for visitors to Pompeii is that administering and preserving such a large and important site is a tall order, and invariably one or more of the top attractions are closed for restoration. Indeed, excavations are still ongoing, and exciting new discoveries are periodically being made.

The easiest way to get to Pompeii is with the Circumvesuviana train service. The station is only a short walk from the main entrance. A free map is available onsite but it is not as easy to follow as it first appears. Audio guides can be purchased. Open Apr-Oct 8:30-7:30 pm; Nov-Mar 8:30-3:30 pm. €10. Reductions €5. ☎ 081 857 5347, www.pompeiisites.org.

Glossary of Latin Terms for Roman Sites	
Calidarium	Hot water bath
Domus	House, residence
Lararium	Temple, shrine
Nymphaeum	Outdoor bathing area
Macellum	Market
Palestra	Gymnasium or sports center

Peristilium	Colonnaded garden in a Roman house
Sacellum	A religious space, sacred enclosure
Tablinum	Meeting & reception room in a Roman house
Tepidarium	Warm water bath
Thermopolium	Shop selling drinks & fast food
Triclinium	Dining room

The Forum

Entering the excavations through the Porta Marina – so named because this route led to the sea – the city walls, part of the defensive structure of the town, can also be seen. Ahead are a number of public and administrative buildings grouped around the Forum. This was the economic heart of the city, and would originally have been surrounded on three sides by an elegant colonnade. Temples, a market, and a law court surround the Forum. Baths were also part of the complex, with the customary separate areas for men and women. They followed the usual sequence: *apodyterium* (dressing room), *frigidarium* (cold bathing room), *tepidarium* (warm room), *caldarium* (hot room).

House of the Tragic Poet

Continuing along the Via del Foro and northward into the Via di Mercurio, this and the two smaller streets parallel to it on either side must have been an upmarket residential area, and contain a number of interesting houses. It is at the House of the Tragic Poet that one of the great symbols of Pompeii can be found: the famous mosaic of a chained dog and the words *Cave Canem* – Beware of the Dog. The atrium-style house is named for its floor mosaic, now in the Naples National Archeological Museum, that depicts a theater rehearsal.

House of Pansa

Like most Pompeiian houses, this has an inner courtyard and a colonnaded garden. The house was subdivided into small rooms that were rented out by the owner, a merchant from

Pompeii
REGION II
REGION III
(UNEXCAVATED)
Via dell'Abbondanza
REGION I
REGION IX
(UNEXCAVATED)
REGION IV
(UNEXCAVATED)
REGION VIII
REGION V
(UNEXCAVATED)
Vicolo dei Vettii
Vicolo di Mercurio
REGION VII
REGION VI
Via Consolare
N
HUNTER PUBLISHING
NOT TO SCALE
© 2006 HUNTER PUBLISHING, INC.

Tour of Pompeii

1. Cemetery of the Nuceria Gate (*Necropoli di Porta Nocera*)
2. Porta Nocera & city wall (*Porta Nocera e cinta muraria*)
3. Place of the Fugitives (*Orto dei Fuggiaschi*)
4. House of the Garden of Hercules (*Casa del Giardino di Ercole*)
5. Amphitheater (*Anfiteatro*)
6. House of Venus in the Sea Shell (*Casa della Venere in Conchiglia*)
7. House of Loreius Tibertinus (*Casa di Octavius Quartio*)
8. House of the ship *Europa* (*Casa della nave* Europa)
9. Temple of Isis (*Tempio di Iside*)
10. Small Theater (*Teatro Piccolo Odeion*)
11. Large Theater (*Teatro Grande*)
12. Doric Temple (*Tempio Dorico*)
13. Triangular Forum (*Foro Triangolare*)
14. Stabian Baths (*Terme Stabiane*)
15. Public Administration Buildings
16. Basilica
17. Marine Port & city wall (*Porta Marina e cinta muraria*)
18. Temple of Apollo (*Tempio di Apollo*)
19. Building of Eumachia (*Edificio di Eumachia*); Temple of Vespasian (*Tempio di Vespasiano-Aedes Genii Augusti*)
20. Memorial garden (*Santuario dei Lari Pubblici*)
21. Temple of Jupiter (*Tempio di Giove*)
22. Meat & Fish Market (*Macellum*)
23. Forum Baths (*Terme del Foro*)
24. Temple of Fortuna Augusta
25. House of the Small Fountain (*Casa della Fontana Piccola*)
26. House of the Faun (*Casa del Fauno*)
27. House of the Vetti family (*Casa dei Vettii*)
28. House of Castor & Pollux (*Casa di Castore & Polluce*); House of Meleagro (*Casa di Meleagro*)
29. House of Sallustio (*Casa di Sallustio*)
30. Herculaneum Gate & city walls (*Porta di Ercolano e cinta muraria*)
31. Cemetery of the Herculaneum Gate (*Necropoli di Porta Ercolano*)
32. Villa of the Mysteries (*Villa dei Misteri*)
33. House of the Ancient Hunt (*Casa della Caccia Antica*)
34. Bakery (*Panificio*)
35. Brothel (*Lupanare*)
36. House of the Ceii brothers (*Casa dei Ceii*) Fullery of Stephanus; House of Larario di Achille (*Casa dei Larario di Achille; Sacello Iliaco*)
37. Gate of Vesuvius (*Porta Vesuvio*)
38. Nolan Gate (*Porta Nola*)
39. Sarno Gate (*Porta Sarno*)
40. Arena (*Palaestra*)
41. Stabian Gate (*Porta Stabiae*)
42. Gladiators' Barracks

Campania. The original décor can no longer be seen, but the lovely Tuscan atrium and a peristyle laid out around a pool suggest the luxurious character of this home.

House of the Small Fountain

This house is worth visiting for its decoration: the glass and shell designs on the fountain *nymphaeum* or bathing area are a rare example of non-floor mosaics. The garden area also contains some small but delightful landscape scenes.

House of the Faun

Mosaic in the House of Faun

The largest, and arguably the most beautiful private house in Pompeii, because of its elegant design and lovely mosaics. The house has a "welcome" mosaic in the atrium and is named after the second-century bronze statue of a dancing faun found here – the original is now in the Naples museum, along with a superb mosaic also taken from the house, depicting the victory of Alexander the Great over the Persian King Darius.

House of Dioscuri

Also known as the House of Castor and Pollux, this was originally several small houses, merged into one by its wealthy owner. The rooms are decorated with elaborate wall paintings, depicting mythological scenes. Some of the paintings, including that of the *Dioscuri* (the name given to the brothers Castor and Pollux) are now in Naples, but the grandeur of this house can still be admired, with its colonnaded atriu, and painted panels in the peristyle.

House of Dioscuri

House of Meleagro

Interesting features of this house include the Corinthian-style living and reception room (*oecus*) decorated with columns, and the original floors, with white tile decoration, in the rooms around the atrium.

House of Apollo

A statue of Apollo found here is now in the Naples Museum, but frescoes on the same theme can be seen along with a small painting of Venus in the *tablinum*. There is also a colorful mosaic in the garden area which depicts Ulysses and Achilles.

House of the Vettii

Zeto & Anfione fresco, House of the Vettii

Not to be missed, because it contains some of the best murals that remain in Pompeii itself (not removed to the Archeological Museum), it is another example of the delightful homes that successful Romans constructed for themselves. Its good state of preservation provides a glimpse of the lifestyle of wealthy residents in Pompeii. Of particular interest are the friezes of Cupids engaged in various workmanlike activities. The kitchen and servants' quarters also provide an interesting glimpse of domestic life in Roman times. The famous painting of *Priapus* (a figure of fertility that looks pornographic to modern viewers) and a statue of him, together with other erotic paintings, were also found here.

Priapus, House of the Vettii

The Lupanare

The brothel in Vicolo del Lupanare is one of the most popular sites in Pompeii. Surprisingly small and uncomfortable-looking rooms with stone beds, where the prostitutes operated, have pictures above the entrances showing sexual scenes, which may have served to indicate the specialties of the occupants. The prostitutes are likely to have been slaves, and were usually of Greek or Oriental origin. The cost of sex has been estimated as equivalent to purchasing two glasses of wine from a *thermopolium*, and the earnings would have gone to the brothel owner.

Fresco, The Lupanare

Stabian Baths

Located at the junction of Vicolo del Lupanare with Via dell'Abbondanza, the oldest thermal complex in the city is still pretty much intact. The outdoor pool, changing room, cold, warm and hot bathing rooms, divided into male and female areas, can all be seen. Beautifully decorated with stuccos and wall paintings, the impressive heating system provides visual evidence of the sophisticated lifestyle of the ancient Romans. Warm air produced by furnaces circulated underneath the floors and through ducts in the walls.

The Theaters

From the baths, the Via dei Teatri leads to the large and small theaters of Pompeii, which could seat 5,000 and 1,300 respectively. They are so well preserved that performances are still held in them during summer. Restored after the AD 62 earthquake, comedies and musical performances would have been held here. Three temples are close-by.

Decorative Styles

Roman wall paintings are divided into four types, corresponding to specific time periods. **First style** (c. 200-60 BC) generally involves the simulation of colored marble on painted plaster. The **second style**, which emerged in the first century BC, is characterized by trompe-l'oeil painting techniques. The **third style** (20 BC-20 AD) reflects the elaborate courtly decoration of the Augustan period, while the **fourth style** (20-79 AD) revives narrative, mythological and panoramic landscape themes from earlier paintings.

The House of Menander

On the corner of the Via Stabiana and Vicolo del Menandro, the house of Menander may have belonged to relatives of Nero's wife, Poppaea Sabina. A number of fourth-style paintings can be seen here, as well as a small family temple. The Greek playwright Menander is shown on a panel in the peristyle. Mosaics in the *caldarium* depict sea monsters.

House of the Ceii

The house is richly decorated in third style, and has a delightful geometrically patterned floor. A hunting scene dominates the garden, and landscapes, representing foreign places, adorn the side walls.

Thermopolium of Vetutius Placidus

Heading west, on one of the principal roads of the city, the Via dell'Abbondanza leads to the amphitheater. On the right-hand side of the street, the *thermopolium* is one of Pompeii's many small food shops, where customers purchased ready meals and drinks. They are distinguished by the large jars, called *dolia*, which are sunk into the counters. Frescoes depicting the gods of trade and of wine can be seen.

House of Octavius Quartus

The villa has large bronze doors, and decorations of Narcissus, Pyramus and Thisbe. The lush garden with two long pools is particularly lovely. This outdoor area was beautifully decorated with statues and frescoes, as well as a large couch for al fresco dining. Tree-lined avenues and three fishponds complete the picture of a superb outdoor space.

House of Venus

The best feature of this house is the wall paintings in the garden depicting a bird fountain, and, in particular, Venus on a pink seashell with two cherubs. They are remarkably well preserved, and it is lovely to see them in their original setting.

The Amphitheater

Turn right into Vicolo dell'Anfiteatro to see this superb, almost intact amphitheater. It could seat 12,000 and dates from 80 BC. Gladiatorial combat took place here. Next door is the *palestra*, a sports hall with a central pool where young men would have exercised. Excavations revealed a number of skeletons here, suggesting that the *palestra* was in use on the fateful day in AD 79.

Villa dei Misteri

Before leaving Pompeii, time should be allocated for a visit to the Villa dei Misteri, at the northeast corner of the excavations. Take the Via Consolare and Via delle Tombe. En route, the **Baker's House** is a popular site, with its vaulted oven.

Also on the Via Consolare are the **houses of Sallustio**, with its garden fresco, and of **the Surgeon**, where a number of medical instruments were found. There are first-style paintings on the exterior walls, and fourth-style frescoes inside. On the Via delle Tombe is the **necropolis of Porta Ercolano**, with tombs of the priestess Mamia, and illustrious citizens of Pompeii. The sumptuous **Villa of Diomedes**, at the end of the Via delle Tombe, offered beautiful views over the garden and sea to its residents, but became a death trap for many of them: 18 bodies were discovered in the basement here. A further walk past an orchard with apricot trees (when the fruit is ripe the owners will sell you a bagful, but only on your way back) leads to the **Villa dei Misteri**, surely the most impressive of Pompeii's palatial homes. The paintings in the complex of rooms are particularly well preserved, and provides a good example of the layout of a large country house in Roman times.

Herculaneum

Located in the modern town of Ercolano, the excavations are less extensive, but the Roman villas are better preserved than those at Pompeii, largely as a result of the 65 vertical feet of mud, lava and ash flow that enveloped and then hardened around them. Some wood, textiles, and papyri emerged intact from the aftermath of the eruption and pyroclastic flows that engulfed Herculaneum. Only part of the original Roman town has been excavated, since contemporary dwellings surround it, but this helps to make Herculaneum a more manageable site for visitors with time constraints. As at Pompeii, work continues, and in 2000 the discovery of 48 more victims enabled scientists to establish that they died instantly from exposure to an intense heat blast without even time to react. Open Mar-Sept 8:30-7:30 pm; Oct-Feb 8:30-5 pm. €10.

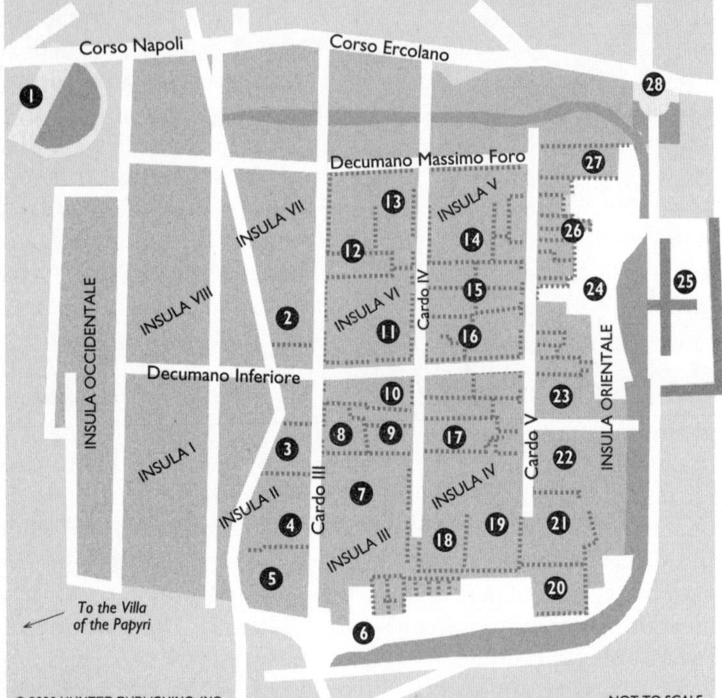

1. Theater
2. *Casa di Galba* (House of Galba)
3. *Casa del Genio* (House of the Genius)
4. *Casa d'Argo* (House of Argus)
5. *Casa d'Aristide* (House of Aristides)
6. *Area Sacra* (sacred area)
7. *Casa del'Albergo* (the large inn)
8. *Casa dello Scheletro* (the skeleton)
9. *Casa a Graticcio* (the woven partition); *Casa dell'Erme di Bronzo* (the bronze Hermes)
10. *Casa di Tramezzo di Legno* (wooden partition)
11. *Terme dei Foro* (forum baths)
12. *Casa dei due Atri* (two Atria); *Sacello degli Augustali* (shrine to Augustus)
13. *Casa dei Salone Nero* (salon of Nero)
14. *Casa con Bottiglie* (the bottles); *Casa dei Bel Cortile* (the fine courtyard); *Casa del Bicentenario* (the bicentennial)
15. *Casa dei Mobile Carbonato* (the charred furniture); *Casa dell'Atrio Corinaio* (Corinthian atrium); *Casa di Nettuno e Anfitrite* (mosaic of Neptune & Amphitryte) *Casa del Sacello di Legno* (wooden shrine)
16. *Casa del Gran Portale* (the large doorway); *Casa dei Taiale* (cloth-merchant); *Casa Sannitica* (Samnite house)
17. *Casa dell'Alcova* (the alcoves); *abitazione e bottega* (residence/shop)
18. *Casa dell'Atrio a Mosaico* (the mosaic atrium)
19. *Casa dei Cervi* (the deer)
20. *Terme Suburbane* (suburban baths)
21. *Casa delle Gemma* (the gem)
22. *Casa dei Rilievo di Telefo* (relief of Telephus)
23. *abitazione e tabernae* (residence/tavern)
24. *Aula* (hall or court)
25. *Palestra* (gymnasium)
26. *Bottegi* (shops)
27. *Aula Superiore* (large hall or court)
28. *Ingresso Scavi* (entrance to the excavation)

House of the Stags

The layout of Herculaneum is relatively simple. It is divided into three parallel streets, *Cardo III, IV* and *V*, which have upper and lower segments (*superiore* and *inferiore*) and are intersected by streets called the *Decumano Inferiore* and the *Decumano Massimo*. The entrance to Herculaneum is on a raised street that crosses the length of the excavations, providing a useful birds-eye view. The entrance leads up some steps into the *Cardo V*. On the left is the House of the Stags which has mosaic and marble flooring, and frescoed walls. When the garden was excavated a number of statues were found: deer being attacked by dogs, a satyr with a wineskin and the famous drunken Hercules, all now in the Museum.

House of the Relief of Telephus

Constructed on three levels, with views over the sea, this is the second-largest house in Herculaneum. Shown at left, a sculptured relief depicting Telephus, son of Hercules, founder of the city, was unearthed here. This Augustan building was damaged in the 62 AD earthquake, and later renovated.

Thermopolium of Priapus

The food shop had a painting of Priapus behind the counter, to ward off evil spiritis. Inhabitants of Herculaneum would have eaten their lunch here, and a jar containing walnuts was found by excavators. The shopkeeper had an entrance to his home directly from the *thermopolium*.

The Palestra

A sporting complex, on two terraces, with a fishpond and fountain, and an area set aside for religious rites, the Palestra was built before 14 AD.

The Pistrinum of Felix

Continuing along *Cardo V Superiore*, a number of bronze baking pans and two millstones were found in this bakery. Two stucco phalluses adorned the entrance, and served as a protection for the property and its inhabitants.

House of the Corinthian Atrium

Shown at right, one of the oldest residences excavated at Herculaneum, the house has an imposing entrance and an atrium with three columns in brick on either side. Marble floors and a fountain, and fourth-style paintings on the walls and ceiling can be seen here.

Taberna Vasaria

Returning along *Cardo V Superior* and turning into *Decumano Inferiore*, two taverns are situated at the entrance to the street. The second may in fact have been a shop selling terra cotta containers, since a number of wine amphorae were found here, carrying Greek inscriptions, although the usual counter for customers is missing.

House with the Large Portal

A number of attractive fourth-style frescoes are still in situ. Paintings also decorated the walls of the garden. There is an exceptional panel fresco in the *triclinium*. Next door, the **Samnite House** has a first-storey suite of rooms that were rented out and given a separate entrance. It is a blend of artistic styles: the entrance has first-style décor, with a second-style ceiling, while the walls of the atrium are painted in fourth style. The pattern of the tiled floors is also of interest.

House of the Wooden Partition

Turning left into *Cardo IV Inferiore*, this house is distinguished by its folding partition between the atrium and the *tablinum*. The wooden structure has supports for hanging oil lamps. In the room to the right of the entrance, note the geometric design of the floor mosaic, and the wall paintings.

House of the Alcove

Across the road, this house has two doors on its street front, probably the result of merging two properties in one. A painting of Ariadne in one of the rooms is the only noteworthy decorative element not stripped from the property by the Bourbon excavators. The *triclinium* is also of interest, as it contains wooden beds and wooden frame doors in a remarkable state of preservation. Remains of the original marble floor can also be seen here.

House of the Mosaic Atrium

This stately residence would have had lovely views, and its elegant décor suggests a wealthy owner. The black and white mosaic floor with its chessboard effect is of special interest. Note the buckling effect – probably due to the pressure of the mud and ash flow that engulfed the town in 79 AD. The garden had a marble fountain and porticos on three sides. It is decorated, like the rest of the house, with fourth-style paintings.

Sacellum of Venus

At the end of the *Cardo IV Inferiore* this small temple dedicated to Venus has a marble altar and frescoes with a garden motif. The *sacellum* had been restored after the 62 AD earthquake.

House of the Bronze Sculpted Head

Returning up *Cardo IV* on the left-hand side, this small house, decorated with third- and fourth-style paintings, is notable for the bronze portrait of the owner that once stood in the atrium. A plaster cast of the original is on display. The *triclinium* has a superb painting of a sea view.

Women's Baths

Continuing into *Cardo IV Superiore*, the lovely mosaic floor of the women's baths is decorated with motifs of Triton and of sea creatures. The changing room, as well as the warm and hot rooms can be seen. Note the shelves for storing garments, and the lovely seats of white and red marble. The *palestra* takes the form of an outdoor courtyard, surrounded by Ionic columns, and covered with stuccoes.

House of Neptune & Amphitrite

Noteworthy for the outstandingly well preserved wall mosaic along the east wall of the exterior *triclinium*. Another mosaic adorns the *nymphaeum* (bathing area).

House of the Black Room

This lovely home, with its views over a garden, has a black mosaic floor in the peristyle. The black room has exceptional fourth-style paintings and a white mosaic floor. A marble table and a wooden *lararium* with marble capitals were also found in this room and removed to the museum.

The Welder's Shop

The tools of trade of the Roman welder or *plumbarius* can be seen here: a crucible for smelting metal, and some terracotta vats where the forged metal would have been cooled. The shop is also of interest for its wooden loft, part of which has been preserved. The welder was repairing a statuette of Bacchus when his work was interrupted forever.

Hall of the Augustals

Turning left into *Decumano Massimo*, past another *thermopolium* and into *Cardo III Superiore*, an inscription on the wall of this building informs us that it was constructed by two brothers, and dedicated to Emperor Augustus. Fourth-style frescoes depict Hercules, Jupiter, Juno and Minerva. A skeleton – probably that of the caretaker – was found lying on a bed in the property.

House with the Double Atrium

Notable for its attractive façade, on which one small window still retains its original ironwork, there is also a terracotta mask on the door.

Men's Baths

Part of the central bath complex, for which the women's section has an entrance on *Cardo IV Superiore*. The *frigidarium* has red walls and a blue dome with yellow niches, while the black and white mosaic of the *tepidarium* features dolphins, an octopus, and a sea god.

House of the Skeleton

On *Cardo III Inferiore*, this house was so-called because a skeleton was found on the upper floor during excavation work in the early 19th century. Frescoed walls and mosaics can still be seen.

House of Argus

The painting to which the name refers has been removed, and clumsy excavation led to the loss of the upper floor. A pantry containing flour and newly-moulded loaves, ready for baking, was found here, along with jars containing olives, almonds and fruit.

House of Aristide

It was from this luxurious residence that the valuable finds from the nearby Villa of the Papyri were brought to the surface. The house is wrongly named: a statue found here represents Aeschines, not Aristide. Built on the slopes of Herculaneum, the house rests on powerful supports.

Villa Oplontis

Oplontis is four miles from Pompeii in the modern town of Torre Annunziata. The Circumvesuviana railway stops at Torre Annunziata and the Roman site is located between the SS 18 (Via Vittorio Veneto) and the Via

Roma. This sumptuous Roman residence is on Via Sepolcri in the modern town of **Torre Annunziata**. The seaside villa boasted 92 rooms, and, like Herculaneum, was buried under a huge mud and ash flow. It may be considered one of the best-preserved of the aristocratic Roman villas, since its recent discovery has enabled more exacting methods of excavation to be employed and, as a result, the original layout and decoration has been retained or replicated very closely. Attributed to Poppaea Sabina, wife of Nero, who was said to have been murdered by him in 65 AD, the intact frescoes and mosaics are exceptional. The restored garden surrounded by porticos is a pleasure to walk in. In addition to the private bath complex, lovely reception rooms, and ornamental pool, the servant/slave quarters can also be seen. Numerous household goods and sculptures were found at the villa. If you only have an hour or two to spare looking at Roman houses, Oplontis is an excellent choice as it provides a ready-made slice of life in antiquity. Open Mar-Sept 8:30-7:30 pm; Oct-Feb 8:30-5 pm. €5. The one-day ticket includes the entry price to Boscoreale and Stabia.

Boscoreale

Roman farmsteads and a museum can be visited at Boscoreale, located at a point around the foot of Vesuvius, equidistant from Torre Annunziata and Pompeii, and a short drive or bus journey from either.

The Roman Country Villas

The hills north of Pompeii were a particularly fertile region in antiquity and a number of Roman countryside villas (*villa rustica*) were excavated at Boscoreale in the late 19th and early 20th centuries. These digs were primarily undertaken in the aim of finding precious objects, and the findings are currently held in museums around the world. For example, in the **D'Acunzo Villa**, a series of bronze statuettes were found, which are today on display in Baltimore MD. Frescoes from the nearby **Villa of Publius Fannius Synistor** are now in the Metropolitan Museum of New York, while magnificent paintings, also taken from this villa, have been disseminated to museums around Italy. More than a hundred items of silver tableware, excavated from the **Villa della Pisanella**, are on display in the Louvre Museum. More recent excavations, conducted according to modern scientific standards, have uncovered the structures of the original buildings and reconstruction work has been undertaken. Artifacts from these investigations are in the adjacent antiquarium. At the **Villa Regina** itself, grapes for the famed *Falernum* wine were produced.

The Antiquarium

The museum itself, known as the Antiquarium, displays finds from the surrounding villas, as well as objects from other Roman excavations in the region. The displays, over two rooms, recreate the ambiance of the Roman countryside, particularly the agricultural activities of the area around Vesuvius. The museum is at 14 Via Settetermini, ☎ 081 536 8796. Open Nov-Mar 8:30-3:30 pm and April-Oct 8:30-6 pm.

The Royal Palace Of Portici

Portici is between San Giorgio a Cremano and Ercolano, both stops on the Circumvesuviana rail network and close to the A3 motorway. From Ercolano, stay on the coastal road to visit

the Royal Palace and the Vesuvian villas. Built between 1738 and 1742, for Charles of Bourbon, the palace has a view of Vesuvius at the front, and backs on to the sea. The site acquired by the king was already occupied by some of his nobles, who had built seaside villas here. These pre-existing structures were incorporated into the palace design and the work was assigned to Giovanni Antonio Medrano. From 1741, it was continued by Antonio Canevari. Another striking feature of the location is its position astride the road – which it still occupies.

The royal apartments were on the upper floors, where some of the 18th-century decoration and paintings can still be seen. Gilded stuccowork adorned the Gold Room, and a Chinese room was decorated with Oriental scenes. Among the few works of art that can still be seen at the palace are paintings by Vincenzo Re, and a fresco in the chapel by Giuseppe Bonito. Treasures from the contemporaneous excavations at Herculaneum were also used in the decoration of the palace.

The gardens were an important part of the design: planting was kept at low height, so as not to block the sea view. Fountains, an outdoor theater, an enclosure for ball games, a zoo, and a chapel were incorporated into the grounds.

Murat renovated the palace according to his own taste in the early 19th century, introducing a Neo-Classical style, and, some years later, the Herculaneum artifacts were moved to the new museum at Naples. The palace passed into state ownership in 1860 and today houses the School of Agriculture of the University of Naples. The building is not open to the public as such, but visitors can wander around to the back to enjoy the view of the sweeping terraces, and up to the richly decorated, but empty, first-floor apartments. In 2004 the Cappella Palatina was opened to the public on Sunday. The organ in the chapel belonged to Wolfgang Amadeus Mozart, who was a guest of the Bourbon royal family.

The Golden Mile Of Vesuvian Villas

The "Golden Mile" or *Miglio d'Oro* of splendid 18th-century villas stretches from San Giovanni a Teduccio to Torre Annunziata. These architectural jewels of the Kingdom of Naples, designed by the grand names of the day – Luigi Vanvitelli, Ferdinando Sanfelice and Domenico Vaccaro – typically had Baroque interiors, Neo-Classical columns, and panoramic gardens, with ponds and fountains. But after 1860, with the fall of the Bourbons, the villas went into slow decline, which was not arrested until the creation of the *Ente per le Ville Vesuviane* (Vesuvian Villas Organization) in 1971 (☎ 081 732 2134, www.villevesuviane.net). This organization's ambitious restoration program is still ongoing; their publicity materials to date are only available in Italian. However, for the diligent traveler, especially if equipped with a car, and some knowledge of Italian, a number of the villas are open to the public free of charge in the mornings and are certainly worth a visit while sightseeing at the better-known Roman sites in the region. There are more than one hundred of these villas listed, but most are in private hands, and obtaining access is not always easy.

Villa d'Elboeuf

On the seafront in Portici, the Villa d'Elboeuf was built by Ferdinando Sanfelice in 1711 for Maurizio Emmanuele di Lorena, Prince of Elboeuf. It was Elboeuf who began the excavations at Herculaneum, and his villa quickly became a repository for the exquisite sculpture and paintings found there. The villa was purchased by the king during the building work for his own palace, which did not have a mooring. The villa has lovely stucco work and a superb circular staircase, but is currently looking rather neglected and is not open to the public. The port itself was constructed by the Bourbons in the 18th century.

Villa Campolieto

One of the most beautiful of the 18th-century villas on the Golden Mile, this was the summer residence of the Dukes of

Casacalenda. In 1977 it was acquired by the Vesuvian Villas Organization, which completed restoration work in 1984. Today conferences and cultural events are held here. Begun by Mario Gioffredo in 1755, and completed by Luigi and Carlo Vanvitelli, notable design features include the monumental stairway, similar to that at Caserta, and the vestibule with central cupola. Among the many works of art that can be seen at the villa are frescoes by Jacopo Cestaro, Fedele Fischietti and Gaetano Magri, and lovely trompe l'oeil ceiling landscapes. The villa is not far from the Herculaneum excavations, at 283 Corso Resina, Ercolano. Open Tue-Sun, 10-1 pm. Free entry.

Villa Favorita

Originally built for the Prince of Jaci, the villa became the property of the king on the former's death, and was redesigned by Ferdinando Fuga as a royal residence. In 1768 a party was held here in celebration of the marriage of Ferdinand IV and Maria Carolina of Austria, and the villa was renamed in her honor. Later acquired by a Turkish Pasha, who purportedly lived here with his seraglio, and then the home of a military institution, the villa is currently undergoing restoration. There are some remarkable furnishings: a marble floor in the Galleria was brought from Tiberius' palace on Capri, and Ferdinand IV decorated the property with silk from San Leucio and paintings. The villa is at 291 Corso Resina, Ercolano, and is set in a vast park, landscaped during Leopold's reign the entrance to which is on Via Gabriele D' Annunzio. Only the park is currently open to visitors, Tue-Sun 10-1 pm.

Villa Ruggiero

Constructed for Baron Petti in the mid-18th century, this is a more rustic dwelling, but has a lovely internal courtyard. There is an elegant portal in piperno (volcanic stone) and white marble, above which is a balcony with a view over Vesuvius, decorated with statues of the four seasons. Located at 41 Via Rossi, Ercolano, the villa is open to the public Tue-Sun 10-1 pm; free entry.

Villas of Torre del Greco

Famous as the place where Giacomo Leopardi stayed in 1836 as a guest of Antonio Ranieri, and where he wrote *La Ginestra* and *Il Tramonto della Luna*, the **Villa delle Ginestra** also had a thermal spa built, as it was on the site of ancient Roman baths. In 1962 Naples University acquired the villa, which is currently undergoing a program of restoration. The villa will, it is hoped, be open to the public in the near future. The 18th-century **Palazzo Vallelonga**, in Via Vittorio Emanuele, is another Vanvitellian jewel of the Miglio d'Oro. The town of **Torre del Greco** is also famous for its coral – known as red gold, and transformed into beautiful carvings. There are still some coral workshops in the town, and a museum devoted to the history of this disappearing craft.

Massa di Somma

It is worth making a detour to the small village of Massa di Somma, close to San Sebastiano al Vesuvio, on the slopes of the volcano. Here, in a square known as Largo Lava, you can see the extraordinary spectacle of a lava flow, many yards thick, which finally ground to a halt at this location during the last great eruption of Vesuvius in the 1940s.

■ Caserta

The Royal Palace of Caserta, its medieval hamlet of Caserta Vecchia, and the nearby model Bourbon village of San Leucio are 26 km/16 miles northeast of Naples. A trip here is well worth the short train, car or bus journey required from your lodgings in Naples or on the coast.

The Royal Palace

The Royal Palace is undoubtedly the Versailles of Naples, and in many respects it surpasses that other great Bourbon edifice in France. The vast 18th-century palace dominates the small town of Caserta. Children may be persuaded to come along, once you inform them that some of the scenes from *Star Wars* were filmed here in 1999. This grand royal creation, with its delightful park, was erected between 1752 and 1774 for the young Charles III, Bourbon King of the Two Sicilies, and is considered to be Luigi Vanvitelli's masterpiece, one of the most majestic buildings in Italy.

Charles' aim in building a palace here was not only to have a royal residence that could compete with Versailles, but to provide his kingdom with a new capital farther from the sea, and thereby more secure from attack than the palace in Naples, which the English fleet had threatened to bombard only a few years previously. The architect he chose for the project was the Naples-born son of Dutch painter Gaspar Van Wittel. Calling himself Vanvitelli, the young Luigi followed the craft of his father and painted frescoes in Rome and theater backdrops, before becoming known as an architect with his work on the restoration of several buildings in various parts of Italy. In 1750 Vanvitelli was commissioned to make a survey of the land in Caserta and on May 22 presented his design for the royal palace. The first stone was laid on January 20, 1752 in the presence of the King and Queen and court dignitaries. The work continued until the end of 1759 when Charles succeeded his brother to the Spanish throne. From then on the palace building languished, under eight-year-old Ferdinand IV and a Regency Council presided over by Bernando Tanucci, which was more concerned to economize. However an eruption of Vesuvius in 1767 again brought the question of a

Above: Ruins of Villa Pollio at Capo di Sorrento

Below: Basilica in the town of Minori on the Amalfi Coast

Above: Beach at Meta di Sorrento

Below: The beach at Palinuro, in the Cilento Valley

Above: View of the Sorrento Peninsula

Below: Garden at Villa Fondi, Sorrento

Above: View from Bellevue Syrene Hotel in Sorrento
Below: Tip of the Sorrento Peninsula, with Capri in the distance

secure site for the palace to the forefront. In 1768 Ferdinand married Maria Carolina of Austria, Queen of France, and the couple spent a few days at Caserta to attend the inauguration of the grand waterfall in the park. Work would continue until

the end of the century. Vanvitelli himself died in 1773 at Caserta and was buried in the humble church of San Francesco di Paola, near his still-unfinished masterpiece. His son Carlo continued to work on the project.

Today the palace is one of the most visited monuments in Italy and covers an area of 44,000 square metres/53,000 square yards. The façade is 245 metres/730 feet long, and the palace complex itself is built around four courtyards. The palace has 1,200 rooms, 1,790 windows and 34 staircases.

The Scalone d'Onore – main staircase – is, in its architectural composition, one of the best works of Vanvitelli. At the foot are white marble lions, the work of Paolo Persico and Tommaso Solari. The Palatine Chapel, inaugurated in the presence of Ferdinand IV on Christmas night 1784, hosted Pope Pius IX in exile, who celebrated mass here on Christmas 1849. The richly decorated royal apartments are adorned with paintings and stuccoes. The former royal residents of the palace from the Bourbon dynasty feature in some of the portraits.

The Throne Room, completed in the reign of Ferdinand II in 1845 by the architect Gaetano Genovese, has stuccoes by Tito Angelini and Tommaso Arnaud. Lovely paintings of the Neapolitan school can be seen in the Sala del Consiglio. The marble busts are of Francesco I and of his wife Maria Isabella. Of special interest is the recently restored Presepe Borbonico, with its 1,200 statuettes, mostly representing famous figures from 18th-century Naples.

The Teatro di Corte, the only room completed by Luigi Vanvitelli himself, was designed to be an exact reproduction of the San Carlo opera house on a smaller scale. The Allied High Command established their headquarters here in World War II.

The grandiose theatricality of the palace is replicated in the stunning park and gardens, also designed by Vanvitelli. It takes around half an hour to walk the length of the garden, but buses shuttle back and forth or more expensive horse-drawn carriages are for hire. Interspersed with grandiose 18th-century fountains, inspired by Greco-Roman mythology, the group of sculptures at the foot of the Grand Cascade are by Andrea Violani, Pietro Solari, Paolo Persico and Angelo Brunelli. The view from here back down to the castle is stunning. Nearby is the lovely English garden, created in the late 18th century for the queen by John Andrew Graefer, hired through the efforts of Sir William Hamilton, and Sir Joseph Banks. ☎ 082 3448084, www.reggiadicaserta.org. Open 8:30 am to 7:30 pm. €6. Bus around the park, €1.

Caserta Vecchia

After a morning spent at the palace, the hilltop medieval village of Caserta Vecchia, 10 km/six miles north of town, is an ideal place to have lunch, and indulge in more sightseeing of a very different kind. Probably built on the site of a Roman village, Caserta Vecchia was occupied in 1062 by Richard I of Aversa, and the Norman period would effectively be its golden age, when the Cathedral of San Michele was constructed. In 1442 the town came under Aragonese control and its importance gradually declined. Features of its splendid past can be seen in the **Duomo**, the **Campanile** and the remaining clutch of Norman-style houses. The 12th-century **Cathedral of San Michele** was begun by Bishop Rainulfo and completed by his successor Nicola in 1153, according to the inscription on the central architrave. A fine example of southern Norman architecture, the cathedral has a tufo stone façade, and a Gothic-style bell tower, added a century later. The **Annunziata church** nearby is also in Gothic style, and has a 17th-century portico. The ruins of a 13th-century castle with six towers can be seen to the east of the village, on the hillside. There are a number of restaurants in the town that exploit medieval themes to the full.

San Leucio

The hill of San Leucio, 3.3 km/two miles northwest of Caserta, was acquired in 1750 by Charles III of Bourbon, who wanted to create a hunting reserve and build a lodge here. The **Casino di Belvedere** was constructed by Ferdinand IV a few years later. Silk weaving was a traditional local artisanal activity carried out at home, and between 1789 and 1799 Ferdinand IV planned to create a model working community here. He set up a silk factory and workers' housing, both of which have been preserved.

■ Places to Eat

The Campi Flegrei

La Misenetta, 2 Via Lungolago, Bacoli, ☎ 081 523 4169. €€. Imaginative dishes are served, such as oyster risotto, aubergine pastry and sea bream with saffron, in a seaside location.

DINING PRICE CHART	
Price for an entrée	
€	€10-29
€€	€30-49
€€€	€50+

Da Giona, 8 Via Dragonara, Capo Miseno, ☎ 081 523 4659. €€. Seafood linguine and baked fish are specialties.

Old Friends, 3 Via Cuma, Fusaro, ☎ 081 804 0115, €€. Pizzas, and steak à la Florentine.

Lo Scoglio, 1 Via Stufe di Nerone, Pozzuoli, ☎ 081 868 8040. €€. Attractive location, and good aperitivi.

L'Angolo del Paradiso, 24 Via G. Marconi, Monte di Procida, ☎ 081 868 3369. €€. Grilled meat and fish; homemade desserts.

The Islands

La Colombaia del Quisisana, 2 Via Camerelle, Capri, ☎ 081 837 0788. €€€. Poolside restaurant at the famed hotel. Open evenings only. Traditional Capri specialties such as ravioli with fresh cherry tomatoes, and fish dishes.

Da Paolino, 11 Via Palazzo a Mare, Marina Grande, Capri, ☎ 081 837 6102. €€€. Classic dishes like fresh fish, aubergine pasta and, for dessert, *delizia al limone*. Closed Wed.

Le Grottelle, 3 Via Matermania, Capri, ☎ 081 837 5719. €€. Local specialties like pasta and beans, or fresh grilled fish.

Da Tonino, 12 Via Dentecale, Capri, ☎ 081 837 6718. €€. Spaghetti with clams, quails Capri-style, and squid are on the menu in this shaded terrace restaurant.

Verginiello, 19 Via Mulo, Capri, ☎ 081 837 7140. €€. Pizzas and typical food from the region; garden and seaview terrace.

Coco Gelo, Piazzale Aragonese, Ischia, ☎ 081 981 1823. €€. Ischian cuisine and fresh fish.

Gennaro, 32 Via Porto, Ischia, ☎ 081 992 917. €€. Fish and homemade desserts.

Il Melograno, 110 Via Mazzella, Forio, Ischia, ☎ 081 998 450. €€. Welcoming atmosphere, with kitchen open until late in the evening.

Dal Pescatore, 5 Piazza O' Troia, Sant'Angelo, Ischia, ☎ 081 999 206. €€. Fish specialties.

Lo Scoglio, 58 Via Cava Ruffano, Sant'Angelo, Ischia, ☎ 081 999 529. €€. Relatively inexpensive dining for this chic location.

Cantinone, 55 Via Roma, Procida, ☎ 081 896 8811. €€. Fish and local specialties.

Crescenzo, 62 Piazza Marina Chiaioella, Procida ☎ 081 896 7255. €€. One of several restaurants on this waterfront location.

Gorgonia, 50 Marina Corricella, ☎ 081 810 1060. €€. Spectacular seafront dining. Busy on weekends.

The Vesuvian Region

Il Principe, 8 Piazza B.Longo, Pompeii, ☎ 081 850 5566, www.ilprincipe.com. €€€. Menus based on ancient Roman cuisine are offered on summer evenings.

President, Piazza Schettini, Pompeii, ☎ 081 850 7245. €€€. Fresh pasta with prawns.

Punta Quattro Venti, 59 Via Marittima, Ercolano, ☎ 081 777 3041. €€. Risotto with zucchini, and other specialties of the house.

Summa Villa, 32 Via Prima Traversa Pizzone Cassante, Somma Vesuviana, ☎ 081 531 7880. €€. Tagliatelle with beans; lemon dessert. Closed Mon and Tues.

Pizzeria Carlo Alberto, 15 Via Carlo Alberto, Pompeii, ☎ 081 863 3231. €. Pizzas, focaccetta and Grappa del Vesuvio.

Caserta

Angolo Verde, 21 Via Redentore, Caserta, ☎ 082 3442 076. €€. A pizzeria with a garden. Closed Fri.

La Castellana, 4 Via Torre, Caserta Vecchia, ☎ 082 3371 230. €€

Antica Locanda, Piazza della Seta, San Leucio, ☎ 082 3305 444. €€. Pasta and risotto specialties.

A Marchesina, Caserta Vecchia, ☎ 082 3764 8684. €. Sandwiches and local wine.

■ Bars & Cafés

The Campi Flegrei

Caffè Serapide, 233 Via Campana, Pozzuoli ☎ 081 526 3200.

Bar Grajales, 264 Piazza Moro, Pozzuoli, ☎ 081 866 1200.

Bar Caffetteria Pino, 5 Via Monteruschello, Pozzuoli, ☎ 081 524 1756.

Brivido Bar, 14 Via Lungo Lago, Bacoli, ☎ 081 523 2669. Pastries and ice creams.

Zanzibar Caffè, 176 Viale Olimpico, ☎ 081 523 2119.

Bar Di Meo, Piazza A. de Gasperi, Baia, ☎ 081 868 7082.

The Islands

Bar Tiberio, Piazza Umberto I, Capri, ☎ 081 837 9268. Good cakes and cocktail snacks.

Buonocore, 35 Via Vittorio Emanuele, Capri, ☎ 081 837 7826. Famed for its traditional Caprese sweets.

Scialapopolo, 31 Via Le Botteghe, Capri, ☎ 081 837 0246. Popular pasticceria.

Calise, Piazza Marina, Casamicciola Terme, ☎ 081 994 080.

Blue Moon, 50 Via Roma, Lacco Ameno, ☎ 081 996 030.

Belmare, Via Maronti, Barano d'Ischia, ☎ 081 905 655.

Bar Roma, 163 Via Roma, Procida, ☎ 081 896 7460. Popular for its sweets.

Bar del Cavaliere, 42 Via Roma, Procida, ☎ 081 810 1074. Great for cocktails. Closed Mon.

The Vesuvian Region

Bar della Stazione, 40 Via dell'Osservatorio, ☎ 081 777 6347. It is worth making a detour to the Bar della Stazione, near the location of the former funicular railway, to have a drink and a chat with the owner Andrea de Gregorio, who has many interesting stories about of life on Vesuvius.

Arturo Bar, 11 Piazza Trieste, Ercolano, ☎ 081 739 3471. Ice creams and pastries.

Bar Dei Papiri, 2 Via A. Consiglio, Ercolano, ☎ 081 732 1002.

Bar Rosso E Nero, 2 Via A. Diaz, Pompeii, ☎ 081 863 1353.

Barret Caffè, 23 Via Roma, Pompeii, ☎ 081 863 4936.

Blu Moon Cafè, 6 Via Cavalcavia del Sarno, Pompei, ☎ 081 850 4003.

Peluso, 6 Via Lepanto, Pompeii, ☎ 081 863 1238. Good sweets and ice creams.

Caserta

Gran Caffè Margherita, 1 Piazza Dante, Caserta, ☎ 082 3321 107. Pastries and sweets.

Antichi Caffè d'Italia di Toraldo, 89 Piazza Vanvitelli, ☎ 082 3279 310.

Bar Adua, 82 Via Roma, ☎ 082 3325 191.

Bar Canzanella, 57 Via G. Verdi, ☎ 082 3325 086.

Bar d'Amico Vincenzo, 200 Corso Trieste, ☎ 082 3326 125.

■ Places To Stay

The Campi Flegrei

Cala Moresca Club, 25 Via del Faro, Capo Miseno, ☎ 081 523 5595. €€. There are 27 rooms, some with sea view. A private path leads to the beach. Features include an attractive swimming pool and a restaurant.

Hotel San Germano, 41 Via Beccadelli, Agnano, ☎ 081 570 5422. €€. This 105-room hotel with conference center attracts mainly business travelers, but if you want to stay outside Naples, while close to transportation links, its pool set in lovely gardens offers a tranquil oasis in the Cami Flegrei.

Dal Tedesco, 12 Via Temporini, Bacoli, ☎ 081 868 7175. €€. A small, nine-room hotel. Its delightful restaurant offers panoramic views of the bay.

Camping Il Vulcano, 161 Via Solfatara, Pozzuoli, ☎ 081 526 7413. €. This campground, on the grounds of the private nature park, with its volcanic attractions, offers bungalows and a pool, as well as tent sites for campers.

HOTEL PRICE CHART	
For a double room for two	
€	€50-150
€€	€151-250
€€€	€251+

The Islands

Capri Palace, 2 Via Capodimonte, Anacapri, ☎ 081 978 0111, www.capri-palace.com. €€€. Dubbed the hotel of the stars, this is five-star luxury.

Grand Hotel Quisisana, 2 Via Camerelle, Capri, ☎ 081 837 0788 www.quisi.com. €€€. A 19th-century sanatorium, and now one of the top hotels of the island.

Mezzatorre Resort Spa, 23 Via San Montano, Lacco Ameno, Ischia, ☎ 081 986 111, www.mezzatorre.it. €€€.

'A **Paziella**, 4 Via Padre Re. Gesualdo, Capri, ☎ 081 837 0044, www.hotellapazziella.com. €€. Good location near the Piazzetta.

Ambassador Weber, 118 Via Marina Piccola, Capri, ☎ 081 837 0141, www.hotelweber.com. €€. All modern conveniences, and gym.

Caesar Augustus, 4 Via G.Orlandi, Anacapri, ☎ 081 837 3395, www.caesar-augustus.com. €€. Great views from this panoramic location.

Grand Hotel Punta Molino Terme, 23 Via Lungomare Colombo, Ischia, ☎ 081 991 1544, www.puntamolino.it. €€. Sea view and private garden.

San Montano, 26 Via Nuova Montevico, Lacco Ameno, Ischia, ☎ 081 994 033, www.sanmontano.com. €€. Panoramic views; thermal treatments.

Cristallo Palace, 1 Via Eddomade, Casamicciola, Ischia, ☎ 081 954 4377, www.cristallopalace.it. €€. Pool, gym and garden.

Celeste, 6 Via Rivoli, Procida, ☎ 081 896 7488, www.hotelceleste.it. €€. Family-owned 35-room hotel, offering home cooking. Near Vivara Island and within walking distance of the beach and the resort of Marina di Chiaiolella.

Riviera Hotel, 38 bis Via G. da Procida, Procida, ☎ 081 810 1812, www.hotelriviera.it. €€. Unpretentious, 25-room hotel on the Chiaiolella hillside. All rooms have views of the sea.

La Tosca, 5 Via D.Birago, Capri, ☎ 081 837 0989. €. Quiet and simple hotel with a view of the Faraglioni from the terrace.

Stella Maris, 27 Via Roma, Capri, ☎ 081 837 0452. €. Rooms with sea view, located 60 feet from the Piazzetta.

Villa Eva, 8 Via La Fabbrica, Anacapri, ☎ 081 8371549, www.villaeva.com. €. Guest house with swimming pool and parking.

Tirrenia Roberts, 27 Via Mulo, Marina Piccola, Capri, ☎ 081 837 0370. €. Rooms with breakfast and a superb pool overlooking the sea at this lovely villa on the Via Mulo, which leads down to Marina Piccola.

Caprihouse, 17 Via Gradoni Sopramonte, Capri, ☎ 338 715 9958, www.caprihouse.it. €. Apartment to rent in Capri.

Le Mìgnole, Via Duca degli Abruzzi – Barano d'Ischia, ☎ 329.644 0984. €. Apartment to rent in Ischia.

Appartamenti America, 12 Via Chiaia di Rose, Sant'Angelo, Ischia, ☎ 081 904 332, www.appartamenti-america.it. €. Apartment in the chic Sant'Angelo. The owners are also proprietors of the popular restaurant across the street.

The Vesuvian Region

Punta Quattro Venti, 59 Via Marittima, Ercolano, ☎ 081 777 3041. €€€. Four-star hotel close to the excavations.

La Mela, 1 Via Panoramica, Boscoreale. ☎ 081 537 2889. €€. Two-star hotel with a popular restaurant, close to the museum of Boscoreale.

Hotel Amleto, 6 Via Bartolo Longo, Pompeii, ☎ 081 863 1004, www.hotelamleto.it. €. Family-run hotel in the town center.

Zeus, Villa dei Misteri, Pompeii, ☎ 081 861 5320. €. Large and well-equipped campsite near the excavations.

Caserta

Europa, 60 Via Roma, Caserta ☎ 082 3325 400. €€. Modern town hotel with 58 rooms, fitness center and sauna.

Jolly, 9 Via Veneto, Caserta ☎ 082 3325 222. €€. Hotel with 107 air-conditioned rooms in an ideal location – 600 yards from the famous royal palace.

Eden, 24 Via Verdi, Caserta ☎ 082 3355 617. €. Unpretentious two-star hotel in Caserta, ideal for budget travelers.

Colleverde, Via Colleverde, Caserta. €. *Agriturismo* farm.

■ Shopping

Clothes, Leather Goods & Accessories

Canfora, Via Camerelle, Capri, ☎ 081 837 0487, www.canforacapri. Boutique selling handmade leather sandals. Jacqueline Onassis, Grace Kelly, Princess Caroline, Naomi Campbell and other celebrities have shopped here.

Mariorita Store, Piazza Vittoria Anacapri, ☎ 081 837 1426, www.mariorita.com. Clothing and handicraft store in the center of Anacapri.

Anna Boutique, Via F. Serena, Capri, ☎ 081 837 0733. Clothing store near the Hotel Quisisana.

Daniel Boutique, 24 Viale Axel Munthe, Anacapri, ☎ 081 837 1744. Specializing in clothing, souvenir, and inlay work, located in the center of Anacapri.

La Perla Gioielli, Piazza Umberto, Capri, ☎ 081 837 0641. Famous clients of this jewelry store in the Piazzetta have included Maria Callas and Clark Gable.

Grazia Vozza, 22 Via Li Campi, Capri, ☎ 081 837 4010, www.graziavozza.com. Jewelry store set on a small street in the center of Capri.

La Fiorente, 4 Via Roma, Capri, ☎ 081 837 7083, www.lafiorentecapri.com. Emeralds, pearls, and delicate coral among precious items on sale here.

Maja Gioielli, 4 Piazzale Aragonese, Ischia, ☎ 081 993 504. Coral jewelry.

L'Angolo, 1 Via Vitt Emanuele, Procida, ☎ 081 896 7202. Craft and gift shops

Carthusia Profumi, 2 Viale Matteotti, Capri, ☎ 081 837 0368, www.carthusia.com. Local perfumes produced from flowers and herbs grown on Capri, reputedly after methods used by the Carthusian monks of San Giacomo.

Galleria dell'Arte, 105 Via G. Orlando, Anacapri, ☎ 081 837 1082, www.capri-miniatura.com. Hand-made and -painted ceramics in this artisanal workshop.

The Seagull, 25 Via Roma, Capri, ☎ 081 837 0852. Hand-painted Italian ceramics, shipped all over the world.

L'Oasi Ceramiche, 1 Via Capodimonte, Anacapri, ☎ 081 8373646. Brightly colored ceramic souvenirs.

Arte & Piastrelle, 9 Via Trieste e Trento, Anacapri, ☎ 328 327 8047. Artistic creations in majolica, tile, stone and marble.

Ceramiche Cianciarelli, 141 Via L. Mazzella, Ischia, ☎ 081 984 674. Ceramic items in pastel colors.

Books, Antiques & Old Prints

Capri Internet Point, 13 Piazza Vittoria, Anacapri, ☎ 081 837 3283. Newspapers, magazines, and souvenirs.

Atelier di Mario Mazzella, 90 Via L. Mazzella, Ischia, ☎ 081 993 244. Watercolors.

Libreria Graziella, Via Vittorio Emanuele, Procida, ☎ 081 896 0378. Food and confectionery.

Mandara, 4 Via Santa Caterina a Chiaia, ☎ 081 417 348. Delicious cheeses and cured meats are among the goodies offered here.

Limoncello di Capri, 79 Via Roma, Capri, ☎ 081 837 5561, www.limoncello.com. The famous lemon liqueur of the Bay of Naples.

Capannina Più, 39 Via Le Botteghe, Capri, ☎ 081 837 8899, www.capannina-capri.com. Gourmet shop selling wines, spirits, local foods and souvenirs.

Ischia Sapori, 3 Via Morgione, Ischia, ☎ 081 984 213. Food products from Ischia including rum babas, limoncello and jams.

Cantine di Pietrarcia, 267 Via Provinciale Panza, Forio, Ischia, ☎ 081 908 206, www.pietratorcia.it. A selection of Ischian wines.

Limoncello di Procida, 8 Piazza dei Martiri, Procida, ☎ 081 896 0556. The name speaks for itself. Limoncello is the famous lemon liqueur of the region.

Sirenetta, 70 Via Roma, Procida, ☎ 081 896 9544. Local food products.

■ Entertainment

Music & Dance

Michelemma, 27 Via Rosini, Pozzuoli, ☎ 081 526 2749. Jazz club and pizzeria, open summer time only. Currently undergoing renovation.

Most Café, 42 Via Pergolesi, Pozzuoli, ☎ 334 359 8158. Ultra-modern bar.

Aramacao, 6 Via Lago d'Averno Pozzuoli, ☎ 081 866 5344. Multi-room disco with Latin music.

Caraibi, 253 Via Campana, Pozzuoli, ☎ 081 526 9444. Live music with a tropical ambience.

La Locura, 3 Via Arco Felice Vecchio Pozzuoli, ☎ 081 586 2870. Bar and disco on two floors.

Musikó, Via Solfatara, Pozzuoli, ☎ 338 283 3817. Live music and terrace with view.

Play Off, 506 Via Miliscola, Lago Lucrino, ☎ 081 868 8586. Sporting complex with piano bar and disco. Tango lessons and shows weekly.

Aqabah, 75 Via Panoramica 75, Monte di Procida, ☎ 347 560 0031. Amphitheater-style disco with panoramic view of the Gulf of Bacoli.

Nabilah, Via Spiaggia Romana, Cuma, ☎ 335 527 8189. Elegant beachside nightclub.

Red Sunset, Molo di Torregaveta, Bacoli, ☎ 081 853 5358. Restaurant and nightclub.

Antica Birreria Kronenbourg, Parco Edenlandia, ☎ 081 239 4090. Live music in the evenings.

Sciuscia, Via Viulo, Ercolano, ☎ 081 777 9898, www.sciusciaclub.it. Restaurant with live shows and a disco on weekends. Sunday night is Latin night.

Baraonda, 6 Via Roma, Capri, ☎ 081 837 7147. Popular discotheque and bar with three zones, for dancing, chatting at the bar, and for relaxing.

Musmé, 61 Via Camerelle, Capri, ☎ 081 837 6011. Dance club in Capri town, frequented by celebrities such as supermodel Naomi Campbell.

Number Two, 1 Via Camerelle, Capri, ☎ 081 837 7078. Energetic dance club.

Underground, 259 Via G. Orlandi, Anacapri, ☎ 081 837 2523. Enjoy hip hop and house music with DJs Antonio and Filippo in this year-round venue.

Zeus, 103 Via G. Orlandi, Anacapri, ☎ 081 837 1169. The most famous nightclub of Capri.

Negombo, San Montano Lacco Ameno, Ischia, ☎ 081 986 390. Nightclub and restaurant.

Neptunus, 11 Via delle Rose Sant'Angelo Ischia, ☎ 081 999 702. Piano bar and restaurant.

Kiwi Jam, Via Luigi Mazzella, Ischia Ponte, ☎ 081 991 698. Music bar open from 10 pm until dawn. Closed Mon.

New Valentino, 97 Corso V Colonna, Ischia, ☎ 081 982 569. Celebrities like Gwyneth Paltrow flock to this lively nightclub in summer, run by the Bondavilli brothers.

Dal Pescatore, Piazzetta Marina Sant'Angelo, Ischia, ☎ 081 999 206. Piano bar.

Ciaomare, 155 Corso Vittoria Colonna, Ischia, ☎ 081 981 465. Piano bar and disco.

■ Adventures

Beaches

Lido Turistico, 56 Via Lido Miliscola, Bacoli, ☎ 081 523 5228. Open 9 am to 3 pm daily for sun loungers, etc. Restaurant is also open in the evening. Pizzeria on site. Music in the evening.

Lido Miliscola, 51 Via Miliscola, Bacoli, ☎ 081 523 3122.

Lo Scoglioni, Via Stufa di Nerone, Bacoli, ☎ 081 868 8040. Lido concession with thermal baths and sauna. €10 for access to the thermal baths including the rental of a sun lounger. Open all year 8 am to midnight. Closed Wed.

La Fontelina, Faraglioni, Capri, ☎ 081.8370845. Chic beach concession, with restaurant serving lunch.

Da Gioia, Località Marina Piccola, Capri, ☎ 081 837 7702, www.dagioiacapri.com. Family-run concession in the Bay of Marina Piccola with solarium on the seafront and restaurant with seafood specialties.

Bagni Tiberio, 41 Via Palazzo a Mare, Capri, ☎ 081 837 0703. Beach club on pebble beach, with restaurant.

Lido del Faro, Località Punta Carena, Anacapri, ☎ 081 837 1798, www.lidofaro.com. Beach club with terrace restaurant overlooking the sea under the lighthouse of Punta Carena, renowned for seafood.

Bagni Nettuno, Località Grotta Azzurra, Anacapri, ☎ 081 837 1362, www.nettuno-capri.com. Located close to the famous Blue Grotto.

Da Gelsomina Migliera, 72 Via Migliara, Anacapri, ☎ 081 837 1499, www.dagelsomina.com. With poolside snack bar and restaurant, overlooking the sea.

Da Franco, Via T Morgera Casamicciola Terme, Ischia, ☎ 081 994 825. Beach with bar. Book in advance for July and August.

Ricciulillo, 22 Lungomare C. Colombo, Ischia, ☎ 081 993 679. Beach club and restaurant with great views of Ischia castle and Capri.

La Conchiglia, 11 Via Pizzaco, Procida, ☎ 081 896 7602. Beach club and restaurant in the lovely Chiaia Bay; hot and cold showers, loungers, sun umbrellas and *pedalos* for rent.

La Capannina, 16 Lungomare C. Colombo, Procida, ☎ 081 896 0253. Snack bar and beach club on the Chiaiolella beach.

Lido di Procida, 6 Lungomare C. Colombo, Procida, ☎ 081 896 7531. Beachside snack bar and restaurant.

Sea Sports & Tours

Associazione Aliseo, 49 Via Lucullo Bacoli, ☎ 081 854 5784, www.associazionealiseo.it. Boat trips to the sunken Roman city with undersea viewing area.

Gruppo Motoscafisti, 282 Piazza Marina Grande, Capri, ☎ 081 837 7714, www.motoscafisticapri.com. Boat service for the Grotta Azzurra and excursions around the island.

Capri Relax Boats, Via Cristoforo Colombo, 64 Marina Grande, Capri, ☎ 081 837 2047. Excursions by sea in traditional wooden boats known as *gozzi*.

Capri Yacht Charter, 3 Piazza Vittoria, 3 Capri, ☎ 333 569 1896, www.capriyachtcharter.com. Motor yacht for hire.

Capri Boats, 31 Via Acquaviva, Capri, ☎ 081 8376471, www.capriboats.com. Tours around the island with lunch in traditional *gozzi* boats.

Sercomar Boat Rental, 64 Via C. Colombo, 64 Capri, ☎ 081 837 8781, www.caprisub.com. Boat excursions around Capri, plus diving lessons.

Ischia Barche, 3 Via Pontano Ischia, ☎ 081 984 854. Boat excursions around the island.

Nautica Ischia Mare, 20 Via Castiglione, Casamicciola, Ischia, ☎ 081 333 1366. Fishing trips and boat excursions.

Protours, Via Marina Chiaiolella, Procida, ☎ 360 664 634, www.protours.it. Water taxi service.

Procida Diving Center, 6 Lungomare C. Colombo, Marina Chiaiolella, ☎ 081 896 8385. Diving courses and trips.

Meditur, Piazza Marina Chiaiolella, Procida, ☎ 081 810 1934. Boat moorings for yacht owners.

Procida Yachting Club, Via Marina Chiaiolella, ☎ 081 810 1481. Daily, monthly and seasonal berthing for yachts.

Walking, Hiking & Horseback Riding

Parco Nazionale del Vesuvio, 8 Piazza Municipio San Sebastiano al Vesuvio, ☎ 081 771 0939, www.parconazionaledelvesuvio.it. Walking, hiking and horseback riding.

Guide Alpine Vulcanologiche della Campania, ☎ 081 777 5720. Tours of volcanic regions of Campania, guided by experts on the subject.

Naples World Wildlife Fund, ☎ 081 726 6511. Guided tours of the Astroni Nature Reserve.

David and Armando Parlato, ☎ 333 800 742 and 338 335 2169. Commercial guides for the Vesuvius region. The National Park of Vesuvius produces fact sheets enabling groups to take walks around the region, but there are also private operators like the Parlato family, who will take tourists on walks up to and around the crater for a fee.

Capritime Tours, 9 Traversa La Guardia, Anacapri, ☎ 081 838 2188, www.capritime.com. Guided walks around the island; day and longer tours available.

Capri Trekking, Anacapri, ☎ 081 837 3407. Guided tours along nature trails; must to be booked and confirmed 20 days before.

Club Sportivo Ippico, Via Mario d'Ambra, Forio, Ischia, ☎ 081 908 518. Horseback riding excursions with guide.

Fitness Centers & Spas

Capri Beauty Farm, 2 Via Capodimonte, Anacapri, ☎ 081 837 3800, www.capribeautyfarm.com. Housed in the five-star Capri Palace Hotel, they offer personalized treatment programs.

Quisi Spa, 2 Via Camerelle, Capri, ☎ 081 837 0788, www.quisiclub.com. A wide range of facial and body treatments at the spa of the Quisisana Hotel.

Sauna Massage by Glauco, 39 via V. Emanuele, Capri, ☎ 081 837 0133. VIP beauty masseur at La Palma Hotel, Glauco's clients have included Kirk Douglas, Nurejev, and Richard Gere.

Athena Fitness, 7 Via Occhio Marino, Capri, ☎ 081 837 5586. Gym open from 9:30 to 9:30, year-round. Personal trainers available.

The Poseidon Gardens, Bay of Citara, Ischia, ☎ 081 908 7111. Hot-water springs and 20 thermal-water pools.

Aphrodite Apollon Thermal Gardens, Sant'Angelo, Ischia, ☎ 081 999 219. Thermal spa at the Hotel Miramare.

Queen Isabel Thermal Baths, Lacco Ameno, Ischia. Connected by sky bridge to the Regina Isabella hotel, the therapy center – on the site of the ancient Roman thermal baths of Santa Restituta – offers programs for health, beauty and relaxation, including mineral and mud baths.

The Sorrento Peninsula

In this Chapter

A getaway destination since Roman times, the magnificent sea views and fragrant citrus groves of the 100-km/60-mile peninsula, dominated by the Lattari hills, continue to attract tourists today. Well situated for excursions to Pompeii, Herculaneum and the ever-popular island of Capri, Sorrento is also a base from which to explore Naples and the Amalfi Coast. The peninsula was reputedly named after the legendary Sirens of Greek mythology who lured passing sailors onto the treacherous rocks. The name Sorrento, in fact, is thought to derive from the Greek, meaning "Land of the Sirens." Known as a destination for sun-worshippers, the peninsula offers up cultural clues to its long history in the ruins of sumptuous Roman villas described by many celebrated visitors and now incorporated into some of the grand hotels. The hordes of young tourists who vacation here are today more interested in the lively bars, restaurants and nightclubs of the coastal resorts, but visitors can also enjoy walks along the craggy coastlines, and into the mountainous interior, or sailing trips around the Bay of Naples from one of the small ports of the peninsula.

The charms of the historic town of Sorrento, which continue to attract the bulk of visitors to the region, more than make up for the crush of tourists in the summer months. However, with efficient and inexpensive transportation between the several coastal resorts on the Circumvesuviana trains or on the SITA buses, you might want to consider basing yourself in the somewhat less expensive and certainly less busy towns around Sorrento.

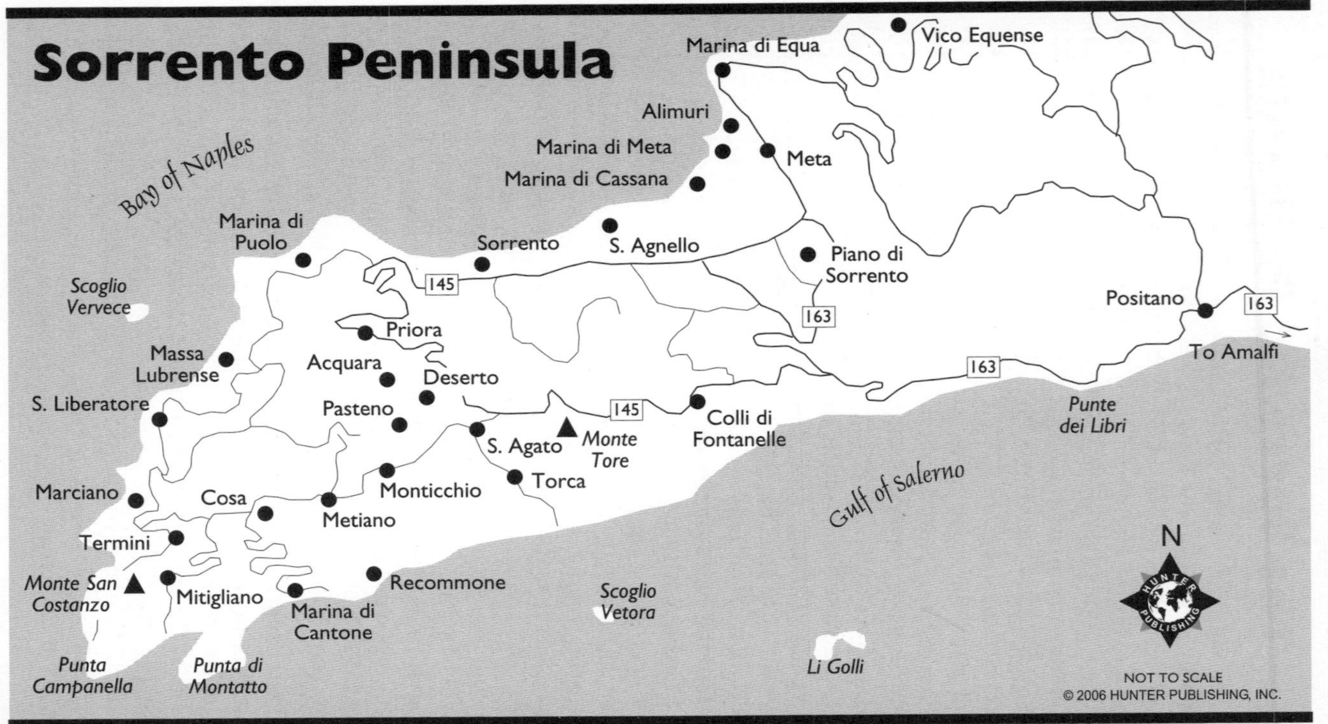
Sorrento Peninsula
Bay of Naples
Marina di Equa
Vico Equense
Alimuri
Marina di Meta
Meta
Marina di Cassana
Marina di Puolo
Sorrento
S. Agnello
Piano di Sorrento
Positano
163
To Amalfi
145
Scoglio Vervece
Priora
Massa Lubrense
Acquara
Deserto
163
S. Liberatore
Pasteno
145
Colli di Fontanelle
Punte dei Libri
S. Agato
Monte Tore
Torca
Marciano
Cosa
Monticchio
Metiano
Gulf of Salerno
Termini
N
Monte San Costanzo
Mitigliano
Recommone
Marina di Cantone
Scoglio Vetora
HUNTER PUBLISHING
Punta Campanella
Punta di Montatto
Li Golli
NOT TO SCALE
© 2006 HUNTER PUBLISHING, INC.

Castellammare di Stabia is a busy port town, known principally for its thermal baths and for the superb Roman villas that can be visited nearby. From both Stabia and **Vico Equense**, journeys to the lovely Monte Faito can be made. Vico has a number of bars and restaurants: the pizzerias are much appreciated by Neapolitans who round off their evening with an ice cream in one of the many *gelaterias*. Dining out is generally much cheaper here than in Sorrento. The beaches of **Meta** and **Piano** are also popular with day-trippers from Naples in the summer.

If you want a rural getaway not too far from the coastal resorts, you might consider a stay in one of the many *agriturismo* properties in the hills around these towns. The elegance that Grand Tour visitors enjoyed, however, really begins at **Sant'Agnello**, within walking distance of Sorrento, and where some of the loveliest cliff-top hotels are found.

On the other side of Sorrento, the district of **Massa Lubrense** stretches to the tip of the peninsula, with its lovely views of the island of Capri. This is the most rugged part of the region, and beautiful drives and walks extend to the protected zone of **Punta Campanella**, up winding paths to Massa itself, then Sant'Agata and down again to the picturesque fishing ports of **Marina della Lobra** and **Marina di Cantone**.

Immortalized by artists and writers, the Sorrento Peninsula, with its remarkable cliffside towns, olive- and citrus-covered hills, and emerald seas, has as many quiet hamlets offering picturesque views as it does bustling promenades lined with lively bars, shops and restaurants. Thus the visitor can pick and choose his vacation to suit, and, whether ensconced in a classic, sea-view Sorrento hotel or in a farmhouse perched on the Lattari slopes, can take advantage of the many faces of this promontory straddling the Gulfs of Naples and Salerno.

■ Castellammare di Stabia

Renowned as a spa resort since ancient times, Stabia also has a medieval castle and stunning Roman villas to visit. The town's museum displays objects from the site. The busy working port is not just a naval yard: there are attractive sea-front restaurants. Try the local specialty, a large biscuit garnished with your choice of delicious pickles.

While the bustling town does not compete for tourists in the same way as the elegant coastal resorts farther along the peninsula, the bargain clothes shops, and no-frills eateries will certainly appeal to travelers on a budget.

The very helpful **tourist office** is in Piazza Matteotti (☎ 081 871 1334). Stabia can be reached on the Circumvesuviana train from either Naples or Sorrento. A cable car service to the summit of Monte Faito is also in the Circumvesuviana railway station.

The Roman Villas

The archeological excavations of Roman **Stabiae** are well worth a visit. They will give you a better understanding of the size and arrangement of these patrician residences than any at Pompeii. Furthermore, unlike Pompeii, they are seldom crowded with visitors and, despite the turnstiles, do not charge an access fee. Frescoes and other artifacts from the villas are housed in the **Antiquarium**, Castellammare's museum. However, this was closed in 2004 with no definite plans for reopening, as it is intended to move the collection to another location. The tourist office in Piazza Matteotti should be able to update you on this. The excavations are about half an hour's walk from town. Take the Via Regina Margherita from the rail station and follow the signs to the Via Passeggiata Archeologica, off of which both sites are located.

The villas and farmhouses of the Roman settlement of Stabiae were a mile or two outside the present town at Varano. The archeological site comprises four residential buildings, set on the hillside with panoramic views over the Gulf of Naples. Buried by the eruption of Vesuvius in 79 AD, they were partly excavated in the 18th century, but only completely uncovered after World War II. Today, the villas can be seen at two locations: the Villa Arianna, with the adjacent second complex, is the first site visitors come to on the Via Passeggiata Archeologica. Farther down the road is Villa San Marco.

The oldest of the buildings is the 13-room **Villa Arianna**, named for a painting of Arianna found in the *triclinium*. In the 1750s Karl Weber excavated the site for the Bourbons, removing many precious artifacts (for example the paintings of Flora and Medea, now in the Naples Museum), but leaving the wall paintings untouched and much of the structure itself still buried. Villa Arianna has four main areas built at different periods: a Tuscan atrium and adjoining rooms, servants' quarters and baths, and a *palestra*. The wall paintings and floor mosaics are superb, and provide one of the best examples we have today of the elegant decorative features of patrician homes in the ancient Roman era. Separated from Villa Arianna by a narrow alley, the ***Secondo Complesso*** consists of a *peristilium* with a portico on three sides, and thermal quarters, including a *calidarium* and a *tepidarium*. Mosaic floors originally found here can today be seen in the Naples Museum.

Villa San Marco is half a mile farther along the road. Also constructed at various times from the era of Augustus, Claudius and Flavius, the rooms around the atrium are decorated with frescoes, but the wrestling cupids that once decorated the thermal quarters are now in the local museum, while the roof art that once adorned the *peristilium* was lost after the structure collapsed during the 1980 earthquake. Nevertheless, the magnificence of the villa can still be admired from the garden and pool, with its portico, off of which lead the beautifully decorated rooms.

Villa Pastore, last of the Roman houses of Stabiae, cannot currently be visited, as it is still buried and awaiting purchase by the state and eviction of tenants in illegal new constructions built around it. Payment to see the current archeological site is made in conjunction with visits to other Roman sites of the region (three sites €5; or the five-site card, valid for three days, including Herculaneum, Pompeii, Oplontis, Stabiae, and Boscoreale, is €18). In fact, when you turn up at Stabiae, your ticket is not checked. ☎ 081 857 5331. Open Nov-Mar 8:30 to 5 pm; Apr-Oct 8:30-7:30.

A number of pizzerias and bars line the Passeggiata Archeologica, but they serve food only in the evening, except in July and August when some of them are open all day. If you feel the need for a refreshing dip with your lunch, try the *Le Piscine* complex, which has an Olympic-style covered swimming pool, sun loungers, restaurant and self-service café. The entrance fee for the pool is €8. Tables are provided for those who wish to bring their own food.

The Terme of Stabia

As an alternative to the swimming pool, on the road back from the excavations, take the Viale delle Terme to sample some of the curative water treatments. The large new thermal bath complex covers a 50-acre site, and offers all types of massage, and fitness routines, steam and Turkish baths, as well as thermal treatments. Entrance to the site is €5, with additional treatments priced individually. Viale delle Terme 3/5, Castellammare di Stabia, ☎ 081 391 3278.

The thermal baths of Stabia date back to Roman times, when the 28 water springs were each considered to have medical properties. The old thermal baths of the town, or *Antiche Terme*, date back to 1833 and are in Piazza Amendola. These are also worth a visit and offer free access for those wishing to drink one of the several types of water offered. All have a slightly salty taste. Open 7 am-6:30 pm. ☎ 081 871 4422. Also in the town is a 16th-century cathedral, and the Palazzo Farnese, now the town hall.

The Quisisana Palace

The Viale delle Terme leads to the Via Panoramica, which winds up and around the town to offer lovely views of Vesuvius and the Bay of Naples. A side-street will take you up old paths to the grandiose former Royal Palace at Quisisana. This is now being restored and is currently not open to visitors. An educational institution is due to be housed here. When the site reopens, the gardens should be well worth a visit. The number of famous visitors to the Quisisana Palace is outstanding. In addition to Bourbon Kings and Queens, Horatio Nelson convalesced here and Prince Christian Frederick of Denmark stayed at the house in 1820. The palace is mentioned in countless Grand Tour travel accounts but has a history dating back to medieval times. The original structure was built by Robert of Anjou in 1310 and was later extended as a residence of the Angevin rulers, in particular of King Ladislao and his sister Giovanna II. Boccaccio set one of the tales of his *Decameron* here.

From Quisisana, a small path winds up to Monte Faito. Steer clear of the uphill wooded areas if you are alone and don't want to be pestered by the clusters of unemployed youths who hang around this area on scooters during summer. There are a number of cool picnic spots along this road.

If you are hiking and plan to spend a night or two exploring Monte Faito on foot, follow the signs marked **Agriturismo Quisisana**, where you can find en-suite rooms offering home-cooked food and superb views of the Bay of Naples. Antonio, who runs the establishment with his family, is a good guide to the area, if you speak some Italian. The farmhouse also has a terrace for al fresco dining and produces olive oil, jam and liqueurs which you will be urged to sample if you opt to take your evening meal here – four courses with local wine and liqueurs included for €25 per person.

The Castle

The Via Panoramica leads on past a splendid medieval castle. Dating from the eighth century, when it was commissioned by the Dukes of Sorrento, the castle was enlarged in 1197. Sadly, today it is in private hands and is not open to visitors. Wedding ceremonies can be arranged here, however.

Print from the 18th century showing the medieval castle, Castellammare di Stabia, for which the city of Castellammare was named.

Madonnna della Libera

From the castle, take the Via Madonna della Libera up to the Santuario Madonna della Libera, which has a café and a wonderful panoramic view over the port and town of Stabia and down to Pozzano with its beautiful church. The sanctuary itself is worth a visit for its 12th-century fresco, painted directly onto the rock face, of the Madonna with baby Jesus and two saints. Continuing along the path to Pozzano, the **Santuario Madonna di Pozzano** is notable for its lovely sacristy by Luigi Vanvitelli.

■ Monte Faito

At Castellammare di Stabia Circumvesuviana station a cable car runs every 20 minutes to the 3,700-foot summit of Monte Faito. Stand at the back of the cable car to get the best views over the town of Stabia and the Gulf of Naples. From Monte Faito, energetic travelers can walk back down to Castellammare or even journey on foot to the first of the Amalfi Coast towns – Positano – a 2½ hour hike. Most travelers opt instead to take a 15 minute walk down to a splendid panoramic spot at the Piazzale dei Capi. There are several cafés and restaurants here, but the **Belvedere Bar** has the best viewpoint and the owner will even give you a plastic cap for your bottled beer if you want to continue walking. The Bar can supply sandwiches as well as cool drinks. If you want a full meal, go to the **Sant'Angelo restaurant and hotel** over the road or back up to the summit for lunch at the picturesque wooden restaurant, among the jostling pine trees, before returning to Stabia on the cable car.

Monte Faito is part of the chain of Lattari mountains, and the Alpine-style villages here offer locals and foreigners alike a cool retreat in summer from the scorching beaches and dusty towns around the Bay of Naples. The conifers, beech, chestnut and cedar woods of the Monti Lattari, the late-flowering plants, prolific birdlife, not to mention the walks down to the resort towns of the Sorrento Peninsula and the Amalfi Coast, make this area a paradise for hikers and nature lovers.

■ Vico Equense

Renowned as a health resort since Roman times, with its thermal waters, sea bathing and mountain walks, Vico Equense is still popular today for all these reasons. Most visitors arrive at the Circumvesuviana rail station, and those wishing to spend some time here are advised to stop first at the **tourist office** in Van San Ciro (☎ 081 879 8826) to pick up a map of the region, which should also provide touring and hiking itineraries.

Museo Mineralogico

Not far from the tourist office at no 2 Via San Ciro, the Mineralogical Museum has more than 2,000 specimens on display. Of particular interest is the lovely collection of crystals and fluorescent rocks, along with the meteorite specimens. Open Tue-Sat 9 am-1 pm and 5-8 pm in summer; 9 am-1 pm and 4-6 pm in winter. Sundays 9 am-1 pm. Closed Mon. Guided tours by arrangement. ☎ 081 801 5668. Note the pretty tiled dome of the Baroque **Church of San Ciro** on Viale Rimembranza.

The Antiquarium

The Antiquarium is a small two-room museum. There is only one guardian, who seems to disappear and shut the museum even during the designated morning opening hours. However, if you look interested and/or desolate enough, one of the other workers, some of whom always seem to be hanging around, might rouse themselves to open up for you. The museum displays pots and an interesting set of Roman ornaments, mostly from necropoli excavated in Via Nicotera. Open (in theory) Mon-Sat 9:30 am-1 pm. Free entry. ☎ 081 801 5752.

Santissima Annunziata

Formerly the cathedral of Vico Equense, the Annunziata is a rare example of a Gothic church on the Sorrento Peninsula. Its campanile dates from the 15th century. Little remains of the frescoes that once adorned the interior, but among the tombs is that of the 14th-century Bishop Cimino, and there are some fine paintings and engraved wooden choir stalls, an 18th-century organ and an *Ecce Homo* attributed to Luca Giordano.

Castello Giusso

Nearby is Castello Giusso, which overlooks the sea. The original medieval structure, dating from the 13th century, dominates the seafront. Much subsequent alteration has produced Catalan and Renaissance architectural features dating from the 16th century. Some of the crenellation was added in the 19th century. The castle is currently divided into private condominiums and is not available for viewing by the public. Immediately to the left after you enter, however, is a public terrace with a good sea view of Marina di Vico.

Castello Giusso

Take the small path to the right of the Cathedral leading toward the little beach resort of Seiano for a good view of the church of Santissima Annunziata itself or to walk down to the

Spiaggia Sporting, if you want a dip in the sea. The terrace of the Sporting Hotel has wonderful views of the Gulf of Naples and of the islands of Procida and Ischia on a clear day.

■ Meta di Sorrento

The fertile plain or *piano* to the east of Sorrento is today divided into three municipalities: Meta di Sorrento, Piano di Sorrento and Sant'Agnello. An ancient town with Greek and Roman origins, Meta was rediscovered by the Goths, Longobards, Byzantines and Saracens. An important port at one time, the Alimuri shipyard dates to the 12th century. A number of the old palazzi in the town belonged to master mariners and shipbuilders and nautical coats of arms are still emblazoned on their venerable façades.

Madonna del Lauro

Built on the site of a temple dedicated to Minerva, where a Paleo-Christian church later stood, the 18th-century Basilica of Madonna del Lauro (Our Lady of the Laurel) is the symbol of Meta, with its Neo-Classical façade, Baroque bell tower and majolica dome. The interior has stucco and gold work, and a number of frescoes by Giuseppe Bonito and Costantino Desiderio. Examples of Neapolitan Baroque art can also be seen in other chapels in Meta, notably **Santa Maria delle Grazie** on Via Cassari and **Santa Maria della Misericordia** in Via Vocale.

The Palazzi of Meta

Walking through the town toward the beach, a number of imposing 18th-century villas can be seen. The **Palazzo Maresca** dates from the early 17th century, while the **Villa Valletta Martina** is an 18th-century dwelling with magnificent portals forming a courtyard which leads to the villa and garden. The **Villa Liguori**, built in 1773, has been enlarged and redesigned over the years, but was damaged in the 1980 earthquake. The **Villa Giuseppina**, dating from 1739, was divided into seven apartments in the 1980s, a common fate of these lovely patrician dwellings.

Camaldoli

A four-hour walk leads from the Corso Italia of Meta along the old access roads to the peninsula and up to **Montechiaro**, the mountain of Sant'Angelo, also called Casini – after the ruins of small dwellings here. From here the road descends to reveal a view of Vico Equense. Follow signs or ask for directions to Alberi. The Strada dei Casini leads to the **Agriturismo La Selva** along a chestnut tree-lined route and **Villa Giusso**, a superb aristocratic dwelling which is also open to paying guests, built on the site of Camaldoli, an old monastery. From here there are wonderful views of the peninsula – from Meta to the Punta Campanella. Note the 16th-century well in the center of the courtyard of Villa Giusso. At the exit of the monastery the trail continues to Via Raffaele Bosco. **San Vito** is a small monastery which has a collection of art. At **San Salvatore** admire the 18th-century organ and altar. The Franciscan convent has a red campanile and, inside, an oratory covered with majolica from the Neapolitan school. From the Via Raffaele Bosco hikers can either descend to **Piano** or continue up to **Pacognano** and go by bus or on foot down to **Marina di Seiano** with its beaches and bathing facilities. The little church of Sant'Antonio in the square is only open on Sundays and during services. Head toward the Saracen tower on Via Murrano to return to the Sorrento road.

■ Piano di Sorrento

The towns of the Sorrento plain have a long history of infighting, although nowadays the competition is mainly confined to tourist quotas. Inhabited since prehistoric times, Piano was first a colony and then a Roman municipality of Sorrento. Requests for autonomy were made from the 13th century onwards, but not until 1808 were the towns separated by order of Giuseppe Bonaparte. **Piano** was then disaffiliated from **Meta** in 1861 and **Sant'Agnello** in 1865, but reunited under Fascist rule until final separation in 1946. In the 19th century, the shipyards of Cassano, and the numerous captains and ship owners of Piano earned the town a good reputation in the naval and commercial worlds. In 1906 the Sorrento tramline linked the peninsula to the wider world, which gave a boost to the tourist industry. Today, quieter than Sorrento, but with a fine, clean beach and good shops, Piano is a tranquil and inexpensive alternative for vacationers wishing to make their base on the peninsula.

Corso Italia

The main street of Piano is the Corso Italia, which links it to Sorrento and Sant'Agnello at one end, and to Meta at the other. Lined with shops, this is a popular street with tourists. Note the superb late 18th-century **Villa Lauro** on the Corso Italia, which has been called the most beautiful example of Neo-Classic architecture on the entire Sorrento Peninsula. Its façade is a listed national monument. Damaged in the 1980 earthquake, the villa has been beautifully restored and is owned by a private company.

San Michele Arcangelo

Take the Via S. Michele to visit the Basilica of the same name. The Circumvesuviana station is reached from a side-street half-way along this road. A little farther down, the 15th-century church has a main door flanked by two pillars that incorporate holy-water fonts decorated with 18th-century alabaster bas reliefs of San Michele. Originally built during the ninth and 10th centuries, the church was destroyed several times by Saracen pirates, then rebuilt in 1405, and again in 1571. The inside of the church is in the form of a Latin cross, with three naves separated from each other by 10 pillars. Note the gilded, panelled ceiling. Above the cross vault was once a dome – destroyed by the 1688 earthquake and replaced by the Saracen Canvas, a ceiling painting, in 1729 – until it too was damaged by the 1980 earthquake.

Villa Fondi

From the church continue along the Via F. S. Ciampa or turn left then right along the Via delle Rose to reach the lovely Villa Fondi on Via Ripa di Cassano, with its splendid coastal views and lovely public gardens. This Neo-Classical villa was begun in 1840. Its monumental façade and great hall were designed by Vanvitelli. Originally owned by the Princes of De Sangro Fondi, it now belongs to the state. The 1980 earthquake damaged the villa, but it has been well restored and today houses a museum. The gardens have a wonderful view of the bay; cultural events are held here during the summer months. There is a café in the garden, and a lovely mosaic *nymphaeum* (bathing area). This is a reconstruction of a Roman structure, found in one of the maritime villas of Marina della Lobra, in Massa Lubrense.

Villa Fondi

Georges Vallet Archeological Museum

Attic amphora

The Villa Fondi houses the Museo Archeologico della Penisola Sorrentina Georges Vallet. This museum brings together artifacts gathered from recent excavations in the Sorrento Peninsula. Its five rooms are divided into prehistoric sections, finds from Classical necropoli, religious, and Roman objects. A number of important discoveries have come from caves in the region, including the Grotta Nicolucci in Sorrento, and the Grotta delle Noglie in Massa Lubrense, as well as recently excavated necropoli at Via Nicotera in Vico Equense, on the Corso Italia and the Mente del Viale dei Platani in Piano di Sorrento, and at Massa Lubrense. In Sorrento itself, excavations revealed a sixth-century BC building at 35 Corso Italia, and at Villa Fiorentino, also on the Corsa Italia, the remains of a Roman-era house were found. Among beautiful statues on display in the museum is the six-foot figure of Pheplophoros found during an excavation of a Sorrentine villa in 1971. It was discovered underneath a solidified bed of lava dating back to the 79 AD eruption of Vesuvius. A very useful model reconstruction of the first century BC Roman villa of Capo di Sorrento which occupied an area of around 5½ acres can be seen here. Today it is known as the baths of Queen Giovanna, or the villa of Pollio Felice. The first floor of the museum leads out onto a terrace, which offers lovely views of the Bay. The museum is closed on Mon. Free entry.

Farther along the Via Ripa di Cassano is the **Hotel Piccola Vienna** and the **Bar Tramonto Rosso**, which has some tables outside with a coastal view. From here you can take the road that winds down to the coast.

Marina di Cassano

The beach at Piano di Sorrento can be reached only by a winding road. There are no stairs, but a small bus runs frequently to and from the town in the peak months of July and August. There is a lift down to the sea, but at the time of writing it had been out of use for some time. Two-thirds of the way downhill under the arch Gabbiano Azzurra is the entrance to the Bagni Tina. Ignore the large signs to the restaurant here – it is closed, and there is only a snack bar serving the beaches. At the end of the winding road is the small **Spiaggia Libera Caterina** – a grey volcanic sand beach which is free to use. The sea here is clear and pleasant to swim in. There is a Salumeria/Paninoteca (sandwich shop) nearby for lunchtime sandwiches. This is a pleasant, relatively quiet beach compared to those of Sorrento – so many of the coastal apartments have washing festooned on them, and little old ladies sitting on the tiny balconies, that it looks like a seaside version of the Quartieri Spagnoli of Naples. The men down below, hard at work in the boat-building yards, reinforce the notion that this fishing hamlet has not been altered as much by tourism as its close proximity to Sorrento would suggest.

Climbing back up to the Via Ripa di Cassano, take Via M Rosella and Via Bagnulo to return to the Corso Italia. En route, note the **Villa Sopramare**. The Maresca family constructed this two-story building in the 18th century, thanks to a legacy from the British crown. Rebuilt several times, the structure is now of an eclectic style. The park annex and terrace overlooking the sea are worth seeing. On Via Bagnuolo, the Neo-Classical **Villa Massa** was given a liberty-style or Art Deco makeover and, viewed behind the railing (it is privately owned) has an attractive tree-filled garden.

LIBERTY STYLE

Better known as Art Deco outside of Italy, this involves use of gemstones and enamelwork, facing of wall mirrors with copperwork and plaques of turquoise enamel or rich blue pottery, furniture with copper panels, leaded lights of clear and stained glass, pewter and silverwork ornamented with enamel.

Santa Teresa

Back on the Corso Italia, take the few steps that lead up to the Church of Santa Teresa and San Giuseppe. Built between 1663 and 1687, the left and right naves have a painting of *St John at the Cross* by Formosa, and a miniature Lourdes grotto.

Chiesa dell'Assunta, Mortora

For travelers with the energy for a walk into the hilly region around Piano di Sorrento, take the Via Cavottole and then Vicoletto Ponte di Mortora for a walk up to the charming parish of Mortora. En route, note the 16th-century **Villa Romano**. On the right, the **Chiesa dell'Assunta** or Church of the Assumption, dating to 1550, has a beautiful Baroque façade decorated with the coat of arms of Pope Leo XIII. The fine crosses on the pillars were executed by a Swiss monk. From here, cross Via Cavone and turn left onto the main road, known as the *Statale* or SS 145. Six hundred yards down the road is the Piazzetta della Trinità.

Chiesa della Trinità

The Holy Trinity Church in the parish of Trinità was built in 1543 and has ancient quadrangular bell-towers. The original stone altar was replaced by the present marble high altar in 1743. The *Holy Trinity* on the canvas altarcloth was painted by Neapolitan artist Mancinelli in 1871. The multi-colored marble canopied pulpit was originally in the church of S

Francesco di Paola in Naples. From here the Amalfitana Road leads to the Colli di San Pietro, where a lovely castle set in a verdant park can be visited.

Castello Colonna

The castle was originally a Benedictine abbey, and was probably abandoned and in ruins for many years before it was acquired by Eduardo Colonna di Paliano, Prince of Summonte, in 1830. Work on the palace, which would be known as Il Castello del Principe, began in 1850 and was completed in 1872. This 19th-century medieval-style castle is one of several constructed in and around Sorrento in the Grand Tour era. One of the few others still standing was built by American writer Marion Crawford in Sant'Agnello. Today, Castello Colonna is used for functions, although part of it has been converted into luxury private accommodation. Fortunately, the swimming pool in the grounds is open to the public, thus enabling tourists to visit this 19th-century folly.

Robert Browning

This area, known as the Colli di San Pietro, is famous for another towering 19th-century figure. In autumn 1844 Robert Browning, the English poet, spent a long period residing in the Colli di San Pietro, perhaps as a guest of Colonna. Browning wrote his beautiful poem, *The Englishman in Italy*, on his return. On the Via San Pietro, a plaque to Robert Browning commemorates his association with this lovely spot. The **Hotel Antico Parco del Principe** is also along this street. Visitors may wish to turn right and follow the signs to the restaurant **Silenzio Cantatore**, which has a lovely sea view. You can take the Via Antonino Aversa beside the castle, to the **beach at Scaricatoio** – a one-hour walk. From here you can see the **Li Galli islands**.

Alternatively, inside the castle grounds, walk past the private houses and take the path up the **Vico Alvano mountain**.

This is about a 1½-hour walk. Each year a procession from the town walks up to the cross on its summit. To return to Piano, take the same route back and then Via dei Platani for a view of the 16th-century **Torre di Legittimo**, by the side of an ancient villa.

■ Sant'Agnello

Named after the patron saint of its lovely Baroque church, Sant'Agnello is famous for its superlative hotels on the tufo cliffs above the delightful Marinella beach. For visitors wishing to recapture the Grand Tour experience, this is definitely the place.

Arriving at Sant'Agnello from the Viale dei Pini, one passes the **Pizzo** on the right, an archeological site with Roman ruins. Unfortunately this is located within a number of private allotments, and unfriendly dogs discourage visitors. As the road turns left towards the sea, the distinctive Neo-Gothic Villa Crawford comes into view.

Villa Crawford

Francis Marion Crawford

Built in 1886 on the site of the Villa De Rentis, this was the home of American novelist Francis Marion Crawford, popular for his works published at the end of the 1800s. Crawford transformed the pre-existing villa into the medieval-style castle that it is today. In the stone, Crawford engraved the words *In Tempestate Securitas.* Villa Crawford became a lively center of the art and intellectual world with numerous important visitors, among them fellow novelist Henry James. On his death in 1909, his daughter Eleonora, wife of the nobleman Pietro Rocca di Roccapadula, inherited the villa. After her death, the villa passed to the Catholic Institute of Maria Ausiliatrice. Crawford is buried in the Sant'Agnello cemetery. When Crawford died not only did a number of Italian newspapers lament his passing, but the former President of the United States, Theodore Roosevelt, whom Crawford counted among his friends, sent a letter of condolence. Five Hollywood films were made of his novels, and he was described as "the most adroit and successful Romantic novelist in the English language" and the "glory of American letters." Yet he has largely been forgotten today.

Church of SS Prisco & Agnello

The pastel yellow and white 15th-century parish church of Sant'Agnello, dedicated to Saints Prisco and Agnello, has three naves, decorated with marbled plasterwork, and paintings by De Castro. The nearby Terrazza Punta San Francesco offers stunning views of the coast, and a café cum wine bar.

Villa Gortchakow

In the extraordinarily beautiful gardens of the Hotel Parco dei Principi is Villa Gortchakow. Built in 1792 for Count Leopold of Bourbon, cousin of the King of Naples, many statues, fountains and Neo-Renaissance terraces were placed in the park surrounding it, now the property of this lovely hotel, and admired by the guests who can afford to stay here.

The Cocumella

The oldest hotel on the Peninsula, and certainly one of the most aristocratic, the Cocumella is notable for the 18th-century Jesuit establishment around which it is built, elements of which are charmingly incorporated. It became a Nautical School after the expulsion of the Jesuits from the Kingdom of Naples, and the site was purchased by Pietro Antonio Gargiulo in 1777. He transformed it into a hotel. Many famous travelers have stayed here – Byron and the Duke of Wellington among them.

■ Sorrento

Sorrento stands on a natural terrace atop a dramatic line of 150-foot white cliffs, on the southern side of the Gulf of

Naples, with a splendid panoramic position. The legendary sunsets, delightful flower gardens, imposing cathedral and distinctive Franciscan church with its 13th-century cloister, are just a few of the charms of a town which has been attracting tourists for hundreds of years. Ruins of the imposing villas of Roman nobles testify to Sorrento's long-held elite status. This was reinforced in the 18th and 19th centuries when the town hosted artists and intellectuals from around the world. Maxim Gorky and Nietszsche are among famous names linked to the town. Today, the tourists are more hedonist than elitist, but alongside the ubiquitous sun loungers, bustling cafés, restaurants, and glitzy nightclubs, visitors can enjoy the quieter pleasures of garden and clifftop walks, or seek out the remaining practitioners of ancient crafts such as lace-making and woodcarving.

The street layout of the old center of Sorrento dates back to Greek and Roman times. The main axes are Via San Cesareo and Via Tasso. The Corso Italia was constructed in the late 19th century, and crosses the town. Piazza Tasso is at the heart of the *Centro Storico*, but the administrative and spiritual center of Sorrento is Piazza Sant'Antonino. Town maps are available at the tourist office – even when closed, they leave the free maps on display. Follow the signs for the **Circolo dei Forestieri (Foreigners' Club)** on Via Luigi de Maio. It has a large terrace with bar and restaurant seating where you can enjoy live music. Have a drink here and enjoy the panoramic view.

Church & Cloister of St. Francis

Cloister of St. Francis

The monastery on this site dates back to the eighth century. The elegant arches of the cloister suggest an interesting blend of architectural styles. During the summer, classical music concerts and art exhibitions are held here. Sorrento's art school, which continues the local marquetry tradition, is today housed in the monastery. The Baroque church has rich stucco decoration, two frescoes of saints, a lovely wooden statue of Saint Francis with Christ on the Cross, and a dome bell tower.

The Villa Communale

The public gardens laid out behind the monastery toward the end of the 19th century offer a superb view of the bay. This pleasant, open space is dotted with trees, flowerbeds and marble busts. From here the grandiose hotels of Sorrento – Tramontano and Excelsior among them – can be seen ranged along the cliffs, and steps or a lift can be taken from the park terrace down to the beach platforms of Marina Piccola.

The Duomo

Dating to the 15th century, but much altered since then, the Cathedral boasts a collection of Neapolitan paintings, including some by Giacomo del Po and a 16th-century marble archbishop's throne. The inlaid woodwork (*intarsia*) of the choir stalls is noteworthy. More recent wooden panels at the main and side entrance attest to the continuing vitality of the craft of marquetry. Ancient Roman columns support the bell tower, while the large multicoloured ceramic clock is the work of modern craftsmen. Torquato Tasso was baptized here. Note the Aragonese coats of arms on the side portal. At 44 Corso Italia, west of Piazza Tasso, the Cathedral is open from 8 am to noon and from 3-10 pm every day. Entrance is free.

Basilica of Sant'Antonino

Saint Antonino Abate is the patron saint of Sorrento – his statue can be seen in the middle of the Piazza that bears his name. The 11th-century Basilica – one of the oldest churches in Sorrento – houses paintings by Giovanni Bernardo Lama and Giacomo Del Po, and a number of Roman artifacts, probably plundered from nearby villas. The columns, for example, are believed to come from the portico of a Roman house. The tomb of Saint Antonino can be seen in the crypt, together with a number of votive paintings of sailors, and in the church lobby two whale ribs are preserved as a tribute to the saint who reputedly rescued a child swallowed by one of these sea mammals. An 18th-century crib and a ninth-century portal are also noteworthy.

Santa Maria delle Grazie

On the opposite side of the square is the church of Santa Maria delle Grazie, founded by a noble Sorrentine – Lady Berardina Donnorso – around 1566. A number of works by southern Italian painters, such as Buono and Caracciolo, can be seen in the church. There is a 16th-century nuns' choir, and apses. Note the lovely majolica floor with its floral design.

Sedil Dominova

Situated at the corner of Via Giuliani, this 16th-century loggia is a rare example of the medieval noble assemblies once dispersed throughout the Gulf of Naples. Today you are more likely to find local card players rather than Sorrentine aristocrats here, but the city's coat of arms and those of local patrician families can still be seen. The 17th-century dome or cupola is decorated with majolica roof tiles, and the end walls are covered with 18th-century frescoes. The corner arches are made of lava.

Museo Correale di Terranova

Located on Via Correale, this 18th-century villa houses the family collection of Alfredo and Pompeo Correale, counts of Terranova. Greek and Roman antiquities, 17th-century Neapolitan paintings, Capodimonte and oriental porcelain, inlaid wood furniture, glassware and clocks are on display here. The marquetry, embroidery and silks provide a glittering demonstration of ancient Sorrentine craftsmanship, many dominated by the doyen of intarsia – Salvatore Gargiulo. In the library, alongside rare works by Torquato Tasso, is a more gruesome reminder of Sorrento's favorite son: his death mask. The gardens of the villa are also well worth a visit. Planted with rare flowers, a path lined with orange trees leads to a belvedere with a lovely coastal view. This is considered by some to be the most attractive provincial museum in Italy. ☎ 081 878 1846. Open 9 am-2 pm. Closed Tues and holidays.

The Valley of the Mills

From Fuorimura Street, behind Tasso Square, an extraordinary natural spectacle is visible – a deep valley, named after the ancient wheat and saw mills once located here. The cleft in the rock dates from a huge volcanic eruption some 35,000 years ago, debris from which progressively filled the valley. At one time Sorrento was bounded by three gorges, and by sea cliffs. Now this is the only remaining gorge. The ruins of the old mills in the valley were a favorite subject of 19th-century artists. They are now abandoned to luxuriant vegetation, dominated by the splendid Phillitis Vulgaris fern.

Greek & Roman Walls

A few feet beneath the Parsano Nuovo gate, the remains of Greek walls can be seen, together with an ancient pre-Roman door. By Roman times, Sorrento was effectively an enclosed city, with five entrance gates defended by towers. One was at Marina Grande, another at Piazza Tasso. The walls remained in place throughout the medieval period, and provided an important defence against marauding Saracen pirates in the mid-16th century, when they were rebuilt and strengthened. A further nine-foot section of the defensive town walls can be seen on Via Sopra le Mura.

Via della Pietà

Palazzo Veniero

This street in the *Centro Storico* boasts some of the most impressive architecture in Sorrento. The 13th-century **Palazzo Veniero** has been sadly neglected, but is a rare example of Byzantine- and Arab-style architecture. Note the large arched windows and inlaid tufo decoration. The 14th-century **Correale Palace** has a characteristic Neapolitan portal in the form of a depressed arch, and a beautifully decorated window. A **second Palazzo Correale** is at the corner of Piazza Tasso and Via Pietà – the inscription on the marble scroll of the portal bears the date 1768. The **Loggia in Vico Calantariaro** is a rare example of Aragonese architecture and betrays 15th-century Tuscan influences.

Palazzo Correale, 14th century, and the Via Pietá

Museobottega della Tarsialignea

Located in a typical 18th-century townhouse on the Via San Nicola, the museum has a collection of principally 19th-century objects and furniture demonstrating the best of the ancient craft of *intarsia*. Paintings and photographs help to explain the development of the local wood inlay industry, alongside explanations of production techniques, materials used and common motifs employed. The work of several of the best local master craftsmen is also on display. ☎ 081 877 1942 for current opening hours.

Other significant buildings of the *Centro Storico* include the **birthplace of Torquato Tasso**. Most of the house fell into the sea in the 17th century but two of the remaining rooms are incorporated in the entrance to the Imperial Tramontano. The home of the famous poet's sister Cornelia, known as the **Casa Fasulo**, is still standing on Via San Nicola, with an intricate portico and a small balcony. The Baroque 18th-century **Church of the Servants of Mary** on Via Sersale houses a wooden statue of Christ, which is carried during the Good Friday procession. Also in Baroque style, the **Chiesa dell'Addolorata**, or Church of Our Lady of Sorrows on Via S Cesareo, has a tufo façade. The **Chiesa del Carmine** on Piazza Tasso has interesting late 18th-century plaster work.

Marina Piccola

The two harbors of Sorrento are known as the Small and Large Marinas. Marina Piccola is closer to Sorrento and has developed from a little fishing village into a major tourist

SM del Carmine Church

gateway – more than one third of foreign visitors traveling around the Gulf of Naples come through this harbor on the ferries and hydrofoils. Close-by are the principal bathing sites of Sorrento. Once private beaches for villa residents and later the clientele of the grand hotels, they are now open to all. To get here, take the road that winds down past the terrace of the Foreigners' Club and the steps that lead to Marina Piccola. The **Bar Ruccio** has tables that are virtually in the water, ideal for those who like to have a drink and sample one of the typical Neapolitan snacks, while contemplating the pleasure craft moored in the harbor. Looking up, you can see the landmark sign of the Hotel Vittoria – one of the symbols of Sorrento for a century or more.

Marina Grande

A pleasant walk to this harbor starts at Piazza Vittoria, along Via Marina to the old Greek gateway that was once the entrance to the town. A series of staircases leads down to the picturesque Marina Grande. The seafaring traditions of Sorrento have been better preserved here, as shown by the proliferation of fishing nets and typical *gozzi sorrentini* or single-sailed boats on the beach. The **Church of Sant'Anna**, the patron of the village, is in the middle of the Marina and, on the Saint's day, the first Sunday after July 26th, pleasure boats throng the bay to see the illuminations and fireworks. There are a number of lively bars and good restaurants in Marina Grande, which is a picturesque location for a traditional Sorrentine dinner.

■ Capo di Sorrento

This limestone promontory at the western edge of the bay of Sorrento is reached by a coastal road that offers spectacular panoramic views. To get here, take the Line A Circumvesuviana bus to Capo di Sorrento. If you choose to walk, you can stop to enjoy the views of Sorrento from the terraces of the hotels on the road leading out of town, and admire some superb villas on the way. Take the Corso Italia out of Sorrento and then the fork to Massa Lubrense. One of the best views of the town is from the terrace restaurant at the **Hotel Tonnarella**. Nearby is the splendid **Villa Rosa**, with its tall tower. A few yards farther on the right is **Il Serito**, where Russian writer Maxim Gorky lived. A sign in Italian and Russian informs passers-by that it was in this residence that the great author from the USSR dedicated himself to his work between 1924 and 1933. Turn right into the ***Calata Punto del Capo***, a cobbled path. A sign with an arrow points toward **Ruderi della Villa Romana di Pollio** (Ruins of the Roman Villa of Pollio). The **SM del Carmine Church** is immediately on your right. The church has a single nave, and a dark-skinned *Madonna*, together with a number of 16th- and 17th-century paintings, and gilded reliquaries of saints. A 10-minute walk leads to the Capo di Sorrento, past some lovely flowers and a superb view of Vesuvius and the Bay of Naples. The narrow lane finally opens onto the ruins of the Roman villa and baths at the tip of a small cape.

Bagni della Regina Giovanna

This lovely picnic spot can also be reached by boat from Sorrento. There is good swimming off the rocks here. The natural outdoor swimming pool reached by steps carved in the rock is known as the Bagni della Regina Giovanna. It is believed that the pool may once have served as a fish tank for the residents of the Roman villa of Pollio Felice. Giovanna, however, was an Angevin queen, believed to have used this place in around 1300 as a quiet retreat and bathing spot.

Pollio Felice Villa

The remains of the famous villa of Pollio Felice, which extend across the promontory at Capo di Sorrento, nowadays play host to prostrate sunbathers, many of whom do not seem to know or care what they lie on. Dating back to the first century AD, ancient ruins of the villa's once-grandiose rooms can be seen, along with the *calidarium* and *nymphaeum*. The archeological site is in a good state of conservation, and scholars have noted that the villa complex included pavilions in the gardens – used for guest lodging, thermal baths, servants' lodgings and for production of oil and wine. In the early Imperial period, when the villa was constructed, the Gulf of Naples had become the preferred getaway for Roman nobles. Pollio, like other wealthy villa-owners of his day, had a private landing place, with fishponds, and his residence was spread over a number of terraces that would have afforded various views of the coast. The beautiful home of Pollio is celebrated in the poetry of Statius. Other Roman villas on this coast have served as foundations for hotels and luxury modern dwellings. The remains of the Roman villa can clearly be seen on the headland, but there are no signs at the spot to indicate how the villa once looked. For this, you need to go into nearby Piano di Sorrento where the **George Vallet Archeological Museum** housed in the Villa Fondi has a model reconstruction of the Pollio Felice Villa.

Model of Pollio Felice Villa

The lively nightspot **Kalimera** is also on Capo di Sorrento, along with a few shops and bars. Swimmers who do not want to pay to use the bathing beaches on Marina Piccola and Marina Grande can sunbathe here, or walk another 100 m/100 yards and along the bath at the side of the Hotel Dania, for the 10-minute shortcut to Marina Puolo.

TORQUATO TASSO

The heart of historic Sorrento, Piazza Tasso, is named after Renaissance poet Torquato Tasso (1544-95), who was born in the town, and whose statue also graces this palm-tree lined square. Best known as the author of *Jerusalem Liberated*, Tasso was persecuted for his writing – which was said to be derisive of his teachers – while still a 20-year-old student at the University of Bologna. He escaped to Mantova and Modena where he was sheltered by a noble family.

■ Massa Lubrense

Massa Lubrense, at the tip of the Sorrento Peninsula and the Amalfi Coast, separated from Capri by a small stretch of water, is a great place for independent travelers – with its networks of trails through olive and citrus groves across 30 hamlets, winding up to panoramic views of the Gulfs of Naples and Salerno, and back down to picturesque fishing villages. Massa, an elegant town, is pushing the tourist opportunities of the region hard, so make sure to visit while it remains the undiscovered jewel of the peninsula. From Sant'Agata's panoramic views and Michelin-starred restaurant to the unique Punta Campanella marine reserve, this is the place to get off the beaten track, by foot or by car. Unlike Sorrento, with its volcanic tufo, the limestone which is characteristic of the Amalfi shoreline begins here, and once again rocky beaches are in evidence.

Marina di Puolo

Within walking distance from Sorrento, this small fishing village occupies the bay between Capo di Sorrento and Capo di Massa. It was known to the Romans, who held sporting competitions on the beach, and it was a subject of dispute between Massa and Sorrento in the medieval period. Today the main activity of Marina di Puolo is tourism, with the usual bars, restaurants and bathing beaches. From here excursions can also be made by boat to the small stony beaches and coves off the cape, where there is greater privacy for swimming and sunbathing.

For drivers there is a panoramic road between Massa and Marina di Puolo. Energetic walkers will also enjoy the four-km/2.4-mile climb up to the town, past gardens, citrus and olive groves and flower fields, and with increasingly lovely views of the coastline. Start out from Piazza Tasso along Via San Cesareo, turn right at the end and make a sharp left up to the main road leading west out of Sorrento. Go right for 150 feet, then left up the cobbled road opposite the International Camping sign. Negotiate the hairpin bends by the three shortcut paths. Continue on the road, climbing away from Sorrento, go straight to Via Priera over the main road and continue for a another 600 feet uphill.

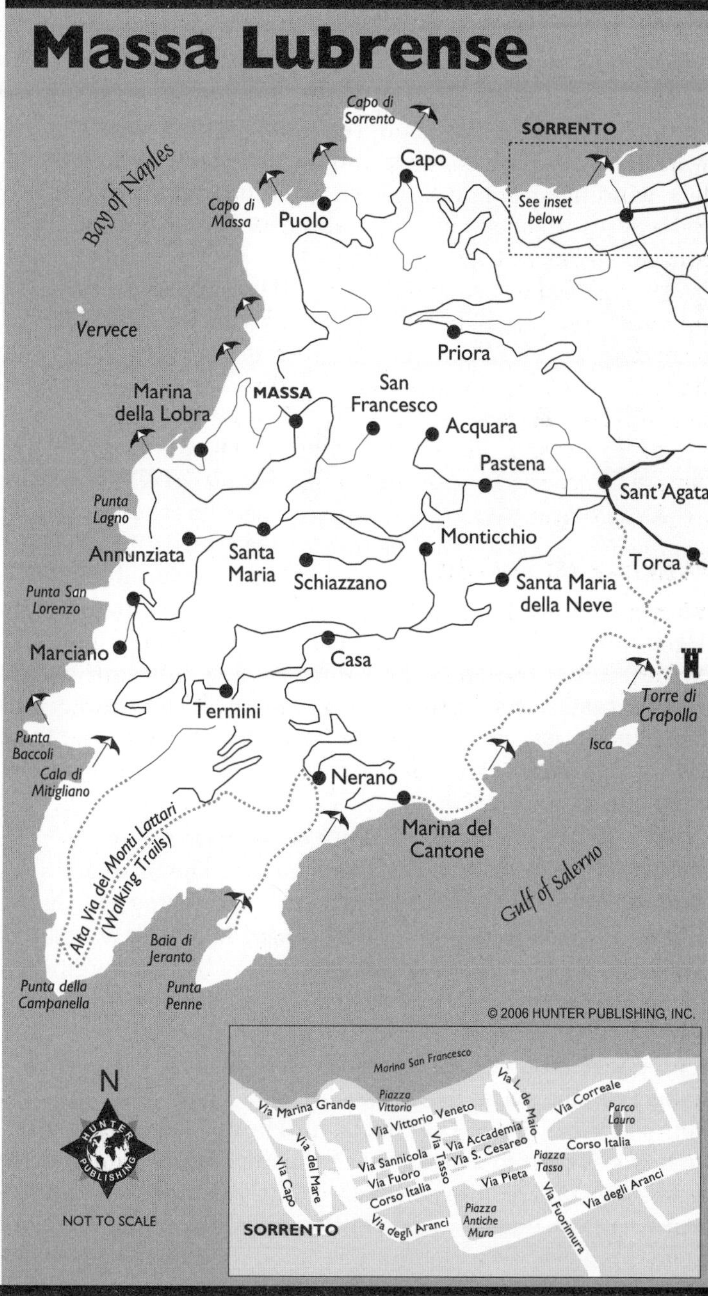
Massa Lubrense
Capo di Sorrento
SORRENTO
Capo
See inset below
Bay of Naples
Capo di Massa
Puolo
Vervece
Priora
Marina della Lobra
MASSA
San Francesco
Acquara
Pastena
Sant'Agata
Punta Lagno
Monticchio
Annunziata
Santa Maria
Schiazzano
Torca
Santa Maria della Neve
Punta San Lorenzo
Marciano
Casa
Termini
Torre di Crapolla
Punta Baccoli
Isca
Cala di Mitigliano
Nerano
Marina del Cantone
Alta Via dei Monti Lattari (Walking Trails)
Gulf of Salerno
Baia di Jeranto
Punta della Campanella
Punta Penne
N
HUNTER PUBLISHING
NOT TO SCALE
Marina San Francesco
Via Marina Grande
Piazza Vittorio
Via Vittorio Veneto
Via L. de Maio
Via Correale
Parco Lauro
Via del Mare
Via Capo
Via Tasso
Via Accademia
Via Sannicola
Via S. Cesareo
Piazza Tasso
Corso Italia
Via Fuoro
Via Pieta
Corso Italia
Via Fuorimura
Via degli Aranci
Piazza Antiche Mura
Via degli Aranci
SORRENTO

Massa Town

Cathedral of Santa Maria delle Grazie

The town of Massa Lubrense, surrounded by agricultural hamlets that have escaped modernization, and beyond the usual tourist trails, is in a panoramic position. Enjoy the view from the belvedere on Piazza Vescovado before visiting the town's major monument – the **Cathedral of Santa Maria delle Grazie**, also on the piazza. It was built in 1512-36 and restored in 1760. Among the works of art housed here is a 16th-century *Madonna* by Marco Cardisco, and a silver bust of the town's patron saint, Cataldo, Bishop of Taranto, by Giuseppe Simoli. Recent restoration work has uncovered 16th-century frescoes, and in the sacristy can be seen 18th-century paintings by Antonio Lanzi. The 18th-century wooden furniture is also of interest.

On Via Palma, the Baroque **Church of Santa Teresa** has a lovely 17th-century brick and tufo façade. The interior stucco work and majolica flooring is well preserved, and the church houses numerous relics of saints, martyred during the Roman period, and taken from catacombs.

Marina della Lobra

A road leads from the center of Massa Lubrense to the coastal village and beach resort of Marina della Lobra. En route, the 16th-century **Church of Santa Maria della Lobra**, considered one of the most beautiful in the Sorrentine peninsula, is worth a visit. The interior houses an attractive 18th-century majolica floor and an important fresco of the *Madonna della Lobra*, brought from Fontanella in 1570. The church has a pretty tiled dome, an unusual wooden ceiling, and a cloister containing Greek and Roman remains. The adventurous may choose to take lodgings which are available in the adjacent monastery. Marina della Lobra has the usual beachside restaurants, and boats for rent that you can take on a swimming excursion to a nearby cove such as Mitigliano.

Santa Maria della Lobra

Punta Campanella

The coastal road does not lead directly to Punta Campanella; indeed current excavations make even the pedestrian paths difficult to access. Hikers and divers are able to visit this protected coastline and marine park with authorized guides, however. Since 1997, this beautiful stretch of coastline has been protected through the creation of the Punta Campanella Marine Park. Walkers will enjoy seeing the migratory birds, as well as the Mediterranean flora, such as myrtle, rosemary, juniper and yellow broom. Divers can enjoy the ocean here, where yellow sea daisies, marine cactus, forests of white and red gorgonia, sea fans and numerous species of fish, including bass, squid and scorpion fish, can be seen. A number of fascinating grottos can also be visited – at Mitigliano the underwater cave has many sea anemones, while the Zaffire grotto near Crapolla boasts waterfalls, stalactites and stalagmites, and an expanse of crystal clear water. On the headland itself, the ruins of the 14th-century **Torre Minerva** can be seen. Constructed by Robert of Anjou as a watchtower, it alerted residents to the arrival of Saracen pirates until the 17th century. According to ancient historians Strabo and Pliny, a temple once stood on this point, erected by the first Greek colonists. A stairway cut out of the rock still bears inscriptions in ancient Greek. The Romans built a villa nearby, along the same lines as their sumptuous Capri getaway residences, with a number of panoramic terraces. They also constructed the road from Sorrento to Punta Campanella; in places the remains of this stone pavement can still be seen. Later, during the Napoleonic Wars, the French placed batteries on the headland while Capri was occupied by the British. Indeed, from here Capri rises majestically across the water, and seems almost close enough to touch.

Termini

From Punta Campanella the *Stradina Lastricata* path takes 45 minutes to reach Termini. At Mount San Costanzo, the hill that overlooks Punta Campanella, there are stunning views down to the coast. The hill has two peaks, and on top of the eastern hill stands the small white 15th-century chapel of **St Costanzo**. There are signs to Punta Campanella on the footpath from Termini which descends through lemon and olive groves. The walk takes two hours in total, returning by the same route. Termini is a great picnic spot, and the starting point for a number of walks around the region. If you need a swim, two km/1.2 miles from Termini are steps, known as the *Cala di Mitigliano*, which lead down to a small beach. Car owners can continue on to Nerano, and down to Marina di Cantone, which has a fine beach.

Nerano

The small cluster of dwellings around the church of San Salvatore, on the main piazza of Nerano, is chiefly of note as the starting point for the pedestrian excursion to Jeranto, and the main access point to the coastal resort of Marina del Cantone. Nerano is an hour's bus journey from Sorrento. For the walk to Jeranto, take the road leading to Cantone Beach, Via A Vespucci and turn right at the paved path – Via Jeranto. As the path climbs, the Li Galli islands come into view. The bay is overlooked by the **Torre di Montalto**, one of the many lookout posts

Torre di Montalto

Above: View from the terrace of the Cocumella, oldest hotel on the Sorrento Peninsula

Below: Marina Puolo beach, Capo di Sorrento

Above: Scrajo Mare, beach bar with loungers and changing rooms, in Stabia

Below: Ceramics shop in Positano, on the Amalfi Coast

Above: Amalfi town and beach

Below: Amalfi panorama

Above: An Amalfi Coast tower, built to warn of pirate raids

Below: View from the terrace of the Hotel San Pietro, near Positano

erected along the coast to warn inhabitants against Saracen raids. The bay itself is another protected site – administered by the FAI, an Italian environmental organization, since 1986. Bounded by Punta Campanella to the west and Punta Penna to the east, the bay itself is stunning. There are three marine grottos, one of which is close to the Capitiello beach. The best beach, however, can only be reached by boat from Marina del Cantone.

Marina del Cantone

Many visitors to the resort arrive by boat, to avoid the winding roads that are the only other way to access Marina del Cantone. Perhaps the difficulty of access makes the pleasure of reaching this delightful resort and enjoying a meal in one of its superb seaside restaurants even more special. The **marina of Recommone**, which is reached by sea, attracts an exclusive clientele. Yacht owners and Amalfi Coast tourists from Positano arrive to dine at the beachfront **Conca del Sogno restaurant**. Car owners can make the journey along a private road from Marina del Cantone.

Sant'Agata

The best panoramic view of the peninsula is from a terraced hill above the village of Sant'Agata sui due Golfi. To reach Sant'Agata by car, take the A3 Naples/Salerno motorway and exit at Castellammare di Stabia, following signs to the Sorrento Peninsula and then, from Meta, signs to Positano for six km/3.6 miles before turning right for Sant'Agata. Sant'Agata was a popular resort in the 19th century, as the fresh air was considered healthy. It is now regaining some status as young residents of the Amalfi Coast move here to avoid the extortionate prices of property in their home towns. The most famous restaurant in southern Italy – **Don Alfonso** – is at the center of this pleasant town, which sits astride the two spectacular gulfs of Naples and Salerno. The town also has a Renaissance-style parish church, with a beautiful marble and mother-of-pearl high altar – considered one of the major works of art on the peninsula. It was originally in the Gerolimini of Naples.

For the best views, drive to the gates of the medieval convent, **Il Deserto**; from there you can park and walk up to the beautiful belvedere for an unbeatable panorama. The entire region from Capri to Ischia and Cape Miseno can be seen from here. The viewpoint is open mornings and from 4 to 8 pm in summer. The church on the way up has wonderful inlaid marble altars. Further views can be had at **Capo di Mondo**, and at the next village, **Fontanelle**, where a short walk along the Via Rocca is rewarded by views of Vesuvius and the Bay of Naples. The Via Belvedere then slopes downhill to provide a view of the Amalfi Coast to Positano.

■ Places to Eat

From small trattorie in the harbor to the glamorous restaurants of the grandiose hotels, the Sorrento Peninsula has a wide range of dining options, many of which are frequented by Italian residents and vacationers as well as the legions of foreign tourists.

Stabia & Vico

Mustafa, Via Marina d'Equa, Seiano, Vico, ☎ 081 802 8602. €€. Friendly restaurant on the waterfront.

DINING PRICE CHART	
Price for an entrée	
€	€10-29
€€	€30-49
€€€	€50+

Gigino Pizza a Metro, 15 Via Nicotera, Vico Equense, ☎ 081 879 8426. €. Try the enormously long pizzas on sale here – by the yard!

Titos Pub, 67 Via Filangieri, Vico, ☎ 081 801 5092. €. Open all day and until 2 am, this is a popular spot for young people, with karaoke on Fridays and a piano player on Saturdays.

Al Belvedere, 13 bis Via Belvedere, Vico, ☎ 081 801 5934. €€. Fine Italian cuisine in this town where there are many good eateries.

Meta & Piano

Da Ninuccio, 31 Via Casa Iaccarino, Meta, ☎ 081 532 1436. €€. Restaurant and pizzeria.

La Conchiglia, 108 Via Cosenza, Meta, ☎ 081 878 6402. €€. Terrace restaurant by the sea.

Tico Tico, 3 Via Caruso, Meta, ☎ 081 532 1837. €€. Beach restaurant and pizzeria.

O'Guarracino, Marina di Cassano, Piano di Sorrento, ☎ 335 718 511. €€. Lovely seafront restaurant, with great fresh seafood and pasta. Open for lunch and dinner. Closed Tues.

Il Chiosco, Via delle Rose, Piano di Sorrento. €€. Al fresco dining under a bamboo shelter. Pizza, pasta, gnocchi.

Il Silenzio Cantatore, 87 Via Meta Amalfi, Piano di Sorrento, ☎ 081 808 3280. €€. Restaurant with panoramic views.

Sant'Agnello

Scintilla del Grand Hotel Cocumella, 7 Via Cocumella, Sant'Agnello, ☎ 081 878 2933. €€€. Exclusive restaurant in the former convent in a lovely location surrounded by gardens and facing the sea.

Da Arturo, Via Marion Crawford, Sant'Agnello, ☎ 081 877 2689. €€. Ristorante and pizzeria.

Il Camino, Piazza Colli di Fontanelle, Sant'Agnello, ☎ 081 808 3844. €. Tasty local cuisine at this unpretentious eatery.

Sorrento

L'Antica Trattoria, Via P. R. Giuliani, Sorrento, ☎ 081 807 1082. €€€. In operation since 1930, and efficiently run by Aldo d'Oria. Chef Fabio Bisanti prepares a range of superb fish dishes and desserts. Vincenzo plays mandolin in the evenings. Closed Mon.

Zi' Ntonio Mare, 180 Via Marina Grande, Sorrento, ☎ 081 807 3033. €€€. The celebrated swimming restaurant offers wood-oven pizzas, and seafood, including pasta with prawns and crawfish. Advisable to book in advance.

Caruso, 12 Via Sant'Antonino, Sorrento, ☎ 081 807 3156. €€€. Good for a special night out. The background music is usually recordings of the famous tenor after whom this restaurant is named.

Il Mulino, 7 Via Furimura, Sorrento, ☎ 081 878 1216. €€. The terrace faces the Valley of the Mills.

O'Parrucchiano, 71 Corso Italia, Sorrento, ☎ 081 878 1321. €€. This family-run restaurant serves traditional Sorrentine food in a citrus grove and daily fresh fish. Try the gnocchi alla sorrentina. Closed Wed off-season.

'O Canonico, 7 Piazza Tasso, Sorrento, ☎ 081 878 3277. €€. In operation since 1898, and run by three generations of the Terminiello family. Serves food prepared according to family recipes, with local wines.

Il Buco, Rampa Marina Piccola, Sorrento, ☎ 081 878 2354. €€. Off Piazza Sant Antonino, and run by Giuseppe Aversa, Il Buco offers a good wine selection to go with well-cooked typical Sorrentine cuisine.

Ristorante Taverna Azzurra, 166 Via Marina Grande, Sorrento, ☎ 081 877 2510. €€. Waterfront restaurant.

Da Cataldo, 202 Via Marina Grande, Sorrento, ☎ 081 878 2170, €€. Sea-facing restaurant, serving tasty Mediterranean dishes.

Osteria del Gatto Nero, 36 Via Santa Maria della Pieta, ☎ 081 878 1582. €. This small eatery for locals offers home cooking at reasonable prices. Closed Mon.

Emilia, 62 Via Marina Grande, Sorrento, ☎ 081 878 14 89. €. Serves good local fish on the sea terrace in summer. Closed Tue.

Di Leva, 31 Via Marina Grande, Sorrento, ☎ 081 878 3826. €. If you are a Sofia Loren fan, come here and look at all the photographs of the film star that line the walls. She paid a visit here in 2004. The geraniums around the restaurant serve as a reminder. Sofia ate a simple pasta dish and fried calamari. She then had the specialty of the house: rose petal ice cream. Why not follow her example at this unpretentious, friendly and reasonably priced family restaurant.

Massa Lubrense

Don Alfonso, 13 Corso S. Agata, S. Agata sui due Golfi, ☎ 081 878 0026. €€€. Rated in the Michelin guide as one of the top three restaurants in Italy, and attracting gourmet clients from around the world. An evening here will be a memorable event. Guests can also book to stay the night if they wish. Closed Mon and Tue off-season.

Franceschiello, 27 Via Partenope Massa Lubrense, ☎ 081 533 9780. €€. Good views from this well-known restaurant. Reputedly where the celebrated dessert *delizia al limone* was first served. Closed Wed off-season.

14 Passi, Via Marina del Cantone, Nerano, ☎ 081 808 1271. €€. Open kitchen offering local dishes. Closed Wed off-season.

Ristorante Miracapri, 13a Via Nastro d'Oro, Termini, ☎ 081 808 1202. €€. The De Turris family keep chilled Massa Lubrense wine on tap and are proud of their unique mobile pizza oven which can be wheeled to your table for a piping-hot lunchtime pizza. Specialty pasta dishes.

La Conca del Sogno, Recommone, Massa Lubrense, ☎ 081 808 1036. €€. Seafront restaurant with lovely views.

Taverna del Capitano, 10 Piazza delle Sirene, Marina del Cantone, ☎ 081 808 1028. €€. Restaurant with seaside views; rooms and sun loungers also available.

Il Cantuccio, 9 Via Vescovado, Marina del Cantone, ☎ 081 808 1228. €€. Seafood specialties, and pasta with zucchini at this lovely sea-view restaurant.

Lo Stuzzichino, 1 Via Deserto, Sant'Agata sui due Golfi, ☎ 081 533 0010. €€. Al fresco dining at this family-run restaurant. Closed Wed.

Aspiett Nu Poc, 12 Via Capo d'Arco, Nerano, Massa, ☎ 081 808 1159. €. Local specialties in this friendly eatery. The name means "Tarry awhile."

Emilia, 9 Via Reola, Sant'Agata sui due Golfi, ☎ 081 808 0643. €. Pizzas at lunchtime and dinner. Closed Tues.

Da Cardillo, 3 Via dei Campi, Sant'Agata sui due Golfi, ☎ 081 533 0417. €. Pizzeria also serving fish and pasta. Garden dining. Closed Mon.

■ Bars & Cafés

Stabia & Vico

Bar Caffè Del Corso, 123, Via G. Bonito, Stabia, ☎ 081 871 1993.

Gran Caffè, 12 Via Roma, Vico, ☎ 081 879 8147. Cakes, coffee, and aperitifs.

Exotic Ice Cream, 107 Via Filangieri, Vico, ☎ 081 801 6400. Sweets and homemade ice creams.

The Aequa Bar, Marina di Aequa, Seiano, Vico. A good place for a hot sandwich and a cold drink with a pleasant sea view. Open from April to October.

Meta & Piano

Bar Gran Caffè Laura, 97 Via A Cosenza, Meta, ☎ 532 1593. Gelateria and bar.

Bar Regina, 144-146 Corso Italia, Meta, ☎ 081 878 6709. Cakes and ice cream.

Bar Elio Guadagnuolo, Via Caracciolo, Meta, ☎ 081 878 8305. Local sweets a specialty.

Bar Delle Rose, Piazza delle Rose, Piano di Sorrento, ☎ 081 878 7272. Homemade ice cream.

Arte Dolce, Via Mortora S Liborio, Piano di Sorrento, ☎ 081 808 3147. Pastries and local sweets.

Casa del Dolce, Piazza Cota, Piano di Sorrento, ☎ 081 878 8038. Pastries and cakes.

Bar Cota, 11/12 Piazza Cota, Piano di Sorrento, ☎ 081 532 3441. Ice cream, coffee and pastries.

Sant'Agnello

Terrazza Bar, Via M Crawford, St Agnello. Stylish modern furniture, and a room with elegant sofas for relaxing. Its real advantage, however, is the large terrace with lovely sea view. A perfect place to start your evening, with a cocktail at sunset.

Bar Capriccio, 3 Via Cocumella, ☎ 081 878 2055.

Bar Turist, 7/8 Corso Italia, ☎ 081 878 2417. Good pastries.

Sorrento

Pasticceria Primavera, Corso Italia 142, Sorrento, ☎ 081 878 3375. Creative confectioner with another branch on Via Fuorimura.

Davide, Via P R Giuliani, Sorrento, ☎ 081 878 1337. Celebrated ice cream parlor.

Bar Villa Comunale, Villa Comunale, Sorrento. A popular spot for a morning coffee.

Bar Ercolano, Piazza Tasso, Sorrento, ☎ 081 807 2951. Central location, with cakes, ice cream and drinks, day or evening.

O'Funzionista, 4 Via Tasso, Sorrento, ☎ 081 807 4083. Sweets like *delizie al limone*, and *torta caprese*.

Massa Lubrense

Di Sarno, 2/4 Viale Filangieri, Massa Lubrense, ☎ 081 878 9244. Bar and ice cream parlor.

Bar Mazzola, 7-9 Massa Turro, Massa Lubrense, ☎ 081 878 9604. Cakes made daily and ice cream.

Bar Fiorentino, 7/9 Via Nastro Azzurro, Sant'Agata sui due Golfi, ☎ 081 878 9157. Ice cream and pastries.

Chalet Li Campi, 8 Via dei Campi, Sant'Agata sui due Golfi, ☎ 081 878 0514. Tea room, garden and ice cream parlor.

Buenos Aires, 2 Via Deserto, Sant'Agata sui due Golfi, ☎ 081 878 0852. Bar and ice cream parlor in a garden.

Angelo's, Marina della Lobra, Massa, ☎ 081 878 9040. Bar and ice cream parlor.

San Francesco, Piazza San Francesco, Massa, ☎ 081 808 9634. Bar and restaurant.

■ Places To Stay

The Sorrento Peninsula has a good range of accommodation to suit every budget – luxury hotels, town apartments, comfortable countryside resorts and campsites, as well as numerous small family hotels with a friendly atmosphere. Villas can be booked for those who want some privacy and perhaps their own swimming pool, away from the bustle of the busy towns, but with easy access to them. Some larger villa-style properties are run by religious orders. The camping sites and "tourist villages" in the countryside are usually within easy reach of the towns. Out-of-town hotels may offer a free shuttle bus service operating several times daily to Sorrento.

HOTEL PRICE CHART	
For a double room for two	
€	€50-150
€€	€151-250
€€€	€251+

Stabia & Vico

Hotel La Medusa, 5 Via Pass. Archeologica, Stabia, ☎ 081 872 3383, www.lamedusahotel.com. €€. This luxury hotel has an elegant lounge, beautiful gardens and swimming pool. Ideally located for the archeological site of Stabiae, La Medusa is a superlative retreat from the dusty excavations and the bustle of town.

Hotel Stabia, 101 Corso Vittorio Emanuele, Stabia, ☎ 081 872 2577. €€. This 92-room hotel is in a 19th-century Neo-Classical building, situated in town, on the seafront. A hotel bus is available for transfers to the thermal baths or local beaches.

Agriturismo Quisisana, 7 Via Pantanella, Quisisana, Stabia, ☎ 081 870 4554, www.agriquisisana.it. €. This family-run establishment on the slopes of Monte Faito offers panoramic views from its 10 comfortable en-suite rooms, and a terrace for al fresco dining. Double rooms with breakfast. An evening meal is supplied if desired, at an inclusive price, with drinks. Ideal if you want to spend a day or two exploring the area.

Hotel Sporting, 127 Via Filangieri, Vico, ☎ 081 879 9661, www.hotel-sporting.it. €. Good views from its restaurant and terrace and run by a charming family. Use of private beach.

Agriturismo La Selva, 51 Via Camaldoli, Vico, ☎ 081 802 4396, www.agriturismolaselva.net. €. Rustic accommodation and home cooking. Beautiful gazebos can be rented for picnics. Speak to Signora Esmeralda Marciano.

Villa Giusso, 51 Via Camaldoli, Vico, ☎ 081 802 4392, www.astapiana.com. €. A historic family palazzo with faded, but elegant, furnishings and family portraiture still intact. A fascinating way to get a glimpse of old aristocratic life in Sorrento. Half-board with dinner is also available. Speak to Signora Giulia.

Villa Cafiero, Colli di San Pietro, Vico, ☎ 081 808 3341, www.villacafiero.it. €. Superb liberty-style villa, built in 1910 and lovingly cared for by Giulia Cacace, who offers bed and breakfast in her wonderful home. Book-lovers will adore the library.

Camping Sant'Antonio, Via Marina d'Equa, Seiano, ☎ 081 802 8570, www.campingsantantonio.it. €. Campsite for tents and caravans. Mobile homes and bungalows can be rented. Cheap and cheerful accommodation right by the Seiano beachfront.

Meta & Piano

Panorama Palace Hotel, 1 Piazza Scarpati, Meta, ☎ 081 878 6833. €€. Beach hotel with pool and solarium.

Hotel Albatros, 54 Madonna di Roselle, Piano di Sorrento, ☎ 081 8787414. €€. Overlooks the Bay of Naples, near the Alimuri and Marina di Cassano beaches. 53 rooms with en-suite facilities, plus a swimming pool and solarium.

Hotel Klein Wien, 4 Ripa di Cassano, Piano di Sorrento, ☎ 081 878 6746, www.kleinwien.it. €. Near the Villa Fondi, with a lovely restaurant that has a panoramic view.

La Ripetta Hotel, Via Ripa di Cassano, Piano di Sorrento, ☎ 081 8088744. €. Of recent construction, on the clifftop overlooking the beach at Piano and with a good view of the coastline.

Nastro Azzurro, 20 Via Nastro Azzurro, Piano, ☎ 081 533 3269. €. Hotel with pool in panoramic hillside location.

Antico Parco del Principe, 8 Via San Pietro, Piano, ☎ 081 533 3310, www.parcodelprincipe.com. €. Not to be confused with the Sant'Agnello hotel. This is a less expensive, hillside hotel, which represents good value for the money.

Costa Alta Villaggio Turistico e Campeggio, 20A Via Madonna di Roselle, Piano di Sorrento, ☎ 081 532 1832. €.

Large complex along the coast with a private beach, and natural grottos. One- or two-room chalets with garden verandas, shower rooms and kitchenettes. The complex also has a restaurant and snack bar, a shop, pool, and tennis court.

I Pini, 242 Corso Italia, Piano di Sorrento, ☎ 081 878 6891, www.campingipini.com. €. Campsite with pool; bungalows and mobile homes available.

Sant'Agnello

Grand Hotel Cocumella, 7 Via Cocumella Sant'Agnello, ☎ 081 878 933. €€€. This Jesuit monastery turned noble family home and then hotel became a meeting point of renown for international visitors to pass the winter. An elevator takes guests down to the private beach and dock. Swimming pool and lovely garden.

Parco dei Principi, 1 Via Rota, Sant'Agnello, ☎ 081 878 4644. €€€. Designed by Gio Ponti, the Parco has kept its geometric 60s décor; but thankfully there is a great seawater outdoor pool, and the lovely gardens with an 18th-century villa in the grounds keep the Grand Tour ambiance alive.

Majestic Palace, 40 Via Crawford, Sant'Agnello, ☎ 081 807 2050. €€. Situated 1,200 feet from the sea, facilities include a swimming pool, sun terrace, Jacuzzi, sauna, and game room. Elegant hall and lounges, plus spacious rooms with all modern conveniences.

Villa Garden Hotel, 7 Via Cappuccini, Sant'Agnello, ☎ 081 878 1387, www.villagardenhotel.com. €€. A clifftop mansion transformed into a hotel with pool, and panoramic restaurant.

Villa Margherita, 17 Via M. Crawford, Sant'Agnello, ☎ 081 878 1381, www.hotelvillamargherita.it. €. Liberty-style (Art Deco) hotel with terrace restaurant. No pool.

Residence Casa Vacanze La Marinella, 93 Via Cappuccini, Sant'Agnello, ☎ 081 877 3980. €. Beach, restaurant, bar and holiday residence.

Il Pino, 30 Viale dei Pini, Sant'Agnello, ☎ 081 878 2776. €. Signora Menno's three-room family-run guesthouse.

Giardino delle Esperidi, 52 Viale dei Pini, Sant'Agnello, ☎ 081 878 3255, www.esperidi.com. €. Studios, chalets and two-bedroom bungalows available. Swimming pool.

Sorrento

Hotel Bellevue Sirene, 5 Piazza della Vittoria, Sorrento, ☎ 081 878 10 24. €€€. A 19th-century hotel built on the remains of a Roman villa. Good views over Marina Grande, as the name suggests, with "Roman baths" and a private beach.

Imperial Tramontano, 1 Via Veneto, Sorrento, ☎ 081 878 25 88. €€€. This very atmospheric and elegant hotel incorporates the historic home of Torquato Tasso.

Grand Hotel Excelsior Vittoria, 34 Piazza Tasso, Sorrento, ☎ 081 878 19 00. €€€. A hotel in four parts, each with a different style, the Vittoria has hosted many celebrities over the years. Roman columns in the garden.

Grand Hotel Flora, 248 Corso Italia, Sorrento, ☎ 081 878 2520. €€€. 130 rooms, with good views over the Bay of Naples. Restaurant, swimming pool, tennis courts.

Antiche Mura, 7 Via Fuorimura, Sorrento, ☎ 081 807 3523. €€. This elegant hotel in the heart of Sorrento offers views over the Vallone dei Mulini, and has the ruins of one of the original defensive towers of Sorrento within its grounds.

Villa Maria, 8 Via Capo, Sorrento, ☎ 081 878 1966. €€. Recently renovated, and with great views over the bay, the rooms are up-to-date and well equipped. Swimming pool, with solarium and Jacuzzi on the terrace. Good restaurant.

La Tonnarella, 31 Via Capo, Sorrento, ☎ 081 878 1153. €€. A cliffside Sorrentine villa that offers glorious views and hosts numerous wedding receptions. Rooms with Jacuzzi bathtubs for a very reasonable price.

La Minervetta, 25 Via Capo, Sorrento, ☎ 081 807 3069. €€. This 12-bedroom hotel began life as a restaurant that still offers great seafood specialties. A good location, with a view over town.

Il Nido, 62 Via Nastro Verde, Sorrento, ☎ 081 878 2766. €. On a hill five km/three miles from the main town of Sorrento but the hotel runs an hourly shuttle bus. The free Internet service is greatly appreciated by younger guests.

Villa Oriana, Via Rubinacci, Sorrento, ☎ 081 878 2468. €. Terrace hotel with good views

Le Sirene, Via degli Aranci, Sorrento, ☎ 081 807 2925. €. Youth hostel offering budget shared sleeping quarters – private rooms are also available at a slightly higher cost.

Residence Villagio Verde, 12 Via Cesarano, Sorrento, ☎ 081 807 3258. €. Bungalows with kitchens that sleep up to four.

Santa Fortunata-Campogaio, 39 Via Capo, Sorrento, ☎ 081 807 3574, www.santafortunata.com. €. Campsite in a good location just outside Sorrento, amid olive and lemon groves. Swimming pool and private rocky beach. Two- to four-person bungalows also available.

Massa Lubrense

La Solara, 118 Via Capo, Marina di Puolo, ☎ 081 538 0000. €€. Well situated, only 800 yards from Puolo Beach and with a shuttle bus operating to Piazza Tasso. Facilities include a large swimming pool – heated in the low season, March-April, October-November.

Villa Lubrense, 31 Via Partenope, Massa Lubrense, ☎ 081 533 9781. €. Comfortable rooms, some with kitchens; two pools with sea view, access to Marina di Puolo beach.

Le Tore, 43 Via Pontone, Sant'Agata sui due Golfi, ☎ 081 808 0637, www.letore.com. €. Accommodation in a rural setting; ideal spot for hikers.

Torre Cangiani, Vigliano, Massa, ☎ 081 533 9849. €. Stay in a 16th-century Saracen tower, overlooking olive and lemon groves.

La Conca del Sogno, Recommone, Massa Lubrense, ☎ 081 808 1036. €. Rooms available above the restaurant are very sensibly priced for the seaside location.

Residence, 2 Piazza delle Sirene, Nerano, ☎ 081 808 2165, www.residencenerano.com. €. Air-conditioned rooms and solarium with lovely sea views.

■ Shopping

Typical products of the Sorrento Peninsula involve lemons – and include liqueurs, chocolate, soap and ceramics with lemon motifs. The Limoncello liqueur can be sampled at one of several micro-distilleries in the town of Sorrento. Clothes shops abound on the Via S. Cesareo in Sorrento and on the Corso Italia at Sant'Agnello and Piano. Bargain hunters should ask around for the times of the weekly local market (Tuesday in Sorrento).

Clothes, Leather Goods & Jewelry

Joy to Wear, 22 Corso Italia, Sorrento, ☎ 081 878 5058. Italian women's wear.

Capricci e Coccole, 22 Via Bagnuole, Sorrento, ☎ 081 534 2144. Clothes and toys for children and all baby products.

Vanna Boutique, 204 Corso Italia, Sorrento, ☎ 081 878 1330. A wide range of Italian women's and men's clothing and accessories.

Adario & Fiorentino Boutique, 128 and 212 Corso Italia, Sorrento, ☎ 081 878 1361. Designer clothing, including Armani, Anna Molinari and Ermenegildo Zegna. Two stores in Sorrento and a third in nearby Sant'Agata. A good selection of bridal wear.

Stile & Sport, 141 Corso Italia, Sorrento, ☎ 081 878 3517. Fred Perry sportswear and other well-known labels for men and women.

Cherie Mode, 3 Via S Ciro, Vico, ☎ 081 801 5545. Clothing and accessories.

Cicalese, 74 Corso Filangieri, Vico, ☎ 081 801 6054. Jewelry store.

Tienet, 13 Via S. Cesareo and 10 Via Luigi De Maio, Sorrento, ☎ 081 877 1962. Two shops selling ties, hats and T-shirts. Tienet, as the name suggests, also has a thriving Internet business, selling quality ties at good prices.

Punto Jeans, 6 Via Marziale Sorrento, ☎ 081 807 2992. Denim and casual wear for youngsters.

Siniscalchi, 203 Corso Italia, Sorrento, ☎ 081 878 3065. This famous store will produce a pair of handmade sandals especially for you.

Balduccelli, 12 Viale Filangieri, Massa Lubrense, ☎ 081 808 9315. Handmade sandals and attractive summer wear for ladies.

Gaia, 38 Corso Italia, Sorrento, ☎ 081 878 1668. Stylish men's and women's shoes.

Sorrento Shoes, 71 Via San Cesareo, Sorrento, ☎ 081 807 2124. Entirely handmade Italian shoes – loafer-style.

Giolleria Di Somma, 114 Corso Italia, Sorrento, ☎ 081 807 3213. Jewelry and accessories by Lalique, Hermes and other top brands.

Craft & Gift Shops

Giglio Asla, 11 Via Rota, Sorrento, ☎ 081 878 5543. Specializes in the local craft of inlaid woodwork – especially jewelry boxes.

Rosbenia, 34 Piazza Laura, Sorrento, ☎ 081 877 2341. Linen ware for table and bedroom. Great for wedding gifts.

Pia Russo, 6 Via Scarpati, Meta, ☎ 081 532 2302. Terracotta and ceramics.

Aprea Mare, 15 Via Santa Lucia, Sorrento, ☎ 081 807 2818. Manufacturers of the world-famous *gozzi* boats.

Cuomo's Lucky Store, 2/7 Piazza Antiche Mura, Sorrento, ☎ 081 878 5649. Sorrento inlaid wood and other Campanian crafts.

Castellano Collezione Casa, 8 Via S. Ciro, Vico, ☎ 081 879 8095. Porcelain and ceramics.

Books, Antiques & Old Prints

Euronews, 69 Corso S. Agata, Sant'Agata sui due Golfi, ☎ 081 808 0066. News agent and stationer.

Punto e Virgola, 51 Corso Italia, Sorrento, ☎ 081 808 6510. News agent and stationer.

L'Indice, 81 Corso Italia, Sorrento, ☎ 081 532 1753. Book and magazine shop.

Food & Drink

Sole di Sorrento & Wine Corner, 12 Via Capo, Sorrento, ☎ 081 807 4731. Very wide range of wines and liqueurs, including, of course, the local *limoncello*.

Correale Distillery, 12 Via Baranica, Sorrento, ☎ 081 807 3203. Homemade *limoncello*, produced with loving care by this family firm.

Nastro D'Oro, 5 Piazza S. Croce, Massa Lubrense, ☎ 081 808 1368. Liqueurs, desserts, jams and gift boxes.

Piemme, 161 Corso Italia, Sorrento, ☎ 081 877 3596. Wine and other local produce.

Mauro Rinaldi, 1/3 Via Luigi di Maio, Sorrento, ☎ 081 807 2199. Lemon, nut, mandarin and fennel are just a few of the liqueurs sold.

Pieme Fabbrica Liquori, 161/163 Corso Italia, Piano di Sorrento, ☎ 081 8072927. Makers of liqueur.

Oleificio Candela, 255 Via A. De Gasperi, Stabia, ☎ 081 871 9416. High quality oil.

Laboratorio Artigianale, 60 Via Angelo Cosenza, Meta, ☎ 081 878 7958. Dairy products.

La Tradizione, 969 Via R Bosco, Vico, ☎ 081 802 8217. Cheese, salami and other delicacies.

Gabriele, 1/5 Corso Umberto, Vico, ☎ 081 801 5285. Dairy products and ice cream.

Apreda, 20 Via del Mare, Sorrento, ☎ 081 878 1334. Dairy products. Get your mozzarella here.

■ Entertainment

The Sorrento Peninsula is a magnet for young and lively tourists, with several nightclubs; in summer people gravitate to beach spots rather than town. There are also classical concerts, annual music and cinema festivals, and theatrical and cultural shows that are more family-oriented. Watersports and walking itineraries are popular in the peninsula. A number of special interest vacations are also available in Sorrento.

Music & Dance

Matilda, 1 Piazza Tasso, Sorrento, ☎ 081 877 3236, www.matildaclub.net. Matilda's has a lively disco catering to a young, casually dressed crowd of Italians and tourists. Arrive at 11 pm to enjoy the **Karaoke Bar**, before going down to the nightclub or the more elegant piano bar. Sunday is Latin Night.

Kalimera, 4 Via Calata Punta Capo, ☎ 081 878 2823, www.kalimera2003.com. Three dance floors; occasional gay and lesbian nights. Restaurant. Closed Mon.

Fauno Club, 1 Piazza Tasso, Sorrento, ☎ 081 8781021. This club also stages the Tarantella show that takes you on a lively journey through the history of the region, including invasions, wars and festivals.

Teatro Tasso, Piazza San Antonino, Sorrento, ☎ 081 807 5525, www. teatrotasso.com. The **Sorrento Musical Show** held here each evening offers a 75-minute performance featuring traditional dances, costumes and songs.

Circolo dei Forestieri, 35 Via L. de Maio, Sorrento, ☎ 081 877 3263. Garden with panoramic sea views. Live music and dancing every evening.

La Mela, 263 Corso Italia, Sorrento, ☎ 081 878 1917. Tarantella shows and nightly discotheque for the under-30s.

Artis Domus, 56 Via S. Nicola, Sorrento, ☎ 081 877 2073. Underground tavern, serving good beer and with live music.

Bollicine Wine Bar & Shop, 9 Via dell'Accademia, Sorrento, ☎ 081 878 4616. Sells wine and gourmet cheeses, becoming a stylish wine bar in the evening, also serving hot food.

Filou Club, 12 Via Santa Maria della Pieta, Sorrento, ☎ 081 878 2083. A lively piano bar.

Kan Kan, Piazza Sant'Antonino, Sorrento, ☎ 081 878 1114. A popular disco.

Melting Pot, 32 Via dei Campi, Sant'Agata, ☎ 081 808 0888. Pub and *birreria*.

Titos Pub, 67 Via Filangieri, Vico, ☎ 081 801 5092.

Kike Bar, The Dock, Marina Lobra, ☎ 328 833 5355. Beer and music on the seafront.

Caffè Osvaldo, 7 Piazza Vescovato, Massa Lubrense, ☎ 081 878 9005. Granitas, snacks and cocktails.

Funiculi Funicula, 16 Via Fontanelle, Marina della Lobra, ☎ 081 878 9392. Live music in the evenings in this bar and restaurant.

Angelo's Bar, 90 Via C. Colombo, Marina della Lobra, ☎ 081 878 9040. Drinks and snacks.

Caffè Gregory, 2 Corso S. Agata. Sant'Agata sui due Golfi, ☎ 081 533 0308I. Ice creams by day and live music by night.

Insolito, Corso Italia, Sorrento, ☎ 081 877 2409. Lounge and wine bar.

■ Adventures

Beaches & Spas

Terme di Stabia, 3/5 Viale delle Terme, Stabia, ☎ 081 391 3111, www.termedistabia.com. Thermal baths.

Scrajo Mare, S 145, Vico Equense, ☎ 081 801 6098. Beach offering loungers, beach umbrellas and changing cabins.

Lido Marinella, 1 Via Caruso, Meta, ☎ 081 532 2030.

Puolo Sole & Mare, Marina di Puolo, ☎ 380 728 2138. Sunbeds, deckchairs; also pedalboats and canoes for rent.

Scrajo Terme, Vico Equense, ☎ 081 801 5731, www.scrajoterme.it. Spa and beauty center with attached hotel and restaurant.

Sea Sports & Tours

Bikini Diving, 145 S.S. Sorrentina, Vico Equense, ☎ 081 801 5555.

Diving Sirene d'Equa, 132 Via Filangieri, Vico Equense, ☎ 081 801 6418.

Sottomarino Tritone, 50 Via delle Rose, Piano di Sorrento, ☎ 081 808 6618. Submarine excursions.

Mediterraneo Yacht Charter, 85 Via Crawford, Sant'Agnello, ☎ 081 807 2947. Operates from the Hotel Mediterraneo. Half-day, full-day and night cruises.

Sorrento Diving Center, 63 Via Marina Piccola, Sorrento, ☎ 081 877 4812.

Diving & Residence Tour, 18 Via Fontanelle, Marina Lobra, ☎ 081 807 2410. Dive center located in the Dive Residence, a small hotel, with two boats. They make two or three dive trips daily.

Villaggio Diving Nettuno, 39 Via A. Vespucci, Marina del Cantone, ☎ 081 801 6418.

Diving Centre, 32 Vico III Rota, Massa, ☎ 081 877 4812. Located in the nature park of Punta Campanella, offering dives between Sorrento and Capri with qualified instructors.

Ulixes, Marine Park, Punta Campanella, ☎ 0333 221 8813 (cell), www.pescaturismo.org.

Cooperative S. Antonio, 47 Via Cantone, Nerano, ☎ 081 808 1638, www.cooperativasantonio.com. Boat rental; excursions to Capri and the Amalfi Coast, visits to the marine reserve of Punta Campanella.

Cala di Puolo, Via Marina di Puolo, Massa, ☎ 081 807 3399, www.divingtour.it. Year-round dive center; rental of wetsuits and other equipment.

Walking, Hiking & Horseback Riding

Comunità Montana, Via Municipio, Tramonti, ☎ 089 876 354. This local organization provides information about walking tours of the region.

Maneggio Vecchio West, 57 Via Radicosa, Agerola, ☎ 081 802 5131. The name literally means "Old West Riding School." It includes a picnic area and games for children. This is a new start-up and they are planning to offer guided tours, biking and trekking in local nature parks as well as on the Amalfi Coast.

WWF, 67 Corso Italia, Sorrento, ☎ 081 807 2533. Maps and guided tours.

Ente Parco Punta Campanella, 40 Viale Filangieri, Massa, ☎ 081 808 9877, www.parchi-marini.it. Information center for the Marine Park.

CRAWFORD - THE MAN AND THE VILLA

Francis Marion Crawford was born in 1854, the Italian-born son of sculptor Thomas Crawford, and his American wife, Louisa Ward. Francis, named after a famous American general, was educated in the USA and England, and traveled widely before returning to Italy and embracing Catholicism. He published his first novel in 1882, and married Elizabeth Berdan in 1884. Having spent the summer of 1885 at the Hotel Cocumella in Sant'Agnello, they decided to settle nearby, and purchased the Villa Renzi, which they renovated and expanded into the castle-like creation which has long been known as Villa Crawford. During his life Crawford wrote more than 50 novels: Robert Louis Stevenson was one of his many admiring readers. The Villa Crawford, eventually placed in the charge of the Catholic church, still stands, an eloquent reminder of a literary past, when writers like Henry James came to call. Crawford left his own tribute to Sorrento in his book, *To Leeward*: "Perhaps in all the orange-scented south there is none more perfect, more sweet with gardens and soft sea-breath, more rich in ancient olive groves, or more tenderly nestled in the bosom of a beautiful Nature."

The Amalfi Coast

In this Chapter

Thirty miles of jaw-dropping magnificence: this remains one of the most dramatic and exciting stretches of coastline in Europe despite the ever-increasing numbers of tourists. John Steinbeck wrote of the Amalfi Coast, "It is a dream place that isn't quite real when you are there." The picturesque villages clinging to sheer mountainsides that drop into turquoise waters are certainly a dazzling sight that you can scarcely believe, and that you will never forget. The spectacular scenery provided by the Lattari limestone cliffs and the terraced groves and vineyards, is further enhanced by the colorful, tiled domes of the churches that grace these picture-postcard tourist resorts, and the white sails of pleasure boats skimming along the shore line.

In his *Decameron*, Boccaccio described this region as "the only delectable part of Italy... full of towns, gardens, springs and wealthy men." This is perhaps truer today than ever before, for after the heyday of the maritime republics in the medieval period, the isolation of Amalfi and surrounding villages prompted a decline in economic importance and population which has only recently revived, through the construction of the cliff-top road linking the region to Naples and Salerno, and the advent of tourism. Nowadays, you need to be wealthy to buy a property on these spectacular hillsides, and even vacationers will find that paradise comes at a price. Fortunately, a reliable and fairly frequent bus service means that day visits are a perfectly acceptable way to enjoy the charms of this spectacular stretch of southern Italy.

For those who do decide to make the Amalfi Coast the base for their visit to the region, there is enough diversity in the several resorts here to suit almost everyone. Indefatigable shop-

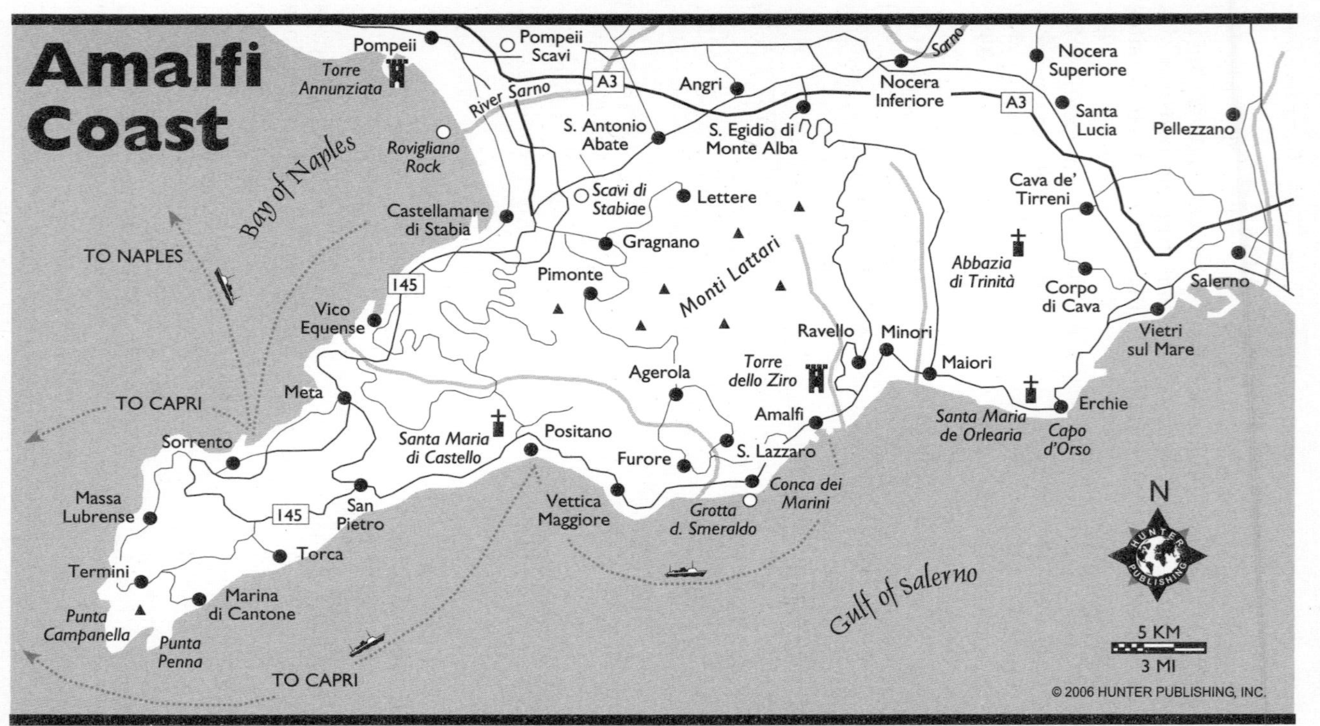
Amalfi Coast
Pompeii
Pompeii Scavi
Torre Annunziata
River Sarno
A3
Angri
Sarno
Nocera Inferiore
Nocera Superiore
Santa Lucia
Pellezzano
Rovigliano Rock
S. Antonio Abate
S. Egidio di Monte Alba
Bay of Naples
Scavi di Stabiae
Lettere
Cava de' Tirreni
Castellamare di Stabia
Gragnano
Monti Lattari
Abbazia di Trinità
TO NAPLES
145
Pimonte
Corpo di Cava
Salerno
Vico Equense
Ravello
Minori
Vietri sul Mare
Maiori
Agerola
Torre dello Ziro
Meta
Erchie
TO CAPRI
Amalfi
Santa Maria de Orlearia
Capo d'Orso
Santa Maria di Castello
Positano
Sorrento
Furore
S. Lazzaro
Conca dei Marini
Massa Lubrense
San Pietro
Vettica Maggiore
Grotta d. Smeraldo
Torca
Termini
Marina di Cantone
Punta Campanella
Punta Penna
Gulf of Salerno
TO CAPRI
N
HUNTER PUBLISHING
5 KM
3 MI
© 2006 HUNTER PUBLISHING, INC.

pers and lovers of glitz and glamor will adore **Positano**, its narrow streets crammed with boutiques so trendy that clothes bought here are judged to have a style of their own, with plenty of bars and clubs where you can show them off. Amalfi offers a good central location, and the benefits of a beach resort with a number of cultural and historic sites thrown in.

Ravello, nestling in the hills above, is unequalled for romance and elegance. Its cool serenity and 19th-century villas and gardens, are a welcome contrast from the bustling waterfronts below. **Maiori**, **Cetara** or **Vietri** would suit families with children clamoring for a beach vacation. Nature lovers and classicists will enjoy excursions to **Paestum** and the **Cilento Valley**, and may choose to stay at the delightful and less crowded beach resorts of **Marina di Pisciotta** and **Palinuro**.

The Amalfi Coast is not directly accessible by train, so bus or car are the only options. But driving along a road that has been described as one of the most beautiful scenic routes in Italy is far from being a chore or a bore, if you approach it in a spirit of adventure.

Buses run regularly on this route and are the easiest way to visit if you are staying in Sorrento. The drivers are highly skilled and usually negotiate the hairpin turns with surprisingly few hold-ups. Watch out for the numerous *Torre Saraceni* on the way. These watchtowers were built in the wake of attacks by the feared Saracens – Turkish and Barbary Coast sea raiders.

■ Positano

The initial view of this enchanting cliffside village, the first of the Amalfi Coast resorts, with its brightly painted houses tumbling down to the small beach, is enough to convince many day-trippers to get off the bus right here. John Steinbeck helped to popularize Positano back in the 1950s, as numerous American artists and writers followed his lead. Since then the resort has rarely been without a clutch of celebrities in residence. Film director Franco Zeffirelli owns a villa in nearby Arienze, where he has hosted Elizabeth Taylor, Placido Domingo and Liza Minnelli. From the bus stop there is a winding road down to the harbor. Positano can also be reached by boat from Naples, Capri and Sorrento.

Steinbeck was unabashed about vaunting the charms of Positano, pointing out that tourist development could not spoil the location because "the cliffs are all taken." Certainly, the resort looks as charming as ever, but there is no doubt that the narrow lanes are chock-full of boutiques, while every square foot of land with a view is converted into a café, and on weekends parked cars stretch hundreds of yards along the coast road above. This is not the place to spend a day in summer if you don't want to be walking three-abreast in the admittedly picturesque lanes, lined on both sides with shops. On sale in them is the glitzy summer-wear, famous enough to be designated the "Positano-style." Sandals, souvenirs, art and ceramics galleries all make the resort a shoppers' heaven. Reputed to be the first place in Italy to introduce the bikini – in 1959 – Positano still thinks of itself as a sartorial trendsetter, though younger visitors might consider it to be stuck in the '60s groove.

The resort has made the most of its spectacular location and offers a choice of accommodations for those visitors who want their own "room with a view." Two of the most famous hotels in Italy are here, offering superlative service, but there are a range of options for the less well-heeled (although this is not the place for budget travelers). Day-trippers can console themselves with a slap-up meal in one of the many restaurants. A tourist office near the main beach is open in the morning (☎ 089 875 067).

Since so many people are in the shops and others are people-watching in the cafés and restaurants, the beaches are not as crowded as might be expected. Expect to pay dearly for a decent spot on the Marina Grande; otherwise the western beach of Fornillo is a five-minute walk away; note the Saracen Tower en route. To the east are several smaller beaches: La Porta, Fiumicello and Arienzo. Don't expect white sand. These are pebble beaches.

Church of Santa Maria Assunta

The splendid yellow, blue and green majolica dome of this parish church dominates almost every photograph of Positano. Medieval in origin, and restored in succeeding centuries, the church has a 16th-century painting by Fabrizio Santafedele, and a lovely Byzantine-style *Black Madonna* with Jesus on her knees above the High Altar. A priceless bust of the patron saint of Positano, San Vito, is also conserved in the church.

Santa Maria Assunta

Medieval relics include a fragment of a mosaic floor in the apse, and a marble slab depicting a sea monster on the doorway of the campanile. More recent paintings by Basil Necitaillov – completed in 1958 and 1960 – portray several of the local inhabitants. The church is near the beach on the Piazza Flavio Gioia. The square is named for a 14th-century son of the village who is venerated as the inventor of the compass, harking back to the great navigation traditions of the Amalfi Coast villagers. Another relic of the past is the large anchor at the entrance of the Ancora Hotel, which is reputed to have been salvaged from a Saracen ship.

Palazzo Murat

This Baroque-style 18th-century villa was built as the summer residence of the flamboyant and short-lived French King of Naples, Joachim Murat, and his wife, Caroline Bonaparte. The antique-filled interior, and picturesque iron-grille balconies which overlook the flower-filled courtyard, are exquisite, and since it has now been converted into a hotel, this is a great opportunity to relive the "olde worlde" experience of the Grand Tour.

Montepertuso

Visitors who want to get away from the crowds, and have energy to spare, can take the footpath from Via Marconi up to the village of Montepertuso. Or take a bus from Piazza dei Mulini – it is 3.3 km/two miles above Positano. Frederick II of

Sicily is believed to have trained his hawks here, and kestrels and falcons can still be seen along the nature trails around the villages, 300-400 yards above sea level. Another scenic path leads to the even higher village of Nocelle, with its piazzetta and picturesque church. The panorama of the coastline from here is superb. It is 1,700 steps back down to the main coast road east of Positano; alternatively, to the east of the village, the famous hiking trail known as *Il Sentiero Degli Dei* – Pathway of the Gods – to Furore can be undertaken. This is a challenging climb, rather than a walk.

The Grottos

Alternative excursions can be taken by boat to the grottos around Positano – Mirabella, Mount Canocchia, Grotto Acquara or to the Li Galli islands. Boat trips also go to the cave at La Porta where Paleolithic and Mesolithic tools were found.

■ Vettica Maggiore

The next stop on the coast road from Positano is this small village, bounded by the towers of **Grado** and Assiola. A cluster of houses leads to the sea. The ornate church of **San Gennaro**, restored in the early 17th century, stands on a large, majolica-paved piazza. Among the important paintings housed here is the *Martyrdom of St Bartholomew* by Giovanni Bernardo Lama. An 18th-century bell tower stands alongside the majolica-tiled dome of the church.

Signs direct travelers to a cliff-side beach. The 13th-century fortification at **Assiola** is also worth a visit, as it is one of the best preserved in the region. The structure, in limestone, was composed of two rooms, one above the other. An old local saying states *Chi vuol vivere sano, la mane a Vettica, la sera a Praiano* – for a healthy life spend the mornings in Vettica and the evenings in Praiano. But this predates the building of the notoriously wild Africana disco near the latter village, so the meaning is unclear!

■ Praiano

On the other side of Assiola is the fishing village of Praiano – a group of white houses on a green slope. With its small beach and nearby sandy coves, Praiano is becoming increasingly popular as its better-known neighbors become overclogged with tourists. At the top of the village, the **Church of San Luca** houses 16th-century paintings by Giovanni Bernardo Lama, the Madonna of the Rosary by Padovano da Montorio, and a late 17th-century silver bust of Saint Luke the Evangelist. The wood pulpit is decorated with paintings of St Peter and St Paul. Medieval nobles once resided in Praiano, and perhaps they too enjoyed visiting the **Marina di Praia**, a seaside hamlet next door. Nowadays this scenic cove hosts a couple of restaurants.

Shortly after leaving Praiano, watch out for the *presepe* – a cluster of model houses built by Michele Castellano – featuring several of the buildings in Praiano itself, including the Trattoria San Gennaro. Close by at **Furore**, a number of steps cut into the rock are the start of a 20-minute cliff walk back to Praiano. More steps lead to the higher levels of the village where the **Church of Sant'Elia Profeta** houses a 15th-century painting by Angelo Antonello, considered to be one of the most important artworks in the region. Furore is also known locally for its wines of the same name, and for its modern sculptures. Marina di Furore has an old paper mill, converted into a museum, and a restaurant at the foot of the cliff.

THE LI GALLI ISLANDS & ISCA

Driving along the first stretch of the Amalfi Coast toward Positano, Isca and the Li Galli islands come into view. Named after the mythical Sirens, Leucosia, Parthenope and Lisia, who were believed to lure sailors on the rocks, they have been refuges for pirates, and in the medieval period watchtowers were built on them. Today, the clear water around the rocky outcrops of Gallo Lungo, La Rotonda, and Castelluccia is popular with swimmers.

■ Conca dei Marini

Conca dei Marini

Rounding the Capo di Conca, on the coast road, Amalfi at last comes into view in all its glory. This dramatic promontory, however, deserves some attention itself. A former Roman province and base of a medieval merchant fleet, more recently Conca dei Marini has become a celebrity retreat. Carlo Ponti built a glorious white villa here, and Gianni Agnelli was known to stop for awhile. Residents built the massive watchtower on the headland of the promontory after the local church – **San Pancrazio** – was ransacked by Turkish pirates in the mid-16th century. Today, the neo-Byzantine church is one of three that can be reached by steps, known locally as a *scalinatella*.

Farther up is the *Convento di Santa Rosa*, now in private hands. In former times, the Augustine nuns were the inventors of a wonderful local pastry – the Santa Rosa confection made with fruit and ricotta. Locals still make the sweet, on the annual saint's day. The Festival of Ravello uses this location for some of its concerts.

Another street leads from the square below to **Sant'Antonio di Padova** – spectacularly perched on a cliff side parapet.

■ Amalfi

This is the best-known of the Amalfi Coast towns. Despite its hustle and bustle, the plaque in the middle of town that reads, "for those natives of Amalfi who are called to Heaven, Judgment Day will be just another day," is still believable. Indeed, the local inhabitants can be forgiven for boasting that their town is heavenly. Its location is certainly so. The grandeur of the Cathedral recalls the glory days of Amalfi when it was an independent and successful maritime Republic, rivaling the Genoa, Venice and Pisa. Nowadays, these four cities together recall their shared history as

Amalfi

centers of medieval trade in an annual boat race. In those days, Amalfi had a population 10 times greater than now, but the tourists seem to more than make up for this loss in the summer months. The crowds of visitors, fortunately, cannot dispel the air of dignity around the dazzling Duomo and Cloister.

A walk to the Valley of the Mills affords another opportunity to escape the crowds, and recollect an ancient industry of the town – paper manufacture. A museum nearby explains the old techniques. Elegant notelets and envelopes are an appropriate souvenir to purchase in Amalfi. Other tributes to the impressive maritime traditions of the town are in the civic museum, where the Tavoliere Amalfitana can be viewed. This is the book of maritime laws that governed the republic, and the rest of the Mediterranean, up to 1570. You can also see the waterfront statue of Flavio Gioia, the Italian navy captain who introduced (and possibly invented) the magnetic compass to Mediterranean sailors in 1302.

Flavio Gioia

Fortunally, cultural relics can also be admired from any of the excellent restaurants and cafés that line the waterfront. To the left the on the hillside, the **Capuchin Convent** can be seen. It has been converted to a hotel which, with its panoramic terrace, was a favorite on the Grand Tour. And to the right, also high up the mountainside, is the imposing **Cimitero Monumentale**. As would be expected in the most popular resort of the Amalfi Coast, one can wine and dine well here. The local wine, called Sammarco, is very good.

The Waterfront

Disembarking from public transport, whether by road or sea, visitors usually begin their tour of Amalfi on the Marina. The square is always bustling with arriving or departing passengers. A tourist office is located here (☎ 089 872 619; open 8 am-2 pm and 4-7 pm). A statue of Flavio Gioia dominates the square (Positano and Amalfi are competing to claim him as their own, on the grounds that he invented the compass). The remains of an Arsenal, where the multi-oared galleys were once constructed in the 10th and 11th centuries, can also be seen on the waterfront.

The Cathedral & Cloister

The heart of Amalfi is the Piazza del Duomo, dominated by the immense, glorious, gold and mosaic cathedral, claimed by some to be the finest in southern Italy. The Arab-Norman façade of the Cathedral has lace-like open arches that are very unusual in Italian sacred architecture. A particular feature is the 11th-century bronze door, from Constantinople. The tiled cupola is typical of Amalfi Coast churches, one of the many delights of the resort towns.

A grandiose flight of stairs leads up to the striped marble and stone façade of the Duomo. By its side is a 13th-century bell tower, and behind this the Chiostro del Paradiso, where the great and good of Amalfi once vied to be interred. The colonnaded garden here, with interlaced arches and sculptures, is very beautiful. The interior of the Cathedral has been extensively renovated in Baroque style. The remains of St Andrew, reportedly brought back from the Holy Land by Cardinal Pietro Capuano in 1208, are buried in the crypt. An extraordinary substance, called Manna, is said to have issued from the saint's bones.

Another story connected to the Cathedral is that in June 1544, when Turkish pirates appeared off Amalfi, local inhabitants' prayers to St Andrew for deliverance were answered when a storm blew up, and drove the pirates off. Since then, June 27 has been celebrated as an annual holiday for Amalfitans. A painting by Ottavio Eliani, on the high altar, commemorates the event. One of the chapel baptismal fonts, in red porphyry, is believed to have been brought here from Paestum.

An adjacent museum houses medieval treasures and ecclesiastical oddities like the bishop of Amalfi's 18th-century sedan chair, brought from Macao. A bejewelled mitre, with pearls and gold, provides further insight into the pampered past of Episcopal potentates.

Bars line the Piazza del Duomo, and it is worth the expense to loiter awhile enjoying the view. In addition to the Cathedral, there is a Baroque 18th-century fountain to admire. Concerts are held in the cloister on summer nights.

The Museo Civico

A 15th-century manuscript copy of the *Tavoliere Amalfitana* (12th century) is kept in the municipal museum on the Piazza Municipio. The Tavoliere is a collection of maritime laws that were extensively used by sailors in the Mediterranean region until the late 16th century. The code is a testament to the pioneering role of Amalfi in the advancement of navigational skills and rules. Other exhibits refer to the role of Flavio Gioia, the merchant traveler who is said to have invented the compass in the 12th century. The ceramic panel on the exterior wall of the museum depicts scenes from local history. ☎ 089 871 066. Open 9 am-1 pm daily. Closed Wed. Free admission.

The Convent Hotels

A favorite place to stay in Amalfi for Grand Tour travelers in the 19th century, was the so-called **Cappuccini Convento**. A medieval monastery, originally founded in the 13th century as the Convento di S. Pietro della Canonica, it passed into the hands of the Capuchins in 1583 and eventually became a hotel. Longfellow wrote a poem about it, and Richard Wagner spent time here. The 13th-century cloister is much-painted and photographed. It is closed to visitors at the moment, but can be seen from the waterfront. The hotel is currently abandoned, and it is hoped that the site will be restored and reopened in the not-too-distant future along with the elevators that used to bring hotel guests directly to the beach.

The **Luna Convento**, now a hotel, was founded in the 13th century – some say by St Francis of Assisi – and is crammed with ancient structures, including a lovely Romanesque cloister, a Baroque chapel and crypt with frescoes, and a converted 15th-century watchtower. This is the most historic hotel on the Amalfi Coast – dating as it does from the early 19th century. A host of famous people have stayed here, from politicians like Bismarck and Mussolini to film stars and writers like Ingrid Bergman and Tennessee Williams. Ibsen is said to have written part of *The Doll's House* while he was in residence.

The Valle dei Mulini

From the Piazza del Duomo, a walk up Via Genova through to the other side of Amalfi, where the souvenir shops give way to lemon groves, leads to the Valley of the Mills. This area was once the center of an ancient paper industry dating from the 12th century, one of the oldest in Europe. The techniques were passed on from the Arabs. In those days, cotton and linen, rather than wood, were the raw materials used to make paper. While most of the old mills have now been converted into private homes, one company, **Cartiera Amatruda**, continues the tradition, and souvenirs of Amalfi-made paper can be purchased in town. On the Via Valle dei Mulini is the **Museo della Carta**, or paper museum. Opened in 1969, it displays antique presses and old prints, together with a few ancient manuscripts. ☎ 089 872 615. 9 am-1 pm, Mon and Fri only. The small **Museo della Civilita Contadina** near here presents archeological finds from surrounding villages. A ceramics factory and a limoncello manufacturer, both using traditional techniques, can also be visited.

If your spirit of adventure has not yet been exhausted, you can continue walking up the **Vallone delle Ferriere**, named after a former ironworks, and follow a nature trail. It leads to the nature reserve run by the World Wildlife Fund. Along the way, a rare fern, *Woodwardia radicans*, can be seen. It is only found here and on the island of Ischia. Continuing on the walk, takes you to the village of **Pontone**.

Woodwardia radicans

An alternative walk from Amalfi, is up the 1,000 or so steps that lead to the village of **Pogerola**. From here there are lovely views of the Gulf.

■ Atrani

The much quieter neighbor of Amalfi, with its one pretty piazza, several churches and sandy beach, Atrani is only a 10-minute walk away, via the Luna Convento, or past the Zaccaria restaurant, and is a lovely refuge from the tourist crowds. Atrani has been designated as "the smallest town in Europe." The 10th-century church of **San Salvatore** has been refurbished in Baroque and Neo-Classical styles, and has a beautifully tiled dome and 11th-century bronze doors, also from Constantinople (like those of the Amalfi cathedral). Another feature of note is the 12th-century marble plaque depicting peacocks, mermaids and birds of prey. Its significance has long since been forgotten, and is the subject of some speculation. The nearby

Atrani

Chiesa dell'Immacolata has Neo-Classical decoration, and a multi-colored marble altar. Finally, the 13th-century church of **Santa Maria Maddalena** has a 19th-century neo-Baroque façade, a majolica-tiled dome, a beautiful marble altar and 16th-century paintings by local artists. Atrani is also known for the colorful ceramics produced here.

AMALFI AND THE COMPASS

Italian sources from the 14th and 15th centuries credit the mariners of Amalfi with the invention of the compass: "Prima dedit nautis, usum magnetis Amalphis" (the people of Amalfi were the first to use the magnet in navigation). In fact it was the Chinese who are believed to have invented the magnetic compass as early as the ninth century, but the famous navigators of the Amalfi Coast certainly appear to have perfected the design.

■ Ravello

Certainly the most romantic of the Amalfi Coast towns and, some would argue, the most spectacular for its cliff-top setting. André Gide wrote that Ravello was closer to the sky than to the sea and, having winced at the hairpin turns as you made your way up here, you will surely agree. In his medieval work, the *Decameron*, Boccaccio described Ravello as a town above the most beautiful coast in Italy, "where many rich men live." This proves not only that this stunning location has been appreciated for centuries, but that it has always been – and remains – a haunt of the mega-wealthy.

Perched on a 350-m/1,000-foot cliff overlooking the sea, this is a cool world of elegant palaces and breathtaking gardens with extraordinary views. It has been immortalized in Wagner's *Parsifal*, and is a backdrop for countless novels, *Lady Chatterley's Lover* by DH Lawrence and the *Immoraliste* by Gide among them. John Huston filmed the movie *Beat the Devil* here, and Gore Vidal is a long-time resident.

Ravello is a 30-minute ride on the Sita buses, which make the hourly journey from Piazza Flavio Gioia in Amalfi. Spare at least an afternoon to see the town, which must be visited on foot – so bring comfortable shoes. There is a tourist office on Piazza Vescovado (☎ 089 857 096, open 8 am to 8 pm). If you can afford to stay over, you will surely enjoy the tranquility of the evening scene on the square, a standing and sitting version of the *passeggiata*, and a perfect place to sip some prosecco or a glass of the local white wine, called Episcopio.

> **Tip:** If you have time and are suitably dressed, consider walking back to the coast. There's a choice of easy paths, including what is billed as "the longest stairway in the world," down to Minori.

San Pantaleone

One of the most important monuments here is the **cathedral**, founded in 1086, and the place where William the Bad was crowned King of Sicily. The pulpit is decorated with Byzantine mosaics. It was rebuilt in the 12th century, and further renovated in 1786. Of special interest are the bronze doors by Barisano da Trani and the marble pulpits, which are superb examples of 13th-century sculpture. On one the story of Jonah is told, and on the other, supported by three sets of lions, are splendid mosaics of dragons and birds. The coat of arms belongs to the Rufolo family. Note also the tribute to an English captain on a commemorative plaque inscribed: "A Divozione di Jean Grant capitano inglese 1925." San Pantaleone's blood, kept in a chapel here, is said to liquefy annually (like that of San Gennaro in Naples) – on July 27th.

San Pantaleone

There is a museum in the crypt, with a 13th-century collection of gold and silver work, sculptures, and the much-admired bust of a noblewoman, probably Sigilgaida Rufolo, the wife of Nicola. Their portraits are also believed to be on the pulpit in the cathedral. ☎ 089 858 311. Open 9:30 am-1 pm and 3-7 pm daily in summer; weekends only in winter.

Villa Rufolo

On the other side of the square, Richard Wagner gained inspiration for the magical garden of Klingsor in his *Parsifal* from this lovely villa. Every year in July, a Wagner festival is held here. It was originally the 13th-century palatial home of the Rufolo family, of which the Moorish cloister and Norman tower are remnants. Some accounts claim that Charles of Anjou and the English Pope Adrian IV (1154-9) stayed here. Described as a "small Alhambra," the present lay-out is the work of a Scottish art expert and botanist, Sir Francis Nevile Reid, who acquired it in 1851. He hired Michele Ruggiero, in charge of excavations at Pompeii, to help him restore the building. The lovely gardens, with terraced flowerbeds, tree-lined avenues and incredible views, are the real draw for visitors. ☎ 089 857 866. Open 9 am to sunset.

Alternatively, take a left by the entrance, and climb up the steps over the tunnel for a free view of the coastline. Following the 1880 visit of Richard Wagner, and the association of his music with the location, an annual **Music Festival** is held here. The Villa makes a superb backdrop for the summer orchestral performances.

Villa Cimbrone

View from Villa Cimbrone

The Via San Francesco, which leads to the Villa Cimbrone, passes the 13th-century Gothic church and monastery of **San Francesco**, rebuilt in the 18th century. Continuing on Via S. Chiara, there is another 13th-century monastery, that of **Santa Chiara**, with a fine majolica floor and a rare *matronaeum*, or women's gallery. Villa Cimbrone is a little farther on from here. The building itself is largely an early 20th-century structure, masquerading as a Gothic-style castle cum palazzo. Its creator, Lord Grimthorpe (Ernest William Beckett), bought the patrician villa that stood on the site in 1904, and transformed the spot, with the help of Nicola Mansi, into a garden that some consider the most beautiful in Italy. The treasure trove of ornamental features includes medieval bas reliefs, 18th-century bronze and marble sculptures (that of Eve, in the grotto is by Tadolini, a pupil of Canova), Roman columns decorated with figures carved in the late Middle Ages, and a 12th-century baptismal font. Japanese cherry trees, cypresses, lavender, rock and rose gardens, camellias, dahlias and hortensia, delight the visitor.

The main Avenue of Immensity leads, under charming pergolas, to the legendary **Belvedere of Infinity**, a grandiose stone parapet, adorned with classical busts. Of this place, Gore Vidal wrote in 1976: "Twenty five years ago I was asked by an American magazine what was the most beautiful place that I had ever seen in all my travels and I said the view from the belvedere of the Villa Cimbrone on a bright winter's day when the sky and the sea were each so vividly blue that it was not possible to tell one from the other." The view – of the entire Bay of Salerno – is indeed unforgettable.

Close by the Belvedere is the **Rondinaia** (swallows' nest), built for Beckett's daughter Lucille in 1925, but now owned by Gore Vidal. Set on eight acres of olive, lemon, and chestnut trees, the Mediterranean-style villa has arched windows and a minaret-like tiled chimney. The villa is on five levels and is built into a cliff face some 1,000 feet above the Gulf of Salerno. Vidal added a pool and sauna in 1984, and has replanted two acres of the land with exotic species, continuing Grimthorpe's work.

The Villa Cimbrone has a guest list which many would envy – Winston Churchill, the Duke and Duchess of Kent, Virginia Woolf and most of the London Bloomsbury set have been here. But none so famously as Greta Garbo in the spring of 1938, escaping (unsuccessfully) from the eyes of the world's media with her lover Leopold Stokowsky. A plaque in the garden commemorates the time of "secret happiness" which she spent here.

San Giovanni del Toro

From the Piazza Duomo, the stepped Via R Wagner or Via Episcopio both lead to Via S Giovanni del Torre. On the Via Episcopio, a 12th-century bishop's residence, formerly the **Villa di Sangro**, is located, where King Victor Emmanuel III is said to have signed his abdication in favor of his son Umberto II. Jacqueline Kennedy stayed here on another occasion. As you

St Catherine of Alexandria, stucco in San Giovanni del

arrive on the Via S.G. del Torre, the **Belvedere Principessa di Piemonte** offers superb views over Minori and the eastern coast. The medieval church of **San Giovanni del Toro**, rebuilt in the 18th century, has a marvelous 12th-century pulpit by Alfano da Termoli, beautifully finished in colorful mosaics. The 14th-century stucco bas-relief of Saint Catherine of Alexandria in one of the chapels is also noteworthy.

■ Scala

A mile from Ravello, across the Valle del Dragone, Scala is the oldest and smallest of the Amalfitan settlements. Once an imposing fortress town, with two castles, and a string of monasteries, Scala was sacked and destroyed by invading armies on a number of occasions, then settled into the more peaceful pursuits of wool production and shoemaking. Scala still has its **Duomo**, however, dedicated to San Lorenzo, and dating from the 12th century. Its Romanesque portal and belfry have survived a 17th-century Baroque renovation. Inside, there is a colorful mosaic pulpit and an 18th-century ceiling, a 13th-century wooden crucifix, and ancient tombs of the local grandees, the Coppolas.

Walks

A number of lovely walks around the region begin from Ravello and Scala. Taking the Via Roma in Ravello, a steep downward walk leads to Minori past cottages and through terraced fields. Alternatively, from Scala, a two-hour walk to Casa Santa Maria dei Monti offers superb views of the Sorrentine Peninsula, but is a hard climb. An easier walk goes from Scala to the miniscule hamlet of Minuta, where the 12th-century Annunziata church has Byzantine frescoes. A stepped path descends via the village of Pontone to Amalfi, an additional 40-minute walk.

THE AMALFI COAST TOWERS

An interesting feature of the Amalfi Coast are the medieval watchtowers. Built to warn inhabitants of pirate raids, some are today in ruins, while others have been restored and converted into tourist attractions, nightclubs or restaurants.

The towers at **Erchie**, **Capo Tummolo** and **Lama del Cane** are good examples of the typical 16th-century square design with barrel or cross-vaulted ceilings and four or five embrasures (crenelated openings for firing weapons) on the upper coping.

■ Minori & Maiori

These resorts do not have the elegance and style of Ravello, Positano and Amalfi, but they do have better beaches, lined with beach concessions, and living costs are slightly lower, all of which is likely to appeal to families. Minori also has the only archeological site on the Amalfi Coast – the remains of a Roman villa and an adjacent museum, well worth a visit – and a boat service to Sorrento and Capri.

Basilica of Santa Trofimena

Minori served as the dockyard of the Amalfi Republic and in the 10th century was designated a bishopric in its own right by Pope John XV. The basilica of Santa Trofimena, near the harbor, was built a century later. Reconstructed in the 19th century, the church houses the relics of the saint of the same name. Each year on July 13th a flotilla of boats honors St Trofimena.

The Antiquarium

This large Roman maritime villa in Minori, covering an area of 3,000 square metres (3,600 square yards), evidently belonged to a rich family – possibly the Vetti brothers of Pompeii – whose name was found on an amphora in the town. The ground floor of their stylish home, complete with garden pool, has been carefully excavated. Visitors can walk around the *viridarium*, as the courtyard garden is called, and some of the rooms, which have traces of frescoes on the wall. Music and theater rooms have decorations of swans, masks, and musical instruments. There is a lovely blue and white mosaic floor in the spa area, but water damage and the use of the rooms as cellars and lime stores by local inhabitants have not helped the conservators. Part of the villa, which dates from the first century AD, is still unexcavated, as it is surrounded by private properties. The Antiquarium, or museum, is built into the structure, and incorporates part of the ancient baths. The museum displays objects from various archeological sites of the Amalfi Coast region. These include finds from underwater sites around the Li Galli islands, from a Roman necropolis and baths at Vietri, and from a rural villa at Tramonti, as well as the Minori villa itself. ☎ 089 852 893. Open 9 am to one hour before sunset. Free entry.

Santa Maria a Mare

The 12th-century church of Santa Maria a Mare, which is a landmark of the coastal resort of Maiori, was named after a wooden icon originally found in the sea. The campanile dates from the 18th century.

Valle di Tramonti

From Maiori or Ravello, intrepid travelers can visit the Valle di Tramonti, which has good views across the Sarno plain to Vesuvius. The area, which includes several hamlets, is known for its excellent farm produce, including cheese and honey. Two km from Maiori, along the lovely coastal road with panoramic views known as the SS 163, you should stop at Capo d'Orso to visit the remains of the **Abbey of Santa Maria de Olearia**. The wall frescoes are rare examples of medieval painting in Campania, but special arrangements may need to be discussed at one of the Amalfi Coast tourist offices if you want to visit the interior.

Just under five miles from Maiori, the fishing village of **Erchie** is a delightful bathing resort, popular with the residents of Salerno. It is divided into two areas by a rocky outcrop, upon which stands an ancient watchtower.

■ Cetara & Vietri

The seaside resorts of the Amalfi Coast become increasingly businesslike as you approach the busy town of Salerno. Cetara is known for its anchovy production and the larger Vietri is celebrated for its majolica and faience work. Fortunately, they are also keen to preserve the natural beauty of their coastal locations and, while they do not have the fame of their neighbors, they attract many visitors in the summer months.

San Pietro

Cetara has all the characteristic charm of an Amalfi Coast fishing village. The church of St Peter has the typical 13th-century bell tower of these parts and is a focal point. Note also the mullioned windows. Furthermore, the beach, like so many on this stretch of the peninsula, is dominated by yet another watchtower, a legacy of the dreaded Saracen invaders. Indeed, the story goes that in the mid-16th century, the Turks actually kidnapped 300 of the local villagers, taking them off on more than 20 galleys into enslavement. It is whispered that the Prince of Salerno was behind the evil deed. The purpose of the tower was to provide warning of further sea raids.

Museo della Ceramica Vietrese

The inhabitants of Vietri have been known for their ceramics skills since the Middle Ages. Their craftsmanship appears to have been highly prized, since archeologists have found evidence of 16th-century ceramic ware produced in Vietri at a number of sites around the region. The town contains many examples of ancient votive tiles, many dating from the 18th century, when it is believed that a new lease on life was given to the industry by the arrival of master tile makers from the Abruzzi and from Naples. The churches of San Giovanni Battista and Confraternita del Rosario are decorated with these historic tiles. A range of tiles from the 17th century to the present day are exhibited in the museum, itself located in a lovely tiled building, otherwise known as the Toretta Belvedere of the **Villa Guariglia**, in the nearby village of **Raito**. The villa served as the lodging of King Victor Emmanuel during the Second World War. Factories and shops all over Vietri sell the ceramic ware for which the town is known, and provide an opportunity to visit workshops and see craftsmen in action.

■ Salerno

This busy industrial city and port has an impressive history, reflected in the numerous monuments of significance. The **Museo Archeologico** helps to shed some light on the Etruscan and Roman origins of the province, while the **Duomo**, the **Castello di Arechi**, and the **Museo della Scuola Medica Salernitana** highlight Salerno's role as a Norman capital, with probably the oldest medical school in Europe. In the Second World War, Salerno was again in the spotlight – on September 8, 1943, Allied troops landed south of the city and, for a few months in 1944, the new Italian government was headquartered here. Unfortunately, the seafront area, bombed during the war, now has a primarily functional appearance but, with a recent make-over by the architect of Barcelona's regeneration, Salerno is well on its way to reclaiming the hearts of travelers. Its efficient transport links, with fast access to Naples and as a gateway to Paestum and the Cilento Valley, certainly are an advantage in this respect.

■ Paestum & the Cilento Valley

The exceptionally well-preserved Greek temples make Paestum one of the most majestic classical sites of Italy. Poseidonia, founded around 600 BC by Greek colonists from Sybaris, later became the Roman settlement of Paestum. Abandoned for centuries – partly as a result of endemic malaria in the region – the site was rediscovered in the 18th century, and became popular with the more adventurous of the Grand Tour visitors. But it was not fully explored and mapped until recently. Located around 40 km/24 miles south of Salerno, and 100 km/60 miles southeast of Naples, Paestum is accessible by rail or car. A trip to the **Doric temples** can be accompanied by a tour of the **National Park of Cilento**, which is nearby. This hilly region, with its lovely, still unspoiled coastline, is dotted with monasteries and medieval ruins. The area is ideal for hikers and offers a unique opportunity to appreciate the cultural and eco-heritage of the Campanian countryside. Paestum and the surrounding area is a UNESCO World Heritage Site.

The Paestum Excavations

The three Doric temples of Paestum are among the best of their kind in the world. There are two entrances to the site: one close to the museum and the other, at the southern end, near the Nettuno restaurant, where most guided tours begin. Before entering, take a moment to admire the city walls, which stretch for five km/three miles around the site of the ancient town, with four entrance gates.

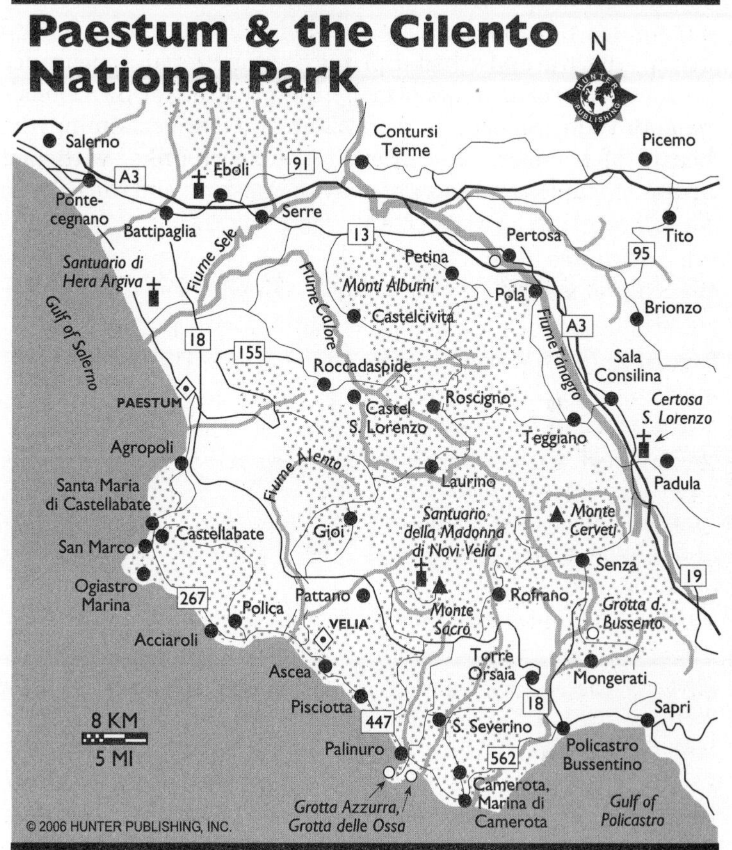

The first monument within the archeological area is the **Temple of Hera**, the oldest at Paestum, dating from around 530 BC. Once believed to be a civic building, it is sometimes described as a basilica. The temple has nine front columns, 18 side columns and two aisles. By its side, the magnificent **Temple of Neptune**, with its 36 fluted columns and virtually intact entablature, has thrown generations of visitors into raptures. Experts have argued over whether it should be renamed a temple to Apollo or Poseidon. A number of small statues and vases found here suggest that it was in fact dedicated to the goddess of fertility, Hera Argiva. Sites devoted to the goddess attracted childless couples, according to one source, who would "flock to the temple of Hera to copulate beneath the night sky, in the belief that making love within the shrine of the goddess will call forth her fertilizing influence and thereby ensure pregnancy."

Temple of Hera detail

In the central area, the **forum** and other civic buildings around it are Roman, as is the third century BC *piscine*, or pool, with its mysterious limestone pillars. Remains of Roman taverns and shops were also found here. To the right, the partially excavated **amphitheater** has been dated to the first century BC. It was later enlarged, but is still much smaller than those at Pompeii and Pozzuoli. An 18th-century road, now called the Via Magna Grecia, straddles the site.

Temple of Ceres

To the left is another circular structure, which is a further remnant of the original Greek city. The **Ekklesia Sterion** was a meeting place, but today it is hard to imagine what went on here, as most of the seats have disappeared. Last but certainly not least, the **Temple of Ceres** (in fact, dedicated to the goddess Athena), stands proudly at the far end of the site. Built around 500 BC, the temple was used as an early Christian burial site, and converted into a church in the Middle Ages. The archeological site is open daily from 9 am to one hour before sunset. During summer, night-time visits around the beautifully-lit temples can also be made. Tours are half-hourly from 9 pm to 12:30 am Thurs-Sat. €14. ☎ 0828 721 113 to book.

Museo Archeologico

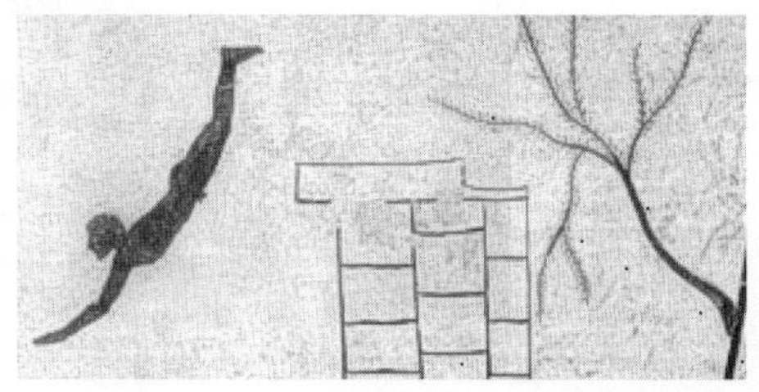

The Diver's Tomb, fresco on the inside lid of a tomb, which may represent diving into the world of the dead

Opened in 1952, the museum is housed in a modern, light building, and exhibits objects from excavations undertaken in and around Paestum. Its most famous exhibit is the so-called **Diver's Tomb**. The name is taken from the superb painting, which has been much reproduced as it is a unique example of classical Greek funerary art. Other decorations on the tomb, which was found in 1968 half a mile from Paestum, represent convivial guests enjoying music and wine. One theory is that the diver was an itinerant musician and, not being a local man, was given an unusual burial. A number of Greek sculptures on show in the museum were found at the **Hera Argiva Sanctuary**, discovered recently at a site near the River Sele, a few miles from Paestum. Panels at the museum also provide a history of the excavations carried out at Paestum from the mid-18th century onwards, although the texts are in Italian only at present; a number of vases, found in local necropoli, are displayed. Open 9 am-7 pm daily. Closed on the first and third Mon of each month. €6, including the visit to the archeological site. ☎ 0828 811 016, www.infopaestum.it.

Silver coin from Paestum, 530-510 BC

Basilica Paleocristiana

At the side of the museum, off the Piazza Basilica – where a welcome café can also be found, this early Christian basilica, also called the Church of the Annunciation, is a symbol of another important facet of Paestum's history: the early arrival of Christianity in the region. The first structure on the site is believed to date back to the fifth or sixth century AD. Long abandoned, it then underwent a number of restorations, the most important of which was carried out in the 18th century. More recent renovation work in the 1960s, revealed the early Christian remains of the basilica. Inside the church, the coat of arms of Pietro Antonio Raimondi, an 18th-century local bishop, can be seen.

The Cilento National Park

South and West of Paestum, covering an area of some 600,000 acres, and incorporating a stretch of lovely coastline, the park is a vast playground, just waiting to be explored by independent travelers and hikers. The words of the Greek philosopher Zenone, written some 2,500 years ago, are still largely true today: "The people of Cilento belong to their land in the same way that that the local plants belong to its soil, they both share the same attributes.... They follow the rhythm of nature around them and, even when nature turns unkind, they adapt to the new conditions and will prosper and propagate right where the damage was strongest." His correspondent replied: "Let us hope for our sake that the people of Cilento will never change their ways and always want to belong to the land instead of wanting the land to belong to them."

This is one of the cradles of ancient European civilization, and many artifacts of its prehistoric inhabitants have been found

Above: Pool at Costa Alta Villaggio Turistico e Campeggio, Piano di Sorrento

Below: Cilento National Park

rrento Peninsula

The Roman Villa San Marco, Stabia

Above: Temple of Ceres at Paestum

Below: Buffalos at Paestum, famous for its yogurt and mozzarella di bufala cheese, made from their milk

in the numerous caves along the Cilento coastline. The region became a favored getaway spot in Greek and Roman times, and Cicero's love for the place, which he knew as Velia, is apparent from his heartfelt letter sent to a friend who lived in this Roman town: "I would be back in Velia in a heartbeat were it not for the sense of duty I have for our Republic.... How it would soothe me to walk through the woods of Velia or alongside the beach that takes us from Porta Marina to the seaport." Many centuries later, Cilento had become a no-go area for travelers, as the feared *briganti* controlled the region, and the lack of Grand Tour visitors with their well-thumbed narratives may help to explain why this area has remained largely undiscovered by foreign visitors.

Cilento is thus the lesser-known face of Campania, yet the variety of its topography, with mountain peaks and hilltop stone villages in its interior, and Mediterranean coastline with sandy beaches punctuated by jagged promontories topped by ancient watchtowers, makes it an ideal vacation spot. The coastal resorts of **Pisciotta**, **Palinuro** and **Camerota** are already well-known to vacationing Italians, but intrepid foreign travelers are increasingly discovering the attractions of the region.

Nowadays, maps of the Cilento National Park, with suggested tour routes, are available – the tourist office at Paestum is happy to supply them. Newly-opened trails take hikers along the coast and through mountain scenery to inland valleys, passing medieval ruins and old villages en route. Part of the development of the park has been the opening of a number of rural museums, which are also shown on the local walking tour map. Possible excursions in the interior include visits to the castle of **Rocca Cilento**, with its panoramic views, the **caves of Castelcivita**, and a visit to the medieval village of **S. Angelo a Fasanella**. For those making their base at one of the coastal resorts, **Palinuro** has an interesting **Antiquarium** or museum, where archeological finds from local Roman necropoli are on display, and it hosts an international music festival every summer. A number of caves are also tourist attractions here and at Marina di Camerota.

The Emerald Grotto

Located between Praiano and Amalfi, this marine cave can be reached by road or by sea (boat trips go from the main resorts). From the street, there is an elevator down to the cave. A boatman escorts visitors into the cave, where the water takes on a green color due to illumination by the sun's rays. It is a lovely natural spectacle, although the repartee of the boatman may not be to everyone's taste. There are stalactites and stalagmites, and an underwater nativity scene. The visit costs €3.

■ Places to Eat

Positano & Praiano

La Cambusa, 24 Piazza A.Vespucci, Positano ☎ 089 875 432. €€€. Beach terrace with great salads, pasta and seafood.

Chez Black, Waterfront, Positano, ☎ 089 875 036. €€. Established seafood restaurant. Pizzas are good if you can't afford the rest.

Al Palazzo, 23 Via dei Mulini, Positano, ☎ 089 875 177. €€. Good venue for candlelit al fresco dining. Adventurous Medinerranean menu.

Ristorante Il Ritrovo, 77 Via Montepertuso, Positano, ☎ 089-812-005. €€. Mountainside location with terrace. Good vegetarian antipasti.

La Buca di Bacco, 8 Via Rampa Teglia, Positano. €€. Beach restaurant and bar. Good place to get a snack at any time.

La Brace, Via G. Capriglione, Praiano, ☎ 089 874226. €€. Great views over Positano from the terrace. Home-cooked food, and good pizzas. Closed Oct-Mar.

Trattoria San Gennaro, 99 Via G. Capriglione, Praiano, ☎ 089 874 293. €. Good choice of local dishes, closed Wed.

Bacco, 9 Via G.B. Lama, Furore, ☎ 089 830 630, www.baccofurore.it. €€. Great fish and pasta.

Amalfi

DINING PRICE CHART	
Price for an entrée	
€	€10-29
€€	€30-49
€€€	€50+

La Caravella, 12 Via Matteo Camera Amalfi, ☎ 089 871 029. €€. Elegant, Michelin-starred restaurant, let down by its roadside location.

Da Gemma, 9 Via Fra Gerardo Sasso, Amalfi, ☎ 089 871 345. €€. Fish soup, fried fish, and pasta dishes. Al fresco dining in summer, near the Duomo. Closed Wed and from Jan 15 to Feb 15.

Zaccaria, Via San Quasimodo, Amalfi, ☎ 089 871807. €€. Popular for fish, on a terrace with view.

Mar di Cobalto, Waterfront, Amalfi, ☎ 089 872 650. €. Reasonably priced meals and snacks with great beach-side location.

A Paranza, 1 Via Dragone, Atrani, ☎ 089 871 840. €€. Considered one of the best fish restaurants on the Amalfi Coast with swordfish specialties, and paccheri (a type of homemade pasta) with prawns and rucola (salad greens called rocket in English). Closed Tues in winter.

La Carcara, 74 Via Castello, Pogerola, ☎ 089 872 796. €€. Fresh fish, gnocchi and pasta. Closed Wed and Jan-Feb.

Osteria da Rispoli, 1 Via Riuolo, Pogerola, ☎ 089 830 080. €€. Enjoy lovely views from the terrace with your risotto alla pescatora or linguine with scampi. Homemade lemon cake and tiramisu. Closed Thurs.

Hostaria di Bacco, 9 Via G.B. Lama, Furore, ☎ 089 830 360. €€. Trattoria and hotel with a panoramic view. One specialty is a meal in which every course features lemon.

Ravello

Rossellini, 28 Via San Giovanni del Toro, Ravello, ☎ 089 818 181. €€€. Creative cuisine on the flower-filled terrace restaurant of Palazzo Sasso.

Cumpa Cosimo, 44 Via Roma, Ravello, ☎ 089 857 156. €€. Trattoria, famed for its pasta dishes at moderate prices.

The Garden, Via Chiunzi, Ravello, ☎ 089 857 226. €€. Terrace with panoramic views.

Palazzo della Marra, 7 Via della Marra, Ravello, ☎ 089 858 302. €€. Local cuisine in an elegant building. Closed mid-Jan to mid-Feb, and on Tues in winter.

Minori & Maiori

Giardinello, 17 Corso Vittorio Emanuele, Minori, ☎ 089 877 050. €€. Garden restaurant serving local and seafood dishes. Closed Wed in winter.

Mammato, Via Amendola, Maiori, ☎ 089 877 036. €€. Closed Tues in low season. Amalfitan specialties and seafood.

Cetara & Vietri

Acqua Pazza, 38 Corso Garibaldi, Cetara, ☎ 089261 606. €€. Local fish specialties, especially anchovies and anchovy sauce (*colatura*).

La Locanda, 52 Corso Umberto I, Vietri, ☎ 089 761 070. €€. Local cuisine, in two air-conditioned rooms. Closed Mon.

La Vela, Lungomare G. Amendola, Cetara, ☎ 089 852 874. €€. Typical local fish-based cuisine.

Paestum & the Valle de Cilento

Nettuno, Via Nettuno, Paestum, ☎ 0828 811 028. €. Conveniently located near the southern entrance of the excavations.

Simposium, 1 Via Nettuno, Paestum, ☎ 0828 722 440. €. Situated on the Via Magna Grecia, also close to the archeological site.

Enoteca Tavernelle, Zone Archeologica, Paestum, ☎ 0828 721 182. €. Pizzeria and ice cream shop.

Carmelo, 562 S.S. Località Isca, Palinuro, ☎ 0974 931 138. €€. Closed Nov, Dec, and Wed in low season. Cilento cuisine with fish specialties.

Pepe, 41 Via della Sirene, Marina di Camerota, ☎ 0974 493 2461. €€. Elegant restaurant, open only in high season.

Valenton, 5 Piazza S. Comenico, Marina di Camerota, ☎ 0974 932 004. €€. Local home cooking, open only in high season.

■ Bars & Cafés

Positano & Praiano

De Martino, 170 Via Pasitea, Positano, ☎ 089 875 082. Cappuccinos and cakes by the sea.

La Zagara, 8 Via Mulini, Positano, ☎ 089 875 964. Fruit granitas in a garden filled with lemon trees.

Amalfi

Andrea Pansa, 40 Piazza Duomo, Amalfi, ☎ 089 871 065. Local sweets are a specialty.

Bar Francese, 20 Piazza Duomo, Amalfi, ☎ 089 871 049. Great location in front of the Duomo.

Gran Caffè, Corso Repubbliche Marinare, Amalfi, ☎ 089 857 874. Tea and aperitifs in this seaside spot.

Il Protontino, Piazza Duomo, Amalfi, ☎ 089 872 590. Great coffees in the Cathedral square.

Gelateria Porto Salvo, Piazza Duomo, Amalfi, ☎ 089-872-445. Great range of fresh ice creams.

Ravello

Bar Schiavo, 2 Piazza Duomo, Ravello, ☎ 089 857 1421. Pleasant café, with a range of cakes.

Bar Klingsor, 4 Via dei Rufolo, Ravello, ☎ 089 857 407.

Bar Calce, 2 Via Roma, Ravello, ☎ 089 857 152.

Minori to Vietri

Gambardella, 37 Corso Vittorio Emanuele, Minori, ☎ 089 877 299. Orange and lemon chocolates are a specialty.

Salvatore di Riso, 28 Piazza Cantilena, Minori, ☎ 089 853 618. A good selection of cakes and sweets.

Bar Del Corso, 72, Corso Regina, Maiori, ☎ 089 877 185.

Bar Sirena, Via G Amendola, Maiori, ☎ 089 877 179.

Bar Caffetteria Napoletana, 56, Corso Umberto, Vietri, ☎ 089 210 107.

Bar Ariston Bar & Caffè, 130 Piazza Matteotti, Vietri, ☎ 089 210 229.

Caffè Dello Sport, 3 Corso Federici, Cetara, ☎ 089 261 485.

Bar Moderno, Piazza S. Francesco, Cetara, ☎ 089 261 102.

Paestum & the Cilento Valley

Bar Anna, Zona Templi, Paestum, ☎ 0828 811 196. Pleasant café bar very close to the archeological zone.

La Basilica Café, Via Magna Graecia, Paestum, ☎ 0828 811 301. Ice creams, sandwiches and pizza in a garden café.

La Ruota del Pavone, Parco Villa Salata, Paestum, ☎ 0828 721 082. Ice creams, drinks and snacks.

■ Places To Stay

Positano & Praiano

Le Sirenuse, 30 Via Cristoforo Colombo, Positano, ☎ 089 875 066, www.sirenuse.it. €€€. Legendary hotel in an 18th-century palazzo, decorated with antiques, and boasting fabulous restaurants. Rooms have whirlpool baths. A new spa/fitness center has been opened.

Hotel San Pietro, 2 Via Laurito, Positano, ☎ 800 735 2478, www.ilsanpietro.it. €€€. Fabulous terraced hotel built into the cliff-face with lovely gardens, terrace pool and private beach. The restaurant is popular with the super-rich residents and celebrity visitors like Michael Douglas and Julia Roberts.

Hotel Palazzo Murat, €€€ 23 Via dei Mulini, Positano, ☎ 089 875 177. This palace was chosen by the French King of Naples to be his summer residence. Centrally located, the courtyard and garden reflect its illustrious past.

Hotel Poseidon, 148 Via Pasitea, Positano, ☎ 089 811 111. €€. Balconies with panoramic views; beauty spa and gym; good-sized car park.

HOTEL PRICE CHART	
For a double room for two	
€	€50-150
€€	€151-250
€€€	€251+

Ostello Brikette, 358 Via G. Marconi, Positano, ☎ 089 875 857. €. Clean, Spartan hostel, with good views from the balcony.

Maria Luisa, Via Fornillo, Positano, ☎ 089 875 023. €. Less central, but good location for the beach.

La Tavolozza, 10 Via C. Colombo, Positano, ☎ 089 875 040. €. Charming and economical.

Hotel Smeraldo, 133 Via G. Capriglione, Praiano, ☎ 089 874 002. €. Lovely sea views from the terrace. No pool.

San Gennaro, 99 Via G. Capriglione, Praiano, ☎ 089 874 293. €. Very reasonable double room with breakfast, in a good location.

La Conca Azzurra, 35 Via Smeraldo, Conca dei Marini, ☎ 089 831 610, www.concaazzurra.it. €. Reasonably priced hotel in this resort, located between Furore and Amalfi.

Tranquillità, Véttica Maggiore, ☎ 089 874 084. €. Campsite with bungalows in a nearby village.

Amalfi

Hotel Santa Caterina, 9 Via S.S. Amalfitana, Amalfi, ☎ 089 871 012, www.hotelsantacaterina.it. €€€. Elegant hotel with period furnishings, and a lift to the beach.

Luna Convento, 33 Via P. Comite, Amalfi, ☎ 089 871 002, www.lunahotel.it. €€. A great deal of history in this former monastery, refurbished to a high standard. Central location with great views.

Grand Hotel Excelsior, Via Papa Leone X, Amalfi, ☎ 089 830 015. €€. Hotel with panoramic views.

Hotel La Bussola, 16 Via Lungomare dei Cavalieri, Amalfi, ☎ 089 871 533. €€. Comfortable hotel in a good location.

Pensione Sole, 2 Largo della Zecca, Amalfi, ☎ 089 871 147. €. Family-run, welcoming guesthouse in the *Centro Storico*.

Pensione La Conchiglia, Piazzale Protontini, Amalfi, ☎ 089 871 856. €. Open at Christmas, and from Easter to October.

A Scalinatella, 12 Piazza Umberto, Atrani, ☎ 089 871492. €. Excellent value guesthouse, with rooms in various town locations.

Ravello

Palazzo Sasso, 28 San Giovanni del Toro, Ravello, ☎ 089 818 181, www.palazzosasso.com. €€€. Superbly restored 12th-century palazzo in a dream location, with great pool and top notch restaurant.

Hotel Palumbo, 16 Via S. G. del Toro, Ravello, ☎ 089 857 244, www.hotel-palumbo.it. €€€. Another aristocratic home on the same street, converted into a lovely hotel. No pool, but private beach club.

Hotel Villa Cimbrone, 26 Via Santa Chiara, Ravello, ☎ 089 857 459, www.villacimbrone.it. €€€. This hotel in the famous villa with superlative gardens, recently hosted Hilary Clinton. The hotel has a small staff, and is a long walk from the center of Ravello.

Villa Maria, 2 Via Santa Chiara, Ravello, ☎ 089 857 255. €€. Edwardian-style villa hotel with panoramic terrace restaurant.

Caruso Belvedere, 2 Via San Giovanni del Toro, Ravello, ☎ 089 857 111. €€. A hotel with a long tradition and matching guest list, Graham Greene among them.

Parsifal, 5 Via G. d'Anna, Ravello, ☎ 089 857144. €€. Great views for a reasonable price.

Minori & Maiori

Villa Romana, 90 Corso Vittorio Emmanuele, Minori, ☎ 089 877 237. €€. Air-conditioned rooms, parking, covered pool, private beach.

Casa Raffaele Conforti, 10 Via Casa Mannini, Maiori, ☎ 089 853 547. €€. Elegantly furnished in a former palazzo, with private beach.

Panorama, 8 Via S. Tecla, Maiori, ☎ 089 877 202. €€. Panoramic views from the roof garden terrace, pool and solarium.

Miramare, 5 Via Nuova Chiunzi, Maiori, ☎ 089 877 225, www.miramaremaiori.it. €€. Central seaside location, with solarium.

Cetara & Vietri

The Cetus, 163 Strada Statale, Cetara, ☎ 089 261 388. €€. Modern design with panoramic restaurant and terrace.

Lloyd's Baia, 2 Via de' Marinis, Vietri, ☎ 089 763 3111. €€. Modern seaside complex, with pool and reserved beach.

La Lucertola, 29 Via C. Colombo, Vietri, ☎ 089 210 837. €€. Panoramic location, with reserved beach and restaurant.

Paestum & the Cilento Valley

Hotel Esplanade, Via Poseidonia, Paestum, ☎ 0828 851 043, www.hotelesplanade.com. €€. Competitive prices for double rooms in this hotel with pool and beach access.

Helios, Zona Archeologica, Paestum, ☎ 0828 811 020. €€. Bungalow-style hotel with pool.

Ariston, 13 Via Laura, Capaccio, ☎ 0828 851 333. €€. Panoramic location, with reserved beach and restaurant.

Delfino, 45, Via Bolivar, Marina di Camerota, ☎ 0974 932 239. €€. Restored palazzo, garden, and private beach.

San Pietro, Corso C. Pisacane, Palinuro, ☎ 0974 931 466. €€. Elegant hotel with saltwater pool and reserved beach.

King's Residence, Baia del Buondormire, Palinuro, ☎ 0974 493 1324. €€. Well located seasonal hotel with covered pool, private beach, and beauty center.

America, 84, Via Bolivar, Marina di Camerota, ☎ 0974 932 131. €€. Modern hotel with access for the disabled; pool, private beach.

Calanca, 60 Via L. Mazzeo, Marina di Camerota, ☎ 0974 128. €€. Rooms with balconies, garden, covered pool and private beach.

La Conchiglia, 52 Via Independenza, Palinuro, ☎ 0974 931 018. €. Newly renovated, with 30 air-conditioned rooms.

Graziella, 68 Via V. Bachelet, Vietri, Capaccio, ☎ 0828 724 351. €. Simple bed and breakfast accommodation, close to Paestum.

Agriturismo Seliano, Via Seliano Paestum, ☎ 0828 724 544, www.agriturismoseliano.it. €. An opportunity to try out local food in a rural location.

Maida, 31 Via Tempa di Lepre, Località Paestum, Capaccio, ☎ 082 872 2953. €. Close to the archeological site of Paestum, and five km/three miles from the sea. Trekking, riding, and other activities are encouraged in this agriturismo development that also sells organic products.

■ Shopping

Clothes, Leather Goods & Jewelry

Antonio della Mura, 36 Via del Saracino, Positano, ☎ 089 875 020. Popular clothes boutique selling designer labels.

Costanzo Avitabile, 1-5 Piazza Amerigo Vespucci, ☎ 089 875 366. Made-while-you-wait Positano sandals.

Sartoria Lampo, 12 Via Pasitea, Positano, ☎ 089 875 021. Beachwear in the Positano style.

La Bottega di Brunella, 72 Via Pasitea, Positano, ☎ 089 875 228. Original clothing for men, women and children.

Emporio Le Sirenuse, 109 Via C. Colombo, Positano, ☎ 089-811-468. Clothes, books and ceramics.

Camo, 9 Piazza Duomo, Ravello, ☎ 089 857 461. Cameos and coral – recent clients for bracelets have been the Princesses of Monaco.

Eurosport, 50 Via Licinella, Paestum. Casual and sport wear.

Craft & Gift Shops

Cafiero, 171 Via Cristoforo Colombo, Positano, ☎ 089 875 838. Glass bottles and vases for home use or as gifts.

Antica Cartiera Amatruda, 11 Piazza Duomo, Amalfi, ☎ 089 872 368. Lovely gifts of notelets in the ancient papermaking tradition of Amalfi.

Antonio Cavaliere, 3 Via Fiume, Amalfi, ☎ 089 871 954. Watercolor paper, with flowers.

La Scuderia Del Duca, 8 Largo Cesareo Console, Amalfi, ☎ 089 872 976. Prints, paper, ceramics and terra-cotta vases.

Criscuolo, 2 Largo Scario, Amalfi, ☎ 871 089. Ceramics and coral work.

Cartiera Cavaliere, 2 Via M. Del Giudice, Amalfi. Traditional paper manufacturing and sales.

Ceramiche d'Arte, 16 Via Dei Rufolo, Ravello, ☎ 089 857 303. Local and designer ceramics.

Ruocco, 23 Corso Vittorio Emanuele, Minori, ☎ 089 521 900. Ceramics made by local craftsmen.

Ceramica Artistica Solimene, 7 Via Madonna degli Angeli, Vietri sul Mare, ☎ 089 210 243. Large warehouse producing and selling ceramics.

Ceramica Margherita, 20 Via Case Sparse, Vietri sul Mare, ☎ 089 210 694. Dinner services, lamps, vases and other ceramic objects.

La Bottega delle Piccole Cose, Via Indipendenza, Palinuro, ☎ 0974 931 741. Terracotta items and other handicrafts.

Books, Antiques & Old Prints

La Libreria, 165 Via C. Colombo, Positano, ☎ 089 811 077.

Miniaci, 18 Via dei Mulini, Positano, ☎ 089 811 771. Centrally located gallery with many landscapes of Positano.

D'Antuono, 11 Piazza Duomo, Amalfi, ☎ 089 872 368. Art books and antique prints.

Libreria Butrico, 74 Via Magna Graecia, Paestum, ☎ 0828 724 631. Books, stationery and souvenirs.

Food & Drink

The countryside around Paestum is famous for production of the sublime mozzarella di bufala cheese and, if you have a car, there are large farms that cater to tourists. You can see the buffaloes and taste wonderful yogurt and cheese made from their milk. For visitors dependent on public transport there are a couple of shops in Paestum that sell mozzarella.

I Sapori di Positano, 6 Via Mulini, Positano, ☎ 089 811 116. Locally made liqueurs, conserves, spices and herbs gift-packaged.

Antichi Sapori d'Amalfi, 39 Piazza Duomo, Amalfi, ☎ 089 872 062. Conserves, honey and liqueurs made with traditional local recipes.

La Valle dei Mulini, 55 Via delle Cartiere, Amalfi, ☎ 873 211. Limoncello and other specialty liqueurs.

Latteria Santa Caterina, 24 Piazza dei Dogi, Amalfi, ☎ 871 249. Provolone, pecora, ricotta and other cheeses.

Gusti & Delizie, 28 Via Roma, Ravello, ☎ 089 857 716. A good selection of the best local wines.

Episcopio, 16 Via S.G. del Toro, Ravello, ☎ 089 857 244. Purchase the local Episcopio wine here.

Profumi della Costiera, 37 Via Trinita, Ravello, ☎ 089 858 167. Limoncello and other liqueurs.

Delfino, 58 Corso Umberto I, Cetara, ☎ 089 261 069. Conserves and liqueurs, including the famous *Colatura*.

La Fattoria del Casaro, 5 Via Licinella, Paestum, ☎ 0828 722 704. Mozzarella manufacturer; garden seating.

Torricelle, Via Magna Grecia, Paestum, ☎ 0828 723 175. Mozzarella di bufala production and sale outlet.

Tenuta Vannulo, 10 Via G Galilei, Capaccio, ☎ 0828 724 765. See the buffaloes, try the yogurt and ice cream, and buy mozzarella.

■ Entertainment

Music & Dance

La Zagara, 6 Via dei Mulini, Positano, ☎ 089 875 964. Café by day, piano bar by night.

Music on the Rocks, 51 Via Grotte dell'Incanto Positano, ☎ 089 875 874. House music in this nightclub by the sea. Open Apr to Oct.

Roccoco Discopub, Valle dei Mulini, Amalfi. Recently opened nightclub.

L'Africana, Praiano. The famous nightclub on the Amalfi Coast, with its glass dance floor over the sea.

Il Ciclope, SS 562 Localita' Mingardo, Marina di Camerota, ☎ 097 493 0318. One of the main theaters of Italian night life since 1972. House and commercial music.

■ Adventures

Beaches

Bagni d'Arienzo, Via Arienzo, Positano, ☎ 089 812 002.

Rispoli, Grotta di Fornillo, Positano, ☎ 089 875 365.

Bagni Mar Di Cobalto, Via Marina Grande, Amalfi, ☎ 089 872 650.

Lido delle Sirene, Piazza le Dei Protontini, Amalfi, ☎ 089 871 489.

Lido Tritone, Via Pellegrino, Vietri Sul Mare ☎ 089 761 575.

Lido Aurora, Via Cristoforo Colombo, Vietri, ☎ 089 211 290.

Lido La Gondola, Via Torre, Paestum, ☎ 0828 811 923.

Lido Marilena, Via Licinella, Paestum, ☎ 0828 811 445.

Bar Lido S. Rita, Lungo Mare Amendola, Maiori, ☎ 089 851 109.

Lido Adriana, Via Erchie, Maiori, ☎ 089 855 030.

Lido Ficocella, 1 Via Ficocella, Palinuro, ☎ 0974 931 051.

Sansone, Via Lago Trasimeno, Picciola, ☎ 089 203 276.

Rosa dei Venti, Via Cristoforo Colombo, Marina di Pisciotta, ☎ 089 210 432.

Sea Sports & Tours

L'Uomo e il Mare, Marina Grande, Positano, ☎ 089 811 613, www.sirene.it. Trips to Li Galli, and local coastal spots.

Noleggio Barche Lucibello, Via Marina Grande, Positano, ☎ 089 875 032, www.lucibello.it. Excursions and rental of motor and rowboats; water skiing.

Capitaneria di Porto, Via del Brigantino, Positano, ☎ 089 875 486. Rental of small boats.

Delegazione di Spiaggia, Municipio, Maiori, ☎ 089 814 211. Boat trips to the sunken Roman city with under-sea level seating.

Posidonia, 11 Lungomare Trieste, Marina di Camerota, ☎ 0973 939 127. Sail and motor boat excursions.

Cooperative Porto, Via Santa Maria, Palinuro, ☎ 0974 938 294. Boat trips.

Pesca Turismo, 19 Via Porto, Palinuro, ☎ 0974 931 604. Day and night excursions to the sea grottos of Cape Palinuro. Fishing trips.

Club Velico Salernitano, Piazza Concordia, Salerno, ☎ 089 236 235.

Lega Navale Italiana, Piazza Concordia, Salerno, ☎ 089 226 694.

Capitaneria di Porto, Via Molo Manfredi, Salerno, ☎ 089 255 000.

Walking, Horseback Riding & Cultural Tours

Comunità Montana Penisola Amalfitana, Via Municipio, Tramonti, ☎ 089 876 354. This local group of hiking enthusiasts offers guided tours and information about walks in the mountains.

Posidonia, 11 Lungomare Trieste, Marina di Camerota, ☎ 0973 939 127. Excursions on foot, and horseback riding in the National Park of Cilento.

Il Sole in Tasca, San Marco di Castellabate, Cenito, ☎ 0974 966 883. Cultural and nature itineraries in the park.

Itinerarte, Via Roma, Teggiano, ☎ 0975 79107, www.itinerarte.it. Trips of one or more days in the Cilento Park.

Nuovo Cilento, San Mauro del Cilento, ☎ 0974 903 239, www.cilentoverde.com. Visits to see traditional oil production, and gastronomic tours.

Index